SPSS® Programming and Data Management

A Guide for SPSS® and SAS® Users

Raynald Levesque

SPSS®

For more information about SPSS® software products, please visit our Web site at *http://www.spss.com* or contact

SPSS Inc.
233 South Wacker Drive, 11th Floor
Chicago, IL 60606-6412
Tel: (312) 651-3000
Fax: (312) 651-3668

2 3 4 5 6 7 8 9 0   06 05 04
ISBN 1-56827-334-7

Preface

Experienced data analysts know that a successful analysis or meaningful report often requires more work in acquiring, merging, and transforming data than in specifying the analysis or report itself. SPSS contains powerful tools for accomplishing and automating these tasks. While much of this capability is available through the graphical user interface, many of the most powerful features are available only through command syntax, the macro facility that extends the power of command syntax, and the scripting facility. Until now, no book or other documentation has focused on those features, and many potential users have been unaware of the power available to them or have not exploited it for lack of examples. This book fills that void.

Using This Book

The contents of this book and the accompanying CD are discussed in Chapter 1. In particular, see the section "Using This Book" if you plan to run the examples on the CD. The CD also contains additional command files, macros, and scripts that are mentioned but not discussed in the book and that can be useful for solving specific problems.

For SAS Users

If you have more experience with SAS than with SPSS for data management, see Chapter 9 for comparisons of the different approaches to handling various types of data management tasks. Quite often, there is not a simple command-for-command relationship between the two programs, although each accomplishes the desired end.

Send Me Comments

I welcome feedback from readers. Please send your suggestions and comments about the book (not the software) to *rlevesque@videotron.ca*. Check my Web site at *http://pages.infinit.net/rlevesqu/* for possible errata and generalizations or improvements of code included on the companion CD.

Acknowledgments

First of all, I wish to thank the SPSS Senior Director of Publications, Bob Gruen, for giving me the opportunity to work on this challenging project. In addition to providing general guidance, Bob reviewed the macros chapter. Jon Peck reviewed and contributed to the scripting chapter. In addition to reviewing all of the remaining chapters, Rick Oliver wrote the sections on importing data from sources other than text files, data transformations, and the new SPSS Output Management System. I enjoyed working with these gentlemen; the book greatly benefited from their technical expertise and communications skills.

I also wish to thank Stephanie Schaller, who provided many sample SAS jobs and helped to define what the SAS user would want to see, as well as Marsha Hollar and Brian Teasley, the authors of the chapter "SPSS for SAS Programmers."

On the nontechnical side, I am grateful to my spouse, Nicole Tousignant, who demonstrated patience and provided support and encouragement during those months when I was handling two jobs and working seven days a week. I dedicate this book to her.

Raynald Levesque

Contents

1 Overview 1

Data Management Tasks 1
Using SPSS Data Management Facilities 3
- Graphical User Interface. 3
- Command Language 4
- Macro Facility 5
- Scripting Facility 5

Working with Command Syntax 5
- Creating Command Syntax Files 5
- Running SPSS Commands 6
- Syntax Rules 7

Using This Book 8
Documentation Resources 8

2 Best Practices and Efficiency Tips 11

Introduction 11
Customizing the Programming Environment 11
- Displaying Commands in the Log 11
- Displaying the Status Bar in Command Syntax Windows 12
- Customizing the Toolbars 13

Protecting the Original Data 16
- Do Not Overwrite Original Variables 16
- Using Temporary Transformations 17
- Using Temporary Variables 18

Using Command Syntax to Document Work 19
- Creating Command Syntax Files 19

Use EXECUTE Sparingly 20
Lag Functions 21
Using $CASENUM to Select Cases 22
MISSING VALUES Command 23
WRITE and XSAVE Commands 24
Using Comments 24
Using SET SEED to Reproduce Random Samples or Values 25
Divide and Conquer 26
Using INCLUDE with a Master Command Syntax File 26
Defining Global Settings 27

3 Getting Data into SPSS 31

Getting Data from Databases. 31
Installing Database Drivers 31
Database Wizard 32
Reading a Single Database Table 33
Reading Multiple Tables. 35
Reading Excel Files 38
Reading a "Typical" Worksheet 38
Reading Multiple Worksheets. 41
Reading Text Data Files 43
Simple Text Data Files 44
Delimited Text Data. 45
Fixed-Width Text Data 49
Text Data Files with Very Wide Records. 53
Reading Different Types of Text Data 54
Reading Complex Text Data Files 56
Mixed Files 56
Grouped Files 57
Nested (Hierarchical) Files 60
Repeating Data 66
Reading SAS Data Files 67

4 Basic Data Management 71

Variable Properties 71
Variable Labels. 75
Value Labels 75
Missing Values. 76
Measurement Level 77
Using Variable Properties As Templates 77
Cleaning and Validating Data 78
Finding and Displaying Invalid Values. 78
Excluding Invalid Data from Analysis 81
Finding and Filtering Duplicates 82
Merging Data Files 87
Merging Files with the Same Cases but Different Variables 87
Merging Files with the Same Variables but Different Cases 90
Updating Data Files by Merging New Values from Transaction Files. 94
Aggregating Data 96
Aggregate Summary Functions 99
Weighting Data 99
Changing File Structure 102
Transposing Cases and Variables 102
Cases to Variables. 106
Variables to Cases. 108
Transforming Data Values 112
Recoding Categorical Variables 113
Banding Scale Variables 113
Simple Numeric Transformations 116
Arithmetic and Statistical Functions. 117
Random Value and Distribution Functions 118
String Manipulation 119
Working with Dates and Times 126
Date Input and Display Formats 127
Date and Time Functions 130

5 Advanced Programming Features 135

Command Syntax Programming Structures 135
Indenting Commands in Programming Structures 136
DO REPEAT 136
VECTOR 140
LOOP 142
Self-Adjusting Command Syntax 149
Using Command Syntax to Write Command Syntax 150
Auto-Adjusting Command Syntax Based on Data Conditions . . . 152
Executing Selective Portions of Command Syntax 160
Excluding Variables from Analysis 163
Debugging Command Syntax 166
Errors Caused by Different Syntax Rules for Different Operational Modes 166
Calculations Affected by Low Default MXLOOPS Setting 167
Missing Values in DO IF - ELSE IF - END IF Structures 169
Disappearing Vectors 170
Locale-Sensitive Decimal Indicators 172

6 Macros 175

A Very Basic Macro 176
Macro Arguments 176
Positional Arguments 178
Tokens 179
Conditional Processing 180
Looping Constructs 182
Macro Expansion. 186
Doing Arithmetic with Macro Variables 187
Macro Examples 188
Importing from MS Access 188

Defining a List of Variables between Two Variables 191
Changing Variable Formats. 193
Reducing a String to Minimum Length 196
Including a Procedure in a Loop 197
Counting Distinct Values across Variables. 200
Recursive Macro (Macro Calling Itself). 202
Random Samples and Selections 204
Generating Simulated Data 213
Working with Many Files 215
Finding All Combinations of Three Letters Out of N 221
Creating Variables Containing Bounds of the CI for the Mean. . . 224
Debugging Macros 228
Printback of the Expanded Syntax. 228
Print Arguments 228
Examples of Error Messages. 229
Other Macro Examples Included with SPSS. 232

7 Scripting 233

Introduction 233
Scripting or OMS? 234
Tasks for Scripting. 235
Automation Objects 235
Script Window. 237
Global Scripts 238
Invoking a Script. 239
Debugging a Script 240
Scripts Included with SPSS 241
Sample Scripts 242
Add File Date to Filename. 242
Run Simple Statistics on All Variables 244
Using a Parameter in the Script Command. 246
An Autoscript That Accepts a Parameter from Syntax 247

Set Data Editor Column Width to Match Data. 249
Set the Length of All String Variables to the Maximum Length of the Data 251
Modify Page Title in Left Pane of Output Window 255
Print Syntax with Path, Date, and Page Numbers 257
Create PowerPoint Presentation 262
Utilities. 268
Empty Designated Output Window. 269
Count Number of Errors 271
Find String in the Viewer Outline 275
Check Viewer for Errors 278
A Challenge: Missing Labels 281
Synchronizing Scripts and Syntax 281
Illustration of the Problem. 281
Synchronizing without the IsBusy Method 284
Other Scripts Included on the CD 286

8 Exporting Data and Results 289

Output Management System 289
Using Output Results as Input Data 290
Transforming OXML with XSLT 299
Exporting Data to Other Applications and Formats 314
Saving Data in SAS Format 314
Saving Data in Excel Format. 315
Writing Data Back to a Database. 315
Saving Data in Text Format 317
Exporting Results to Other Applications and Formats. 317
Customizing HTML 318

9 SPSS for SAS Programmers 319

Reading Data 319
Reading Database Tables. 319
Reading Excel Files 323
Reading Text Data 325
Merging Data Files 326
Merging Files with the Same Cases but Different Variables 326
Merging Files with the Same Variables but Different Cases 327
Aggregating Data 329
Assigning Variable Properties. 331
Variable Labels. 331
Value Labels 332
Cleaning and Validating Data 333
Finding and Displaying Invalid Values. 334
Finding and Filtering Duplicates 336
Transforming Data Values 337
Recoding Data 337
Banding Data. 339
Numeric Functions. 340
Random Number Functions. 342
String Concatenation 343
String Parsing 344
Working with Dates and Times 345
Calculating and Converting Date and Time Intervals 345
Adding to or Subtracting from One Date to Find Another Date. . . 347
Extracting Date and Time Information. 348

Index 351

Chapter

1

Overview

Most researchers and others who work regularly with data recognize that much more of their time goes into various stages of acquiring and preparing data than into building models and producing reports. SPSS offers a rich set of tools for carrying out those data management tasks. This book offers many examples of how these tools can be used to bring in data from almost any source, clean it, transform it, merge it with other data, and get it into the kind of shape required to produce reliable models and informative reports. It is intended for use with other documentation resources that go into more detail about specific features but have fewer extended examples.

For readers who may be more familiar with the data management commands in the SAS system, Chapter 9 provides examples that demonstrate how some common data management tasks are handled in both SAS and SPSS.

Data Management Tasks

The data management, or data preparation, tasks that you need to perform may be quite simple or quite complex. They will typically involve some or all of the following:

Get and define the data. Getting data requires reading it from a source, such as a database, spreadsheet, text file, or file saved by another analysis program. Defining it means providing the information that SPSS needs to analyze it correctly and present meaningful reports and analyses. In many cases, that information comes directly from the source, but you may want to provide additional metadata that describes the data, such as descriptive value labels, missing value codes, and level of measurement for selected variables.

Combine data from various sources. You can read data from multiple database tables directly into SPSS. You can also combine multiple SPSS data files to add cases or add information to each case.

Clean the data. Data often come with duplicate records, missing information, and impossible (or highly unlikely) values or combinations of values. Checking for these anomalies helps to ensure valid results in analyses.

Aggregate, select, sort, and weight cases. Often, you want to work with just a sample or selection of the data, or you want to aggregate the data so that each case represents a subgroup of a large original file. By saving aggregated files and merging them back to the original data, you can compare individual values to group means or other statistics. Weighting cases allows you to give some more influence than others in analyses.

Transform data. Often, the variables that you want to test or report aren't actually in your original data but are functions of existing variables: ratios between variables, ages calculated from birth dates, counts of positive responses or missing responses across multiple questions, last names when you have names such as "Harold B. Williams," and so on. Or, variables may not be coded consistently. You might also want to collapse a lot of infrequently used values into one category. SPSS offers a powerful set of facilities for transforming data values and selecting which cases should be analyzed.

Restructure data for analysis. Various reports and analytical procedures require that the data be organized in a particular way. For example, independent samples tests typically require that all of the measured values be in one variable and that one or more classifying variables indicate which sample each value belongs to; if you have one variable for each sample (such as one column for those who accepted an offer and another column for those who did not), you need to restructure your data. The opposite may be true if you want to compare two or more measurements on the same cases.

Export data and results. After preparing the data and running reports and/or analyses, you can export both the data and the results to other applications. You can even export results as data for further analysis in SPSS or other applications.

Using SPSS Data Management Facilities

SPSS provides facilities for performing all of the tasks mentioned in the previous section, and a good deal more.

Graphical User Interface

Many SPSS data management tasks are most easily performed through the graphical user interface that provides dialog boxes and wizards to aid with specifications.

- The File menu contains the options for reading data into the system.
- The Data menu provides options for file-level tasks, such as merging two or more data files together, aggregating data, restructuring data files, and selecting subsets of cases.
- The Transform menu, as shown in Figure 1-1, provides options for case-level transformations, such as recoding data values and computing new data values (see Figure 1-2).

Figure 1-1
Transform menu

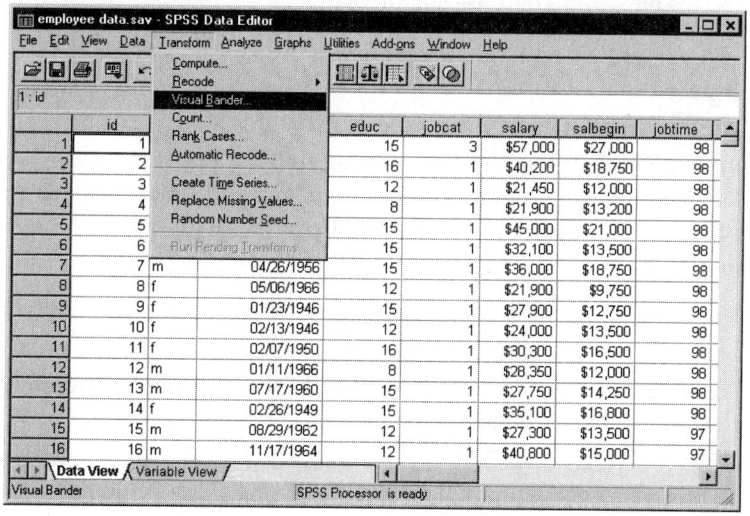

Figure 1-2
Recoding scale values into banded categories

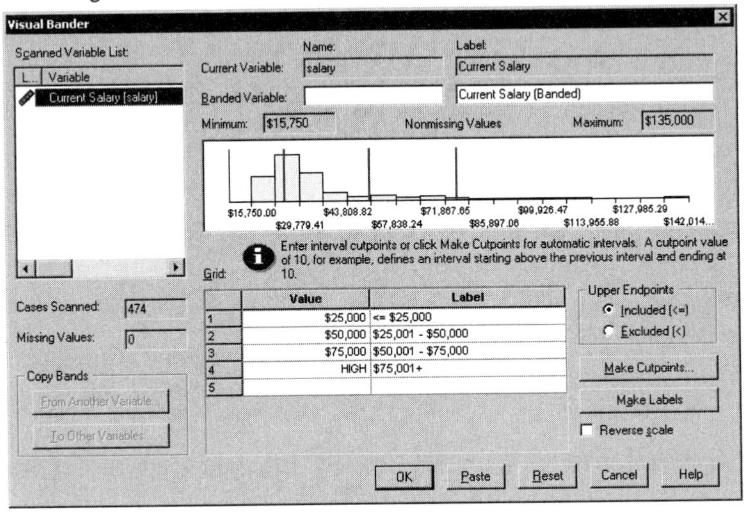

This book docs *not* discuss the graphical user interface in any great detail. The Help system provides detailed tutorials about using the graphical user interface, and almost all dialog boxes have Help buttons that display dialog-box-specific Help topics.

Command Language

The primary emphasis of this book is on using the SPSS command language, or command syntax, to write programs to solve data management problems. Although the command language may not be as user-friendly as the graphical user interface, it has several distinct advantages:

- You can save command files and run them repeatedly and in unattended batch mode.
- Some data management facilities are available only through the command language and are not available via the menus and dialog boxes.
- Command syntax provides documentation of your work, making it clear how you obtained your results and making it possible to reproduce them.

Macro Facility

SPSS has a macro facility that can be used to streamline the coding of repetitive commands and build command streams that can be run many times with varied parameters. You could, for example, create a complex command stream in which a variable or filename appears multiple times, define that stream as a macro with the name as an argument, and then call that stream as part of a job simply by naming the macro and specifying the name as an argument. Or, you could define a stream that iterates across a list of names. See Chapter 6 for more information about the macro facility.

Scripting Facility

In addition to the command language and the macro facility, you can also automate many tasks with the SPSS scripting facility using standard programming languages, such as Visual Basic and C++.

Working with Command Syntax

If you haven't worked with SPSS command syntax before, there are a few things you should know. A detailed introduction to SPSS command syntax is available in the "Universals" section in the *SPSS Command Syntax Reference*.

Creating Command Syntax Files

An SPSS command file is a simple text file. You can use any text editor to create a command syntax file, but SPSS provides a number of tools to make your job easier. Most features available in the graphical user interface have command syntax equivalents, and there are several ways to reveal that underlying command syntax:

- **Use the Paste button.** Make selections from the menus and dialog boxes, and then click the Paste button instead of the OK button. This will paste the underlying commands into a command syntax window.
- **Record commands in the log.** Select Display commands in the log on the Viewer tab in the Options dialog box (Edit menu, Options). As you run analyses, the commands for your dialog box selections will be recorded and displayed in the log in the Viewer window. You can then copy and paste the commands from the Viewer into a syntax window or text editor.

- **Retrieve commands from the journal file.** Most actions that you perform in the graphical user interface (and all commands that you run from a command syntax window) are automatically recorded in the journal file in the form of command syntax. The default name of the journal file is *spss.jnl*. The default location varies, depending on your operating system. Both the name and location of the journal file are displayed on the General tab in the Options dialog box (Edit menu, Options).

Running SPSS Commands

Once you have a set of commands, you can run the commands in a number of ways:

- Highlight the commands that you want to run in a command syntax window and click the Run button.
- Invoke one command file from another with the INCLUDE command (see Chapter 2 for more information).
- Use the Production Facility to create production jobs that can run unattended and even start unattended (and automatically) using common scheduling software. See the Help system for more information about the Production Facility.
- Use SPSSB (available only with the server version) to run command files from a command line and automatically route results to different output destinations in different formats. See the SPSSB documentation supplied with the SPSS server software for more information.

Figure 1-3
Command syntax in a syntax window

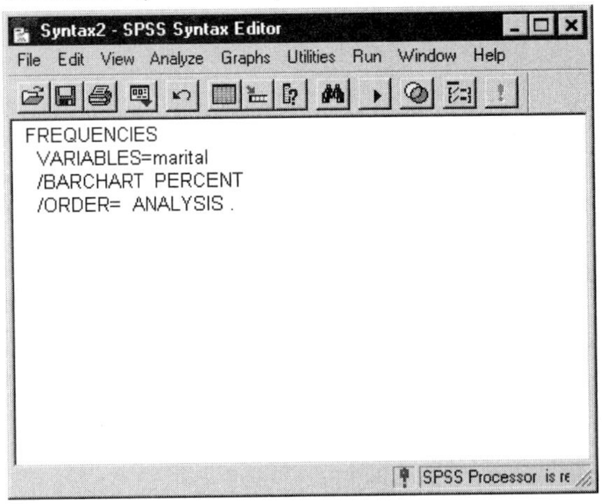

Syntax Rules

Commands run from a command syntax window during a typical SPSS session must follow the **interactive** command syntax rules:

- Each command must start on a new line.
- Each command must end with a period (.).

Commands files run via SPSSB or the Production Facility or invoked via the INCLUDE command must follow the **batch** command syntax rules:

- Each command must start in the first column of a new line.
- Each command continuation line must be indented at least one space.
- The command terminator (a period) is optional.

If you adhere to the batch rules and also include a period at the end of each command, your command syntax will run in either mode. Command syntax pasted from dialog box selections is compatible with both interactive and batch modes.

CASE doesn't MaTTeR (mostly)

For the most part, SPSS command syntax is not case sensitive.

- Commands and keywords are not case sensitive. Examples in this book display command names and keywords in upper case simply to distinguish them from user-specified parameters.
- Variable names can be defined with any mixture of upper- and lowercase characters, and case is preserved for display purposes.
- Commands that refer to existing variable names are not case sensitive. For example, FREQUENCIES VARIABLES = newvar and frequencies variables = NEWVAR are functionally equivalent.
- String values are case sensitive. This includes string data values and quoted strings. For example, the conditional statement IF (stringvar="abc") is false if the value of stringvar is *"Abc"*.

Using This Book

This book is intended for use with SPSS release 12.0 or later. Many examples will work with earlier versions, but some commands and features (such as OMS, the Visual Bander, and variable names longer than eight bytes) are not available in versions prior to release 12.0.

Most of the examples shown in this book are designed as hands-on exercises that you can perform yourself. The CD that comes with the book contains the command files and data files used in the examples. All of the sample files are contained in the *examples* folder.

- *\examples\commands* contains SPSS command syntax files.
- *\examples\data* contains data files in a variety of formats.
- *\examples\scripts* contains sample scripts.

All of the sample command files that contain file access commands assume that you have copied the examples folder to your *c:* drive. For example:

```
GET FILE='c:\examples\data\duplicates.sav'.
SORT CASES BY ID_house(A) ID_person(A) int_date(A) .
AGGREGATE OUTFILE = 'C:\temp\tempdata.sav'
```

Many examples, such as the one above, also assume that you have a *c:\temp* folder for writing temporary files. You can access command and data files from the accompanying CD, substituting the drive location for *c:* in file access commands. For commands that write files, however, you need to specify a valid folder location on a device for which you have write access.

Documentation Resources

The *SPSS Base User's Guide* documents the data management tools available through the graphical user interface. The material is similar to that available in the Help system. In addition to the chapters on "Data Files," "Data Preparation," "Data Transformations," and "File Handling and File Transformations," see:

- "Production Facility" for information about running unattended batch-mode SPSS jobs.
- "Scripting Facility" for an introduction to scripting.

The *SPSS Command Syntax Reference*, which is installed as a PDF file with the SPSS system and is available in print, is a complete guide to the specifications for each SPSS command. The guide provides many examples illustrating individual commands. It has only a few extended examples illustrating how commands can be combined to accomplish the kinds of tasks that analysts frequently encounter. Sections of the *SPSS Command Syntax Reference* of particular interest include:

- The DEFINE—!ENDDEFINE command, which covers the macro facility.
- The appendix "Using the Macro Facility," which includes additional examples.
- The appendix "Defining Complex Files," which covers the commands specifically intended for reading common types of complex files.
- The INPUT PROGRAM—END INPUT PROGRAM command, which provides rules for working with input programs.

For additional information about scripting, see the *SPSS for Windows Developer's Guide*, which is included on the SPSS installation CD in the *SPSS\developer* folder.

Chapter

2

Best Practices and Efficiency Tips

Introduction

If you haven't worked with SPSS command syntax before, you will probably start with simple jobs that perform a few basic tasks. Since it is easier to develop good habits while working with small jobs than to try to change bad habits once you move to more complex situations, you may find the information in this chapter helpful.

Some of the practices suggested in this chapter are particularly useful for large projects involving thousands of lines of code, many data files, and production jobs run on a regular basis and/or multiple data sources.

Customizing the Programming Environment

There are a few global settings and customization features that may make working with command syntax a little easier.

Displaying Commands in the Log

By default, commands that have been run are not displayed in the log, which can make it difficult to interpret error messages. To display commands in the log, use the command:

```
SET PRINTBACK = ON.
```

Or, using the graphical user interface:

▶ From the menus, choose:

Edit
 Options...

▶ Click the Viewer tab.

▶ Click (check) Display commands in the log.

Figure 2-1
Log with and without commands displayed

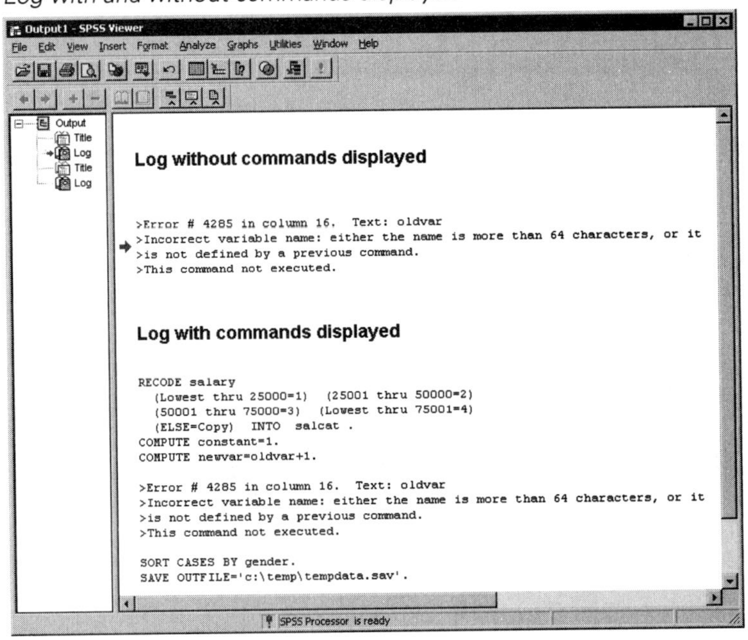

Displaying the Status Bar in Command Syntax Windows

In addition to various status messages, the status bar at the bottom of a command syntax window displays the current line number and character position within the line. Since error messages typically contain information about the column position where an error was encountered, the column position information in the status bar can help you to pinpoint errors. (*Note*: You may have to increase the width of the command syntax window to see this information.)

The status bar is displayed by default. If it is currently not displayed, select Status Bar from the View menu in the command syntax window.

Figure 2-2
Status bar in command syntax window with current line number and column position displayed

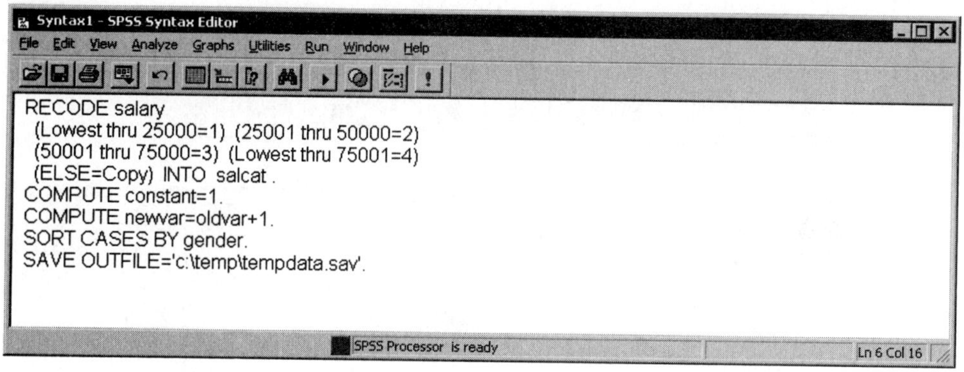

Customizing the Toolbars

SPSS provides a simple drag-and-drop interface for creating customized toolbars that use buttons as shortcuts for virtually any menu item. You can also create custom buttons that run specific command syntax files or script files. To create customized toolbars:

- From the menus, choose:

  View
  Toolbars...

- Select the window type for which you want to create or modify a toolbar.

- Click Customize to modify an existing toolbar, or click New Toolbar to create a completely new toolbar.

  For detailed information about customizing toolbars, click the Help button in any of the toolbar customization dialog boxes.

Example

The following toolbar combines items from the File, Run, and Help menus, all added to the syntax window toolbar simply by dragging and dropping selections from list boxes to the toolbar. It also contains one custom toolbar button that runs a script.

Figure 2-3
Customized toolbar

- The first two buttons are shortcuts to the following menu selections:

  File
    New
      Data

  and

  File
    New
      Syntax

  Both selections are often useful when writing and debugging command syntax.

- The next four buttons are shortcuts to the Run menu items that you can use to run different segments of a command syntax file: Current, Selection, To End, and All.

- After the Run buttons, the next two buttons display the command syntax chart for the current command (your cursor location) and the PDF version of the detailed *SPSS Command Syntax Reference*, respectively. Clicking the latter button displays the first page of the guide, not the section for the current command; the icon shown has been edited to depict an open book rather than the default generic icon provided for "user-defined" items.

  These two items may be a little hard to find when creating customized toolbars. The item for adding a button for context-sensitive syntax charts is Syntax Help in the Help category in the Customize Toolbar dialog box, and the item for adding a button for the *SPSS Command Syntax Reference* PDF is in the User-Defined category (although it is not actually "user-defined").

- The last button is a custom control that launches a script called *CountNumberOfErrors.SBS*, located in the *commands\scripts* folder. This script calculates and displays the number of errors encountered in a designated block of commands. For more information about this script, see "Count Number of Errors" on p. 271 in Chapter 7.

Additional Utility Scripts

The accompanying CD contains additional utility scripts that you may want to include as custom controls on your toolbar.

DeleteStatisticsAndCaseProcessingSummary.sbs. Deletes Statistics and Case Processing tables from the Viewer. (As an alternative, you could use the OMS command to simply prevent these table types from ever appearing in the Viewer, using the VIEWER=NO setting.)

EmptyDesignatedOutputWindow.sbs. Deletes all of the contents of the designated Viewer window and displays the number of errors encountered so far in the session.

ExportViewerToSingleExcelSheet.sbs. Exports visible SPSS pivot tables, standard charts, and interactive charts to Excel. Before executing this script, open a worksheet in Excel and select the cell/row in which pasting should start.

ShowMXERRS.sbs. Runs the command SHOW MXERRS, which displays the number of errors encountered in the session in the designated Viewer window.

FindErrorMessages.sbs. Find error messages in logs and text blocks. Warnings objects and items that are not visible are not included.

FindOutlineText.sbs. Searches for the specified text string in the outline pane of the designated Viewer window. The search is not case sensitive.

ReplaceLeftPanePageTitle.sbs. Replaces "Page Title" in the outline pane with a portion of the content of the page title. This is useful for placing quick references in the outline pane to locate given areas of the output. It has no effect if no page titles have been created. Page titles are different from the object titles that also appear in the outline. They are created by the TITLE command or, in the Viewer, by selecting Page Title from the Insert menu.

PrintSyntaxFile.sbs. Saves and prints the currently designated syntax window. The filename, path, date, timestamp, and page numbers are printed

ConvertSyntaxToScript.sbs. Converts the command syntax of the designated syntax window into the corresponding script format. The resulting command syntax is pasted at the end of the designated syntax window.

Protecting the Original Data

The original data file should be protected from modifications that may alter or delete original variables and/or cases. If the original data are in an external file format (for example, text, Excel, or database), there is little risk of accidentally overwriting the original data while working in SPSS. However, if the original data are in SPSS-format data files (*.sav*), there are many transformation commands that can modify or destroy the data, and it is not difficult to inadvertently overwrite the contents of an SPSS-format data file. Overwriting the original data file may result in a loss of data that cannot be retrieved.

There are several ways in which you can protect the original data, including:

- Storing a copy in a separate location, such as on a CD, that can't be overwritten.
- Using the operating system facilities to change the read-write property of the file to read-only. If you aren't familiar with how to do this in the operating system, you can use Mark File Read Only on the File menu or the new PERMISSIONS subcommand on the SAVE command.

The ideal situation is then to load the original (protected) data file into SPSS and do *all* data transformations, recoding, and calculations using SPSS. The objective is to end up with one or more command syntax files that start from the original data and produce the required results without any manual intervention.

Do Not Overwrite Original Variables

It is often necessary to recode or modify original variables, and it is good practice to assign the modified values to new variables and keep the original variable unchanged. For one thing, this allows comparison of the initial and modified values to verify that the intended modifications were carried out correctly. The original values can subsequently be discarded if required.

Example

```
*These commands overwrite existing variables.
COMPUTE var1=var1*2.
RECODE var2 (1 thru 5 = 1) (6 thru 10 = 2).
*These commands create new variables.
COMPUTE var1_new=var1*2.
RECODE var2 (1 thru 5 = 1) (6 thru 10 = 2)(ELSE=COPY)
  /INTO var2_new.
```

- The difference between the two COMPUTE commands is simply the substitution of a new variable name on the left side of the equals sign.
- The second RECODE command includes the INTO subcommand, which specifies a new variable to receive the recoded values of the original variable. ELSE=COPY makes sure that any values not covered by the specified ranges are preserved.

Using Temporary Transformations

You can use the TEMPORARY command to temporarily transform existing variables for analysis. The temporary transformations remain in effect through the first command that reads the data (for example, a statistical procedure), after which the variables revert to their original values.

Example

```
*temporary.sps.
data list free /var1 var2.
begin data
1 2
3 4
5 6
7 8
9 10
end data.
TEMPORARY.
COMPUTE var1=var1+5.
RECODE var2 (1 thru 5=1) (6 thru 10=2).
FREQUENCIES
  /VARIABLES=var1 var2
  /STATISTICS=MEAN STDDEV MIN MAX.
DESCRIPTIVES
  /VARIABLES=var1 var2
  /STATISTICS=MEAN STDDEV MIN MAX.
```

- The transformed values from the two transformation commands that follow the TEMPORARY command will be used in the FREQUENCIES procedure.
- The original data values will be used in the subsequent DESCRIPTIVES procedure, yielding different results for the same summary statistics.

Using Temporary Variables

For transformations that require intermediate variables, use scratch (temporary) variables for the intermediate values. Any variable name that begins with a pound sign (#) is treated as a scratch variable that is discarded at the end of the series of transformation commands when SPSS encounters an EXECUTE command or other command that reads the data (such as a statistical procedure).

Example

```
*scratchvar.sps.
DATA LIST FREE / var1.
BEGIN DATA
1 2 3 4 5
END DATA.
COMPUTE factor=1.
LOOP #tempvar=1 TO var1.
- COMPUTE factor=factor * #tempvar.
END LOOP.
EXECUTE.
```

Figure 2-4
Result of loop with scratch variable

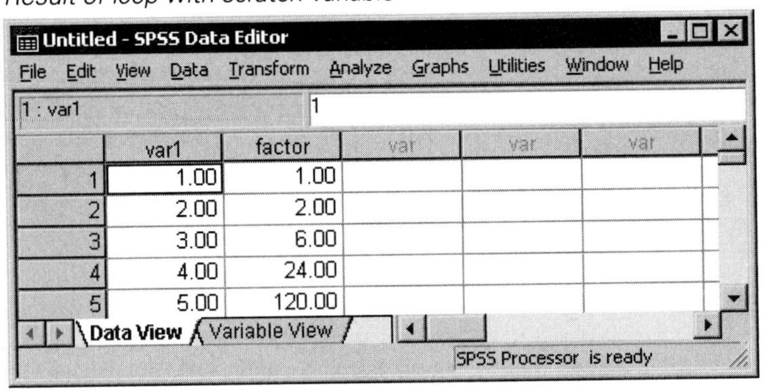

- The loop structure computes the factorial for each value of *var1* and puts the factorial value in the variable *factor*.
- The scratch variable *#tempvar* is used as an index variable for the loop structure.
- For each case, the COMPUTE command is run iteratively up to the value of *var1*.
- For each iteration, the current value of the variable *factor* is multiplied by the current loop iteration number stored in *#tempvar*.

- The EXECUTE command runs the transformation commands, after which the scratch variable is discarded.

The use of scratch variables doesn't technically "protect" the original data in any way, but it does prevent the data file from getting cluttered with extraneous variables. If you need to remove temporary variables that still exist after reading the data, you can use the DELETE VARIABLES command to eliminate them.

Using Command Syntax to Document Work

Contrary to what many new SPSS users generally expect, it is often almost as easy—and sometimes even easier—to create a command syntax file (which is a program) as it is to select menu and dialog box options. Command syntax also has a number of distinct advantages:

- **Documentation.** The commands represent step-by-step documentation of how you obtained your results.
- **Verification.** Anyone can easily rerun the command syntax and compare the results.
- **Reuse.** You can automate common tasks performed on a routine basis.

Creating Command Syntax Files

If you're new to SPSS command syntax, there are a number of tools to help you get started. Most features available in the graphical user interface have command syntax equivalents, and there are several ways to reveal that underlying command syntax:

- **Use the Paste button.** Make selections from the menus and dialog boxes, and then click the Paste button instead of the OK button. This will paste the underlying commands into a command syntax window.
- **Record commands in the log.** Select Display commands in the log on the Viewer tab in the Options dialog box (Edit menu, Options). As you run analyses, the commands for your dialog box selections will be recorded and displayed in the log in the Viewer window. You can then copy and paste the commands from the Viewer to a syntax window or text editor. See "Displaying Commands in the Log" on p. 11 for more information.

- **Retrieve commands from the journal file.** Most actions that you perform in the graphical user interface (and all commands that you run from a command syntax window) are automatically recorded in the journal file in the form of command syntax. The default name of the journal file is *spss.jnl*. The default location varies, depending on your operating system. Both the name and location of the journal file are displayed on the General tab in the Options dialog box (Edit menu, Options).
- **Use the script define_variables.sbs.** Use this script (located in the *examples\scripts* folder) to generate variable definition command syntax based on the current properties of the working data file. If you use Variable View in the Data Editor to define variable properties, such as variable labels, value labels, and missing values, there is no Paste button and none of these actions will be recorded in the log or journal. This script generates the equivalent command syntax based on the defined properties of the variables in the working data file.

Use EXECUTE Sparingly

SPSS is designed to work with large data files (the current version can accommodate 2.15 billion cases). Since going through every case of a large data file takes time, the software is also designed to minimize the number of times it has to read the data. Statistical and charting procedures always read the data, but most transformation commands (for example, COMPUTE, RECODE, COUNT, SELECT IF) do not require a separate data pass.

The default behavior of the graphical user interface, however, is to read the data for each separate transformation so that you can see the results in the Data Editor immediately. Consequently, every transformation command generated from the dialog boxes is followed by an EXECUTE command. So, if you create command syntax by pasting from dialog boxes or copying from the log or journal, your command syntax may contain a large number of superfluous EXECUTE commands that can significantly increase the processing time for very large data files.

In most cases, you can remove virtually all of the auto-generated EXECUTE commands, which will speed up processing, particularly for large data files and jobs that contain many transformation commands.

To turn off the automatic, immediate execution of transformations and the associated pasting of EXECUTE commands:

▶ From the menus, choose:

Edit
 Options...

▶ Click the Data tab.

▶ Click Calculate values before used.

Lag Functions

One notable exception to the above rule is transformation commands that contain lag functions. In a series of transformation commands without any intervening EXECUTE commands or other commands that read the data, lag functions are calculated after all other transformations, regardless of command order. While this might not be a consideration most of the time, it requires special consideration in the following cases:

- The lag variable is also used in any of the other transformation commands.
- One of the transformations selects a subset of cases and deletes the unselected cases, such as SELECT IF or SAMPLE.

Example

```
*lagfunction.sps.
*create some data.
DATA LIST FREE /var1.
BEGIN DATA
1 2 3 4 5
END DATA.
COMPUTE var2=var1.
********************************.
*Lag without intervening EXECUTE.
COMPUTE lagvar1=LAG(var1).
COMPUTE var1=var1*2.
EXECUTE.
********************************.
*Lag with intervening EXECUTE.
COMPUTE lagvar2=LAG(var2).
EXECUTE.
COMPUTE var2=var2*2.
EXECUTE.
```

Figure 2-5
Results of lag functions displayed in Data Editor

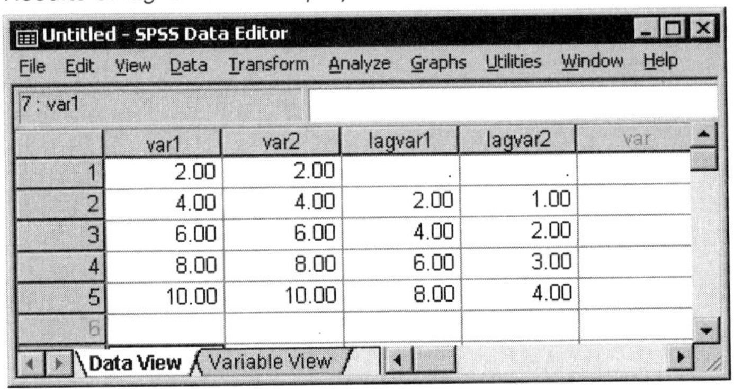

- Although *var1* and *var2* contain the same data values, *lagvar1* and *lagvar2* are very different from each other.
- Without an intervening EXECUTE command, *lagvar1* is based on the transformed values of *var1*.
- With the EXECUTE command between the two transformation commands, the value of *lagvar2* is based on the original value of *var2*.
- Any command that reads the data will have the same effect as the EXECUTE command. For example, you could substitute the FREQUENCIES command and achieve the same result.

In a similar fashion, if the set of transformations includes a command that selects a subset of cases and deletes unselected cases (for example, SELECT IF), lags will be computed after the case selection. You will probably want to avoid case selection criteria based on lag values—unless you EXECUTE the lags first.

Using $CASENUM to Select Cases

The value of the system variable *$CASENUM* is dynamic. If you change the sort order of cases, the value of *$CASENUM* for each case changes. If you delete the first case, the case that formerly had a value of 2 for this system variable now has the value 1. Using the value of *$CASENUM* with the SELECT IF command can be a little tricky because SELECT IF deletes each unselected case, changing the value of *$CASENUM* for all remaining cases.

For example, a SELECT IF command of the general form:

```
SELECT IF ($CASENUM > [positive value]).
```

will delete all cases because, regardless of the value specified, the value of *$CASENUM* for the current case will never be greater than 1. When the first case is evaluated, it has a value of 1 for *$CASENUM* and is therefore deleted because it doesn't have a value greater than the specified positive value. The erstwhile second case then becomes the first case, with a value of 1, and is consequently also deleted, and so on.

The simple solution to this problem is to create a new variable equal to the original value of *$CASENUM*. However, command syntax of the form:

```
COMPUTE CaseNumber=$CASENUM.
SELECT IF (CaseNumber > [positive value]).
```

will still delete all cases because each case is deleted before the value of the new variable is computed. The correct solution is to insert an EXECUTE command between COMPUTE and SELECT IF, as in:

```
COMPUTE CaseNumber=$CASENUM.
EXECUTE.
SELECT IF (CaseNumber > [positive value]).
```

MISSING VALUES Command

If you have a series of transformation commands (for example, COMPUTE, IF, RECODE) followed by a MISSING VALUES command that involves the same variables, you may want to place an EXECUTE statement before the MISSING VALUES command. This is because the MISSING VALUES command changes the dictionary before the transformations take place.

Example

```
IF (x = 0) y = z*2.
MISSING VALUES x (0).
```

The cases where x = 0 would be considered user-missing on x, and the transformation of y would not occur. Placing an EXECUTE before MISSING VALUES allows the transformation to occur before 0 is assigned missing status.

WRITE and XSAVE Commands

In some circumstances, it may be necessary to have an EXECUTE command after a WRITE or an XSAVE command. See "Using XSAVE in a Loop to Build a Data File" on p. 148 and "Using Command Syntax to Write Command Syntax" on p. 150 in Chapter 5 for more information.

Using Comments

It is always a good practice to include explanatory comments in your code. In SPSS, you can do this in several ways:

```
COMMENT Get summary stats for scale variables.
* An asterisk in the first column also identifies comments.
FREQUENCIES
  VARIABLES=income ed reside
  /FORMAT=LIMIT(10) /*avoid long frequency tables
  /STATISTICS=MEAN /*arithmetic average*/ MEDIAN.
* A macro name like !mymacro in this comment may invoke the macro.
/* A macro name like !mymacro in this comment will not invoke the
   macro*/.
```

- The first line of a comment can begin with the keyword COMMENT or with an asterisk (*).
- Comment text can extend for multiple lines and can contain any characters. The rules for continuation lines are the same as for other commands. Be sure to terminate a comment with a period. See "Syntax Rules" on p. 7 in Chapter 1 for more information.
- Use /* and */ to set off a comment within a command.
- The closing */ is optional when the comment is at the end of the line. The command can continue onto the next line just as if the inserted comment was a blank.
- To ensure that comments that refer to macros by name don't accidently invoke those macros, use the /* [comment text] */ format.

Using SET SEED to Reproduce Random Samples or Values

When doing research work involving random numbers—for example, when randomly assigning cases to experimental treatment groups—you should explicitly set the random number seed value if you want to be able to reproduce the same results.

The random number generator is used by the SAMPLE command to generate random samples and is used by many distribution functions (for example, NORMAL, UNIFORM) to generate distributions of random numbers. The generator begins with a **seed**, a large integer. Starting with the same seed, the system will repeatedly produce the same sequence of numbers and will select the same sample from a given data file. At the start of each session, the seed is set to a value that may vary or may be fixed, depending on your current settings. The seed value changes each time a series of transformations contains one or more commands that use the random number generator.

Example

To repeat the same random distribution within a session or in subsequent sessions, use SET SEED before each series of transformations that use the random number generator to explicitly set the seed value to a constant value.

```
*set_seed.sps.
GET FILE = 'c:\examples\data\onevar.sav'.
SET SEED = 123456789.
SAMPLE .1.
LIST.
SHOW SEED.
GET FILE = 'c:\examples\data\onevar.sav'.
SET SEED = 123456789.
SAMPLE .1.
LIST.
```

- Before the first sample is taken the first time, the seed value is explicitly set with SET SEED.
- The LIST command causes the data to be read and the random number generator to be invoked once for each original case. The result is an updated seed value.
- The second time the data file is opened, SET SEED sets the seed to the same value as before, resulting in the same sample of cases.
- Both SET SEED commands are required since you aren't likely to know what the initial seed value is unless you set it yourself.

Note: This example opens the data file before each SAMPLE command because successive SAMPLE commands are *cumulative* within the working data file.

Divide and Conquer

A time-proven method of winning the battle against programming bugs is to split the tasks into separate, manageable pieces. It is also easier to navigate around a syntax file of 200–300 lines than one of 2,000–3,000 lines.

Therefore, it is good practice to break down a program into separate stand-alone files, each performing a specific task or set of tasks. For example, you could create separate command syntax files to:

- Prepare and standardize data.
- Merge data files.
- Perform tests on data.
- Report results for different groups (for example, gender, age group, income category).

Using the INCLUDE command and a master command syntax file that specifies all of the other command files, you can partition all of these tasks into separate command files.

Using INCLUDE with a Master Command Syntax File

The INCLUDE command provides a method for linking multiple syntax files together, making it possible to reuse blocks of command syntax in different projects by using a "master" command syntax file that consists primarily of INCLUDE commands that refer to other command syntax files.

Example

```
INCLUDE FILE = "c:\examples\data\prepare data.sps".
INCLUDE FILE = "c:\examples\commands\combine data.sps".
INCLUDE FILE = "c:\examples\commands\do tests.sps".
INCLUDE FILE = "c:\examples\commands\report groups.sps".
```

- Each INCLUDE command specifies a file that contains SPSS command syntax.
- Each included file must use **batch mode** syntax rules; that is, each command must begin in the first column, and command continuation lines must be indented at least one space.
- You should use absolute paths to specify file locations, even if all of the files are located in the same folder. See "Defining Global Settings" on p. 27 for information about using macros to specify paths.

Error Handling with INCLUDE Files

One minor drawback of using INCLUDE instead of putting all of the command syntax into one large file is that processing of an included file stops when the first error in the file is encountered. In many cases, this is not what you want. For example, in normal command processing, such as:

```
FREQUENCIES VARIABLES = catvar1, catvar2, 3catvar.
DESCRIPTIVES VARIABLES = scalevar1, scalevar2.
```

the second command will run even though the first command generates a warning message (*3catvar* is not a legal variable name since it starts with a number; so, that variable can't exist in any data file). In an included file, however, the second command (and any subsequent commands in the included file) will not run.

Defining Global Settings

In addition to using INCLUDE to create modular master command syntax files, you can define global settings that will enable you to use those same command files for different reports and analyses.

Example

You can create a separate command syntax file that contains a set of macros that define global variables for file paths, client name, output language, and so on. When you need to change any settings, you change them once in the macro definition file, leaving the bulk of the command syntax files unchanged. This example uses simple string substitution macros, where the defined strings will be substituted wherever the macro names appear in subsequent commands during the session. See Chapter 6 for more information.

```
*define_globals.sps.
DEFINE !pathd()'c:\examples\data\'!ENDDEFINE.
DEFINE !pathsyn()'c:\examples\commands\'!ENDDEFINE.
DEFINE !pathpgm()'c:\Program Files\SPSS\'!ENDDEFINE.
DEFINE !pathtmp()'d:\temp\'!ENDDEFINE.

DEFINE !enddate()DATE.DMY(1,1,2004)!ENDDEFINE.
DEFINE !olang()English!ENDDEFINE.
DEFINE !client()"ABC Inc"!ENDDEFINE
DEFINE !title()TITLE !client.!ENDDEFINE.
```

- The first two DEFINE commands define the paths for the data and command syntax files.
- !pathpgm contains the path to the SPSS folder. This path can be useful if you use any of the command syntax or script files that are installed with SPSS.
- !pathtmp contains the path of a temporary folder. It is very useful to define a temporary folder path and use it to save any intermediary files created by the various command syntax files making up the project. The main purpose of this is to avoid crowding the data folders with useless files, some of which might be very large. Note that here the !pathtmp resides on the *d:* drive. When possible, it is more efficient to keep the temporary and main folders on different hard drives.
- !enddate contains the end date of the period covered by the data file. This can be useful to calculate ages or other duration variables as well as to add footnotes to tables or graphs.
- !olang specifies the output language.
- !client contains the client's name. This can be used in titles of tables or graphs.
- !title specifies a TITLE command, using the value of the macro *!client* as the title text.

The master command syntax file might then look something like this:

```
INCLUDE FILE = "c:\examples\commands\define_globals.sps".
!title.
INCLUDE FILE = !pathd + "prepare data.sps".
INCLUDE FILE = !pathsyn + "combine data.sps".
INCLUDE FILE = !pathsyn + "do tests.sps".
INCLUDE FILE = !pathsyn + "report groups.sps".
```

- The first INCLUDE runs the command syntax file that defines all of the global settings. This needs to be run before any commands that invoke the macros defined in that file.
- !title will print the client's name at the top of each page of output.
- !pathd and !pathsyn in the remaining INCLUDE commands insert the defined paths before the filenames. The plus sign (+) concatenates the string represented by the macro and the quoted string for the filename into a single quoted string.

Note: Using absolute paths or macros that represent those paths is the most reliable way to make sure that SPSS finds the necessary files. Relative paths may not work as you might expect, since they refer to the current directory, which can change frequently.

Global Subroutines

You can create much more sophisticated macros than these simple string substitution macros, including macros that take arguments that you specify in the macro calls. As a general rule, you may find it most useful to keep most macros in separate files, distinct from your regular command syntax files. You can then use the macro files as a library of global subroutines.

Example

This macro executes one set of commands for a list of categorical variables that you supply and another set of commands for a list of scale variables that you supply. This might be useful if you routinely generate the same descriptive and summary statistics as a preliminary step before further analysis, where the only thing that differs is the variables used in the summaries.

```
*macro_lib1.sps.
DEFINE !sumstat (catvars = !CHAREND('/')
  /scalevars = !CMDEND)
!IF (!catvars ~=!NULL) !THEN
frequencies variables = !catvars
    /barchart.
!IFEND
!IF (!scalevars ~= !NULL) !THEN
frequencies variables = !scalevars
   /format = notable
   /statistics = mean median min max
   /histogram.
!IFEND
!ENDDEFINE.
```

- The macro contains two arguments: one for handling categorical variables and one for handling scale variables.
- catvars = !CHAREND('/') specifies that any text in the macro call between catvars = and the next forward slash encountered in the macro call will be used wherever !catvars appears in the macro.
- scalevars = !CMDEND specifies that any text in the macro call that appears after scalevars = will be used wherever !scalevars appears in the macro.
- Two FREQUENCIES commands are defined in the macro: one to use for categorical variables and one to use for scale variables.

- The !IF statements make sure that the macro call includes a list of *catvars* and/or *scalevars* before running the respective FREQUENCIES command. This provides more flexibility, since the macro call can then contain one list of either kind or both lists without generating any errors.

You could then invoke the macro in several ways:

```
***First run the file that defines the macro***.
INCLUDE FILE="c:\examples\commands\macro_lib1.sps".

***now run the macro with both catvars and scalevars***.
!sumstat catvars  = marital gender jobcat
    /scalevars = income age edyears.

***now run it with just catvars***.
!sumstat catvars  = marital gender jobcat.
***and now just scalevars***.
!sumstat scalevars  = income age edyears.
```

The first macro call would generate two FREQUENCIES commands; the other two would each generate one FREQUENCIES command. In each case, the variables listed in the macro call would be used in the VARIABLES subcommand. Macros are discussed in greater detail in Chapter 6.

Chapter

3

Getting Data into SPSS

Before you can work with data in SPSS, you need some data to work with. There are several ways to get data into the application:

- Open a data file that has already been saved in SPSS format.
- Enter data manually in the Data Editor.
- Read a data file from another source, such as a database, text data file, spreadsheet, or SAS.

Opening an SPSS-format data file is simple, and manually entering data in the Data Editor is not likely to be your first choice, particularly if you have a large amount of data. This chapter focuses on how to read data files created and saved in other applications and formats.

Getting Data from Databases

SPSS relies on ODBC (open database connectivity) to read data from databases. ODBC is an open standard with versions available on many platforms, including Windows, UNIX, and Macintosh.

Installing Database Drivers

You can read data from any database format for which you have a database driver. In local analysis mode, the necessary drivers must be installed on your local computer. In distributed analysis mode (available with the server version), the drivers must be installed on the remote server.

ODBC database drivers for a wide variety of database formats are included on the SPSS installation CD, including:

- Access
- Btrieve
- DB2
- dBASE
- Excel
- FoxPro
- Informix
- Oracle
- Paradox
- Progress
- SQL Base
- SQL Server
- Sybase

Most of these drivers can be installed by installing the SPSS Data Access Pack. You can install the SPSS Data Access Pack from the Autoplay menu on the SPSS installation CD.

If you need a Microsoft Access driver, you will need to install the Microsoft Data Access Pack. An installable version is located in the Microsoft Data Access Pack folder on the SPSS installation CD.

Before you can use the installed database drivers, you may also need to configure the drivers using the Windows ODBC Data Source Administrator. For the SPSS Data Access Pack, installation instructions and information on configuring data sources are located in the *Installation Instructions* folder on the SPSS installation CD.

Database Wizard

It's probably a good idea to use the Database Wizard (File menu, Open Database) the first time you retrieve data from a database source. At the last step of the wizard, you can paste the equivalent commands into a command syntax window. Although the SQL generated by the wizard tends to be overly verbose, it also generates the CONNECT string, which you might never figure out without the wizard.

Reading a Single Database Table

SPSS reads data from databases by reading database tables. You can read information from a single table or merge data from multiple tables in the same database. A single database table has basically the same two-dimensional structure as an SPSS data file: records are cases and fields are variables. So reading a single table can be very simple.

Example

This example reads a single table from an Access database. It reads all records and fields in the table.

```
*access1.sps.
GET DATA /TYPE=ODBC /CONNECT=
 'DSN=MS Access Database;DBQ=C:\examples\data\dm_demo.mdb;'+
 'DriverId=25;FIL=MS Access;MaxBufferSize=2048;PageTimeout=5;'
 /SQL = 'SELECT * FROM CombinedTable'.
EXECUTE.
```

- The GET DATA command is used to read the database.
- TYPE=ODBC indicates that an ODBC driver will be used to read the data. This is required for reading data from any database, and it can also be used for other data sources with ODBC drivers, such as Excel workbooks (see "Reading Multiple Worksheets" on p. 41).
- CONNECT identifies the data source. For this example, the CONNECT string was copied from the command syntax generated by the Database Wizard. The entire string must be enclosed in single or double quotes. In this example, we have split the long string onto two lines using a plus sign (+) to combine the two strings.
- The SQL subcommand can contain any SQL statements supported by the database format. Each line must be enclosed in single or double quotes.
- SELECT * FROM CombinedTable reads all of the fields (columns) and all records (rows) from the table named *CombinedTable* in the database.
- Any field names that are not valid SPSS variable names are automatically converted to valid variable names, and the original field names are used as variable labels. In this database table, many of the field names contain spaces, which are removed in the variable names.

Figure 3-1
Database field names converted to valid variable names

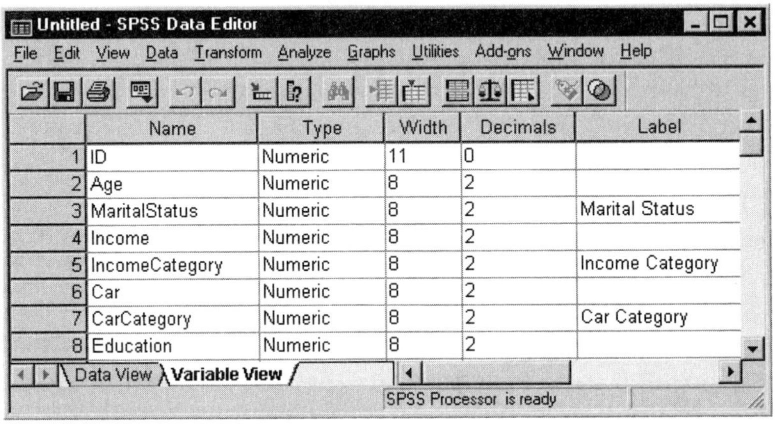

Example

Now we'll read the same database table—except this time, we'll read only a subset of fields and records.

```
*access2.sps.
GET DATA /TYPE=ODBC /CONNECT=
 'DSN=MS Access Database;DBQ=C:\examples\data\dm_demo.mdb;'+
 'DriverId=25;FIL=MS Access;MaxBufferSize=2048;PageTimeout=5;'
 /SQL =
 'SELECT  Age,  Education,  [Income Category]'
 ' FROM CombinedTable'
 ' WHERE ([Marital Status] <> 1 AND Internet = 1 )'.
EXECUTE.
```

- The SELECT clause explicitly specifies only three fields from the file; so the working data file will contain only three variables.
- The WHERE clause will select only records where the value of the *Marital Status* field is not 1 and the value of the *Internet* field is 1. In this example, that means only unmarried people who have Internet service will be included.

Two additional details in this example are worth noting:

- The field names *Income Category* and *Marital Status* are enclosed in brackets. Since these field names contain spaces, they must be enclosed in brackets or quotes. Since single quotes are already being used to enclose each line of the SQL statement, the alternative to brackets here would be double quotes.
- We've put the FROM and WHERE clauses on separate lines to make the code easier to read; however, in order for this command to be read properly, each of those lines also has a blank space between the starting single quote and the first word on the line. When the command is processed, all of the lines of the SQL statement are merged together in a very literal fashion. Without the space before WHERE, the program would attempt to read a table named *CombinedTableWhere*, and an error would result. As a general rule, you should probably insert a blank space between the quotation mark and the first word of each continuation line.

Reading Multiple Tables

You can combine data from two or more database tables by "joining" the tables. The working data file can be constructed from more than two tables, but each "join" defines a relationship between only two of those tables:

- **Inner join.** Records in the two tables with matching values for one or more specified fields are included. For example, a unique ID value may be used in each table, and records with matching ID values are combined. Any records without matching identifier values in the other table are omitted.
- **Left outer join.** All records from the first table are included regardless of the criteria used to match records.
- **Right outer join.** Essentially the opposite of a left outer join. So the appropriate one to use is basically a matter of the order in which the tables are specified in the SQL SELECT clause.

Example

In the previous two examples, all of the data resided in a single database table. But what if the data were divided between two tables? This example merges data from two different tables: one containing demographic information for survey respondents and one containing survey responses.

```
*access_multtables1.sps.
GET DATA /TYPE=ODBC /CONNECT=
 'DSN=MS Access Database;DBQ=C:\examples\data\dm_demo.mdb;'+
  'DriverId=25;FIL=MS Access;MaxBufferSize=2048;PageTimeout=5;'
 /SQL =
 'SELECT  * FROM DemographicInformation, SurveyResponses'
 ' WHERE DemographicInformation.ID=SurveyResponses.ID'.
EXECUTE.
```

- The SELECT clause specifies all fields from both tables.
- The WHERE clause matches records from the two tables based on the value of the *ID* field in both tables. Any records in either table without matching *ID* values in the other table are excluded.
- The result is an inner join in which only records with matching *ID* values in both tables are included in the working data file.

Example

In addition to one-to-one matching, as in the previous inner join example, you can also merge tables with a one-to-many matching scheme. For example, you could match a table in which there are only a few records representing data values and associated descriptive labels with values in a table containing hundreds or thousands of records representing survey respondents.

In this example, we read data from an SQL Server database, using an outer join to avoid omitting records in the larger table that don't have matching identifier values in the smaller table.

```
*sqlserver_outer_join.sps.
GET DATA /TYPE=ODBC
 /CONNECT= 'DSN=SQLServer;UID=;APP=SPSS For Windows;'
  'WSID=ROLIVERLAP;Network=DBMSSOCN;Trusted_Connection=Yes'
 /SQL =
  'SELECT  SurveyResponses.ID,  SurveyResponses.Internet,'
  ' [Value Labels].[Internet Label]'
  ' FROM SurveyResponses LEFT OUTER JOIN [Value Labels]'
  ' ON SurveyResponses.Internet'
  ' = [Value Labels].[Internet Value]'.
```

Figure 3-2
SQL Server tables to be merged with outer join

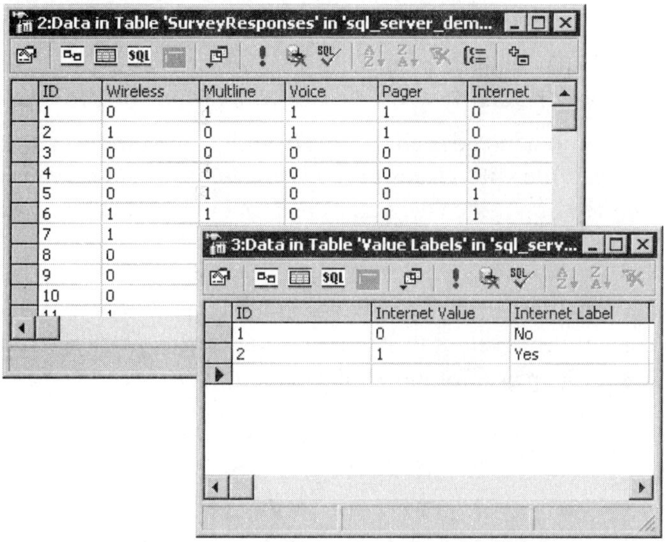

Figure 3-3
Working data file in SPSS

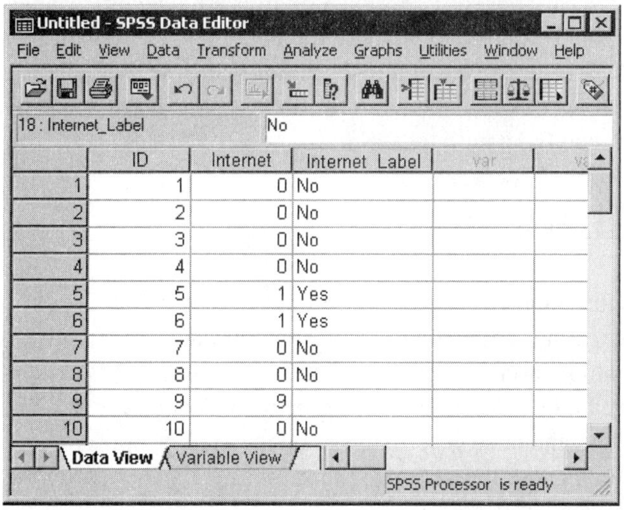

- FROM SurveyResponses LEFT OUTER JOIN [Value Labels] will include all records from the table *SurveyResponses* even if there are no records in the *Value Labels* table that meet the matching criteria.

- ON SurveyResponses.Internet = [Value Labels].[Internet Value] matches records based on the value of the field *Internet* in the table *SurveyResponses* and the value of the field *Internet Value* in the table *Value Labels*.
- The resulting working data file has an *InternetLabel* value of *No* for all cases with a value of 0 for *Internet* and *Yes* for all cases with a value of 1 for *Internet*.
- Since the left outer join includes all records from *SurveyResponses*, there are cases in the working data file with values of 8 or 9 for *Internet* and no value (a blank string) for *InternetLabel*, since the values of 8 and 9 do not occur in the *Internet Value* field in the table *Value Labels*.

Now that the value labels are in the working data file in the form of a separate variable, it's possible to convert those values to standard value labels (see "Importing from MS Access" on p. 188 in Chapter 6 for more information).

Reading Excel Files

SPSS can read individual Excel worksheets and multiple worksheets in the same Excel workbook. The basic mechanics of reading Excel files are relatively straightforward—rows are read as cases and columns are read as variables. However, reading a typical Excel spreadsheet—where the data may not start in row 1, column 1—requires a little extra work, and reading multiple worksheets requires treating the Excel workbook as a database. In both instances, we can use the GET DATA command to read the data into SPSS.

Reading a "Typical" Worksheet

When reading an individual worksheet, SPSS reads a rectangular area of the worksheet, and everything in that area must be data-related. The first row of the area may or may not contain variable names (depending on your specifications); the remainder of the area must contain the data to be read. A typical worksheet, however, may also contain titles and other information that may not be appropriate for an SPSS data file and may even cause the data to be read incorrectly if you don't explicitly specify the range of cells to read.

Example

Figure 3-4
Typical Excel worksheet

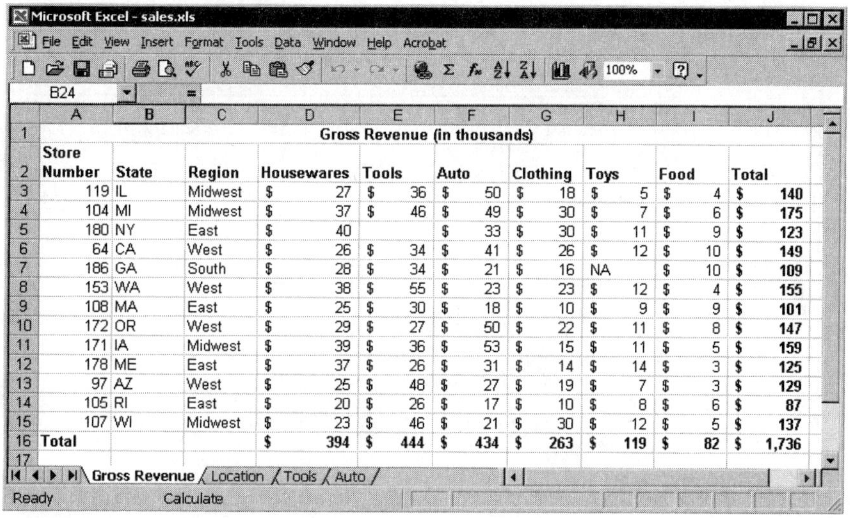

Store Number	State	Region	Housewares	Tools	Auto	Clothing	Toys	Food	Total
119	IL	Midwest	$ 27	$ 36	$ 50	$ 18	$ 5	$ 4	**$ 140**
104	MI	Midwest	$ 37	$ 46	$ 49	$ 30	$ 7	$ 6	**$ 175**
180	NY	East	$ 40		$ 33	$ 30	$ 11	$ 9	**$ 123**
64	CA	West	$ 26	$ 34	$ 41	$ 26	$ 12	$ 10	**$ 149**
186	GA	South	$ 28	$ 34	$ 21	$ 16	NA	$ 10	**$ 109**
153	WA	West	$ 38	$ 55	$ 23	$ 23	$ 12	$ 4	**$ 155**
108	MA	East	$ 25	$ 30	$ 18	$ 10	$ 9	$ 9	**$ 101**
172	OR	West	$ 29	$ 27	$ 50	$ 22	$ 11	$ 8	**$ 147**
171	IA	Midwest	$ 39	$ 36	$ 53	$ 15	$ 11	$ 5	**$ 159**
178	ME	East	$ 37	$ 26	$ 31	$ 14	$ 14	$ 3	**$ 125**
97	AZ	West	$ 25	$ 48	$ 27	$ 19	$ 7	$ 3	**$ 129**
105	RI	East	$ 20	$ 26	$ 17	$ 10	$ 8	$ 6	**$ 87**
107	WI	Midwest	$ 23	$ 46	$ 21	$ 30	$ 12	$ 5	**$ 137**
Total			**$ 394**	**$ 444**	**$ 434**	**$ 263**	**$ 119**	**$ 82**	**$ 1,736**

To read this spreadsheet without the title row or total row and column:

```
*readexcel.sps.
GET DATA
   /TYPE=XLS
   /FILE='c:\examples\data\sales.xls'
   /SHEET=NAME 'Gross Revenue'
   /CELLRANGE=RANGE 'A2:I15'
   /READNAMES=on .
```

- The TYPE subcommand identifies the file type as Excel, version 5 or later. (For earlier versions, use GET TRANSLATE.)
- The SHEET subcommand identifies which worksheet of the workbook to read. Instead of the NAME keyword, you could use the INDEX keyword and an integer value indicating the sheet location in the workbook. Without this subcommand, the first worksheet is read.
- The CELLRANGE subcommand indicates that SPSS should start reading at column A, row 2, and read through column J, row 15.
- The READNAMES subcommand indicates that the first row of the specified range contains column labels to be used as variable names.

Figure 3-5
Excel worksheet read into SPSS

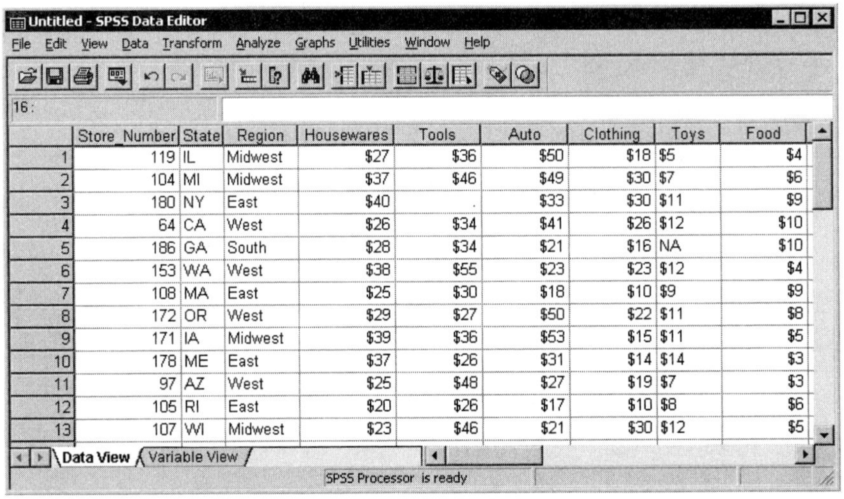

	Store_Number	State	Region	Housewares	Tools	Auto	Clothing	Toys	Food
1	119	IL	Midwest	$27	$36	$50	$18	$5	$4
2	104	MI	Midwest	$37	$46	$49	$30	$7	$6
3	180	NY	East	$40	.	$33	$30	$11	$9
4	64	CA	West	$26	$34	$41	$26	$12	$10
5	186	GA	South	$28	$34	$21	$16	NA	$10
6	153	WA	West	$38	$55	$23	$23	$12	$4
7	108	MA	East	$25	$30	$18	$10	$9	$9
8	172	OR	West	$29	$27	$50	$22	$11	$8
9	171	IA	Midwest	$39	$36	$53	$15	$11	$5
10	178	ME	East	$37	$26	$31	$14	$14	$3
11	97	AZ	West	$25	$48	$27	$19	$7	$3
12	105	RI	East	$20	$26	$17	$10	$8	$6
13	107	WI	Midwest	$23	$46	$21	$30	$12	$5

- The Excel column label *Store Number* is automatically converted to the SPSS variable name *Store_Number*, since variable names cannot contain spaces. The original column label is retained as the variable label.
- The original data type from Excel is preserved whenever possible, but since data type is determined at the individual cell level in Excel and at the column (variable) level in SPSS, this isn't always possible.
- When SPSS encounters mixed data types in the same column, the variable is assigned the string data type; so the variable *Toys* in this example is assigned the string data type.

READNAMES Subcommand

The READNAMES subcommand tells SPSS to treat the first row of the spreadsheet or specified range as either variable names (ON) or data (OFF). This subcommand will *always* affect the way the Excel spreadsheet is read, even when it isn't specified, since the default setting is ON.

- With READNAMES=ON (or in the absence of this subcommand), if the first row contains data instead of column headings, SPSS will attempt to read the cells in that row as variable names instead of as data: alphanumeric values will be used to create variable names; numeric values will be ignored, and default variable names will be assigned.

- With READNAMES=OFF, if the first row does, in fact, contain column headings or other alphanumeric text, then those column headings will be read as data values, and all of the variables will be assigned the string data type.

Reading Multiple Worksheets

An Excel file (workbook) can contain multiple worksheets, and you can read multiple worksheets from the same workbook by treating the Excel file as a database. This requires an ODBC driver for Excel.

Figure 3-6
Multiple worksheets in same workbook

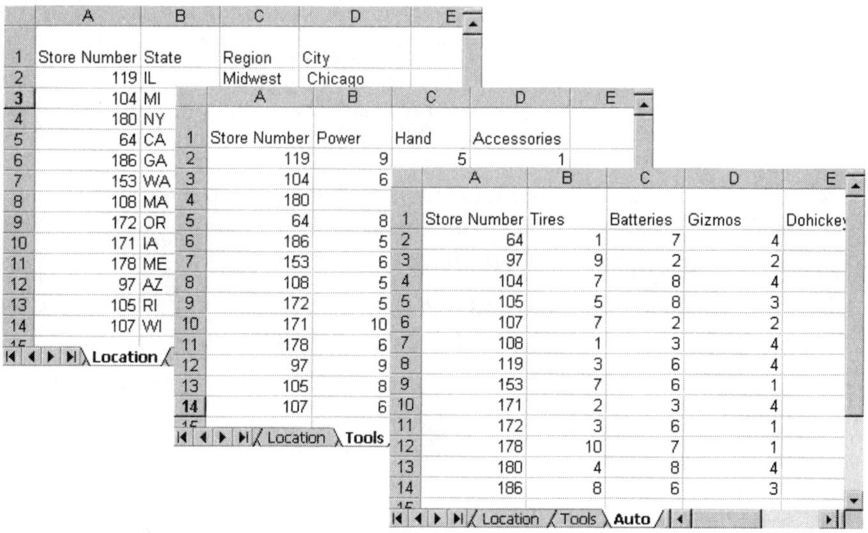

When reading multiple worksheets, you lose some of the flexibility available for reading individual worksheets:

- You cannot specify cell ranges.
- The first non-empty row of each worksheet should contain column labels that will be used as variable names.
- Only basic data types—string and numeric—are preserved, and all string variables are set to the maximum string width (255 characters). ("Changing the Defined Width of a String Variable" on p. 125 in Chapter 4 provides a method to automatically adjust the length of a string variable to the length of the longest observed string value.)

Example

In this example, the first worksheet contains information about store location, and the second and third contain information for different departments. All three contain a column, *Store Number*, that uniquely identifies each store, so the information in the three sheets can be merged correctly regardless of the order in which the stores are listed on each worksheet.

```
*readexcel2.sps.
GET DATA
  /TYPE=ODBC
  /CONNECT=
    'DSN=Excel Files;DBQ=c:\examples\data\sales.xls;' +
    'DriverId=790;MaxBufferSize=2048;PageTimeout=5;'
    /SQL =
    'SELECT  Location$.[Store Number], State, Region, City,'
    ' Power, Hand, Accessories,'
    ' Tires, Batteries, Gizmos, Dohickeys'
    ' FROM [Location$], [Tools$], [Auto$]'
    ' WHERE [Tools$].[Store Number]=[Location$].[Store Number]'
    ' AND [Auto$].[Store Number]=[Location$].[Store Number]'.
```

- If these commands look like random characters scattered on the page to you, try using the Database Wizard (File menu, Open Database) and, in the last step, paste the commands into a syntax window.
- Even if you are familiar with SQL statements, you may want to use the Database Wizard the first time to generate the proper CONNECT string.
- The SELECT statement specifies the columns to read from each worksheet, as identified by the column headings. Since all three worksheets have a column labeled *Store Number*, the specific worksheet from which to read this column is also included.
- If the column headings can't be used as variable names, you can either let SPSS automatically create valid variable names or use the AS keyword followed by a valid variable name. In this example, *Store Number* is not a valid SPSS variable name; so a variable name of *Store_Number* is automatically created, and the original column heading is used as the variable label.
- The FROM clause identifies the worksheets to read.
- The WHERE clause indicates that the data should be merged by matching the values of the column *Store Number* in the three worksheets.

Figure 3-7
Merged worksheets in SPSS

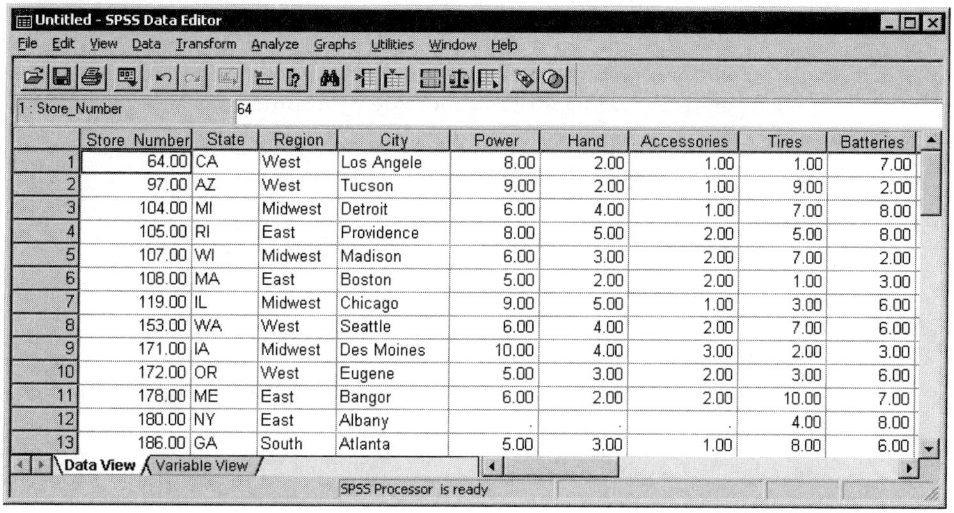

	Store Number	State	Region	City	Power	Hand	Accessories	Tires	Batteries
1	64.00	CA	West	Los Angele	8.00	2.00	1.00	1.00	7.00
2	97.00	AZ	West	Tucson	9.00	2.00	1.00	9.00	2.00
3	104.00	MI	Midwest	Detroit	6.00	4.00	1.00	7.00	8.00
4	105.00	RI	East	Providence	8.00	5.00	2.00	5.00	8.00
5	107.00	WI	Midwest	Madison	6.00	3.00	2.00	7.00	2.00
6	108.00	MA	East	Boston	5.00	2.00	2.00	1.00	3.00
7	119.00	IL	Midwest	Chicago	9.00	5.00	1.00	3.00	6.00
8	153.00	WA	West	Seattle	6.00	4.00	2.00	7.00	6.00
9	171.00	IA	Midwest	Des Moines	10.00	4.00	3.00	2.00	3.00
10	172.00	OR	West	Eugene	5.00	3.00	2.00	3.00	6.00
11	178.00	ME	East	Bangor	6.00	2.00	2.00	10.00	7.00
12	180.00	NY	East	Albany	.	.	.	4.00	8.00
13	186.00	GA	South	Atlanta	5.00	3.00	1.00	8.00	6.00

Reading Text Data Files

A text data file is simply a text file that contains data. Text data files fall into two broad categories:

- "Simple" text data files, in which all variables are recorded in the same order for all cases, and all cases contain the same variables. This is basically how all data files appear once they are read into SPSS.
- "Complex" text data files, including files in which the order of variables may vary between cases and hierarchical or nested data files in which some records contain variables with values that apply to one or more cases contained on subsequent records that contain a different set of variables (for example, city, state, and street address on one record, and name, age, and gender of each household member on subsequent records).

Text data files can be further subdivided into two more categories:

- **Delimited.** Spaces, commas, tabs, or other characters are used to separate variables. The variables are recorded in the same order for each case but not necessarily in the same column locations. This is also referred to as **freefield** format. Some applications export text data in CSV (comma-separated values) format; this is a delimited format.

- **Fixed width.** Each variable is recorded in the same column location on the same line (record) for each case in the data file. No delimiter is required between values. In fact, in many text data files generated by computer programs, data values may appear to run together without even spaces separating them. The column location determines which variable is being read.

Complex data files are typically also fixed-width format data files.

Simple Text Data Files

In most cases, the Text Wizard (File menu, Read Text Data) provides all of the functionality you need to read simple text data files. You can preview the original text data file and resulting SPSS data file as you make your choices in the wizard, and you can paste the command syntax equivalent of your choices into a command syntax window at the last step.

Two commands are available for reading text data files: GET DATA and DATA LIST. In many cases, they provide the same functionality, and the choice of one versus the other is a matter of personal preference. In some instances, however, you may need to take advantage of features in one command that aren't available in the other.

GET DATA

Use GET DATA instead of DATA LIST if:

- The file is in CSV format.
- The text data file is very large.

DATA LIST

Use DATA LIST instead of GET DATA if:

- The text data is "inline" data contained in a command syntax file using BEGIN DATA-END DATA.
- The file has a complex structure, such as a mixed or hierarchical structure. (See "Reading Complex Text Data Files" on p. 56.)
- You want to use the TO keyword to define a large number of sequential variable names (for example, var1 TO var1000).

Many examples in other chapters use DATA LIST to define sample data simply because it supports the use of inline data contained in the command syntax file rather than in an external data file, making the examples self-contained, requiring no additional files to work.

Delimited Text Data

In a simple delimited (or "freefield") text data file, absolute position of each variable isn't important; only the relative position matters. Variables should be recorded in the same order for each case, but the actual column locations aren't relevant. More than one case can appear on the same record, and/or some records can span multiple records, while others do not.

Example

One of the advantages of delimited text data files is that they don't require a great deal of structure. The sample data file, *simple_delimited.txt*, looks like this:

```
1 m 28 1 2 2 1 2 2 f 29 2 1 2 1 2
003 f 45 3 2 1 4 5 128 m 17 1 1
1 9 4
```

The DATA LIST command to read the data file is:

```
*simple_delimited.sps.
DATA LIST FREE
   FILE = 'c:\examples\data\simple_delimited.txt'
   /id (F3) sex (A1) age (F2) opinion1 TO opinion5 (5F).
EXECUTE.
```

- FREE indicates that the text data file is a delimited file, in which only the order of variables matters. By default, commas and spaces are read as delimiters between data values. In this example, all of the data values are separated by spaces.
- Eight variables are defined; so after reading eight values, the next value is read as the first variable for the next case, even if it's on the same line. If the end of a record is reached before eight values have been read for the current case, the first value on the next line is read as the next value for the current case. In this example, four cases are contained on three records.
- If all of the variables were simple numeric variables, you wouldn't need to specify the format for any of them, but if there are any variables for which you need to

specify the format, any preceding variables also need format specifications. Since you need to specify a string format for *sex*, you also need to specify a format for *id*.

- In this example, you don't need to specify formats for any of the numeric variables that appear after the string variable, but the default numeric format is F8.2, which means values are displayed with two decimals even if the actual values are integers. (F2) specifies an integer with a maximum of two digits, and (5F) specifies five integers, each containing a single digit.

The "defined format for all preceding variables" rule can be quite cumbersome, particularly if you have a large number of simple numeric variables interspersed with a few string variables or other variables that require format specifications. There's a shortcut you can use to get around this rule:

```
DATA LIST FREE
  FILE = 'c:\examples\data\simple_delimited.txt'
  /id * sex (A1) age opinion1 TO opinion5.
```

The asterisk indicates that all preceding variables should be read in the default numeric format (F8.2). In this example, it doesn't save much over simply defining a format for the first variable, but if *sex* were the last variable instead of the second, it could be useful.

Example

One of the drawbacks of DATA LIST FREE is that if a single value for a single case is accidently missed in data entry, all subsequent cases will be read incorrectly, since values are read sequentially from the beginning of the file to the end regardless of what line each value is recorded on. For delimited files in which each case is recorded on a separate line, you can use DATA LIST LIST, which will limit problems caused by this type of data entry error to the current case.

The data file, *delimited_list.txt*, contains one case that has only seven values recorded, whereas all of the others have eight:

```
001 m 28 1 2 2 1 2
002 f 29 2 1 2 1 2
003 f 45 3 2 4 5
128 m 17 1 1 1 9 4
```

The **DATA LIST** command to read the file is:

```
*delimited_list.sps.
DATA LIST LIST
  FILE='c:\examples\data\delimited_list.txt'
  /id(F3) sex (A1) age opinion1 TO opinion5 (6F1).
EXECUTE.
```

Figure 3-8
Text data file read with DATA LIST LIST

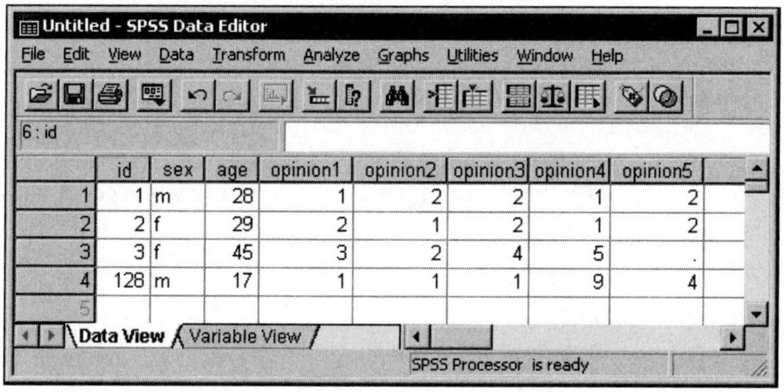

	id	sex	age	opinion1	opinion2	opinion3	opinion4	opinion5
1	1	m	28	1	2	2	1	2
2	2	f	29	2	1	2	1	2
3	3	f	45	3	2	4	5	.
4	128	m	17	1	1	1	9	4
5								

- Eight variables are defined; so eight values are expected on each line.
- The third case, however, has only seven values recorded. The first seven values are read as the values for the first seven defined variables. The eighth variable is assigned the system-missing value.

You don't know which variable for the third case is actually missing. In this example, it could be any variable after the second variable (since that's the only string variable, and an appropriate string value was read), making all of the remaining values for that case suspect; so a warning message is issued whenever a case doesn't contain enough data values:

```
>Warning # 1116
>Under LIST input, insufficient data were contained on one record to
>fulfill the variable list.
>Remaining numeric variables have been set to the system-missing
>value and string variables have been set to blanks.

>Command line: 6  Current case: 3  Current splitfile group: 1
```

CSV Delimited Text Files

A CSV file uses commas to separate data values and encloses values that include commas in quotation marks. Many applications export text data in this format. To read CSV files correctly, you need to use the GET DATA command.

Example

The file *CSV_file.csv* was exported from Microsoft Excel:

```
ID,Name,Gender,Date Hired,Department
1,"Foster, Chantal",f,10/29/1998,1
2,"Healy, Jonathan",m,3/1/1992,3
3,"Walter, Wendy",f,1/23/1995,2
4,"Oliver, Kendall",f,10/28/2003,2
```

This data file contains variable descriptions on the first line and a combination of string and numeric data values for each case on subsequent lines, including string values that contain commas. The GET DATA command syntax to read this file is:

```
*delimited_csv.sps.
GET DATA  /TYPE = TXT
  /FILE = 'C:\examples\data\CSV_file.csv'
  /DELIMITERS = ","
  /QUALIFIER = '"'
  /ARRANGEMENT = DELIMITED
  /FIRSTCASE = 2
  /VARIABLES = ID F3 Name A15 Gender A1
   Date_Hired ADATE10 Department F1.
```

- DELIMITERS = "," specifies the comma as the delimiter between values.
- QUALIFIER = '"' specifies that values that contain commas are enclosed in double quotes so that the embedded commas won't be interpreted as delimiters.
- FIRSTCASE=2 skips the top line that contains the variable descriptions; otherwise, this line would be read as the first case.
- ADATE10 specifies that the variable *Date_Hired* is a date variable of the general format mm/dd/yyyy. See "Reading Different Types of Text Data" on p. 54 for more information about data formats.

Note: The command syntax in this example was adapted from the command syntax generated by the Text Wizard (File menu, Read Text Data), which automatically generated valid SPSS variable names from the information on the first line of the data file.

Fixed-Width Text Data

In a fixed-width data file, variables start and end in the same column locations for each case. No delimiters are required between values, and there is often no space between the end of one value and the start of the next. For fixed-width data files, the command that reads the data file (GET DATA or DATA LIST) contains information on the column location and/or width of each variable.

Example

In the simplest type of fixed-width text data file, each case is contained on a single line (record) in the file. In this example, the text data file *simple_fixed.txt* looks like this:

```
001 m 28 12212
002 f 29 21212
003 f 45 32145
128 m 17 11194
```

Using DATA LIST, the command syntax to read the file is:

```
*simple_fixed.sps.
DATA LIST FIXED
  FILE='c:\examples\data\simple_fixed.txt'
  /id 1-3 sex 5 (A) age 7-8 opinion1 TO opinion5 10-14.
EXECUTE.
```

- The keyword FIXED is included in this example, but since it is the default format, it can be omitted.
- The forward slash before the variable *id* separates the variable definitions from the rest of the command specifications (unlike other commands where subcommands are separated by forward slashes). The forward slash actually denotes the start of each record that will be read, but in this case there is only one record per case.
- The variable *id* is located in columns 1 through 3. Since no format is specified, the standard numeric format is assumed.
- The variable *sex* is found in column 5. The format (A) indicates that this is a string variable, with values that contain something other than numbers.
- The numeric variable *age* is in columns 7 and 8.
- opinion1 TO opinion5 10-14 defines five numeric variables, with each variable occupying a single column: *opinion1* in column 10, *opinion2* in column 11, etc.

You could define the same data file using variable width instead of column locations:

```
*simple_fixed_alt.sps.
DATA LIST FIXED
  FILE='c:\examples\data\simple_fixed.txt'
  /id (F3, 1X) sex (A1, 1X) age (F2, 1X)
   opinion1 TO opinion5 (5F1).
EXECUTE.
```

- id (F3, 1X) indicates that the variable *id* is in the first three column positions, and the next column position (column 4) should be skipped.
- Each variable is assumed to start in the next sequential column position; so *sex* is read from column 5.

Figure 3-9
Fixed-width text data file displayed in Data Editor

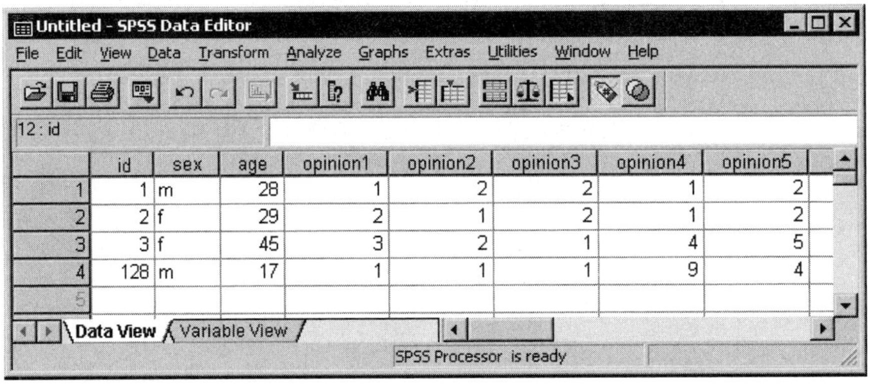

Example

Reading the same file with GET DATA, the command syntax would be:

```
*simple_fixed_getdata.sps.
GET DATA  /TYPE = TXT
 /FILE = 'C:\examples\data\simple_fixed.txt'
 /ARRANGEMENT = FIXED
 /VARIABLES =/1  id 0-2 F3 sex 4-4 A1 age 6-7 F2
  opinion1 9-9 F opinion2 10-10 F opinion3 11-11 F
  opinion4 12-12 F opinion5 13-13 F.
```

- The first column is column 0 (in contrast to DATA LIST, in which the first column is column 1).
- There is no "default" data type. You must explicitly specify the data type for all variables.

- You must specify both a start and an end column position for each variable, even if the variable occupies only a single column (for example, sex 4-4).
- All variables must be explicitly specified; you cannot use the keyword TO to define a range of variables.

Reading Selected Portions of a Fixed-Width File

With fixed-format text data files, you can read all or part of each record and/or skip entire records

Example

In this example, each case takes two lines (records), and the first line of the file should be skipped because it doesn't contain data. The data file, *skip_first_fixed.txt*, looks like this:

```
Employee age, department, and salary information
John Smith
26 2 40000
Joan Allen
32 3 48000
Bill Murray
45 3 50000
```

The DATA LIST command syntax to read the file is:

```
*skip_first_fixed.sps.
DATA LIST FIXED
 FILE = 'c:\examples\data\skip_first_fixed.txt'
  RECORDS=2
  SKIP=1
  /name 1-20 (A)
  /age 1-2 dept 4 salary 6-10.
EXECUTE.
```

- The RECORDS subcommand indicates that there are two lines per case.
- The SKIP subcommand indicates that the first line of the file should not be included.
- The first forward slash indicates the start of the list of variables contained on the first record for each case. The only variable on the first record is the string variable *name*.
- The second forward slash indicates the start of the variables contained on the second record for each case.

Figure 3-10
Fixed-width, multiple-record text data file displayed in Data Editor

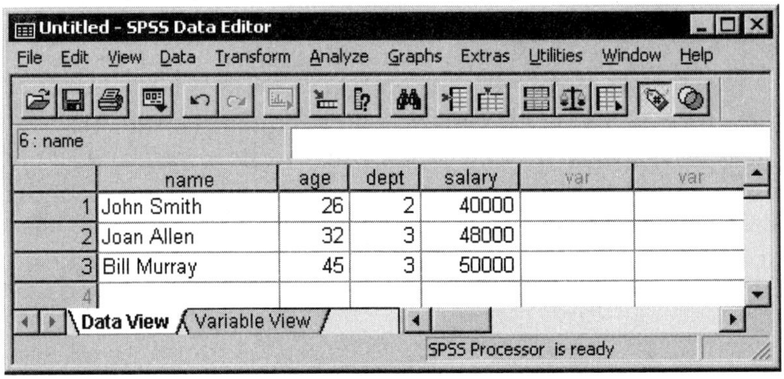

Example

With fixed-width text data files, you can easily read selected portions of the data. For example, using the *skip_first_fixed.txt* data file from the above example, you could read just the age and salary information.

```
*selected_vars_fixed.sps.
DATA LIST FIXED
 FILE = 'c:\examples\data\skip_first_fixed.txt'
  RECORDS=2
  SKIP=1
  /2 age 1-2 salary 6-10.
EXECUTE.
```

- As in the previous example, the command specifies that there are two records per case and that the first line in the file should not be read.
- /2 indicates that variables should be read from the second record for each case. Since this is the only list of variables defined, the information on the first record for each case is ignored, and the employee's name is not included in the data to be read.
- The variables *age* and *salary* are read exactly as before, but no information is read from columns 3–5 between those two variables because the command does not define a variable in that space; so the department information is not included in the data to be read.

DATA LIST FIXED and Implied Decimals

If you specify a number of decimals for a numeric format with DATA LIST FIXED and some data values for that variable do not contain decimal indicators, those values are assumed to contain **implied** decimals.

Example

```
*implied_decimals.sps.
DATA LIST FIXED /var1 (F5.2).
BEGIN DATA
123
123.0
1234
123.4
end data.
```

- The values of 123 and 1234 will be read as containing two implied decimals positions, resulting in values of 1.23 and 12.34.
- The values of 123.0 and 123.4, however, contain **explicit** decimal indicators, resulting in values of 123.0 and 123.4.

DATA LIST FREE (and LIST) and GET DATA /TYPE=TEXT do *not* read implied decimals; so a value of 123 with a format of F5.2 will be read as 123.

Text Data Files with Very Wide Records

Some machine-generated text data files with a large number of variables may have a single, very wide record for each case. If the record width exceeds 8,192 columns/characters, you need to specify the record length with the FILE HANDLE command before reading the data file.

```
*wide_file.sps.
*Read text data file with record length of 10,000.
*This command will stop at column 8,192.
DATA LIST FIXED
  FILE='c:\examples\data\wide_file.txt'
  /var1 TO var1000 (1000F10).
EXECUTE.

*Define record length first.
FILE HANDLE  wide_file NAME = 'c:\examples\data\wide_file.txt'
  /MODE = CHARACTER /LRECL = 10000.
DATA LIST FIXED
  FILE = wide_file
  /var1 TO var1000 (1000F10).
EXECUTE.
```

- Each record in the data file contains 1,000 10-digit values, for a total record length of 10,000 characters.
- The first DATA LIST command will read only the first 819 values (8,190 characters), and the remaining variables will be set to the system-missing value. A warning message is issued for each variable that is set to system-missing, which in this example means 181 warning messages.
- FILE HANDLE assigns a "handle" of *wide_file* to the data *file wide_file.txt.*
- The LRECL subcommand specifies that each record is 10,000 characters wide.
- The FILE subcommand on the second DATA LIST command refers to the file handle *wide_file* instead of the actual filename, and all 1,000 variables are read correctly.

Reading Different Types of Text Data

SPSS can read text data recorded in a wide variety of formats. Some of the more common formats are listed in the following table:

Table 3-1
Common text data types

Type	Example	Format Specification
Numeric	123	F3
	123.45	F6.2
Period as decimal indicator, comma as thousands separator	12,345	COMMA6
	1,234.5	COMMA7.1
Comma as decimal indicator, period as thousands separator	123,4	DOT6
	1.234,5	DOT7.1
Dollar	$12,345	DOLLAR7
	$12,234.50	DOLLAR9.2
String (alphanumeric)	Female	A6
International Date	28-OCT-1986	DATE11
American Date	10/28/1986	ADATE10
Date and Time	28 October, 1986 23:56	DATETIME22

For more information on date and time formats, see "Date and Time" in the "Universals" section of the *SPSS Command Syntax Reference*. For a complete list of data formats supported by SPSS, see "Variables" in the "Universals" section of the *SPSS Command Syntax Reference*.

Example

```
*delimited_formats.sps.
DATA LIST LIST (" ")
  /numericVar (F4) dotVar(DOT7.1) stringVar(a4) dateVar(DATE11).
BEGIN DATA
1 2 abc 28/10/03
111 2.222,2 abcd 28-OCT-2003
111.11 222.222,222 abcdefg 28-October-2003
END DATA.
EXECUTE.
```

Figure 3-11
Different data types displayed in Data Editor

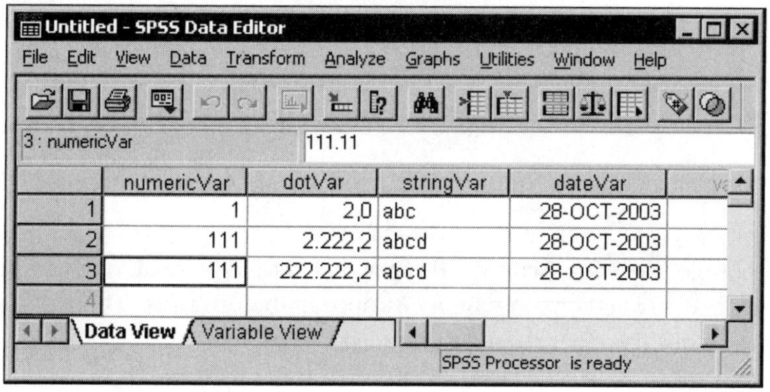

- All of the numeric and date values are read correctly even if the actual values exceed the maximum width (number of digits and characters) defined for the variables.
- Although the third case appears to have a truncated value for *numericVar*, the entire value of 111.11 is stored internally. Since the defined format is also used as the display format, and (F4) defines a format with no decimals, 111 is displayed instead of the full value. Values aren't actually truncated for display; they're rounded. A value of 111.99 would display as 112.
- The *dateVar* value of 28-October-2003 is displayed as 28-OCT-2003 to fit the defined width of 11 digits/characters.
- For string variables, the defined width is more critical than with numeric variables. Any string value that exceeds the defined width is truncated; so only the first four characters for *stringVar* in the third case are read. Warning messages are displayed in the log for any strings that exceed the defined width.

Reading Complex Text Data Files

"Complex" text data files come in a variety of flavors, including:

- Mixed files in which the order of variables isn't necessarily the same for all records and/or some record types should be skipped entirely.
- Grouped files in which there are multiple records for each case that need to be grouped together.
- Nested files in which record types are related to each other hierarchically.

Mixed Files

A mixed file is one in which the order of variables may differ for some records and/or some records may contain entirely different variables or information that shouldn't be read.

Example

In this example, there are two record types that should be read: one in which *state* appears before *city* and one in which *city* appears before *state*. There is also an additional record type that shouldn't be read.

```
*mixed_file.sps.
FILE TYPE MIXED RECORD = 1-2.
- RECORD TYPE 1.
-  DATA LIST FIXED
    /state 4-5 (A) city 7-17 (A) population 19-26 (F).
- RECORD TYPE 2.
-  DATA LIST FIXED
    /city 4-14 (A) state 16-17 (A) population 19-26 (F).
END FILE TYPE.
BEGIN DATA
01 TX Dallas      3280310
01 IL Chicago     8008507
02 Ancorage    AK 257808
99 What am I doing here?
02 Casper      WY 63157
01 WI Madison     428563
END DATA.
EXECUTE.
```

- The commands that define how to read the data are all contained within the FILE TYPE - END FILE TYPE structure.
- MIXED identifies the type of data file.

- RECORD = 1-2 indicates that the record type identifier appears in the first two columns of each record.
- Each DATA LIST command reads only records with the identifier value specified on the preceding RECORD TYPE command. So if the value in the first two columns of the record is 1 (or 01), *state* comes before *city*, and if the value is 2, *city* comes before *state*.
- The record with the value 99 in the first two columns is not read, since there are no corresponding RECORD TYPE and DATA LIST commands.

You can also include a variable that contains the record identifier value by including a variable name on the RECORD subcommand of the FILE TYPE command, as in:

```
FILE TYPE MIXED /RECORD = recID 1-2.
```

You can also specify the format for the identifier value, using the same type of format specifications as the DATA LIST command. For example, if the value is a string instead of a simple numeric value:

```
FILE TYPE MIXED /RECORD = recID 1-2 (A).
```

Grouped Files

In a grouped file, there are multiple records for each case that should be grouped together based on a unique case identifier. Each case usually has one record of each type. All records for a single case must be together in the file.

Example

In this example, there are three records for each case. Each record contains a value that identifies the case, a value that identifies the record type, and a grade or score for a different course.

```
* grouped_file.sps.
* A case is made up of all record types.
FILE TYPE GROUPED RECORD=6 CASE=student 1-4.
RECORD TYPE 1.
- DATA LIST /english 8-9 (A).
RECORD TYPE 2.
- DATA LIST /reading 8-10.
RECORD TYPE 3.
- DATA LIST /math 8-10.
END FILE TYPE.
```

```
BEGIN DATA
0001 1 B+
0001 2 74
0001 3 83
0002 1 A
0002 3 71
0002 2 100
0003 1 B-
0003 2 88
0003 3 81
0004 1 C
0004 2 94
0004 3 91
END DATA.
EXECUTE.
```

- The commands that define how to read the data are all contained within the FILE TYPE - END FILE TYPE structure.
- GROUPED identifies the type of data file.
- RECORD = 6 indicates that the record type identifier appears in column 6 of each record.
- CASE student 1-4 indicates that the unique case identifier appears in the first four columns and assigns that value to the variable *student* in the working data file.
- The three RECORD TYPE and subsequent DATA LIST commands determine how each record is read, based on the value in column 6 of each record.

Figure 3-12
Grouped data displayed in Data Editor

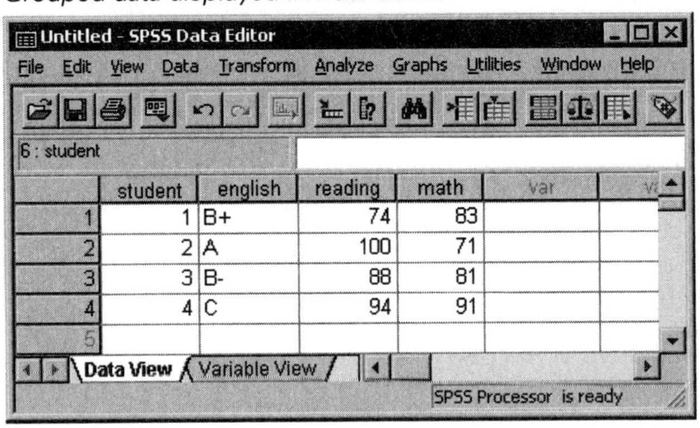

Example

In order to correctly read a grouped data file, all records for the same case must be contiguous in the source text data file. If the they are not, you need to sort the data file before reading it as a grouped data file. You can do this by reading the file as a simple text data file, sorting it and saving it, and then reading it again as a grouped file.

```
*grouped_file2.sps.
* Data file is sorted by record type instead of by
  identification number.

DATA LIST FIXED
  /alldata 1-80 (A) caseid 1-4.

BEGIN DATA
0001 1 B+
0002 1 A
0003 1 B-
0004 1 C
0001 2 74
0002 2 100
0003 2 88
0004 2 94
0001 3 83
0002 3 71
0003 3 81
0004 3 91
END DATA.

SORT CASES BY caseid.
WRITE OUTFILE='c:\temp\tempdata.txt'
 /alldata.
EXECUTE.

* read the sorted file.
FILE TYPE GROUPED FILE='c:\temp\tempdata.txt'
 RECORD=6 CASE=student 1-4.
- RECORD TYPE 1.
-  DATA LIST /english 8-9 (A).
- RECORD TYPE 2.
-  DATA LIST /reading 8-10.
- RECORD TYPE 3.
-  DATA LIST /math 8-10.
END FILE TYPE.
EXECUTE.
```

- The first DATA LIST command reads all of the data on each record as a single string variable.
- In addition to being part of the string variable spanning the entire record, the first four columns are also read as the variable *caseid*.

- The data file is then sorted by *caseid*, and the string variable *alldata*, containing all of the data on each record, is written to the text file *tempdata.txt*.
- The sorted file, *tempdata.txt*, is then read as a grouped data file, just like the inline data in the previous example.

The maximum width of a string variable is 255 characters; so for a file with records wider than 255 characters, you would need to modify the job slightly to read and write multiple string variables. For example, if the record width is 1,200:

```
DATA LIST FIXED
  /string1 to string6 1-1200 (A) caseid 1-4.
```

This would read the file as six 200-character string variables. (If the record length exceeds 8,192, you need to use the FILE HANDLE command to specify the record length. See the *SPSS Command Syntax Reference* for more information.)

Nested (Hierarchical) Files

In a nested file, the record types are related to each other hierarchically. The record types are grouped together by a case identification number that identifies the highest level—the first record type—of the hierarchy. Usually, the last record type specified—the lowest level of the hierarchy—defines a case. For example, in a file containing information on a company's sales representatives, the records could be grouped by sales region. Information from higher record types may be spread to each case. For example, the sales region information can be spread to the records for each sales representative in the region.

Example

In this example, sales data for each sales representative are nested within sales regions (cities), and those regions are nested within years.

```
*nested_file1.sps.
FILE TYPE NESTED RECORD=1(A).
- RECORD TYPE 'Y'.
- DATA LIST / Year 3-6.

- RECORD TYPE 'R'.
- DATA LIST / Region 3-13 (A).

- RECORD TYPE 'P'.
- DATA LIST / SalesRep 3-13 (A) Sales 20-23.
END FILE TYPE.

BEGIN DATA
Y 2002
R Chicago
P Jones            900
P Gregory          400
R Baton Rouge
P Rodriguez        300
P Smith            333
P Grau             100
END DATA.
EXECUTE.
```

Figure 3-13
Nested data displayed in Data Editor

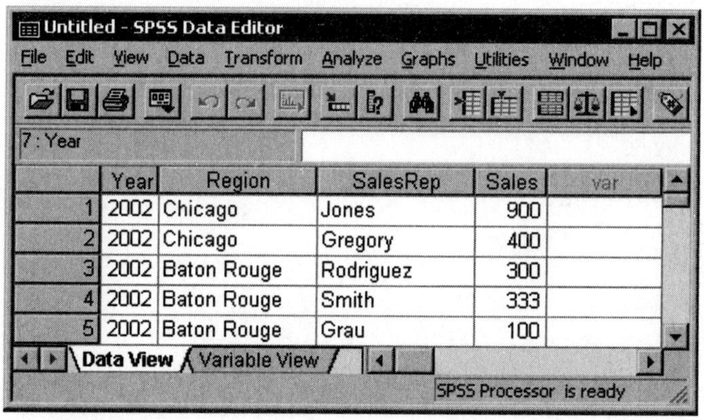

- The commands that define how to read the data are all contained within the FILE TYPE - END FILE TYPE structure.
- NESTED identifies the type of data file.

- The value that identifies each record type is a string value in column 1 of each record.
- The order of the RECORD TYPE and associated DATA LIST commands defines the nesting hierarchy, with the highest level of the hierachy specified first. So 'Y' (year) is the highest level, followed by 'R' (region), and finally 'P' (person).
- Eight records are read, but one of those contains year information and two identify regions; so the working data file contains five cases, all with a value of 2002 for *Year*, two in the Chicago *Region* and three in Baton Rouge.

Using INPUT PROGRAM to Read Nested Files

The previous example imposes some strict requirements on the structure of the data. For instance, the value that identifies the record type must be in the same location on all records, and it must also be the same type of data value (in this example, a one-character string).

Instead of using a FILE TYPE structure, we can read the same data with an INPUT PROGRAM, which can provide more control and flexibility.

Example

This first input program reads the same data file as the FILE TYPE NESTED example and obtains the same results in a different manner.

```
* nested_input1.sps.
INPUT PROGRAM.
- DATA LIST FIXED END=#eof /#type 1 (A).
- DO IF #eof.
-  END FILE.
- END IF.
- DO IF #type='Y'.
-  REREAD.
-  DATA LIST /Year 3-6.
-  LEAVE Year.
- ELSE IF #type='R'.
-  REREAD.
-  DATA LIST / Region 3-13 (A).
-  LEAVE Region.
- ELSE IF #type='P'.
-  REREAD.
-  DATA LIST / SalesRep 3-13 (A) Sales 20-23.
-  END CASE.
- END IF.
END INPUT PROGRAM.
```

```
BEGIN DATA
Y 2002
R Chicago
P Jones              900
P Gregory            400
R Baton Rouge
P Rodriguez          300
P Smith              333
P Grau               100
END DATA.
EXECUTE.
```

- The commands that define how to read the data are all contained within the INPUT PROGRAM structure.
- The first DATA LIST command reads the temporary variable *#type* from the first column of each record.
- END=#eof creates a temporary variable named *#eof* that has a value of 0 until the end of the data file is reached, at which point the value is set to 1.
- DO IF #eof evaluates as true when the value of *#eof* is set to 1 at the end of the file, and an END FILE command is issued, which tells the INPUT PROGRAM to stop reading data. In this example, this isn't really necessary, since we're reading the entire file; however, it will be used later when we want to define an end point prior to the end of the data file.
- The second DO IF-ELSE IF-END IF structure determines what to do for each value of *type*.
- REREAD reads the same record again, this time reading either *Year*, *Region*, or *SalesRep* and *Sales*, depending on the value of *#type*.
- LEAVE retains the value(s) of the specified variable(s) when reading the next record. So the value of *Year* from the first record is retained when reading *Region* from the next record, and both of those values are retained when reading *SalesRep* and *Sales* from the subsequent records in the hierarchy. So the appropriate values of *Year* and *Region* are spread to all of the cases at the lowest level of the hierarchy.
- END CASE marks the end of each case. So after reading a record with a *#type* value of 'P', the process starts again to create the next case.

Example

In this example, the data file reflects the nested structure by indenting each nested level; so the values that identify record type do not appear in the same place on each record. Furthermore, at the lowest level of the hierarchy, the record type identifier is the last value instead of the first. Here, an INPUT PROGRAM provides the ability to read a file that cannot be read correctly by FILE TYPE NESTED.

```
*nested_input2.sps.
INPUT PROGRAM.
- DATA LIST FIXED END=#eof
   /#yr 1 (A) #reg 3(A) #person 25 (A).
- DO IF #eof.
-   END FILE.
- END IF.
- DO IF #yr='Y'.
-   REREAD.
-   DATA LIST /Year 3-6.
-   LEAVE Year.
- ELSE IF #reg='R'.
-   REREAD.
-   DATA LIST / Region 5-15 (A).
-   LEAVE Region.
- ELSE IF #person='P'.
-   REREAD.
-   DATA LIST / SalesRep 7-17 (A) Sales 20-23.
-   END CASE.
- END IF.
END INPUT PROGRAM.

BEGIN DATA
Y 2002
  R Chicago
      Jones         900  P
      Gregory       400  P
  R Baton Rouge
      Rodriguez     300  P
      Smith         333  P
      Grau          100  P
END DATA.
EXECUTE.
```

- This time, the first DATA LIST command reads three temporary variables at different locations, one for each record type.
- The DO IF-ELSE IF-END IF structure then determines how to read each record based on the values of *#yr*, *#reg*, or *#person*.
- The remainder of the job is essentially the same as the previous example.

Example

Using the input program, we can also select a random sample of cases from each region and/or stop reading cases at a specified maximum.

```
*nested_input3.sps.
INPUT PROGRAM.
COMPUTE #count=0.
- DATA LIST FIXED END=#eof
   /#yr 1 (A) #reg 3(A) #person 25 (A).
- DO IF #eof OR #count = 1000.
-  END FILE.
- END IF.
- DO IF #yr='Y'.
-  REREAD.
-  DATA LIST /Year 3-6.
-  LEAVE Year.
- ELSE IF #reg='R'.
-  REREAD.
-  DATA LIST / Region 5-15 (A).
-  LEAVE Region.
- ELSE IF #person='P' AND UNIFORM(1000) < 500.
-  REREAD.
-  DATA LIST / SalesRep 7-17 (A) Sales 20-23.
-  END CASE.
-  COMPUTE #count=#count+1.
- END IF.
END INPUT PROGRAM.

BEGIN DATA
Y 2002
  R Chicago
      Jones          900  P
      Gregory        400  P
  R Baton Rouge
      Rodriguez      300  P
      Smith          333  P
      Grau           100  P
END DATA.
EXECUTE.
```

- COMPUTE #count=0 initializes a case-counter variable.
- ELSE IF #person='P' AND UNIFORM(1000) < 500 will read a random sample of approximately 50% from each region, since UNIFORM(1000) will generate a value less than 500 approximately 50% of the time.
- COMPUTE #count=#count+1 increments the case counter by 1 for each case that's included.
- DO IF #eof OR #count = 1000 will issue an END FILE command if the case counter reaches 1,000, limiting the total number of cases in the working data file to no more than 1,000.

Since the source file must be sorted by year and region, limiting the total number of cases to 1,000 (or any value) may omit some years or regions within the last year entirely.

Repeating Data

In a repeating data file structure, multiple cases are constructed from a single record. Information common to each case on the record may be entered once and then spread to all of the cases constructed from the record. In this respect, a file with a repeating data structure is like a hierarchical file, with two levels of information recorded on a single record rather than on separate record types.

Example

In this example, we read essentially the same information as in the examples of nested file structures, except now all of the information for each region is stored on a single record.

```
*repeating_data.sps.
INPUT PROGRAM.
DATA LIST FIXED
  /Year 1-4 Region 6-16 (A) #numrep 19.
REPEATING DATA STARTS=22 /OCCURS=#numrep
  /DATA=SalesRep 1-10 (A) Sales 12-14.
END INPUT PROGRAM.

BEGIN DATA
2002 Chicago     2  Jones      900Gregory    400
2002 Baton Rouge 3  Rodriguez  300Smith      333Grau       100
END DATA.
EXECUTE.
```

- The commands that define how to read the data are all contained within the INPUT PROGRAM structure.
- The DATA LIST command defines two variables, *Year* and *Region*, that will be spread across all of the cases read from each record. It also defines a temporary variable, *#numrep*.
- On the REPEATING DATA command, STARTS=22 indicates that the case starts in column 22.
- OCCURS=#numrep uses the value of the temporary variable, *#numrep* (defined on the previous DATA LIST command), to determine how many cases to read from

each record. So two cases will be read from the first record, and three will be read from the second.

- The DATA subcommand defines two variables for each case. The column locations for those variables are relative locations. For the first case, column 22 (specified on the STARTS subcommand) is read as column 1. For the next case, column 1 is the first column after the end of the defined column span for the last variable in the previous case, which would be column 36 (22 + 14 = 36).

The end result is a working data file that looks remarkably similar to the data file created from the hierarchical source data file.

Figure 3-14
Repeating data displayed in Data Editor

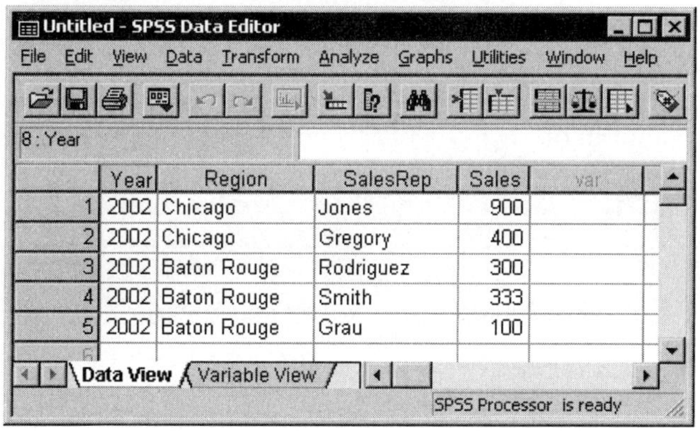

Reading SAS Data Files

SPSS can read the following types of SAS files:

- SAS long filename, versions 7 and 8
- SAS short filenames, versions 7 and 8
- SAS version 6 for Windows
- SAS version 6 for UNIX
- SAS Transport

The basic structure of a SAS data file is very similar to an SPSS data file—rows are cases (observations), and columns are variables—and reading SAS data files requires only a single, simple command: GET SAS.

Example

In its simplest form, the GET SAS command has a single subcommand that specifies the SAS filename.

```
*get_sas.sps.
GET SAS DATA='C:\examples\data\gss.sd2'.
```

- SAS variable names that do not conform to SPSS variable-naming rules are converted to valid SPSS variable names.
- SAS variable labels specified on the LABEL statement in the DATA step are used as variable labels in SPSS.

Figure 3-15
SAS data file with variable labels in SPSS

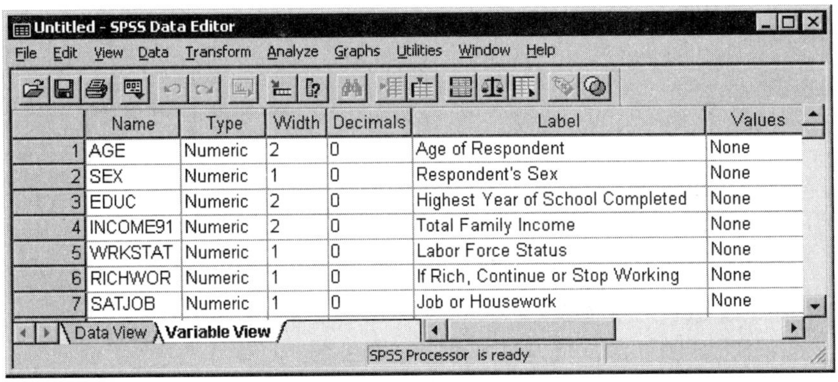

Example

SAS value formats are similar to SPSS value labels, but SAS value formats are saved in a separate file; so if you want to use value formats as value labels, you need to use the FORMATS subcommand to specify the formats file.

```
*get_sas2.sps.
GET SAS DATA='C:\examples\data\gss.sd2'
 FORMATS='c:\examples\data\GSS_Fmts.sd2'.
```

- Labels assigned to single values are retained.
- Labels assigned to a range of values are ignored.
- Labels assigned to SAS keywords LOW, HIGH, and OTHER are ignored.
- Labels assigned to string variables and non-integer numeric values are ignored.
- Labels over 60 characters long are truncated.

Figure 3-16
SAS value formats used as value labels

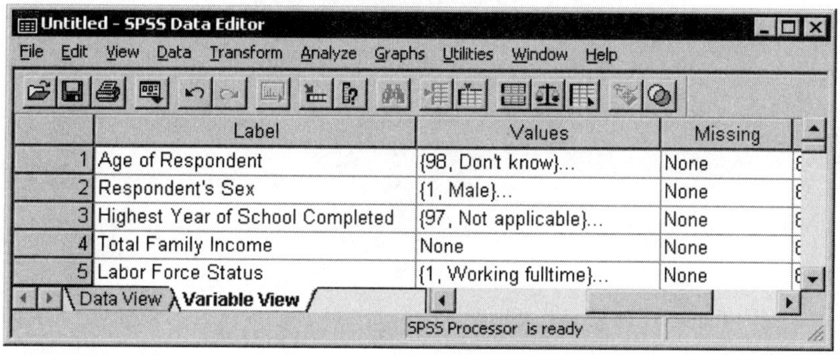

Chapter

4

Basic Data Management

Basic data management encompasses a wide variety of tasks that you may want or need to perform after getting your data into SPSS and before you generate any reports or analyses, including:

- Assigning variable properties, such as descriptive variable labels, value labels, and missing value codes
- Cleaning and validating data
- Merging, aggregating, and restructuring data files
- Recoding data, combining categories, and banding scale variables into ranges
- Transforming numeric values with arithmetic, statistical, and random value functions
- Combining string values, extracting substrings from string values, and converting numeric strings to numeric variables
- Converting string and/or numeric values to dates, calculating durations based on date differences, and extracting specific information from date variables, such as the day of the week associated with a date

Variable Properties

In addition to basic data type (numeric, string, date, etc.), you can assign other properties that describe the variables and their associated values. In a sense, these properties can be considered **metadata**—data that describe the data. These properties are automatically saved with the data when you save the data as an SPSS-format data file.

Example

```
*define_variables.sps.
DATA LIST LIST
  /id (F3) Interview_date (ADATE10) Age (F3) Gender (A1)
   Income_category (F1) Religion (F1) opinion1 to opinion4 (4F1).
BEGIN DATA
150 11/1/2002 55 m 3 4 5 1 3 1
272 10/24/02 25 f 3 9 2 3 4 3
299 10-24-02 900 f 8 4 2 9 3 4
227 10/29/2002 62 m 9 4 2 3 5 3
216 10/26/2002 39 F 7 3 9 3 2 1
228 10/30/2002 24 f 4 2 3 5 1 5
333 10/29/2002 30 m 2 3 5 1 2 3
385 10/24/2002 23 m 4 4 3 3 9 2
170 10/21/2002 29 f 4 2 2 2 2 5
391 10/21/2002 58 m 1 3 5 1 5 3
END DATA.
FREQUENCIES VARIABLES=opinion3 Income_Category.
VARIABLE LABELS
  Interview_date "Interview date"
  Income_category "Income category"
  opinion1 "Would buy this product"
  opinion2 "Would recommend this product to others"
  opinion3 "Price is reasonable"
  opinion4 "Better than a poke in the eye with a sharp stick".
VALUE LABELS
  Gender "m" "Male" "f" "Female"
  /Income_category 1 "Under 25K" 2 "25K to 49K"
   3 "50K to 74K" 4 "75K+" 7 "Refused to answer"
   8 "Don't know" 9 "No answer"
  /Religion 1 "Catholic" 2 "Protestant" 3 "Jewish"
   4 "Other" 9 "No answer"
  /opinion1 TO opinion4 1 "Strongly Disagree"
   2 "Disagree" 3 "Ambivalent" 4 "Agree"
   5 "Strongly Agree" 9 "No answer".
MISSING VALUES
  Income_category (7, 8, 9)
  Religion opinion1 TO opinion4 (9).
VARIABLE LEVEL
  Income_category, opinion1 to opinion4 (ORDINAL)
  Religion (NOMINAL).
FREQUENCIES VARIABLES=opinion3 Income_Category.
```

Figure 4-1
Frequency tables before assigning variable properties

opinion3

		Frequency	Percent	Valid Percent	Cumulative Percent
Valid	1	1	10.0	10.0	10.0
	2	3	30.0	30.0	40.0
	3	2	20.0	20.0	60.0
	4	1	10.0	10.0	70.0
	5	2	20.0	20.0	90.0
	9	1	10.0	10.0	100.0
	Total	10	100.0	100.0	

Income_category

		Frequency	Percent	Valid Percent	Cumulative Percent
Valid	1	1	10.0	10.0	10.0
	2	1	10.0	10.0	20.0
	3	2	20.0	20.0	40.0
	4	3	30.0	30.0	70.0
	7	1	10.0	10.0	80.0
	8	1	10.0	10.0	90.0
	9	1	10.0	10.0	100.0
	Total	10	100.0	100.0	

- The first FREQUENCIES command, run before any variable properties are assigned, produces the preceding frequency tables.
- For both variables in the two tables, the actual numeric values do not mean a great deal by themselves, since the numbers are really just codes that represent categorical information.
- For *opinion3*, the variable name itself does not convey any particularly useful information either.
- The fact that the reported values for *opinion3* go from 1 to 5 and then jump to 9 may mean something, but you really cannot tell what.

Figure 4-2
Frequency tables after assigning variable properties

Price is reasonable

		Frequency	Percent	Valid Percent	Cumulative Percent
Valid	Strongly Disagree	1	10.0	11.1	11.1
	Disagree	3	30.0	33.3	44.4
	Ambivalent	2	20.0	22.2	66.7
	Agree	1	10.0	11.1	77.8
	Strongly Agree	2	20.0	22.2	100.0
	Total	9	90.0	100.0	
Missing	No answer	1	10.0		
Total		10	100.0		

Income category

		Frequency	Percent	Valid Percent	Cumulative Percent
Valid	Under 25K	1	10.0	14.3	14.3
	25K to 49K	1	10.0	14.3	28.6
	50K to 74K	2	20.0	28.6	57.1
	75K+	3	30.0	42.9	100.0
	Total	7	70.0	100.0	
Missing	Refused to answer	1	10.0		
	Don't know	1	10.0		
	No answer	1	10.0		
	Total	3	30.0		
Total		10	100.0		

- The second FREQUENCIES command is exactly the same as the first, except this time it is run after a number of properties have been assigned to the variables.
- By default, any defined variable labels and value labels are displayed in output instead of variable names and data values. You can also choose to display variable names and/or data values, or display both names/values and variable and value labels. (See the SET command and the TVARS and TNUMBERS subcommands in the *SPSS Command Syntax Reference*.)
- User-defined missing values are flagged for special handling. Many procedures and computations automatically exclude user-defined missing values. In this example, missing values are displayed separately and are not included in the computation of valid percent or cumulative percent.
- If you save the data as an SPSS-format data file, variable labels, value labels, missing values, and other variable properties are automatically saved with the data file. You do not need to reassign variable properties every time you open the data file.

Variable Labels

The VARIABLE LABELS command provides descriptive labels up to 255 bytes long. Variable names can be up to 64 bytes long, but variable names cannot contain spaces and cannot contain certain characters. For more information, see "Variables" in the "Universals" section of the *SPSS Command Syntax Reference*.

```
VARIABLE LABELS
  Interview_date "Interview date"
  Income_category "Income category"
  opinion1 "Would buy this product"
  opinion2 "Would recommend this product to others"
  opinion3 "Price is reasonable"
  opinion4 "Better than a poke in the eye with a sharp stick".
```

- The variable labels *Interview date* and *Income category* do not provide any additional information, but they appear better in output than the variable names with underscores where spaces would normally be.
- For the four opinion variables, the descriptive variable labels are more informative than the generic variable names.

Value Labels

You can use the VALUE LABELS command to assign descriptive labels for each value of a variable. This is particularly useful if your data file uses numeric codes to represent non-numeric categories. For example, *income_category* uses the codes 1 through 4 to represent different income ranges, and the four opinion variables use the codes 1 through 5 to represent level of agreement/disagreement.

```
VALUE LABELS
  Gender "m" "Male" "f" "Female"
  /Income_category 1 "Under 25K" 2 "25K to 49K"
   3 "50K to 74K" 4 "75K+" 7 "Refused to answer"
   8 "Don't know" 9 "No answer"
  /Religion 1 "Catholic" 2 "Protestant" 3 "Jewish"
   4 "Other" 9 "No answer"
  /opinion1 TO opinion4 1 "Strongly Disagree"
   2 "Disagree" 3 "Ambivalent" 4 "Agree"
   5 "Strongly Agree" 9 "No answer".
```

- Value labels can be up to 60 characters long.
- For string variables, both the values and the labels need to be enclosed in quotes. Also, remember that string values are case sensitive; "f" "Female" is *not* the same as "F" "Female".
- You cannot assign value labels to long string variables (string variables longer than eight characters).
- Use ADD VALUE LABELS to define additional value labels without deleting existing value labels.

Missing Values

The MISSING VALUES command identifies specified data values as **user-missing**. It is often useful to know why information is missing. For example, you might want to distinguish between data missing because a respondent refused to answer and data missing because the question did not apply to that respondent. Data values specified as user-missing are flagged for special treatment and are excluded from most calculations.

```
MISSING VALUES
  Income_category (7, 8, 9)
  Religion opinion1 TO opinion4 (9).
```

- You can assign up to three discrete (individual) missing values, a range of missing values, or a range plus one discrete value.
- Ranges can be specified only for numeric variables.
- You cannot assign missing values to long string variables (string variables longer than eight characters).

Measurement Level

You can assign measurement levels (nominal, ordinal, scale) to variables with the VARIABLE LEVEL command. Currently, only a few procedures are affected by defined measurement level (IGRAPH, CTABLES), and the only distinction those procedures (and some dialog boxes in the graphical user interface) make is between scale and categorical (nominal, ordinal).

```
VARIABLE LEVEL
  Income_category, opinion1 to opinion4 (ORDINAL)
  Religion (NOMINAL).
```

- By default, all new string variables are assigned a nominal measurement level, and all new numeric variables are assigned a scale measurement level. In our example, there is no need to explicitly specify a measurement level for *Interview_date* or *Gender*, since they already have the appropriate measurement levels (scale and nominal, respectively).
- The numeric opinion variables are assigned the ordinal measurement level because there is a meaningful order to the categories.
- The numeric variable *Religion* is assigned the nominal measurement level because there is no meaningful order of religious affiliation. No religion is "higher" or "lower" than another religion.

Using Variable Properties As Templates

You can reuse the assigned variable properties in a data file as templates for new data files or other variables in the same data file, selectively applying different properties to different variables.

Example

The data and the assigned variable properties at the beginning of this chapter are saved in the SPSS-format data file *variable_properties.sav*. In this example, we apply some of those variable properties to a new data file with similar variables.

```
*apply_properties.sps.
DATA LIST LIST
 /id (F3) Interview_date (ADATE10) Age (F3) Gender (A1) Income_category (F1)
  attitude1 to attitude4(4F1).
```

```
BEGIN DATA
456 11/1/2002 55 m 3 5 1 3 1
789 10/24/02 25 f 3 2 3 4 3
131 10-24-02 900 f 8 2 9 3 4
659 10/29/2002 62 m 9 2 3 5 3
217 10/26/2002 39 f 7 9 3 2 1
399 10/30/2002 24 f 4 3 5 1 5
END DATA.
APPLY DICTIONARY
  /FROM 'C:\examples\data\variable_properties.sav'
  /SOURCE VARIABLES = Interview_date Age Gender Income_category
  /VARINFO ALL.
APPLY DICTIONARY
  /FROM 'C:\examples\data\variable_properties.sav'
  /SOURCE VARIABLES =  opinion1
  /TARGET VARIABLES =  attitude1 attitude2 attitude3 attitude4
  /VARINFO LEVEL MISSING VALLABELS.
```

- The first APPLY DICTIONARY command applies all variable properties from the specified SOURCE VARIABLES in *variable_properties.sav* to variables in the new data file with matching names and data types. For example, *Income_category* in the new data file now has the same variable label, value labels, missing values, and measurement level (and a few other properties) as the variable of the same name in the source data file.
- The second APPLY DICTIONARY command applies selected properties from the variable *opinion1* in the source data file to the four attitude variables in the new data file. The selected properties are measurement level, missing values, and value labels.
- Since it is unlikely that the variable label for *opinion1* would be appropriate for all four attitude variables, the variable label is not included in the list of properties to apply to the variables in the new data file.

Cleaning and Validating Data

Real data often contain real errors—and many of these errors can be caught by simple cleaning routines.

Finding and Displaying Invalid Values

Invalid—or at least questionable—data values can include anything from simple out-of-range values to complex combinations of values that should not occur.

Example

All of the variables in a file may have values that appear to be valid when examined individually, but certain combinations of values for different variables may indicate that at least one of the variables has either an invalid value or at least one that is suspect. For example, a pregnant male clearly indicates an error in one of the values, whereas a pregnant female older than 55 may not be invalid but should probably be double-checked.

```
*invalid_data3.sps.
DATA LIST FREE /age gender pregnant.
BEGIN DATA
25 0 0
12 1 0
80 1 1
47 0 0
34 0 1
9 1 1
19 0 0
27 0 1
END DATA.
VALUE LABELS gender 0 'Male' 1 'Female'
  /pregnant 0 'No' 1 'Yes'.
COMPUTE valueCheck = 0.
DO IF pregnant = 1.
- DO IF gender = 0.
-   COMPUTE valueCheck = 1.
- ELSE IF gender = 1.
-   DO IF age > 55.
-      COMPUTE valueCheck = 2.
-   ELSE IF age < 12.
-      COMPUTE valueCheck = 3.
-   END IF.
- END IF.
END IF.
VALUE LABELS valueCheck
  0 'No problems detected'
  1 'Male and pregnant'
  2 'Age > 55 and pregnant'
  3 'Age < 12 and pregnant'.
FREQUENCIES VARIABLES = valueCheck.
```

- The variable *valueCheck* is first set to 0.
- The outer DO IF structure restricts the actions for all transformations within the structure to cases recorded as pregnant (pregnant = 1).
- The first nested DO IF structure checks for males (gender = 0) and assigns those cases a value of 1 for *valueCheck*.
- For females (*gender = 1*), a second nested DO IF structure, nested within the previous one, is initiated, and *valueCheck* is set to 2 for females over the age of 55 and 3 for females under 12.

- The VALUE LABELS command assigns descriptive labels to the numeric values of *valueCheck*, and the FREQUENCIES command generates a table that summarizes the results.

Figure 4-3
Frequency table summarizing invalid or suspect values detected

valueCheck

		Frequency	Percent	Valid Percent	Cumulative Percent
Valid	No problems detected	4	50.0	50.0	50.0
	Male and pregnant	2	25.0	25.0	75.0
	Age > 55 and pregnant	1	12.5	12.5	87.5
	Age < 12 and pregnant	1	12.5	12.5	100.0
	Total	8	100.0	100.0	

Example

A data file contains a variable *quantity* that represents the number of products sold to a customer, and the only valid values for this variable are integers. The following command syntax checks for and then reports all cases with non-integer values.

```
*invalid_data.sps.
*First we provide some simple sample data.
DATA LIST FREE /quantity.
BEGIN DATA
1 1.1 2 5 8.01
END DATA.
*Now we look for non-integers values
 in the sample data.
COMPUTE filtervar=(MOD(quantity,1)>0).
FILTER BY filtervar.
SUMMARIZE
  /TABLES=quantity
  /FORMAT=LIST CASENUM NOTOTAL
  /CELLS=COUNT.
FILTER OFF.
```

Figure 4-4
Table listing all cases with non-integer values

	Case Number	quantity
1	2	1.10
2	5	8.01
N		2

- The COMPUTE command creates a new variable, *filtervar*. If the remainder (the MOD function) of the original variable (*quantity*) divided by 1 is greater than 0, then the expression is true and *filtervar* will have a value of 1, resulting in all non-integer values of *quantity* having a value of 1 for *filtervar*. For integer values, *filtervar* is set to 0.
- The FILTER command filters out any cases with a value of 0 for the specified filter variable. In this example, it will filter out all of the cases with integer values for *quantity*, since they have a value of 0 for *filtervar*.
- The SUMMARIZE command simply lists all of the nonfiltered cases, providing both the case number and the value of *quantity* for each case, and a table listing all of the cases with non-integer values.
- The second FILTER command turns off filtering, making all cases available for subsequent procedures.

Excluding Invalid Data from Analysis

With a slight modification, you can change the computation of the filter variable in the above example to filter out cases with invalid values:

```
COMPUTE filtrvar=(MOD(quantity,1)=0).
FILTER BY filtrvar.
```

- Now all cases with integer values for *quantity* have a value of 1 for the filter variable, and all cases with non-integer values for *quantity* are filtered out because they now have a value of 0 for the filter variable.
- This solution filters out the entire case, including valid values for other variables in the data file. If, for example, another variable recorded total purchase price, any case with an invalid value for *quantity* would be excluded from computations involving total purchase price (such as average total purchase price), even if that case has a valid value for total purchase price.

A better solution is to assign invalid values to a user-missing category, which identifies values that should be excluded or treated in a special manner for that specific variable, leaving other variables for cases with invalid values for *quantity* unaffected.

```
*invalid_data2.sps.
DATA LIST FREE /quantity.
BEGIN DATA
1 1.1 2 5 8.01
END DATA.
IF (MOD(quantity,1) > 0) quantity = (-9).
MISSING VALUES quantity (-9).
VALUE LABELS quantity -9 "Non-integer values".
```

- The IF command assigns a value of –9 to all non-integer values of *quantity*.
- The MISSING VALUES command flags *quantity* values of –9 as user-missing, which means these values will either be excluded or treated in a special manner by most procedures.
- The VALUE LABELS command assigns a descriptive label to the user-missing value.

Finding and Filtering Duplicates

Duplicate cases may occur in your data for many reasons, including:

- Data entry errors in which the same case is accidently entered more than once.
- Multiple cases share a common primary ID value but have different secondary ID values, such as family members who live in the same house.
- Multiple cases represent the same case, but with different values for variables other than those that identify the case, such as multiple purchases made by the same person or company for different products or at different times.

The Identify Duplicate Cases dialog box (on the Data menu) provides a number of useful features for finding and filtering duplicate cases. You can paste the command syntax from the dialog box selections into a command syntax window and then refine the criteria used to define duplicate cases.

Example

In the data file *duplicates.sav*, each case is identified by two ID variables: *ID_house*, which identifies each household, and *ID_person*, which identifies each person within the household. If multiple cases have the same value for both variables, then they represent the same case. In this example, that is not necessarily a coding error since the same person may have been interviewed on more than one occasion.

The interview date is recorded in the variable *int_date*, and for cases that match on both ID variables, we want to ignore all but the most recent interview.

```
* duplicates_filter.sps.
GET FILE='c:\examples\data\duplicates.sav'.
SORT CASES BY ID_house(A) ID_person(A) int_date(A) .
MATCH FILES  /FILE = *
  /BY ID_house ID_person /LAST = MostRecent .
FILTER BY MostRecent .
EXECUTE.
```

- SORT CASES sorts the data file by the two ID variables and the interview date. The end result is that all cases with the same household ID are grouped together, and within each household, cases with the same person ID are grouped together. Those cases are sorted by ascending interview date; for any duplicates, the last case will be the most recent interview date.
- Although MATCH FILES is typically used to merge two or more data files, you can use FILE=* to match the working data file with itself. In this case, that is useful not because we want to merge data files but because we want another feature of the command—the ability to identify the LAST case for each value of the key variables specified on the BY subcommand.
- BY ID_house ID_person defines a match as cases having the same values for those two variables. The order of the BY variables must match the sort order of the data file. In this example, the two variables are specified in the same order on both the SORT CASES and MATCH FILES commands.
- LAST = MostRecent assigns a value of 1 for the new variable *MostRecent* to the last case in each matching group and a value of 0 to all other cases in each matching group. Since the data file is sorted by ascending interview date within the two ID variables, the most recent interview date is the last case in each matching group. If there is only one case in a "group," then it is also considered the "last" case and is assigned a value of 1 for the new variable *MostRecent*.

- FILTER BY MostRecent filters out any cases with a value of 0 for *MostRecent*, which means that all but the case with the most recent interview date in each duplicate group will be excluded from reports and analyses. Filtered out cases are indicated with a slash through the row number in Data View in the Data Editor.

Figure 4-5
Filtered duplicate cases in Data View

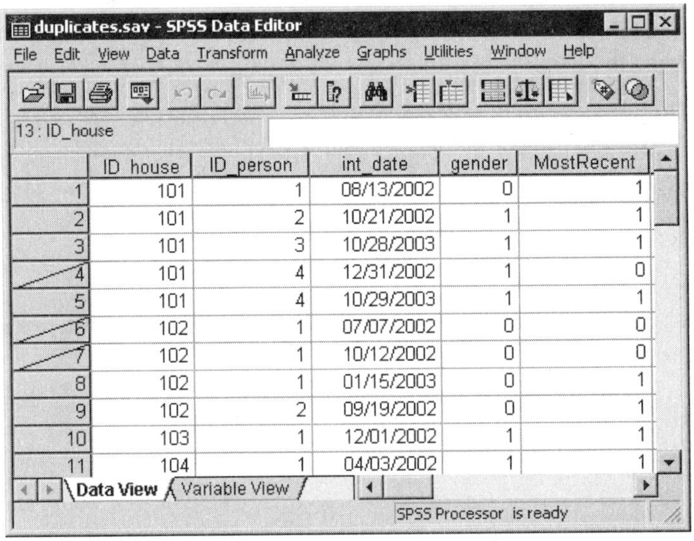

Example

You may not want to automatically exclude duplicates from reports; you may want to examine them before deciding how to treat them. You could simply omit the FILTER command at the end of the previous example and look at each group of duplicates in the Data Editor, but if there are many variables and you are interested in examining only the values of a few key variables, that might not be the optimal approach.

This example counts the number of duplicates in each group and then displays a report of a selected set of variables for all duplicate cases, sorted in descending order of the duplicate count, so the cases with the largest number of duplicates are displayed first.

```
*duplicates_count.sps.
GET FILE='c:\examples\data\duplicates.sav'.
SORT CASES BY ID_house(A) ID_person(A) int_date(A) .
AGGREGATE OUTFILE = 'C:\temp\tempdata.sav'
  /PRESORTED
  /BREAK = ID_house ID_person
  /DuplicateCount = N.
MATCH FILES /FILE = *
  /TABLE = 'C:\temp\tempdata.sav'
  /BY ID_house ID_person.
SORT CASES BY DuplicateCount (D).
TEMPORARY.
SELECT IF (DuplicateCount > 1).
SUMMARIZE
  /TABLES=ID_house ID_person int_date DuplicateCount
  /FORMAT=LIST NOCASENUM TOTAL
  /TITLE='Duplicate Report'
  /CELLS=COUNT.
```

- Since the criteria for identifying duplicates is the same as in the previous example, the SORT CASES command is the same in this example.
- The AGGREGATE command is used to create a table lookup file that will contain the two ID variables plus a new variable that represents the number of cases for each pair of ID values.
- Since the data file is already sorted by the aggregate grouping variables, we can use the PRESORTED subcommand to save processing time.
- The BREAK subcommand creates one case in the table lookup file for each group of cases with matching values on the two ID variables; so the table lookup file will contain one case for each pair of ID values.
- DuplicateCount = N creates a new variable that represents the number of cases for each pair of ID values.
- The MATCH FILES command adds the variable *DuplicateCount* from the table lookup file to the working data file, matching cases based on the values of the two ID variables.
- The TABLE subcommand identifies the file to be merged as a table lookup file.
- Each case in the working data file receives the value of *DuplicateCount* from the variable in the table lookup file with the same pair of ID variable values. For example, the *DuplicateCount* value of 3 from the single case in the table lookup file with values of 102 and 1 for *ID_house* and *ID_person*, respectively, is assigned to the three cases in the working data file with the same two ID variable values.

Figure 4-6
Table lookup file merged with working data file

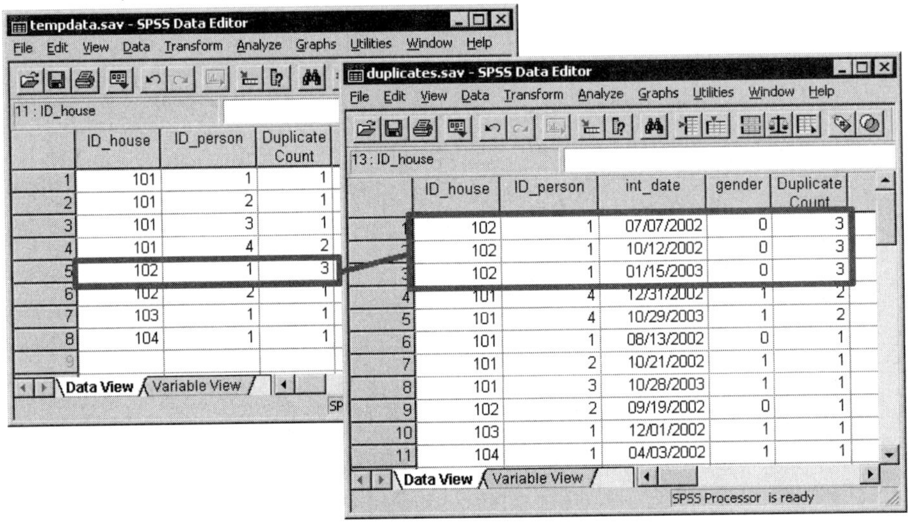

- The second SORT CASES command sorts the data file in descending order of the values of *DuplicateCount*, so cases with the largest numbers of duplicates will be displayed first in the subsequent report.
- The TEMPORARY command specifies that any subsequent transformations will be in effect only for the next procedure that reads the data, after which the data file will be restored to its previous state.
- SELECT IF (DuplicateCount > 1) selects only duplicate cases. Without the preceding TEMPORARY command, all nonduplicate cases would be deleted from the working data file for the remainder of the session.
- The SUMMARIZE command produces a report of the two ID variables, the interview date, and the number of duplicates in each group for all duplicate cases. It also displays the total number of duplicates. The cases are displayed in the current file order, which is descending order of the duplicate count value.

Figure 4-7
Summary report of duplicate cases

Duplicate Report

	Household ID	Person ID	Interview date	DuplicateCount
1	102	1	07/07/2002	3
2	102	1	10/12/2002	3
3	102	1	01/15/2003	3
4	101	4	12/31/2002	2
5	101	4	10/29/2003	2
Total N	5	5	5	5

Merging Data Files

You can merge two or more SPSS-format data files in several ways:

- Merge files with the same cases but different variables.
- Merge files with the same variables but different cases.
- Update values in a master data file with values from a transaction file.

Merging Files with the Same Cases but Different Variables

The MATCH FILES command merges two or more data files that contain the same cases but different variables. For example, demographic data for survey respondents might be contained in one data file, and survey responses for surveys taken at different times might be contained in multiple additional data files. The cases are the same (respondents), but the variables are different (demographic information and survey responses).

This type of data file merge is similar to joining multiple database tables, except you are merging multiple SPSS-format data files rather than database tables. For more information on joining database tables, see "Reading Multiple Tables" on p. 35 in Chapter 3.

One-to-One Matches

The simplest type of match assumes that there is basically a one-to-one relationship between cases in the files being merged—for each case in one file, there is a corresponding case in the other file.

Example

This example merges a data file containing demographic data with another file containing survey responses for the same cases.

```
*match_files1.sps.
*first make sure files are sorted correctly.
GET FILE='C:\examples\data\match_response1.sav'.
SORT CASES BY id.
SAVE OUTFILE='C:\examples\data\match_response1.sav'.
GET FILE='C:\examples\data\match_demographics.sav'.
SORT CASES BY id.
*now merge the survey responses with the demographic info.
MATCH FILES /FILE=*
  /FILE='C:\examples\data\match_response1.sav'
  /BY id.
EXECUTE.
```

- SORT CASES BY id is used to sort both files in the same case order. Cases are merged sequentially, so both files must be sorted in the same order to make sure that cases are merged correctly. The file containing survey responses is saved in the sorted order, and then the file containing demographic information is opened and sorted.
- MATCH FILES merges the two files. FILE=* indicates the working data file (the demographic data file).
- The BY subcommand matches cases by the value of the ID variable in both files. In this example, this is not technically necessary, since there is a one-to-one correspondence between cases in the two files and the files are sorted in the same case order. However, if the files are *not* sorted in the same order and no key variable is specified on the BY subcommand, the files will be merged incorrectly with no warnings or error messages; whereas, if a key variable is specified on the BY subcommand and the files are not sorted in the same order of the key variable, the merge will fail and an appropriate error message will be displayed. If the files contain a common case identifier variable, it is a good practice to use the BY subcommand.
- Any variables with the same name are assumed to contain the same information, and only the variable from the first data file is included in the merged data file. In this example, the variable *id* is present in both data files, and the merged data file contains the values of the variable from the first data file (and in this case, the values are identical anyway).

Example

Expanding the previous example, we will merge the same two data files plus a third data file that contains survey responses from a later date. Two aspects of this third file warrant special attention:

- The variable names for the survey questions are the same as the variable names in the survey response data file from the earlier date.
- One of the cases that is present in both the demographic data file and the first survey response file is missing from the new survey response data file.

```
*match_files2.sps.
GET FILE='C:\examples\data\match_response1.sav'.
SORT CASES BY id.
SAVE OUTFILE='C:\examples\data\match_response1.sav'.
GET FILE='C:\examples\data\match_response2.sav'.
SORT CASES BY id.
SAVE OUTFILE='C:\examples\data\match_response2.sav'.
GET FILE='C:\examples\data\match_demographics.sav'.
SORT CASES BY id.
MATCH FILES /FILE=*
  /FILE='C:\examples\data\match_response1.sav'
  /FILE='C:\examples\data\match_response2.sav'
  /RENAME  opinion1=opinion1_2 opinion2=opinion2_2
   opinion3=opinion3_2 opinion4=opinion4_2
  /BY id.
EXECUTE.
```

- As before, all of the files are sorted by values of the ID variable.
- MATCH FILES specifies three data files this time: the working data file that contains the demographic information and the two data files containing survey responses from two different dates.
- The RENAME command after the FILE subcommand for the second survey response file provides new names for the survey response variables in that file. This is necessary to include these variables in the merged file. Otherwise, they would be excluded because the original variable names are the same as the variable names in the first survey response data file.
- The BY subcommand is necessary in this example because one case is missing (id = 184) from the second survey response file, and without using the BY variable to match cases, the files would be merged incorrectly.
- All cases are included in the merged file. The case missing from the second survey response file is assigned the system-missing value for the variables from that file (*opinion1_2 - opinion4_2*).

Figure 4-8
Merged files displayed in Data Editor

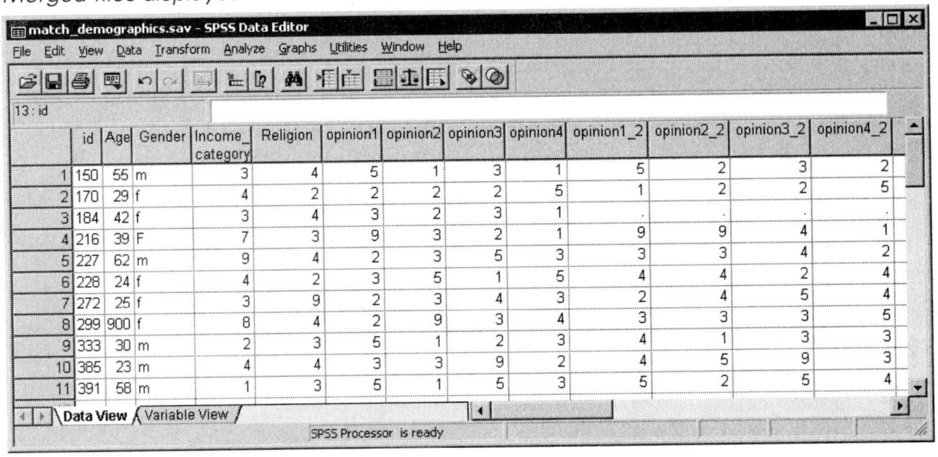

	id	Age	Gender	Income_category	Religion	opinion1	opinion2	opinion3	opinion4	opinion1_2	opinion2_2	opinion3_2	opinion4_2
1	150	55	m	3	4	5	1	3	1	5	2	3	2
2	170	29	f	4	2	2	2	2	5	1	2	2	5
3	184	42	f	3	4	3	2	3	1	.	.	.	.
4	216	39	F	7	3	9	3	2	1	9	9	4	1
5	227	62	m	9	4	2	3	5	3	3	3	4	2
6	228	24	f	4	2	3	5	1	5	4	4	2	4
7	272	25	f	3	9	2	3	4	3	2	4	5	4
8	299	900	f	8	4	2	9	3	4	3	3	3	5
9	333	30	m	2	3	5	1	2	3	4	1	3	3
10	385	23	m	4	4	3	3	9	2	4	5	9	3
11	391	58	m	1	3	5	1	5	3	5	2	5	4

Table Lookup (One-to-Many) Matches

A **table lookup file** is a file in which data for each "case" can be applied to multiple cases in the other data file(s). For example, if one file contains information on individual family members (such as gender, age, education) and the other file contains overall family information (such as total income, family size, location), you can use the file of family data as a table lookup file and apply the common family data to each individual family member in the merged data file.

Specifying a file with the TABLE subcommand instead of the FILE subcommand indicates that the file is a table lookup file. The examples of counting duplicate cases in "Finding and Filtering Duplicates" on p. 82 and writing aggregate summary values back to the original file in "Aggregating Data" on p. 96 use MATCH FILES with a table lookup file.

Merging Files with the Same Variables but Different Cases

The ADD FILES command merges two or more data files that contain the same variables but different cases. For example, regional revenue for two different company divisions might be stored in two separate data files. Both files have the same variables (region indicator and revenue) but different cases (each region for each division is a case).

Example

ADD FILES relies on variable names to determine which variables represent the "same" variables in the data files being merged. In the simplest example, all of the files contain the same set of variables, using the exact same variable names, and all you need to do is specify the files to be merged. In this example, the two files both contain the same two variables, with the same two variable names: *Region* and *Revenue*.

```
*add_files1.sps.
ADD FILES
  /FILE = 'c:\examples\data\catalog.sav'
  /FILE =' c:\examples\data\retail.sav'
    /IN = Division.
EXECUTE.
VALUE LABELS Division 0 'Catalog' 1 'Retail Store'.
```

Figure 4-9
Cases from one file added to another file

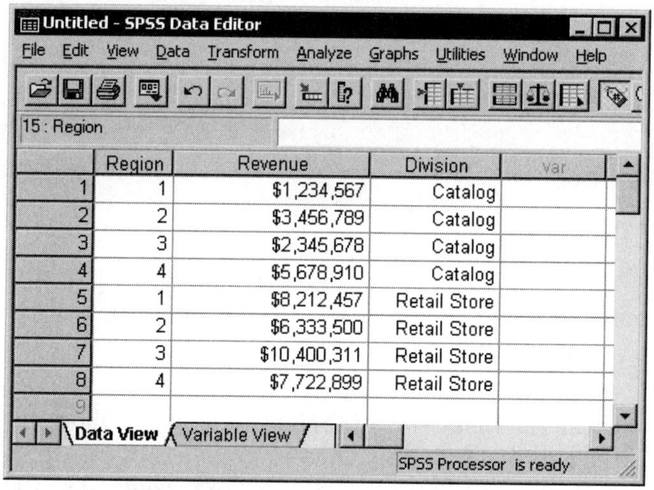

- Cases are added to the working data file in the order the source data files are specified on the ADD FILES command; all of the cases from *catalog.sav* appear first, followed by all of the cases from *retail.sav*.
- The IN subcommand after the FILE subcommand for *retail.sav* creates a new variable named *Division* in the merged data file, with a value of 1 for cases that come from *retail.sav* and a value of 0 for cases that come from *catalog.sav*. (If the IN subcommand was placed immediately after the FILE subcommand for *catalog.sav*, the values would be reversed.)

- The VALUE LABELS command provides descriptive labels for the *Division* values of 0 and 1, identifying the division for each case in the merged file.

Example

Now that we've had a good laugh over the likelihood that all of the files have the exact same structure with the exact same variable names, let's look at a more realistic example. What if the revenue variable had a different name in one of the files, and one of the files contained additional variables not present in the other files being merged?

```
*add_files2.sps.
***first throw some curves into the data***.
GET FILE = 'c:\examples\data\catalog.sav'.
RENAME VARIABLES (Revenue=Sales).
SAVE OUTFILE = 'c:\temp\temp1.sav'.
GET FILE = 'c:\examples\data\retail.sav'.
COMPUTE ExtraVar = 9.
SAVE OUTFILE = 'c:\temp\temp2.sav'.
***show default behavior***.
ADD FILES
  /FILE = 'c:\temp\temp1.sav'
  /FILE = 'c:\temp\temp2.sav'
    /IN = Division.
EXECUTE.
***now treat Sales and Revenue as same variable***.
***and drop ExtraVar from the merged file***.
ADD FILES
  /FILE = 'c:\temp\temp1.sav'
    /RENAME (Sales = Revenue)
  /FILE = 'c:\temp\temp2.sav'
    /IN = Division
    /DROP ExtraVar
 /BY Region.
EXECUTE.
```

- All of the commands prior to the first ADD FILES command simply modify the original data files to contain minor variations—*Revenue* is changed to *Sales* in one data file, and an extra variable, *ExtraVar*, is added to the other data file.
- The first ADD FILES command is similar to the one in the previous example and shows the default behavior if nonmatching variable names and extraneous variables are not accounted for—the merged data file has five variables instead of three, and it also has a lot of missing data. *Sales* and *Revenue* are treated as different variables, resulting in half the cases having values for *Sales* and half the cases having values for *Revenue*—and cases from the second data file have values for *ExtraVar*, but cases from the first data file do not, since this variable does not exist in that file.

Figure 4-10
Probably not what you want when you add cases from another file

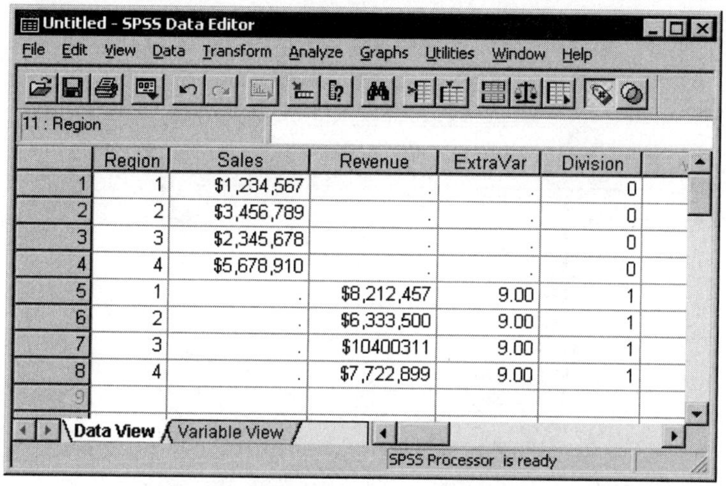

- In the second ADD FILES command, the RENAME subcommand after the FILE subcommand for *temp1.sav* will treat the variable *Sales* as if its name were *Revenue*, so the variable name will match the corresponding variable in *temp2.sav*.
- The DROP subcommand following the FILE subcommand for *temp2.sav* (and the associated IN subcommand) will exclude *ExtraVar* from the merged file. (The DROP subcommand must come after the FILE subcommand for the file that contains the variables to be excluded.)
- The BY subcommand adds cases to the merged data file in ascending order of values of the variable *Region*, instead of adding cases in file order. You could achieve the same result using SORT CASES after all of the cases have been added to the merged data file, but the BY subcommand is more efficient for data files with a large number of cases, since it does not require an additional data pass.

Figure 4-11
Cases added in order of Region variable instead of file order

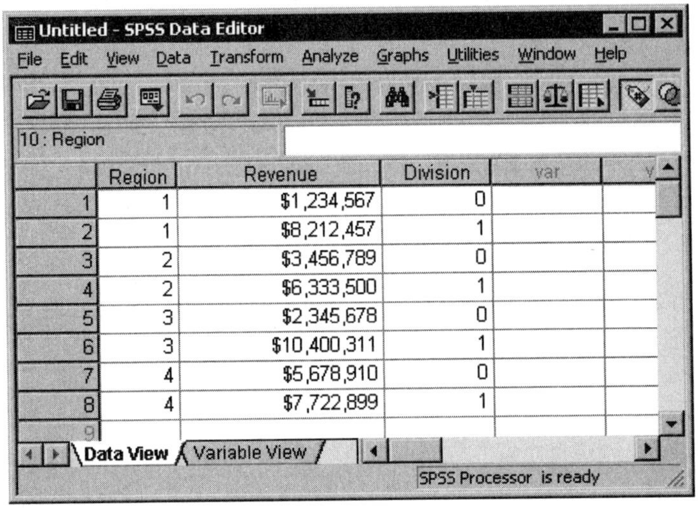

Updating Data Files by Merging New Values from Transaction Files

You can use the UPDATE command to replace values in a master file with updated values recorded in one or more files called transaction files.

```
*update.sps.
NEW FILE.
GET FILE = 'c:\examples\data\update_transaction.sav'.
SORT CASE BY id.
SAVE OUTFILE = 'c:\examples\data\update_transaction.sav'.
GET FILE = 'c:\examples\data\update_master.sav'.
SORT CASES BY id.
UPDATE /FILE = *
  /FILE = 'c:\examples\data\update_transaction.sav'
  /IN = updated
  /BY id.
EXECUTE.
```

- SORT CASES BY id is used to sort both files in the same case order. Cases are updated sequentially, so both files must be sorted in the same order.
- The first FILE subcommand on the UPDATE command specifies the master data file. In this example, FILE = * specifies the working data file.
- The second FILE subcommand specifies the transaction file from which to obtain updated values.

- The IN subcommand immediately following the second FILE subcommand creates a new variable called *updated* in the master data file; this variable will have a value of 1 for any cases with updated values and a value of 0 for cases that have not changed.
- The BY subcommand matches cases by *id*. This subcommand is required. Transaction files often contain only a subset of cases, and a key variable is necessary to match cases in the two files.

Figure 4-12
Original file, transaction file, and update file

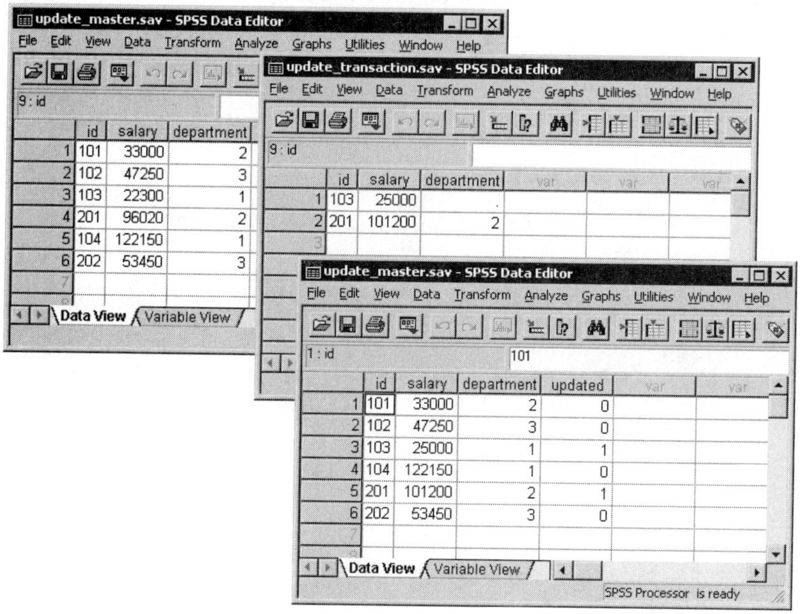

	id	salary	department
1	101	33000	2
2	102	47250	3
3	103	22300	1
4	201	96020	2
5	104	122150	1
6	202	53450	3

	id	salary	department
1	103	25000	.
2	201	101200	2

	id	salary	department	updated
1	101	33000	2	0
2	102	47250	3	0
3	103	25000	1	1
4	104	122150	1	0
5	201	101200	2	1
6	202	53450	3	0

- The *salary* values for the cases with the *id* values of 103 and 201 are both updated.
- The *department* value for case 201 is updated, but the *department* value for case 103 is *not* updated. System-missing values in the transaction files do not overwrite existing values in the master file, so the transactions files can contain partial information for each case.

Aggregating Data

The AGGREGATE command creates a new data file where each case represents one or more cases from the original data file. You can save the aggregated data to a new file or replace the working data file with aggregated data.

Example

In this example, information was collected for every person living in a selected sample of households. In addition to information for each individual, each case contains a variable that identifies the household. You can change the unit of analysis from individuals to households by aggregating the data based on the value of the household ID variable.

```
*aggregate1.sps.
***create some sample data***.
DATA LIST FREE (" ")
  /ID_household (F3) ID_person (F2) Income (F8).
BEGIN DATA
101 1 12345 101 2 47321 101 3 500 101 4 0
102 1 77233 102 2 0
103 1 19010 103 2 98277 103 3 0
104 1 101244
END DATA.
***now aggregate based on household id***.
AGGREGATE
  /OUTFILE = *
  /BREAK = ID_household
  /Household_Income = SUM(Income)
  /Household_Size = N.
```

- OUTFILE = * replaces the working data file with the aggregated data.
- BREAK = ID_household combines cases based on the value of the household ID variable.
- Household_Income = SUM(Income) creates a new variable in the aggregated file that is the total income for each household.
- Household_Size = N creates a new variable in the aggregated file that is the number of original cases in each aggregated case.

Figure 4-13
Original and aggregated data

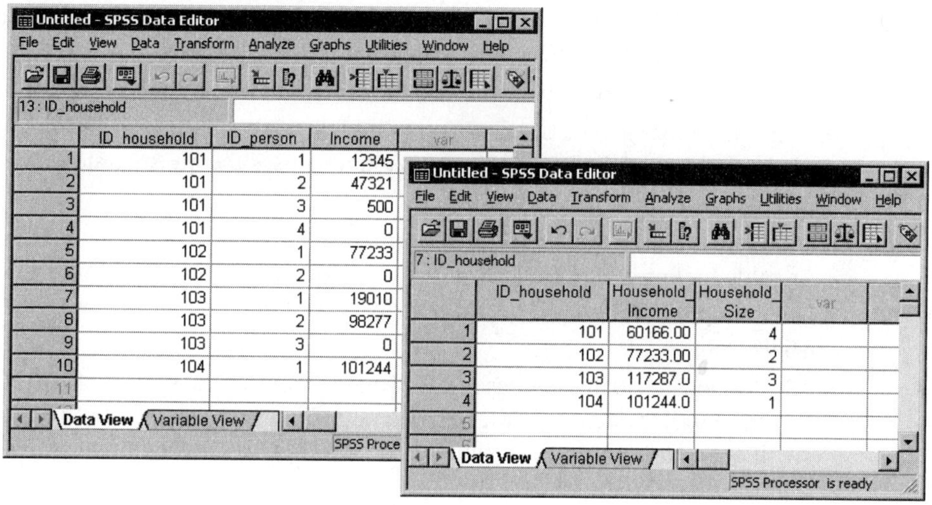

	ID_household	ID_person	Income
1	101	1	12345
2	101	2	47321
3	101	3	500
4	101	4	0
5	102	1	77233
6	102	2	0
7	103	1	19010
8	103	2	98277
9	103	3	0
10	104	1	101244

	ID_household	Household_Income	Household_Size
1	101	60166.00	4
2	102	77233.00	2
3	103	117287.0	3
4	104	101244.0	1

Example

You can also use AGGREGATE with MATCH FILES to add group summary information to the original data file. For example, you could create two new variables in the original data file that contain the number of people in the household and the per capita income for the household (total income divided by number of people in the household).

```
*aggregate2.sps.
DATA LIST FREE (" ")
  /ID_household (F3) ID_person (F2) Income (F8).
BEGIN DATA
101 1 12345 101 2 47321 101 3 500 101 4 0
102 1 77233 102 2 0
103 1 19010 103 2 98277 103 3 0
104 1 101244
END DATA.
SORT CASES BY ID_household.
SAVE OUTFILE = 'c:\temp\tempdata.sav'.
AGGREGATE
  /OUTFILE = *
  /BREAK = ID_household
  /per_capita_Income = MEAN(Income)
  /Household_Size = N.
***merge the two files together***.
MATCH FILES
  /FILE = 'c:\temp\tempdata.sav'
  /TABLE = *
  /BY ID_Household.
EXECUTE.
```

- The first part of this example is essentially the same as the previous example. The only difference is that we need to save the original data in a file, sorted by the household ID variable, before overwriting the working data file with the aggregated data. The MATCH FILES command will merge cases based on the values of *ID_household*, and both files must be sorted by this variable or the merge will fail.
- Instead of using the SUM function to add all of the income values in each household, the AGGREGATE command now uses the MEAN function to obtain the per capita household incomes.
- TABLE = * on the MATCH FILES command uses the aggregated working data file as a table lookup file. This indicates a one-to-many matching scheme—each "case" in the aggregated table lookup file may correspond to multiple cases in the original data file.
- BY ID_household merges cases based on the value of the household ID variable. For example, all four cases in the original data file with a value of 101 for ID_household will get a *Household_Size* value of 4 from the one case in the aggregate file with an *ID_household* value of 101.

Figure 4-14
Aggregate summary data merged with original data

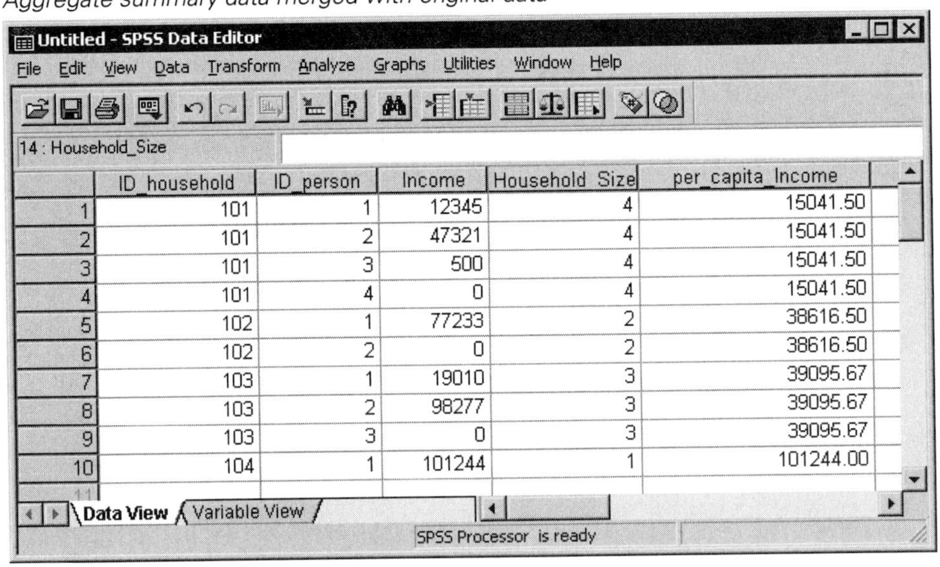

	ID_household	ID_person	Income	Household_Size	per_capita_Income
1	101	1	12345	4	15041.50
2	101	2	47321	4	15041.50
3	101	3	500	4	15041.50
4	101	4	0	4	15041.50
5	102	1	77233	2	38616.50
6	102	2	0	2	38616.50
7	103	1	19010	3	39095.67
8	103	2	98277	3	39095.67
9	103	3	0	3	39095.67
10	104	1	101244	1	101244.00

Aggregate Summary Functions

The new variables created when you aggregate a data file can be based on a wide variety of numeric and statistical functions applied to each group of cases defined by the BREAK variables, including:

- Number of cases in each group
- Sum, mean, median, and standard deviation
- Minimum, maximum, and range
- Percent of cases between, above, and/or below specified values
- First and last non-missing value in each group
- Number of missing values in each group

For a complete list of aggregate functions, see the AGGREGATE command in the *SPSS Command Syntax Reference.*

Weighting Data

The WEIGHT command simulates case replication by treating each case as if it were actually the number of cases indicated by the value of the weight variable. You can use a weight variable to adjust the distribution of cases to more accurately reflect the larger population or to simulate raw data from aggregated data.

Example

A sample data file contains 52% males and 48% females, but you know that in the larger population the real distribution is 49% males and 51% females. You can compute and apply a weight variable to simulate this distribution.

```
*weight_sample.sps.
***create sample data of 52 males, 48 females***.
NEW FILE.
INPUT PROGRAM.
- STRING gender (A6).
- LOOP #I =1 TO 100.
-   DO IF #I <= 52.
-     COMPUTE gender='Male'.
-   ELSE.
-     COMPUTE Gender='Female'.
-   END IF.
-   COMPUTE AgeCategory = TRUNC(UNIFORM(3)+1).
-   END CASE.
- END LOOP.
- END FILE.
END INPUT PROGRAM.
FREQUENCIES VARIABLES=gender AgeCategory.
***create and apply weightvar***.
***to simulate 49 males, 51 females***.
DO IF gender = 'Male'.
- COMPUTE weightvar=49/52.
ELSE IF gender = 'Female'.
- COMPUTE weightvar=51/48.
END IF.
WEIGHT BY weightvar.
FREQUENCIES VARIABLES=gender AgeCategory.
```

- Everything prior to the first FREQUENCIES command simply generates a sample data file with 52 males and 48 females.
- The DO IF structure sets one value of *weightvar* for males and a different value for females. The formula used here is: *desired proportion/observed proportion*. For males, it is 49/52 (0.94), and for females, it is 51/48 (1.06).
- The WEIGHT command weights cases by the value of *weightvar*, and the second FREQUENCIES command displays the weighted distribution.

Note: In this example, the weight values have been calculated in a manner that does not alter the total number of cases. If the weighted number of cases exceeds the original number of cases, tests of significance are inflated; if it is smaller, they are deflated. More flexible and reliable weighting techniques are available in the Complex Samples option.

Example

You want to calculate measures of association and/or significance tests for a crosstabulation, but all you have to work with is the summary table, not the raw data used to construct the table. The table looks like this:

	Male	Female	Total
Under $50K	25	35	60
$50K +	30	10	40
Total	55	45	100

You then read the data into SPSS, using rows, columns, and cell counts as variables; then, use the cell count variable as a weight variable.

```
*weight.sps.
DATA LIST LIST /Income Gender count.
BEGIN DATA
1, 1, 25
1, 2, 35
2, 1, 30
2, 2, 10
END DATA.
VALUE LABELS
  Income 1 'Under $50K' 2 '$50K+'
  /Gender 1 'Male' 2 'Female'.
WEIGHT BY count.
CROSSTABS TABLES=Income by Gender
  /STATISTICS=CC PHI.
```

- The values for *Income* and *Gender* represent the row and column positions from the original table, and *count* is the value that appears in the corresponding cell in the table. For example, 1, 2, 35 indicates that the value in the first row, second column is 35. (The total row and column are not included.)
- The VALUE LABELS command assigns descriptive labels to the numeric codes for *Income* and *Gender*. In this example, the value labels are the row and column labels from the original table.
- The WEIGHT command weights cases by the value of *count*, which is the number of cases in each cell of the original table.
- The CROSSTABS command produces a table very similar to the original and provides statistical tests of association and significance.

Figure 4-15
Crosstabulation and significance tests for reconstructed table

Income * Gender Crosstabulation

		Gender		Total
		Male	Female	
Income	Under $50K	25	35	60
	$50K+	30	10	40
Total		55	45	100

Symmetric Measures

		Value	Approx. Sig.
Nominal by Nominal	Phi	-.328	.001
	Cramer's V	.328	.001
	Contingency Coefficient	.312	.001
N of Valid Cases		100	

Changing File Structure

SPSS expects data to be organized in a certain way, and different types of analysis may require different data structures. Since your original data can come from many different sources, the data may require some reorganization before you can create the reports or analyses that you want.

Transposing Cases and Variables

You can use the FLIP command to create a new data file in which the rows and columns in the original data file are transposed so that cases (rows) become variables and variables (columns) become cases.

Example

Although SPSS expects cases in the rows and variables in the columns, applications such as Excel don't have that kind of data structure limitation. So what do you do with an Excel file in which cases are recorded in the columns and variables are recorded in the rows? For example, what if the Excel file looks like Figure 4-16?

Figure 4-16
Excel file with cases in columns, variables in rows

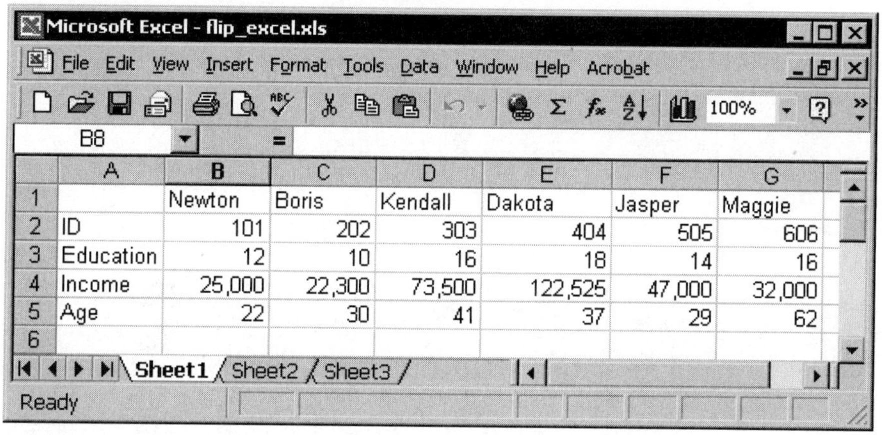

Here are the commands to read the Excel spreadsheet and transpose the rows and columns:

```
*flip_excel.sps.
GET DATA /TYPE=XLS
  /FILE='C:\examples\data\flip_excel.xls'
  /READNAMES=ON .
FLIP VARIABLES=Newton Boris Kendall Dakota Jasper Maggie
  /NEWNAME=V1.
RENAME VARIABLES (CASE_LBL = Name).
```

- READNAMES=ON in the GET DATA command reads the first row of the Excel spreadsheet as variable names. Since the first cell in the first row is blank, it is assigned a default variable name of *V1*.
- The FLIP command creates a new working data file in which all of the variables specified will become cases and all cases in the file will become variables.
- The original variable names are automatically stored as values in a new variable called *CASE_LBL*. The subsequent RENAME VARIABLES command changes the name of this variable to *Name*.
- NEWNAME=V1 uses the values of variable *V1* as variable names in the transposed data file.

Figure 4-17
Original and transposed data in Data Editor

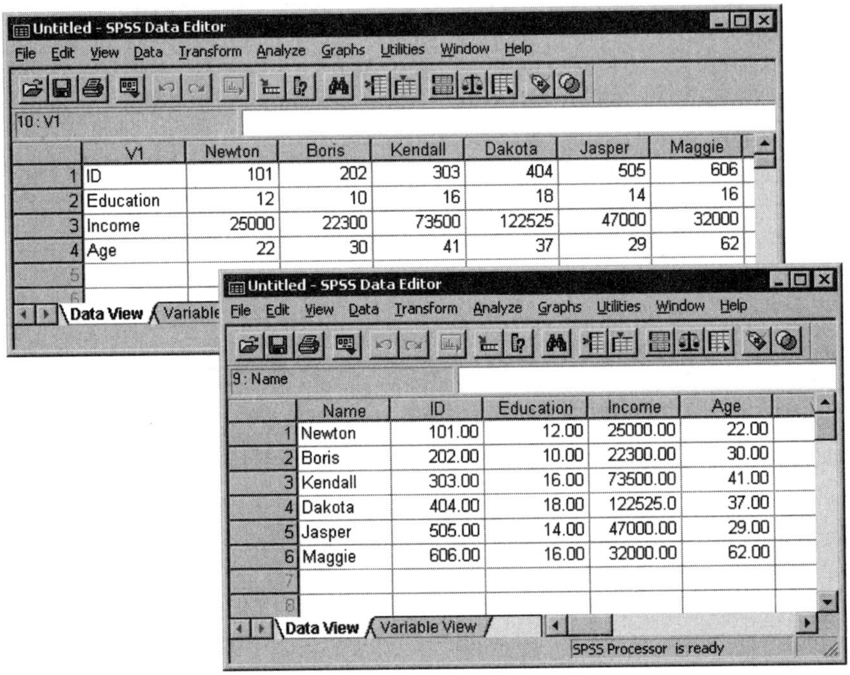

Example

This example uses the values of the variable *CASE_LBL* (automatically generated by the FLIP command) to sort the variables in the original data file in alphabetic order.

```
*sort_variables.sps.
GET FILE='c:\examples\data\employee data.sav'.
N OF CASES 1.
FLIP.
SORT CASES BY case_lbl.
DO IF $casenum = 1.
- WRITE OUTFILE='c:\temp\reorder.sps'
    /'ADD FILES FILE=* /KEEP='case_lbl.
- ELSE.
- WRITE OUTFILE='c:\temp\reorder.sps'
    /' 'case_lbl.
END IF.
EXECUTE.
GET FILE='c:\examples\data\employee data.sav'.
INCLUDE 'c:\temp\reorder.sps'.
EXECUTE.
```

- N OF CASES 1 discards all but the first case. The case data is not important at this point, and the fewer variables you create when flipping the file, the less time and resources it takes. Also, we use N OF CASES instead of SELECT IF $CASENUM=1 because the former takes effect immediately, whereas the latter reads the entire data file, which can be time consuming for large data files.
- FLIP creates a data file with two variables. The only one of interest is *CASE_LBL*, the string variable automatically created by FLIP that contains the original variable names.
- The SORT CASES command sorts the flipped file in alphabetic order of *CASE_LBL* values.
- The DO IF structure generates a series of WRITE commands that build a command syntax file.
- For the first case, the WRITE command writes out the literal string:
  ADD FILES FILE = * /KEEP=
  followed by the value of *CASE_LBL* for the first case in the flipped file.
- For all remaining cases, a space followed by the value of *CASE_LBL* is written to the command syntax file.
- The EXECUTE command closes the generated command syntax file.
- Finally, we open the original data file again and run the generated command syntax file with an INCLUDE command, which sorts the variables in alphabetical order by specifying all of the variables in the file in alphabetical order on the KEEP subcommand of the ADD FILES command.

The generated command syntax file looks like this:

```
ADD FILES FILE=* /KEEP=bdate
 educ
 gender
 id
 jobcat
 jobtime
 minority
 prevexp
 salary
 salbegin
```

Note: The generated command does not end with a period. Since this command is run via an INCLUDE command, the period at the end of the command is not required. Ending the command with a period would require a more complicated job, since you would need code to check for the last case and to write out the period after the last case.

Cases to Variables

Sometimes you may have a need to restructure your data in a slightly more complex manner than simply flipping rows and columns.

Many statistical techniques in SPSS are based on the assumption that cases (rows) represent independent observations and/or that related observations are recorded in separate variables rather than separate cases. If a data file contains groups of related cases, you may not be able to use the appropriate statistical techniques (for example, Paired Samples T Test or Repeated Measures GLM) because the data are not organized in the required fashion for those techniques.

In this example, we use a data file that is very similar to the data used in the AGGREGATE example, "Aggregating Data" on p. 96; information was collected for every person living in a selected sample of households. In addition to information for each individual, each case contains a variable that identifies the household. Cases in the same household represent related observations, not independent observations, and we want to restructure the data file so that each group of related cases is one case in the restructured file and new variables are created to contain the related observations.

Figure 4-18
Data file before restructuring cases to variables

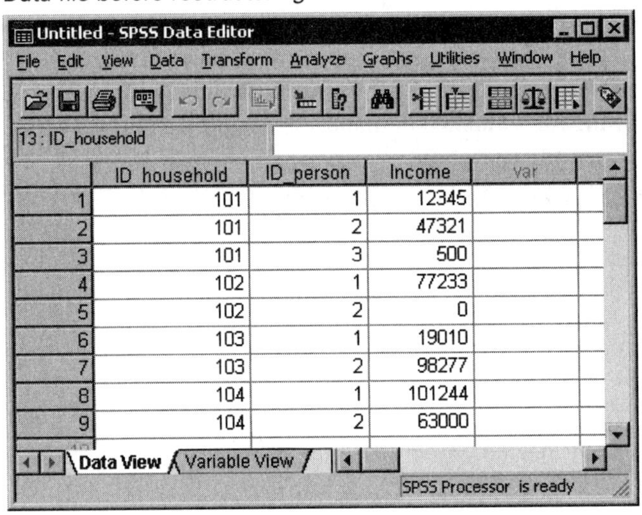

The CASESTOVARS command combines the related cases and produces the new variables.

```
*casestovars.sps.
GET FILE = 'c:\examples\data\casestovars.sav'.
SORT CASES BY ID_household.
CASESTOVARS
 /ID = ID_household
 /INDEX = ID_person
 /SEPARATOR = "_"
 /COUNT = famsize.
VARIABLE LABELS
  Income_1 "Husband/Father Income"
  Income_2 "Wife/Mother Income"
  Income_3 "Other Income".
```

- SORT CASES sorts the data file by the variable that will be used to group cases in the CASESTOVARS command. The data file must be sorted by the variable(s) specified on the ID subcommand of the CASESTOVARS command.
- The ID subcommand of the CASESTOVARS indicates the variable(s) that will be used to group cases together. In this example, all cases with the same value for *ID_household* will become a single case in the restructured file.
- The optional INDEX subcommand identifies the original variables that will be used to create new variables in the restructured file. Without the INDEX subcommand, all unique values of all non-ID variables will generate variables in the restructured file. In this example, only values of *ID_person* will be used to generate new variables. Index variables can be either string or numeric. Numeric index values must be non-missing, positive integers; string index values cannot be blank.
- The SEPARATOR subcommand specifies the character(s) that will be used to separate original variable names and the values appended to those names for the new variable names in the restructured file. By default, a period is used. You can use any characters that are allowed in a valid variable name (which means the character cannot be a space). If you do not want any separator, specify a null string (SEPARATOR = "").
- The COUNT subcommand will create a new variable that indicates the number of original cases represented by each combined case in the restructured file.
- The VARIABLE LABELS command provides descriptive labels for the new variables in the restructured file.

Figure 4-19
Data file after restructuring cases to variables

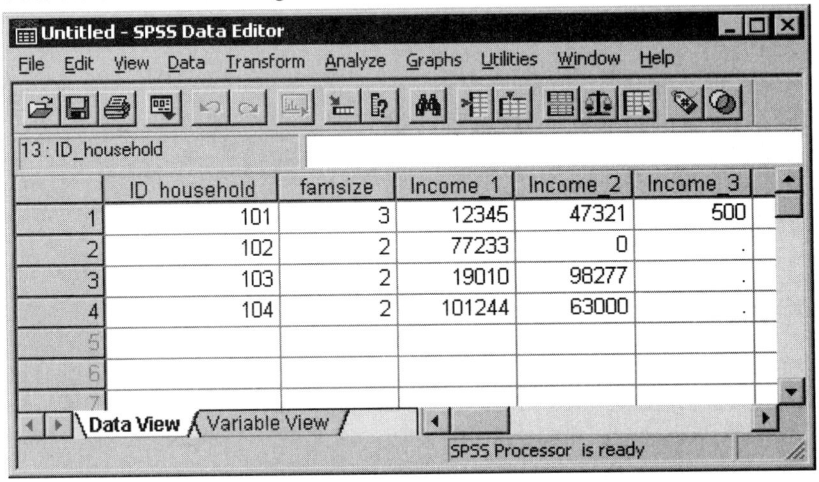

	ID_household	famsize	Income_1	Income_2	Income_3
1	101	3	12345	47321	500
2	102	2	77233	0	.
3	103	2	19010	98277	.
4	104	2	101244	63000	.
5					
6					
7					

Variables to Cases

The previous example turned related cases into related variables for use with statistical techniques that compare and contrast related samples. But sometimes you may need to do the exact opposite—convert variables that represent unrelated observations to variables.

Example

A simple Excel file contains two columns of information: income for males and income for females. There is no known or assumed relationship between male and female values that are recorded in the same row; the two columns represent independent (unrelated) observations, and we want to create cases (rows) from the columns (variables) and create a new variable that indicates the gender for each case.

Figure 4-20
Data file before restructuring variables to cases

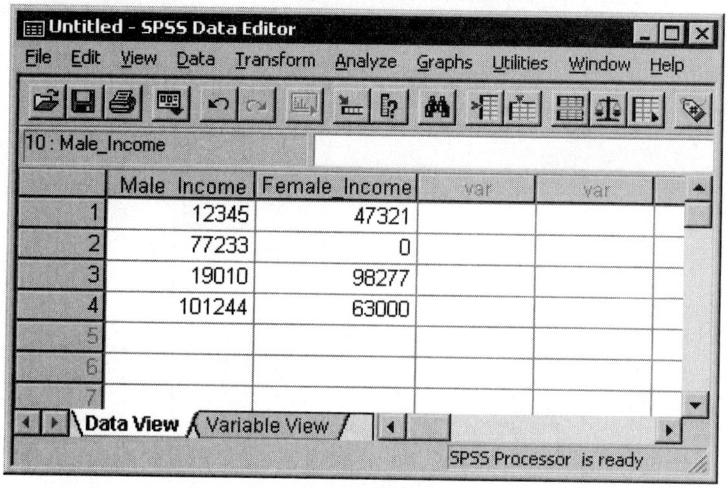

The VARSTOCASES command creates cases from the two columns of data.

```
*varstocases1.sps.
GET DATA /TYPE=XLS
 /FILE = 'c:\examples\data\varstocases.xls'
 /READNAMES = ON.
VARSTOCASES
 /MAKE Income FROM Male_Income Female_Income
 /INDEX = Gender.
VALUE LABELS Gender 1 'Male' 2 'Female'.
```

- The MAKE subcommand creates a single income variable from the two original income variables.
- The INDEX subcommand creates a new variable named *Gender* with integer values that represent the sequential order in which the original variables are specified on the MAKE subcommand. A value of 1 indicates that the new case came from the original male income column, and a value of 2 indicates that the new case came from the original female income column.
- The VALUE LABELS command provides descriptive labels for the two values of the new gender variable.

Figure 4-21
Data file after restructuring variables to cases

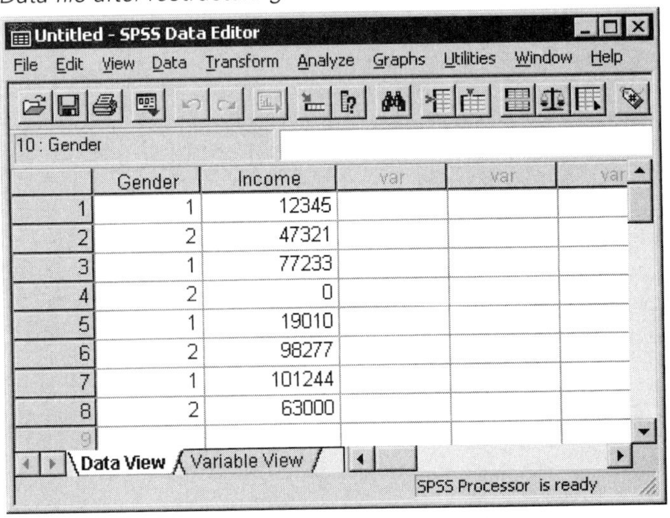

Example

In this example, the original data contain separate variables for two measures taken at three separate times for each case. This is the correct data structure for most procedures that compare related observations—but there is one important exception: Linear Mixed Models (available in the Advanced Statistics option) requires a data structure in which related observations are recorded as separate cases.

Figure 4-22
Related observations recorded as separate variables

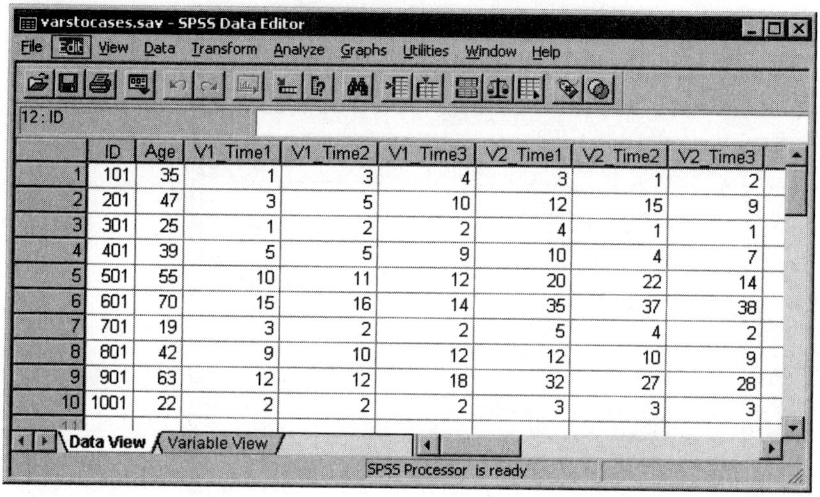

	ID	Age	V1_Time1	V1_Time2	V1_Time3	V2_Time1	V2_Time2	V2_Time3
1	101	35	1	3	4	3	1	2
2	201	47	3	5	10	12	15	9
3	301	25	1	2	2	4	1	1
4	401	39	5	5	9	10	4	7
5	501	55	10	11	12	20	22	14
6	601	70	15	16	14	35	37	38
7	701	19	3	2	2	5	4	2
8	801	42	9	10	12	12	10	9
9	901	63	12	12	18	32	27	28
10	1001	22	2	2	2	3	3	3

```
*varstocases2.sps.
GET FILE = 'c:\examples\data\varstocases.sav'.
VARSTOCASES  /MAKE V1 FROM V1_Time1 V1_Time2 V1_Time3
 /MAKE V2 FROM V2_Time1 V2_Time2 V2_Time3
 /INDEX = Time
 /KEEP = ID Age.
```

- The two MAKE subcommands create two variables, one for each group of three related variables.
- The INDEX subcommand creates a variable named *Time* that indicates the sequential order of the original variables used to create the cases, as specified on the MAKE subcommand.
- The KEEP subcommand retains the original variables *ID* and *Age*.

Figure 4-23
Related variables restructured into cases

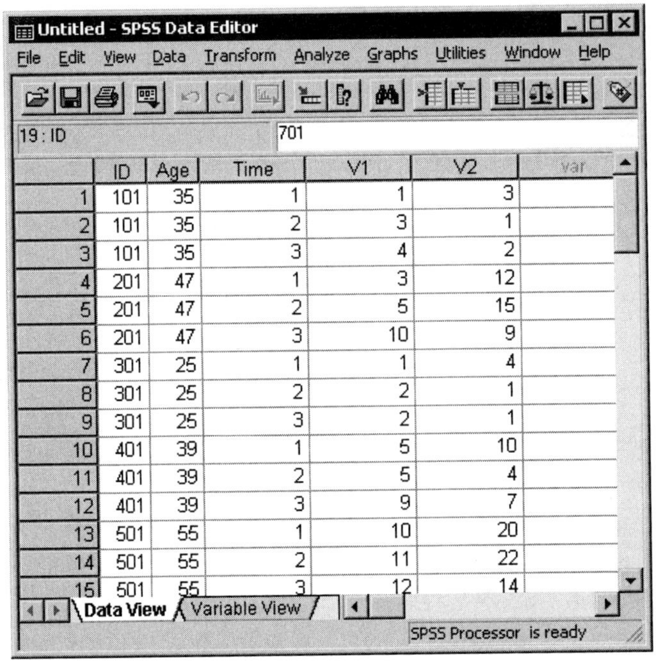

Transforming Data Values

In an ideal situation, your raw data are perfectly suitable for the reports and analyses you need. Unfortunately, this is rarely the case. Preliminary analysis may reveal inconvenient coding schemes or coding errors, or data transformations may be required in order to coax out the true relationship between variables.

You can perform data transformations ranging from simple tasks, such as collapsing categories for reports, to more advanced tasks, such as creating new variables based on complex equations and conditional statements.

Recoding Categorical Variables

You can use the RECODE command to change, rearrange, and/or consolidate values of a variable. For example, questionnaires often use a combination of high-low and low-high rankings. For reporting and analysis purposes you probably want these all coded in a consistent manner.

```
*recode.sps.
DATA LIST FREE /opinion1 opinion2.
BEGIN DATA
1 5
2 4
3 3
4 2
5 1
END DATA.
RECODE opinion2
 (1 = 5) (2 = 4) (4 = 2) (5 = 1)
 (ELSE = COPY)
 INTO opinion2_new.
EXECUTE.
VALUE LABELS opinion1 opinion2_new
  1 'Really bad' 2 'Bad' 3 'Blah'
  4 'Good' 5 'Terrific!'.
```

- The RECODE command essentially reverses the values of *opinion2*.
- ELSE = COPY retains the value of 3 (which is the middle value in either direction) and any other unspecified values, such as user-missing values, which would otherwise be set to system-missing for the new variable.
- INTO creates a new variable for the recoded values, leaving the original variable unchanged.

Banding Scale Variables

Creating a small number of discrete categories from a continuous scale variable is sometimes referred to as **banding**. For example, you can recode salary data into a few salary range categories. Although it is not difficult to write command syntax to band a scale variable into range categories, we recommend that you try the Visual Bander, available on the Transform menu, because it can help you make the best recoding choices by showing the actual distribution of values and where your selected category boundaries occur in the distribution. It also provides a number of different banding methods and can automatically generate descriptive labels for the banded categories.

Figure 4-24
Visual Bander

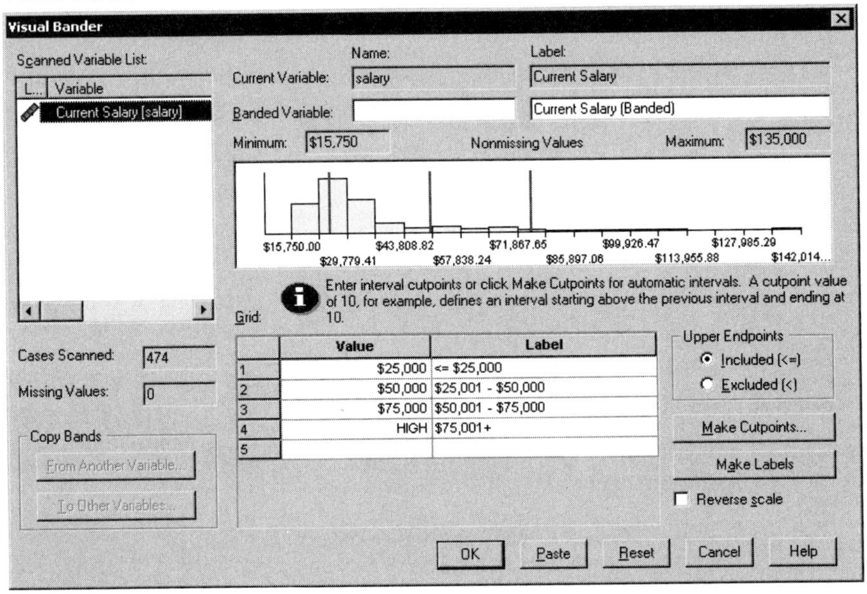

- The histogram shows the distribution of values for the selected variable. The vertical lines indicate the banded category divisions for the specified range groupings.
- In this example, the range groupings were automatically generated using the Make Cutpoints dialog box, and the descriptive category labels were automatically generated with the Make Labels button.
- You can use the Make Cutpoints dialog box to create banded categories based on equal width intervals, equal percentiles (equal number of cases in each category), or standard deviations.

Figure 4-25
Make Cutpoints dialog box

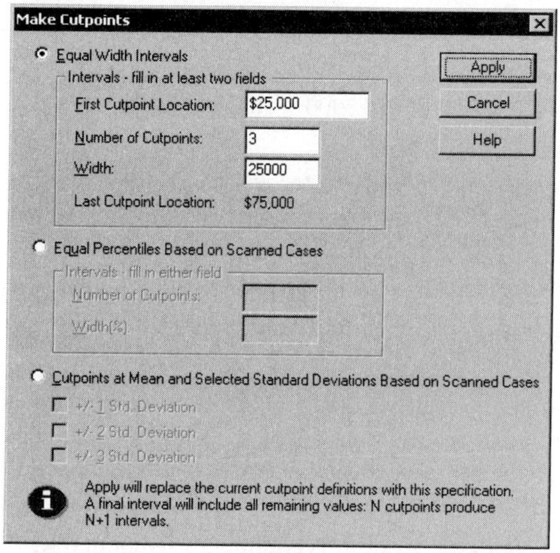

You can use the Paste button in the Visual Bander to paste the command syntax for your selections into a command syntax window. The RECODE command syntax generated by the Visual Bander provides a good model for a proper recoding method.

```
*visual_bander.sps.
GET FILE = 'c:\examples\data\employee data.sav'.
***commands generated by Visual Bander***.
RECODE salary
   ( MISSING = COPY ) ( LO THRU 25000 =1 ) ( LO THRU 50000 =2 )
   ( LO THRU 75000 =3 ) ( LO THRU HI = 4 )
   INTO salary_category.
VARIABLE LABELS salary_category 'Current Salary (Banded)'.
FORMAT salary_category (F5.0).
VALUE LABELS salary_category
   1  '<= $25,000'
   2  '$25,001 - $50,000'
   3  '$50,001 - $75,000'
   4  '$75,001+'
   0   'missing'.
MISSING VALUES salary_category ( 0 ).
VARIABLE LEVEL salary_category ( ORDINAL ).
EXECUTE.
```

- The RECODE command encompasses all possible values of the original variable.

- MISSING = COPY preserves any user-missing values from the original variable. Without this, user-missing values could be inadvertently combined into a non-missing category for the new variable.
- The general recoding scheme of LO THRU *value* ensures that no values fall through the cracks. For example, 25001 THRU 50000 would not include a value of 25000.50.
- Since the RECODE expression is evaluated from left to right and each original value is recoded only once, each subsequent range specification can start with LO because this means the lowest remaining value that has not already been recoded.
- LO thru HI includes all remaining values (other than system-missing) not included in any of the other categories, which in this example should be any salary value above $75,000.
- INTO creates a new variable for the recoded values, leaving the original variable unchanged. Since banding or combining/collapsing categories can result in loss of information, it is a good idea to create a new variable for the recoded values rather than overwriting the original variable.
- The VALUE LABELS and MISSING VALUES commands generated by the Visual Bander preserve the user-missing category and its label from the original variable.

Simple Numeric Transformations

You can perform simple numeric transformations using the standard programming language notation for addition, subtraction, multiplication, division, exponents, etc.

```
*numeric_transformations.sps.
DATA LIST FREE /var1.
BEGIN DATA
1 2 3 4 5
END DATA.
COMPUTE var2 = 1.
COMPUTE var3 = var1*2.
COMPUTE var4 = ((var1*2)**2)/2.
EXECUTE.
```

- COMPUTE var2 = 1 creates a constant with a value of 1.
- COMPUTE var3 = var1*2 creates a new variable that is twice the value of *var1*.
- COMPUTE var4 = ((var1*2)**2)/2 first multiplies *var1* by 2, then squares that value, and finally divides the result by 2.

Arithmetic and Statistical Functions

In addition to simple arithmetic operators, you can also transform data with a wide variety of functions, including arithmetic and statistical functions.

```
*numeric_functions.sps.
DATA LIST LIST (",") /var1 var2 var3 var4.
BEGIN DATA
1, , 3, 4
5, 6, 7, 8
9, , , 12
END DATA.
COMPUTE Square_Root = SQRT(var4).
COMPUTE Remainder = MOD(var4, 3).
COMPUTE Average = MEAN.3(var1, var2, var3, var4).
COMPUTE Valid_Values = NVALID(var1 TO var4).
COMPUTE Trunc_Mean = TRUNC(MEAN(var1 TO var4)).
EXECUTE.
```

- All functions take one or more arguments, enclosed in parentheses. Depending on the function, the arguments can be constants, expressions, and/or variable names—or various combinations thereof.
- SQRT(var4) returns the square root of the value of *var4* for each case.
- MOD(var4, 3) returns the remainder (modulus) from dividing the value of *var4* by 3.
- MEAN.3(var1, var2, var3, var4) returns the mean of the four specified variables, provided that at least three of them have non-missing values. The divisor for the calculation of the mean is the number of non-missing values.
- NVALID(var1 TO var4) returns the number of valid, non-missing values for the inclusive range of specified variables. For example, if only two of the variables have non-missing values for a particular case, the value of the computed variable is 2 for that case.
- TRUNC(MEAN(var1 TO var4)) computes the mean of the values for the inclusive range of variables and then truncates the result. Since no minimum number of non-missing values is specified for the MEAN function, a mean will be calculated (and truncated) as long as at least one of the variables has a non-missing value for that case.

Figure 4-26
Variables computed with arithmetic and statistical functions

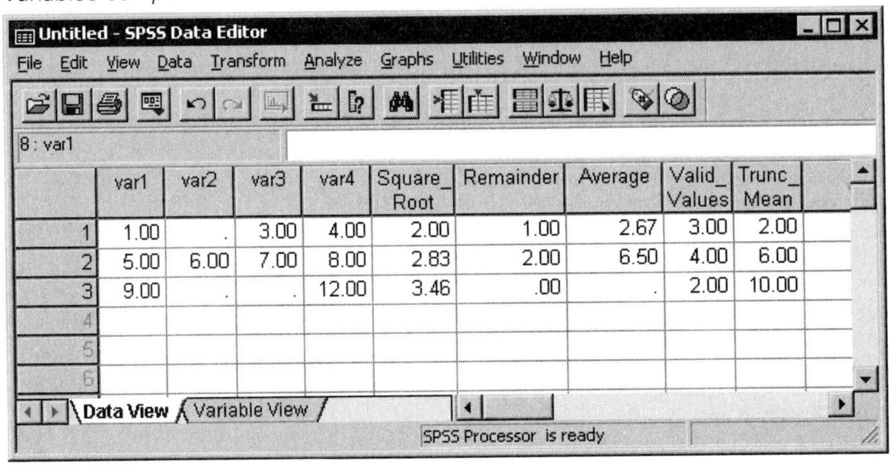

For a complete list of arithmetic and statistical functions, see "Transformation Expressions" in the "Universals" section of the *SPSS Command Syntax Reference.*

Random Value and Distribution Functions

Random value and distribution functions generate random values based on the specified type of distribution and parameters, such as mean, standard deviation, or maximum value.

```
*random_functons.sps.
NEW FILE.
SET SEED 987987987.
*create 1,000 cases with random values.
INPUT PROGRAM.
- LOOP #I=1 TO 1000.
-   COMPUTE Uniform_Distribution = UNIFORM(100).
-   COMPUTE Normal_Distribution = RV.NORMAL(50,25).
-   COMPUTE Poisson_Distribution = RV.POISSON(50).
-   END CASE.
- END LOOP.
- END FILE.
END INPUT PROGRAM.
FREQUENCIES VARIABLES = ALL
  /HISTOGRAM /FORMAT = NOTABLE.
```

- The INPUT PROGRAM uses a LOOP structure to generate 1,000 cases.
- For each case, UNIFORM(100) returns a random value from a uniform distribution with values that range from 0 to 100.
- RV.NORMAL(50, 25) returns a random value from a normal distribution with a mean of 50 and a standard deviation of 25.
- RV.POISSON(50) returns a random value from a Poisson distribution with a mean of 50.
- The FREQUENCIES command produces histograms of the three variables that show the distributions of the randomly generated values.

Figure 4-27
Histograms of randomly generated values for different distributions

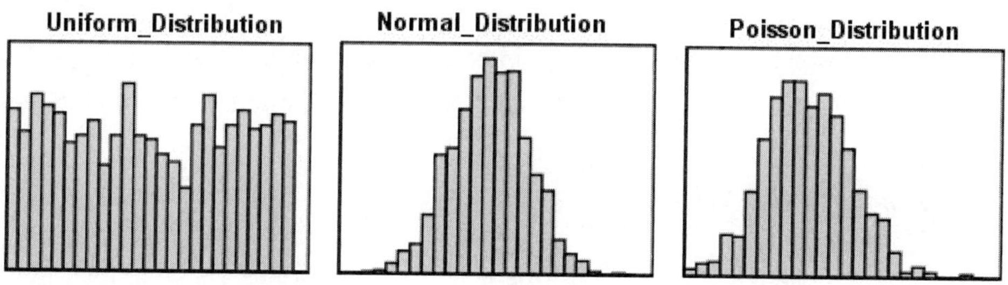

Random variable functions are available for a variety of distributions, including Bernoulli, Cauchy, Weibull, and others. For a complete list of random variable functions, see "Random Variable and Distribution Functions" in the "Universals" section of the *SPSS Command Syntax Reference*.

String Manipulation

Since just about the only restriction you can impose on string variables is the maximum number of characters, string values may often be recorded in an inconsistent manner and/or contain important bits of information that would be more useful if they could be extracted from the rest of the string.

Changing the Case of String Values

Perhaps the most common problem with string values is inconsistent capitalization. Since string values are case sensitive, a value of "male" is *not* the same as a value of "Male." This example converts all values of a string variable to lowercase letters.

```
*string_case.sps.
DATA LIST FREE /gender (A6).
BEGIN DATA
Male Female
male female
MALE FEMALE
END DATA.
COMPUTE gender=LOWER(gender).
EXECUTE.
```

- The LOWER function converts all uppercase letters in the value of *gender* to lowercase letters, resulting in consistent values of "male" and "female."
- You can use the UPCASE function to convert string values to all uppercase letters.

Combining String Values

You can combine multiple string and/or numeric values to create new string variables. For example, you could combine three numeric variables for area code, exchange, and number into one string variable for telephone number with dashes between the values.

```
*concat_string.sps.
DATA LIST FREE /tel1 tel2 tel3 (3F4).
BEGIN DATA
111 222 3333
222 333 4444
333 444 5555
555 666  707
END DATA.
STRING telephone (A12).
COMPUTE telephone =
  CONCAT((STRING(tel1, N3)), "-",
              (STRING(tel2, N3)), "-",
              (STRING(tel3, N4))).
EXECUTE.
```

- The STRING command defines a new string variable that is 12 characters long. Unlike new numeric variables, which can be created by transformation commands, you must define new string variables before using them in any transformations.

- The COMPUTE command combines two string manipulation functions to create the new telephone number variable.
- The CONCAT function concatenates two or more string values. The general form of the function is CONCAT(string1, string2, ...). Each argument can be a variable name, an expression, or a literal string enclosed in quotes.
- Each argument of the CONCAT function must evaluate to a string; so we use the STRING function to treat the numeric values of the three original variables as strings. The general form of the function is STRING(value, format). The value argument can be a variable name, a number, or an expression. The format argument must be a valid numeric format. In this example, we use N format to support leading zeros in values (for example, 0707).
- The dashes in quotes are literal strings that will be included in the new string value; a dash will be displayed between the area code and exchange and between the exchange and number.

Figure 4-28
Original numeric values and concatenated string values

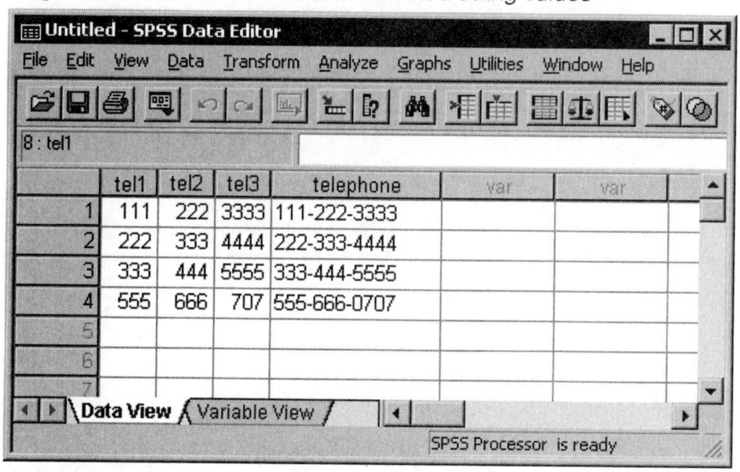

Taking Strings Apart

In addition to being able to combine strings, you can also take them apart. For example, you could take apart a 12-character telephone number, recorded as a string (because of the embedded dashes), and create three new numeric variables for area code, exchange, and number.

If all of the values were in the form *nnn-nnn-nnnn* with no spaces, it would be fairly easy to extract each segment of the telephone number, but some of the values have leading spaces or spaces before and after the dashes.

```
*substr_index.sps.
***Create some inconsistent sample numbers***.
DATA LIST FREE (",") /telephone (A16).
BEGIN DATA
111-222-3333
222 - 333 - 4444
 333-444-5555
444 - 555-6666
555-666-0707
END DATA.
***Now extract the component parts***.
COMPUTE tel1 =
  NUMBER(SUBSTR(telephone, 1, INDEX(telephone, "-")-1), F5).
COMPUTE tel2 =
  NUMBER(SUBSTR(telephone, INDEX(telephone, "-")+1,
         RINDEX(telephone, "-")-(INDEX(telephone, "-")+1)), F5).
COMPUTE tel3 =
  NUMBER(SUBSTR(telephone, RINDEX(telephone, "-")+1), F5).
EXECUTE.
FORMATS tel1 tel2 (N3) tel3 (N4).

***Alternate method***.
STRING #telstr(A16).
COMPUTE #telstr = telephone.
VECTOR tel(3,f4).
LOOP #i = 1 to 2.
- COMPUTE #dash = INDEX(#telstr,"-").
- COMPUTE tel(#i) = NUMBER(SUBSTR(#telstr,1,#dash-1),f10).
- COMPUTE #telstr = SUBSTR(#telstr,#dash+1).
END LOOP.
COMPUTE tel(3) = NUMBER(#telstr,f10).
EXECUTE.
FORMATS tel1 tel2 (N3) tel3 (N4).
```

- The NUMBER function converts a number expressed as a string to a numeric value. The basic format is NUMBER(value, format). The value argument can be a variable name, a number expressed as a string in quotes, or an expression. The format argument must be a valid numeric format; this format is used to determine the numeric value of the string. In other words, the format argument says, "Read the string as if it were a number in this format."
- The value argument for the NUMBER function for all three new variables is an expression using the SUBSTR function. The general form of the function is SUBSTR(value, position, length). The value argument can be a variable name, an expression, or a literal string enclosed in quotes. The position argument is a number

that indicates the starting character position within the string. The optional length argument is a number that specifies how many characters to read starting at the value specified on the position argument. Without the length argument, the string is read from the specified starting position to the end of the string value. So SUBSTR("abcd", 2, 2) would return "bc," and SUBSTR("abcd", 2) would return "bcd."

- INDEX and RINDEX functions are used to determine starting position and/or length for the three new variables. The general form of these commands is [R]INDEX(haystack, needle). The haystack argument can be a variable name or a literal string enclosed in quotes. The needle argument can be a literal string enclosed in quotes or an expression. Both arguments must evaluate to strings. The function returns a numeric value that represents the starting position of needle within haystack. For INDEX, the number is the starting position of the first occurrence of needle, and for RINDEX it's the starting position of the *last* occurrence of needle. So INDEX("abcabc", "b") would return a value of 2 and RINDEX("abcabc", "b") would return a value of 5.
- For *tel1*, SUBSTR(telephone, 1, INDEX(telephone, "-")-1) defines a substring starting with the first character in the value of *telephone* and ending with the last character prior to the first dash.
- For *tel3*, (SUBSTR(telephone, RINDEX(telephone, "-")+1) defines a substring starting with the first character after the last dash in the value of *telephone*. In the absence of a length argument, the remainder of the string value is read.
- Extracting the value of *tel2* is a little more complicated, since it's in the middle of the original string value. The starting position is the first character after the first dash: INDEX(telephone, "-")+1. The length is the difference between that value and the starting position of the second dash: RINDEX(telephone, "-")-(INDEX(telephone, "-")+1)).
- FORMATS assigns N format to the three new variables for numbers with leading zeros (for example, 0707).

Figure 4-29
Substrings extracted and converted to numbers

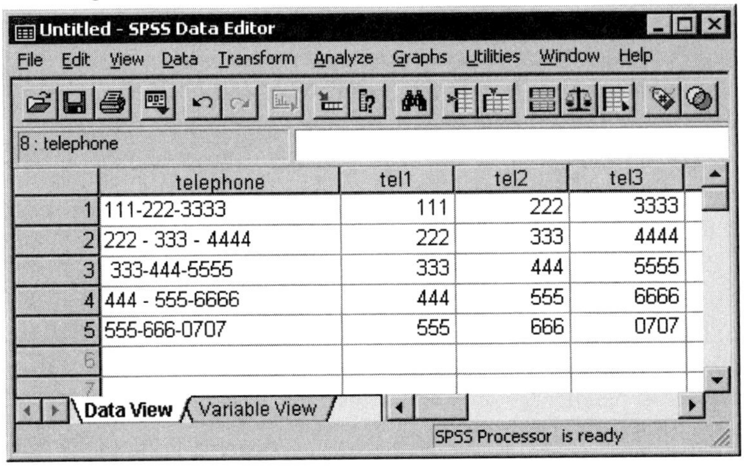

The alternative method eliminates the need to use a somewhat complicated expression to extract a substring from the middle of the string value by using a temporary variable and changing the value of the temporary variable to the remaining portion(s) of the string value as each segment is extracted.

- A temporary (scratch) string variable, *#telstr* is declared and set to the value of the original string telephone number.
- The VECTOR command creates three numeric variables—*tel1*, *tel2*, and *tel3*—and creates a vector containing those variables.
- The LOOP structure iterates twice to produce the values for *tel1* and *tel2*.
- COMPUTE #dash = INDEX(#telstr,"-") creates another temporary variable, *#dash*, that contains the position of the first dash in the string value.
- On the first iteration, COMPUTE tel(#i) = NUMBER(SUBSTR(#telstr,1,#dash-1),f10) extracts everything prior to the first dash, converts it to a number, and sets *tel1* to that value.
- COMPUTE #telstr = SUBSTR(#telstr,#dash+1) then sets *#telstr* to the remaining portion of the string value *after* the first dash.
- On the second iteration, COMPUTE #dash... sets *#dash* to the position of the "first" dash in the modified value of *#telstr*. Since the area code and the original first dash have been removed from *#telstr*, this is the position of the dash between the exchange and the number.

- COMPUTE tel(#)... sets *tel2* to the numeric value of everything up to the "first" dash in the modified version of *#telstr*, which is everything after the first dash and before the second dash in the original string value.
- COMPUTE #telstr... then sets *#telstr* to the remaining segment of the string value—everything after the "first" dash in the modified value, which is everything after the second dash in the original value.
- After the two loop iterations are complete, COMPUTE tel(3) = NUMBER(#telstr,f10) sets *tel3* to the numeric value of the final segment of the original string value.

Changing the Defined Width of a String Variable

When reading in data from text files or databases, the width of string variables is sometimes set higher than necessary. In some cases, string variables are automatically set to the maximum string width—255 characters. This can make the string variables awkward to work with. The following example counts the number of characters in each string value, ignoring trailing spaces, and changes the string variable width to the maximum character count.

```
*string_length.sps.
DATA LIST FREE /stringvar (A10).
BEGIN DATA
a ab abc a abcde ab abcdefg
END DATA.
COMPUTE strlength=LENGTH(RTRIM(stringvar)).
SORT CASES BY strlength (D).
DO IF ($casenum = 1).
WRITE OUTFILE = 'c:\temp\temp.sps'
  /"STRING newstring  (A" strlength (N3) ")."
  /"COMPUTE newstring = stringvar."
  /"MATCH FILES FILE=* /DROP stringvar strlength.".
END IF.
EXECUTE.
INCLUDE FILE = 'c:\temp\temp.sps'.
```

- The COMPUTE command creates a new numeric variable, *strlength*, that is the number of characters in each string value.
- The LENGTH function has the general form LENGTH(string), and it returns the number of characters in the string argument. The value of the argument can be a variable name, an expression, or a literal string.
- RTRIM strips off any trailing blanks in the string value. This is necessary because string values are right-padded to the defined width of the string variable, so without

it, LENGTH(varname) will always return the defined width of the string variable, which does not help in this case.

- The SORT CASES command sorts the cases in descending order of the new variable *strlength*; the case with the longest string value for *stringvar* will be the first case in the working data file.
- DO IF ($casenum = 1) restricts the transformations in the DO IF structure to the first case in the file, which is the case with the highest value for *strlength*.
- The WRITE command creates a command syntax file that declares a new string variable *newstring* with a defined width set to the value of *strlength*. We need to create a new string variable because you cannot change the defined width of an existing variable.
- N3 format is used to write the value of *strlength* because we know the value will be somewhere between one and three digits long (since the maximum string width is 255 characters), and we need to write the value without any preceding blanks. Using the default F8.2 format for *strlength* would result in a format specification of (A   7), which is invalid. N format fills out the values to the defined width with leading zeros, resulting in a format specification of (A007).
- The COMPUTE command generated by the WRITE command copies the contents of *stringvar* into *newstring*, and then MATCH FILES is used to delete the intermediate variable *strlength* and the now redundant original string variable *stringvar*.
- The INCLUDE command runs the command syntax file created by the WRITE command, creating the new string variable with the more appropriate width specification.

Working with Dates and Times

Dates and times come in a wide variety of formats, ranging from different display formats (for example, 10/28/1986 versus 28-OCT-1986) to separate entries for each component of a date or time (for example, a day variable, a month variable, and a year variable). A wide variety of features are available for dealing with dates and times, including:

- Support for multiple input and display formats for dates and times.
- Storing dates and times internally as consistent numbers regardless of the input format, making it possible to compare date/time values and calculate the difference between values even if they were not entered in the same format.

- Functions that can convert string dates to real dates, extract portions of date values (such as simply the month or year) or other information that is associated with a date (such as day of the week), and create calendar dates from separate values for day, month, and year.

Date Input and Display Formats

SPSS automatically converts date information from databases, Excel files, and SAS files to equivalent SPSS date format variables. SPSS can also recognize dates in text data files stored in a variety of formats. All you need to do is specify the appropriate format when reading the text data file.

Table 4-1
*Some of the date and time formats recognized by SPSS**

Date Format	General Form	Example	SPSS Date Format Specification
International date	dd-mmm-yyyy	28-OCT-2003	DATE
American date	mm/dd/yyyy	10/28/2003	ADATE
Sortable date	yyyy/mm/dd	2003/10/28	SDATE
Julian date	yyyyddd	2003301	JDATE
Time	hh:mm:ss	11:35:43	TIME
Days and time	dd hh:mm:ss	15 08:27:12	DTIME
Date and time	dd-mmm-yyyy hh:mm:ss	20-JUN-2003 12:23:01	DATETIME
Day of week	(name of day)	Tuesday	WKDAY
Month of year	(name of month)	January	MONTH

*For a complete list of date and time formats, see "Date and Time" in the "Universals" section of the *SPSS Command Syntax Reference*.

Example

```
DATA LIST FREE(" ")
 /StartDate(ADATE) EndDate(DATE).
BEGIN DATA
10/28/2002 28-01-2003
10-29-02 15,03,03
01.01.96 01/01/97
1/1/1997 01-JAN-1998
END DATA.
```

- Both two- and four-digit year specifications are recognized. Use SET EPOCH to set the starting year for two-digit years.
- Dashes, periods, commas, slashes, or blanks can be used as delimiters in the day-month-year input.
- Months can be represented in digits, Roman numerals, or three-character abbreviations, and they can be fully spelled out. Three-letter abbreviations and fully spelled out month names must be English month names; month names in other languages are not recognized.
- In time specifications, colons can be used as delimiters between hours, minutes, and seconds. Hours and minutes are required but seconds are optional. A period is required to separate seconds from fractional seconds. Hours can be of unlimited magnitude, but the maximum value for minutes is 59 and for seconds 59.999….
- Internally, dates and date/times are stored as the number of seconds from October 14, 1582, and times are stored as the number of seconds from midnight.

Note: SET EPOCH has no effect on existing dates in the file. You must set this value before reading or entering date values. The actual date stored internally is determined when the date is read; changing the epoch value afterward will not change the century for existing date values in the file.

Using FORMATS to Change the Display of Dates

Dates in SPSS are often referred to as date-format variables because the dates you see are really just display formats for underlying numeric values. Using the FORMATS command, you can change the display formats of a date-format variable, including changing to a format that displays only a certain portion of the date, such as the month or day of the week.

Example

```
FORMATS StartDate(DATE11).
```

- A date originally displayed as 10/28/02 would now be displayed as 10-OCT-2002.
- The number following the date format specifies the display width. DATE9 would display as 10-OCT-02.

Some of the other format options are shown in the following table:

Table 4-2
Changing display format with FORMATS

Original Display Format	New Format Specification	New Display Format
10/28/02	SDATE11	2002/10/28
10/28/02	WKDAY7	MONDAY
10/28/02	MONTH12	OCTOBER
10/28/02	MOYR9	OCT 2002
10/28/02	QYR6	4 Q 02

The underlying values remain the same; only the display format changes with the FORMATS command.

Converting String Dates to Date-Format Numeric Variables

Under some circumstances, SPSS may read valid date formats as string variables instead of date-format numeric variables. For example, if you use the Text Wizard to read text data files, by default the wizard reads dates as string variables. If the string date values conform to one of the recognized date formats, it is easy to convert the strings to date-format numeric variables.

Example

```
COMPUTE numeric_date = NUMBER(string_date, ADATE)
FORMATS numeric_date (ADATE10).
```

- The NUMBER function indicates that any numeric string values should be converted to those numbers.
- ADATE tells the program to assume that the strings represent dates of the general form mm/dd/yyyy. It is important to specify the date format that corresponds to the way the dates are represented in the string variable, since string dates that do not conform to that format will be assigned the system-missing value for the new numeric variable.
- The FORMATS command specifies the date display format for the new numeric variable. Without this command, the values of the new variable would be displayed as very large integers.

Date and Time Functions

A large number of date and time functions are available, including:

- Aggregation functions to create a single date variable from multiple other variables representing day, month, and year.
- Conversion functions to convert from one date/time measurement unit to another—for example, converting a time interval expressed in seconds to number of days.
- Extraction functions to obtain different types of information from date and time values—for example, obtaining just the year from a date value, or the day of the week associated with a date.

Note: Date functions that take date values or year values as arguments interpret two-digit years based on the century defined by SET EPOCH. By default, two-digit years assume a range beginning 69 years prior to the current date and ending 30 years after the current date. When in doubt, use four-digit year values.

Aggregating Multiple Date Components into a Single Date-Format Variable

Sometimes, dates and times are recorded as separate variables for each unit of the date. For example, you might have separate variables for day, month, and year or separate hour and minute variables for time. You can use the DATE and TIME functions to combine the constituent parts into a single date/time variable.

Example

```
COMPUTE datevar=DATE.MDY(month, day, year).
COMPUTE monthyear=DATE.MOYR(month, year).
COMPUTE time=TIME.HMS(hours, minutes).
FORMATS datevar (ADATE10) monthyear (MOYR9) time(TIME9).
```

- DATE.MDY creates a single date variable from three separate variables for month, day, and year.
- DATE.MOYR creates a single date variable from two separate variables for month and year. Internally, this is stored as the same value as the first day of that month.
- TIME.HMS creates a single time variable from two separate variables for hours and minutes.
- The FORMATS command applies the appropriate display formats to each of the new date variables.

For a complete list of DATE and TIME functions, see "Date and Time" in the "Universals" section of the *SPSS Command Syntax Reference*.

Calculating and Converting Date and Time Intervals

Since dates and times are stored internally in seconds, the result of date and time calculations is also expressed in seconds. But if you want to know how much time elapsed between a start date and an end date, you probably do not want the answer in seconds. You can use CTIME functions to calculate and convert time intervals from seconds to minutes, hours, or days.

Example

```
*date_functions.sps.
DATA LIST FREE (",")
  /StartDate (ADATE12) EndDate (ADATE12)
  StartDateTime(DATETIME20) EndDateTime(DATETIME20)
  StartTime (TIME10) EndTime (TIME10).
BEGIN DATA
3/01/2003, 4/10/2003
01-MAR-2003 12:00, 02-MAR-2003 12:00
09:30, 10:15
END DATA.
COMPUTE days = CTIME.DAYS(EndDate-StartDate).
COMPUTE hours = CTIME.HOURS(EndDateTime-StartDateTime).
COMPUTE minutes = CTIME.MINUTES(EndTime-StartTime).
EXECUTE.
```

- CTIME.DAYS calculates the difference between *EndDate* and *StartDate* in days—in this example, 40 days.
- CTIME.HOURS calculates the difference between *EndDateTime* and *StartDateTime* in hours—in this example, 24 hours.
- CTIME.MINUTES calculates the difference between *EndTime* and *StartTime* in minutes—in this example, 45 minutes.

Calculating Number of Years between Dates

There is no function to convert time intervals to years because not all years contain the same number of seconds, but it does not take much work to calculate the number of years between two dates (assuming each year has an average of 365.25 days) using the CTIME.DAYS function.

Example

```
COMPUTE years = CTIME.DAYS(EndDate-StartDate)/365.25.
COMPUTE age =TRUNC(CTIME.DAYS($TIME-BirthDate)/365.25).
```

- The number of years between *EndDate* and *StartDate* is obtained by calculating the number of days and then dividing by 365.25. (The .25 accounts for leap years.)
- Age is calculated by subtracting *BirthDate* from the current date, which we obtain from the system variable *$TIME*. Once again, we divide by 365.25, but then we use the TRUNC function to truncate the result, keeping only the integer portion, since age is typically reported in whole years, based on the previous birthday (not the nearest birthday).

Adding to or Subtracting from a Date to Find Another Date

If you need to calculate a date a certain length of time before or after a given date, you can use the TIME.DAYS function.

Example

Prospective customers can use your product on a trial basis for 30 days, and you need to know when the trial period ends—and just to make it interesting, if the trial period ends on a Saturday or Sunday, you want to extend it to the following Monday.

```
*date_functions2.sps.
DATA LIST FREE (" ") /StartDate (ADATE10).
BEGIN DATA
10/29/2003 10/30/2003
10/31/2003 11/1/2003
11/2/2003 11/4/2003
11/5/2003 11/6/2003
END DATA.
COMPUTE expdate = StartDate + TIME.DAYS(30).
execute.
FORMATS expdate (ADATE10).
***if expdate is Saturday or Sunday, make it Monday***.
DO IF (XDATE.WKDAY(expdate) = 1).
+  COMPUTE expdate = expdate + TIME.DAYS(1).
ELSE IF (XDATE.WKDAY(expdate) = 7).
+  COMPUTE expdate = expdate + TIME.DAYS(2).
END IF.
EXECUTE.
```

- TIME.DAYS(30) adds 30 days to *StartDate*, and then the new variable *expdate* is given a date display format.
- The DO IF structure uses an XDATE.WKDAY extraction function to see if *expdate* is a Sunday (1) or a Saturday (7), and then adds one or two days, respectively.

Extracting Date Information

A great deal of information can be extracted from date and time variables. In addition to using XDATE functions to extract the more obvious pieces of information, such as year, month, day, hour, etc., you can obtain information such as day of the week, week of the year, or quarter of the year.

Example

```
*date_functions3.sps.
DATA LIST FREE (",")
  /StartDateTime (datetime25).
BEGIN DATA
29-OCT-2003 11:23:02
1 January 1998 1:45:01
21/6/2000 2:55:13
END DATA.
COMPUTE dateonly=XDATE.DATE(StartDateTime).
FORMATS dateonly(ADATE10).
COMPUTE hour=XDATE.HOUR(StartDateTime).
COMPUTE DayofWeek=XDATE.WKDAY(StartDateTime).
COMPUTE WeekofYear=XDATE.WEEK(StartDateTime).
COMPUTE quarter=XDATE.QUARTER(StartDateTime).
EXECUTE.
```

Figure 4-30
Extracted date information

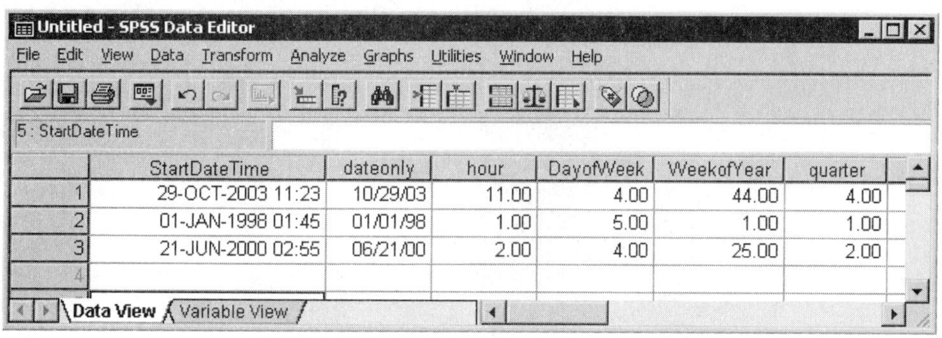

- The date portion extracted with XDATE.DATE returns a date expressed in seconds; so we also include a FORMATS command to display the date in a readable date format.
- Day of the week is an integer between 1 (Sunday) and 7 (Saturday).
- Week of the year is an integer between 1 and 53 (January 1–7 = 1).

For a complete list of XDATE functions, see “Date and Time” in the “Universals” section of the *SPSS Command Syntax Reference*.

Chapter

5

Advanced Programming Features

SPSS command syntax offers many powerful programming features, and many of these features aren't available in the point-and-click graphical user interface. This chapter describes some of those features, including:

- Programming structures, including loops, vectors, and if/then/else processing.
- Command syntax that automatically adjusts to different data conditions.

This chapter also provides information on how to avoid common programming errors and tips for debugging command syntax.

The *SPSS Command Syntax Reference* is an essential resource when writing command syntax. An electronic version (PDF format) is automatically installed with SPSS and can be accessed from the Help menu:

Help
  Command Syntax Reference

Be sure to read the "Universals" section; it contains essential information that will help you understand and use the rest of the manual.

Command Syntax Programming Structures

As with other programming languages, SPSS contains standard programming structures that can be used to do many things. These include the ability to:

- Perform actions only if some condition is true (if/then/else processing).
- Repeat actions.
- Create an array of elements.
- Use loop structures.

Indenting Commands in Programming Structures

Indenting commands nested within programming structures is a fairly common convention that makes code easier to read and debug. For compatibility with batch production mode, however, each SPSS command should begin in the first column of a new line. You can indent nested commands by inserting a plus (+) or minus (–) sign in the first column of each indented command, as in:

```
DO REPEAT tempvar = var1, var2, var3.
+   COMPUTE tempvar = tempvar/10.
+   DO IF (tempvar >= 100).   /*Then divide by 10 again.
+      COMPUTE tempvar = tempvar/10.
+   END IF.
END REPEAT.
```

DO REPEAT

A DO REPEAT structure allows you to repeat the same group of transformations multiple times, thereby reducing the number of commands that you need to write. The basic format of the command is:

```
DO REPEAT stand-in variable = variable or value list
     /optional additional stand-in variable(s) …
transformation commands
END REPEAT PRINT.
```

- The transformation commands inside the DO REPEAT structure are repeated for each variable or value assigned to the stand-in variable.
- Multiple stand-in variables and values can be specified in the same DO REPEAT structure by preceding each additional specification with a forward slash.
- The optional PRINT keyword after the END REPEAT command is useful when debugging command syntax, since it displays the actual commands generated by the DO REPEAT structure.
- Note that when a stand-in variable is set equal to a list of variables, the variables do not have to be consecutive in the data file. So DO REPEAT may be more useful than VECTOR in some circumstances. (See “VECTOR” on p. 140.)

Example

This example sets two variables to the same value.

```
* do_repeat1.sps.

***create some sample data***.
DATA LIST LIST /var1 var3 id var2.
BEGIN DATA
3 3 3 3
2 2 2 2
END DATA.
***real job starts here***.
DO REPEAT v=var1 var2.
- COMPUTE v=99.
END REPEAT.
EXECUTE.
```

Figure 5-1
Two variables set to the same constant value

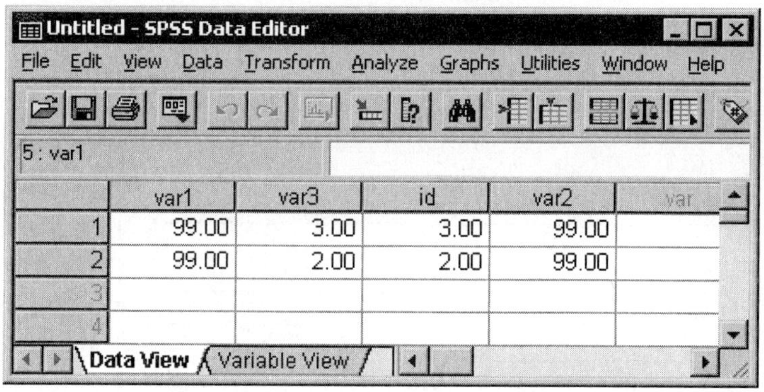

- The two variables assigned to the stand-in variable *v* are assigned the value 99.
- If the variables don't already exist, they are created.

Example

You could also assign different values to each variable by using two stand-in variables: one that specifies the variables and one that specifies the corresponding values.

```
* do_repeat2.sps.
***create some sample data***.
DATA LIST LIST /var1 var3 id var2.
BEGIN DATA
3 3 3 3
2 2 2 2
END DATA.
***real job starts here***.
DO REPEAT v=var1 TO var2 /val=1 3 5 7.
- COMPUTE v=val.
END REPEAT PRINT.
EXECUTE.
```

Figure 5-2

Different value assigned to each variable

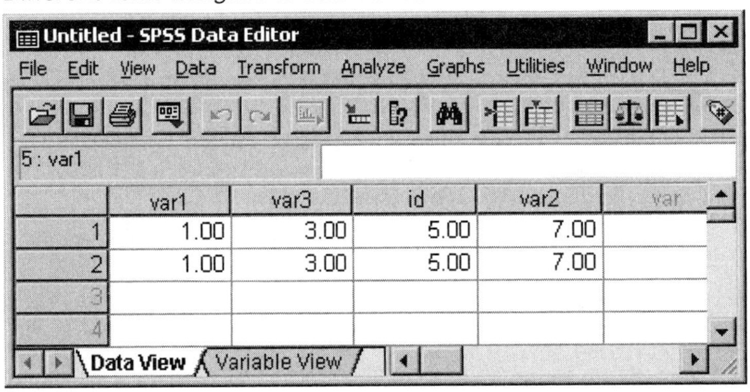

- The COMPUTE command inside the structure is repeated four times, and each value of the stand-in variable *v* is associated with the corresponding value of the variable *val*.
- The PRINT keyword displays the generated commands in the log item in the Viewer.

Figure 5-3
Commands generated by DO REPEAT displayed in the log

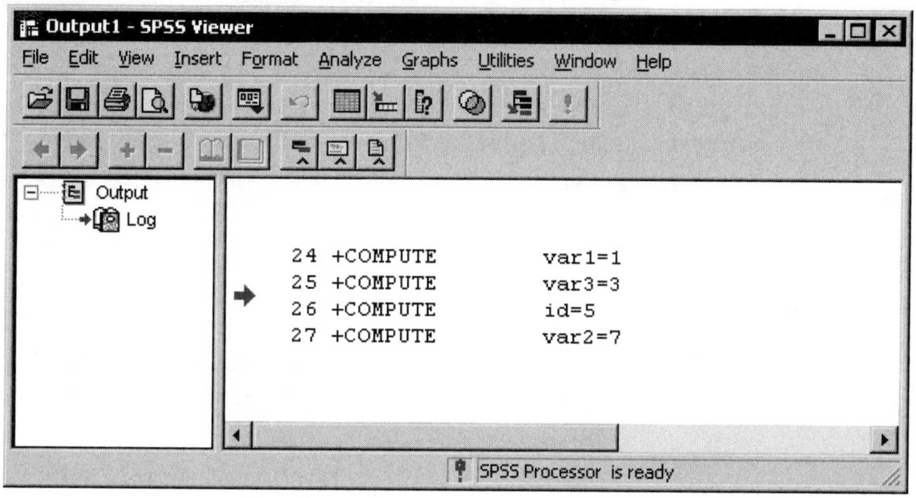

ALL Keyword and Error Handling

You can use the keyword ALL to set the stand-in variable to all variables in the working data file; however, since not all variables are created equal, actions that are valid for some variables may not be valid for others, resulting in errors. For example, some functions are valid only for numeric variables, and other functions are valid only for string variables.

You can suppress the display of error messages with the command SET ERRORS = NONE, which can be useful if you know your command syntax will create a certain number of harmless error conditions for which the error messages are mostly noise. This does not, however, tell the program to ignore error conditions; it merely prevents error messages from being displayed in the output. This distinction is important for command syntax run via an INCLUDE command (which includes any jobs run via the production facility), which will terminate on the first error encountered regardless of the setting for displaying error messages.

VECTOR

Vectors are a convenient way to sequentially refer to consecutive variables in the working data file. For example, if *age*, *sex*, and *salary* are three consecutive numeric variables in the data file, we can define a vector called *VectorVar* for those three variables. We can then refer to these three variables as *VectorVar(1)*, *VectorVar(2)*, and *VectorVar(3)*. This is often used in LOOP structures but can also be used without a LOOP.

Example

You can use the MAX function to find the highest value among a specified set of variables. But what if you also want to know which variable has that value—and if more than one variable has that value, how many variables have that value? Using VECTOR and LOOP, you can get the information you want.

```
*vectors.sps.

***create some sample data***.
DATA LIST FREE
  /FirstVar SecondVar ThirdVar FourthVar FifthVar.
BEGIN DATA
1 2 3 4 5
10 9 8 7 6
1 4 4 4 2
END DATA.

***real job starts here***.
COMPUTE MaxValue=MAX(FirstVar TO FifthVar).
COMPUTE MaxCount=0.

VECTOR VectorVar=FirstVar TO FifthVar.
LOOP #cnt=5 to 1 BY -1.
- DO IF MaxValue=VectorVar(#cnt).
-    COMPUTE MaxVar=#cnt.
-    COMPUTE MaxCount=MaxCount+1.
- END IF.
END LOOP.
EXECUTE.
```

- For each case, the MAX function in the first COMPUTE command sets the variable *MaxValue* to the maximum value within the inclusive range of variables from *FirstVar* to *FifthVar*. In this example, that happens to be five variables.
- The second COMPUTE command initializes the variable *MaxCount* to 0. This is the variable that will contain the count of variables with the maximum value.
- The VECTOR command defines a vector in which *VectorVar(1)* = *FirstVar*, *VectorVar(2)* = the next variable in the file order... *VectorVar(5)* = *FifthVar*. *Note*: Unlike some other programming languages, vectors in SPSS start at 1, not 0.
- The LOOP structure defines a loop that will be repeated five times, decreasing the value of the temporary variable *#cnt* by 1 for each loop. On the first loop, *VectorVar(#cnt)* equals *VectorVar(5),* which equals *FifthVar*; on the last loop, it will equal *VectorVar(1)*, which equals *FirstVar*.
- If the value of the current variable equals the value of *MaxValue*, then the value of *MaxVar* is set to the current loop number represented by *#cnt*, and *MaxCount* is incremented by 1.
- The final value of *MaxVar* represents the position of the first variable in file order that contains the maximum value, and *MaxCount* is the number of variables that have that value.
  (LOOP #cnt = 1 TO 5 would set *MaxVar* to the position of the *last* variable with the maximum value.)
- The vector exists only until the next EXECUTE command or procedure that reads the data.

Figure 5-4
Highest value across variables identified with VECTOR and LOOP

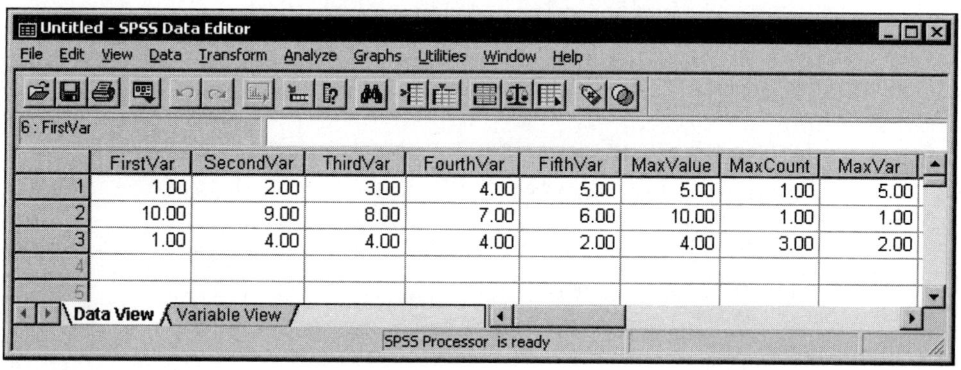

Creating Variables with VECTOR

You can use the short form of the VECTOR command to create multiple new variables. The short form is VECTOR followed by a variable name prefix and, in parentheses, the number of variables to create. For example:

```
VECTOR newvar(100).
```

will create 100 new variables, named *newvar1, newvar2, ...newvar100.*

LOOP

The LOOP-END LOOP structure performs repeated transformations specified by the commands within the loop until it reaches a specified cutoff. The cutoff can be determined in a number of ways:

```
*loop1.sps.
*create sample data, 4 vars = 0.
DATA LIST FREE /var1 var2 var3 var4 var5.
BEGIN DATA
0 0 0 0 0
END DATA.
***Loops start here***.
*Loop that repeats until MXLOOPS value reached.
SET MXLOOPS=10.
LOOP.
- COMPUTE var1=var1+1.
END LOOP.
*Loop that repeats 9 times, based on indexing clause.
LOOP #I = 1 to 9.
- COMPUTE var2=var2+1.
END LOOP.
*Loop while condition not encountered.
LOOP IF (var3 < 8).
- COMPUTE var3=var3+1.
END LOOP.
*Loop until condition encountered.
LOOP.
- COMPUTE var4=var4+1.
END LOOP IF (var4 >= 7).
*Loop until BREAK condition.
LOOP.
- DO IF  (var5 < 6).
-   COMPUTE var5=var5+1.
- ELSE.
-   BREAK.
- END IF.
END LOOP.
EXECUTE.
```

- An unconditional loop with no indexing clause will repeat until it reaches the value specified on the SET MXLOOPS command. The default value is 40.
- LOOP #I=1 to 9 specifies an indexing clause that will repeat the loop nine times, incrementing the value of *#I* by 1 for each loop. LOOP #tempvar=1 to 10 BY 2 would repeat five times, incrementing the value of *#tempvar* by 2 for each loop.
- LOOP IF continues as long as the specified condition is not encountered. This corresponds to the programming concept of "do while."
- END LOOP IF continues until the specified condition is encountered. This corresponds to the programming concept of "do until."
- A BREAK command in a loop ends the loop. Since BREAK is unconditional, it is typically used only inside of conditional structures in the loop, such as DO IF-END IF.

Indexing Clauses

The indexing clause limits the number of iterations for a loop by specifying the number of times the program should execute commands within the loop structure. The indexing clause is specified on the LOOP command and includes an indexing variable followed by initial and terminal values.

The indexing variable can do far more than simply define the number of iterations. The current value of the indexing variable can be used in transformations and conditional statements within the loop structure. So it is often useful to define indexing clauses that:

- Use the BY keyword to increment the value of the indexing variable by some value other than the default of 1, as in:
  LOOP #i = 1 TO 100 BY 5.
- Define an indexing variable that *decreases* in value for each iteration, as in:
  LOOP #j = 100 TO 1 BY -1.

Loops that use an indexing clause are not constrained by the MXLOOPS setting. An indexing clause that defines 1,000 iterations will be iterated 1,000 times even if the MXLOOPS setting is only 40.

The loop structure described in "VECTOR" on p. 140 uses an indexing variable that decreases for each iteration. The loop structure described in "Using XSAVE in a Loop to Build a Data File" on p. 148 has an indexing clause that uses an arithmetic function to define the ending value of the index. Both examples use the current value of the indexing variable in transformations in the loop structure.

Nested Loops

You can nest loops inside of other loops. A nested loop is run for every iteration of the parent loop. For example, a parent loop that defines 5 iterations and a nested loop that defines 10 iterations will result in a total of 50 iterations for the nested loop (10 times for each iteration of the parent loop).

Example

Many statistical tests rely on assumptions of normal distributions and the **Central Limit Theorem**, which basically states that even if the distribution of the population is *not* normal, repeated random samples of a sufficiently large size will yield a distribution of sample means that *is* normal.

We can use an input program and nested loops to demonstrate the validity of the Central Limit Theorem. For this example, we'll assume that a sample size of 100 is "sufficiently large."

```
*loop_nested.sps.
NEW FILE.
SET SEED 987987987.
INPUT PROGRAM.
- VECTOR UniformVar(100).
- *parent loop creates cases.
- LOOP #I=1 TO 100.
-  *nested loop creates values for each variable in each case.
-  LOOP #J=1 to 100.
-   COMPUTE UniformVar(#J)=UNIFORM(1000).
-  END LOOP.
-  END CASE.
- END LOOP.
- END FILE.
END INPUT PROGRAM.
COMPUTE UniformMean=MEAN(UniformVar1 TO UniformVar100).
COMPUTE NormalVar=500+NORMAL(100).
FREQUENCIES
  VARIABLES=NormalVar UniformVar1 UniformMean
  /FORMAT=NOTABLE
  /HISTOGRAM  NORMAL
  /ORDER = ANALYSIS.
```

- The first two commands simply create a new, empty working data file and set the random number seed to consistently duplicate the same results.
- INPUT PROGRAM-END INPUT PROGRAM is used to generate cases in the data file.
- The VECTOR command creates a vector called *UniformVar*, and it also creates 100 variables, named *UniformVar1, UniformVar2, ...UniformVar100.*

- The outer LOOP creates 100 cases via the END CASE command, which creates a new case for each iteration of the loop. END CASE is part of the input program and can be used only within an INPUT PROGRAM-END INPUT PROGRAM structure.
- For each case created by the outer loop, the nested LOOP creates values for the 100 variables. For each iteration, the value of *#J* increments by one, setting *UniformVar(#J)* to *UniformVar(1)*, then *UniformVar(2)*, etc., which in turn stands for *UniformVar1, UniformVar2*, etc.
- The UNIFORM function assigns each variable a random value based on a uniform distribution. This is repeated for all 100 cases, resulting in 100 cases and 100 variables, all containing random values based on a uniform distribution. So the distribution of values within each variable and across variables within each case is non-normal.
- The MEAN function creates a variable that represents the mean value across all variables for each case. This is essentially equivalent to the distribution of sample means for 100 random samples, each containing 100 cases.
- For comparison purposes, we use the NORMAL function to create a variable with a normal distribution.
- Finally, we create histograms to compare the distributions of the variable based on a normal distribution (*NormalVar*), one of the variables based on a uniform distribution (*UniformVar1*), and the variable that represents the distribution of sample means (*UniformMean*).

Figure 5-5
Demonstrating the Central Limit Theorem with nested loops

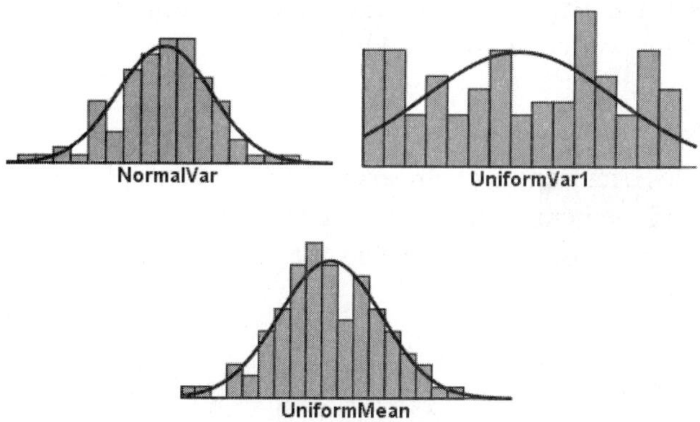

As you can see from the histograms, the distribution of sample means represented by *UniformMean* is approximately normal, despite the fact that it was generated from samples with uniform distributions similar to *UniformVar1*.

Conditional Loops

You can define conditional loop processing with LOOP IF or END LOOP IF. The main difference between the two is that, given equivalent conditions, END LOOP IF will produce one more iteration of the loop than LOOP IF.

Example

```
*loop_if1.sps.
DATA LIST FREE /X.
BEGIN DATA
1 2 3 4 5
END DATA.
SET MXLOOPS=10.
COMPUTE Y=0.
LOOP IF (X~=3).
- COMPUTE Y=Y+1.
END LOOP.
COMPUTE Z=0.
LOOP.
- COMPUTE Z=Z+1.
END LOOP IF (X=3).
EXECUTE.
```

- LOOP IF (X~=3) does nothing when *X* is 3; so the value of *Y* is not incremented and remains 0 for that case.
- END LOOP IF (X=3) will iterate once when *X* is 3, incrementing *Z* by 1, yielding a value of 1.
- For all other cases, the loop is iterated the number of times specified on SET MXLOOPS, yielding a value of 10 for both *Y* and *Z*.

Example

This examples replaces occurrences of ampersands (&) in a string variable with a dash (-). For each case, the loop iterates until there are no more ampersands in the string variable or until the number of iterations equals the number specified on SET MXLOOPS—*whichever occurs first.*

```
*loop_if2.sps.
***create sample data, including a string variable***.
DATA LIST FREE /numvar(f2) stringvar(a15).
BEGIN DATA
1 "A & B"
2 "A & B & C"
3 "A & B & C & D"
END DATA.
```

```
***real job starts here***.
SET MXLOOPS = 2.
LOOP IF INDEX(stringvar,"&")>0.
- COMPUTE SUBSTR(stringvar,INDEX(stringvar,"&"),1)="-".
END LOOP.
EXECUTE.
```

- MXLOOPS is set to a very low value just to illustrate a point.
- The INDEX function returns a value that indicates the position of the first occurrence of the string "&" in the value of *stringvar* for the current case. If the value of *stringvar* contains no ampersands, then INDEX returns a value of 0. As long as there is at least one ampersand, the index value is greater than 0. So the loop will continue to iterate until there are no more ampersands in the string or until the value of MXLOOPS is reached.
- The SUBSTR function, when used on the left side of the equals sign, replaces the specified substring with the value on the right side of the equals sign, leaving the rest of the string intact. The first argument of the function specifies the variable containing the string; the second argument specifies the starting position of the substring to replace, for which we've used the INDEX function to identify the position of the first ampersand; and the third argument specifies the number of characters to replace, which in this case is only 1.
- Since MXLOOPS is set to 2, only the first two of the three ampersands in the third case are replaced.

Figure 5-6
Result of loop that replaces ampersands with dashes

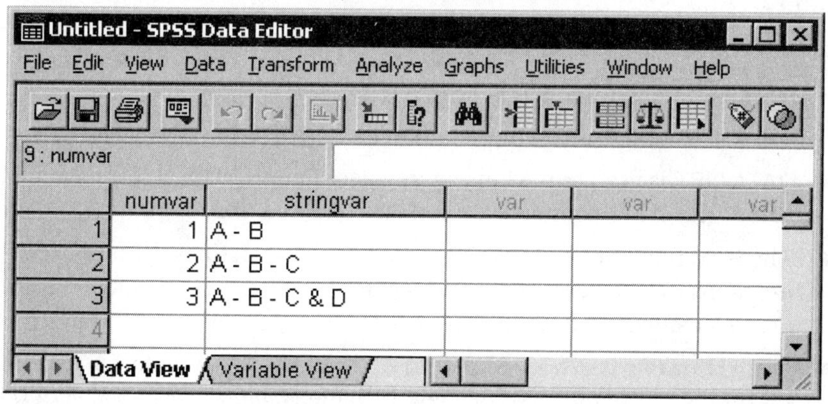

Using XSAVE in a Loop to Build a Data File

You can use XSAVE in a loop structure to build a data file, writing one case at a time to the new data file.

Example

This example constructs a data file of casewise data from aggregated data. The aggregated data file comes from a table that reports the number of males and females by age. Since SPSS works best with raw (casewise) data, we need to "disaggregate" the data, creating one case for each person and a new variable that indicates gender for each case.

In addition to using XSAVE to build the new data file, this example also uses a function in the indexing clause to define the ending index value.

```
*loop_xsave.sps.
DATA LIST FREE
 /Age Female Male.
BEGIN DATA
20 2 2
21 0 0
22 1 4
23 3 0
24 0 1
END DATA.
LOOP #cnt=1 to SUM(Female, Male).
- COMPUTE Gender = (#cnt > Female).
- XSAVE OUTFILE="c:\temp\tempdata.sav"
    /KEEP Age Gender.
END LOOP.
EXECUTE.
GET FILE='c:\temp\tempdata.sav'.
COMPUTE IdVar=$CASENUM.
FORMATS Age Gender (F2.0) IdVar(N3).
EXECUTE.
```

- DATA LIST is used to read the aggregated, tabulated data. For example, the first "case" (record) represents two females and two males aged 20.
- The SUM function in the LOOP indexing clause defines the number of loop iterations for each case. For example, for the first case, the function returns a value of 4; so the loop will iterate four times.
- On the first two iterations, the value of the indexing variable *#cnt* is not greater than the number of females; so the new variable *Gender* takes a value of 0 for each of those iterations, and the values 20 and 0 (for *Age* and *Gender*) are saved to the new data file for the first two cases.

- During the subsequent two iterations, the comparison #cnt > Female is true, returning a value of 1, and the next two variables are saved to the new data file with the values of 20 and 1.
- This process is repeated for each case in the aggregated data file. The second case results in no loop iterations and consequently no cases in the new data file; the third case produces five new cases, etc.
- Since XSAVE is a transformation, we need an EXECUTE command after the loop ends to finish the process of saving the new data file.
- The FORMATS command specifies a format of N3 for the ID variable, displaying leading zeros for one- and two-digit values. GET FILE opens the data file that we created, and the subsequent COMPUTE command creates a sequential ID variable based on the system variable $CASENUM, which is the current row number in the data file.

Figure 5-7
Tabular source data and new "disaggregated" data file

Age	Female	Male
20.00	2.00	2.00
21.00	.00	.00
22.00	1.00	4.00
23.00	3.00	.00
24.00	.00	1.00

Age	Gender	IdVar
20	0	001
20	0	002
20	1	003
20	1	004
22	0	005
22	1	006
22	1	007
22	1	008
22	1	009
23	0	010
23	0	011
23	0	012
24	1	013

Self-Adjusting Command Syntax

If you want to create powerful, flexible command syntax files that can be used for different data files under different circumstances, you need to have conditional code that provides the appropriate command branching. This section illustrates some typical conditions that you may encounter and methods for handling them, including methods for generating entirely new command syntax files that run auto-generated commands based on various conditions.

Using Command Syntax to Write Command Syntax

A command syntax file (**.sps*) can be a simple text file with the extension *.sps*. Since we can write text files with SPSS command syntax, we can write command syntax files using command syntax.

Example

Suppose we have a numeric variable *var1* and a string variable *lab1*. Cases with a given value of *var1* have the same value of *lab1*. We want to use the values of *lab1* as value labels for *var1*.

```
*write_syntax.sps.
DATA LIST FIXED /var1 1-2 (F) lab1 4-21(A).
BEGIN DATA
17 value label for 17
17 value label for 17
   Missing
21 value label for 21
32 value label for 32
32 value label for 32
END DATA.
SORT CASES BY var1.
MATCH FILES FILE=* /BY=var1 /FIRST=first.
EXECUTE.
STRING #quot(A1) #lab_out(A62) #lab2(A60).
COMPUTE #lab2=LTRIM(lab1)/* limit label to 60 characters */.
COMPUTE #quot="'".
DO IF NOT SYSMIS(var1).
- DO IF first=1.
-  COMPUTE #lab_out=CONCAT(#quot,RTRIM(#lab2),#quot).
-  WRITE OUTFILE 'c:\temp\temp.sps'
   /"ADD VALUE LABELS var1 " var1
   /" " #lab_out ".".
- END IF.
END IF.
EXECUTE.
INCLUDE FILE = 'c:\temp\temp.sps'.
```

- SORT CASES sorts the data by the value of *var1*. This will put all cases with the same values together and is required for the following MATCH FILES command, since the file must be sorted by the key variable(s) specified on the BY subcommand.
- Although MATCH FILES is typically used to merge two or more data files, you can use FILE=* to match the working data file with itself. In this case, that's useful, because we don't want to merge data files but we do want another feature of the

command—the ability to identify the FIRST case for each value of the key variable specified on the BY subcommand.

- The STRING command creates three temporary string variables: *#quot, #lab_out,* and *#lab2*. Unlike numeric variables, string variables must be defined before they can be specified in any transformations. The defined length of *#lab_out* is 62 characters because it will contain the value label based on the value of *lab1* plus two quotation marks, and value labels can be up to 60 characters long.
- #lab2=LTRIM(lab1) sets the temporary variable *#lab2* to the first 60 characters of *lab1*; so the value labels won't exceed the 60-character limit.
- The outer DO IF weeds out any cases with system-missing values for *var1* because that would result in invalid syntax when we write out the value label definitions.
- The inner DO IF looks for unique values of *var1* by looking for the first instance of each value, based on the value of the logical variable *first* defined by the FIRST subcommand of MATCH FILES; so the value label for each value will be defined only once.
- The CONCAT function creates a concatenated string from the values of *#quot*, *#lab2*, and *#quot* again, which is basically the value of *lab1* (or a portion thereof) enclosed in quotes. RTRIM strips off any trailing blanks in the value of *#lab2*.
- The WRITE command writes out a series of ADD VALUE LABELS commands to a text file using the values of *var1* and *#lab_out* to complete the command specifications.
- The INCLUDE command then executes the commands in the text file created by the WRITE command.

The command syntax file generated by the WRITE command looks like this:

```
ADD VALUE LABELS var1 17
 'value label for 17'                                                    .
ADD VALUE LABELS var1 21
 'value label for 21'                                                    .
ADD VALUE LABELS var1 32
 'value label for 32'                                                    .
```

You may notice the command terminators (.) way over on the right. By default, the WRITE command uses the print format of each variable, and since the format of *#lab_out* is A62, the WRITE command assumes that 62 characters are needed to write the value of the variable.

Auto-Adjusting Command Syntax Based on Data Conditions

You can create code that checks for various data conditions and branches accordingly, including command files that generate and run different commands based on the presence or absence of specific data values and/or variables.

Conditional INCLUDE Processing Based on Data Values

This example is designed to avoid command syntax errors caused by conditions that result in no cases being selected for analysis. The INCLUDE file *syntax_when_88.sps* contains the following commands:

```
SELECT IF var1=88.
FREQUENCIES VARIABLES=var1.
```

If no cases in the data file have a value of 88, this will result in an error. So we check to make sure there is at least one case with a value of 88 for *var1* and then generate the appropriate INCLUDE command.

```
*conditional_include.sps.
GET FILE='c:\examples\data\when_88.sav'.
COMPUTE testvar=(var1 = 88).
SORT CASES BY testvar(D).
DO IF $CASENUM=1.
-   DO IF testvar=1.
-     WRITE OUTFILE='c:\temp\temp.sps'
        /"INCLUDE FILE = 'c:\examples\commands\syntax_when_88.sps'.".
-   ELSE.
-     WRITE OUTFILE='c:\temp\temp.sps'
        /"INCLUDE FILE =
        'c:\examples\commands\syntax_when_no_88.sps'.".
-   END IF.
END IF.
EXECUTE.
INCLUDE FILE = 'c:\temp\temp.sps'.
*******************************************
  (To see result for other condition, change
    when_88.sav to when_no_88.sav)
 *******************************************.
```

- COMPUTE testvar(var1=88) returns a value of 1 for *testvar* for any case with a value of 88 for *var1* and 0 for all other non-missing values.
- SORT CASES BY testvar(D) sorts the data in descending order of *testvar* values; so any cases with a value of 1 will be sorted to the top. (Cases with the system-missing value will sort to the bottom in descending order.)

- The outer DO IF structure is executed for only the first case.
- The inner DO IF structure executes different WRITE commands based on the value of *testvar* for the first case. If the value is 1, then the file contains at least one case with a value of 88 for *var1*, and the file *temp.sps* will contain an INCLUDE command that specifies the command syntax file *syntax_when_88.sps*. Otherwise, the file will contain an INCLUDE command that specifies a different file.
- The INCLUDE command includes the generated command syntax file *temp.sps*, which contains another INCLUDE command, with a file specification based on the presence or absence of the value 88 for *var1* in the working data file.

For a more general solution to this kind of problem using macros, see "run syntax only when there are cases.sps" in "Other Macro Examples Included with SPSS" on p. 232 in Chapter 6.

Conditional INCLUDE Processing Based on Presence/Absence of a Variable

You can also specify conditional INCLUDE commands based on the presence or absence of a specified variable. In this example, we will insert a command to include a certain command syntax file only if the specified variable is not present in the working data file.

```
*macro_var_not_exist.sps.
SET MPRINT OFF.

DEFINE !exist (varname=!TOKENS(1))
- SAVE OUTFILE='c:\temp\tempdata.sav'.
- N OF CASES 1.
- FLIP.
- COMPUTE varcheck=(UPCASE(case_lbl) = !QUOTE(!UPCASE(!varname))).
- SORT CASES BY varcheck(d).
- DO IF $casenum=1.
-   DO IF varcheck=1.
-     WRITE OUTFILE='c:\temp\temp.sps'
       /'* Nothing to do, variable exists.'.
-   ELSE.
-     WRITE OUTFILE='c:\temp\temp.sps'
       /'* Variable does not exist, must include file.'
       /"INCLUDE 'c:\examples\commands\var_not_exist.sps'.".
-   END IF.
- END IF.
- EXECUTE.
- GET FILE='c:\temp\tempdata.sav'.
- INCLUDE 'c:\temp\temp.sps'.
!ENDDEFINE.
```

Here's the command file that uses the macro:

```
*use_macro_var_not_exist.sps.
INCLUDE
   FILE= 'c:\examples\commands\macro_var_not_exist.sps'.
GET FILE='c:\examples\data\employee data.sav'.
***Variable specified below exists in data file
   so var_not_exist.sps not run.
!exist varname=educ.
***Variable specified below does not exist,
   so var_not_exist.sps is run.
!exist varname=notexist.
```

And here's the command file that will be included if the variable doesn't exist.

```
*var_not_exist.sps.
**************************************************
 This file would run some commands if the
 specified variable doesn't exist
**************************************************.
*[insert your commands here].
```

- The macro first saves a copy of the working data file as *tempdata.sav* and then deletes all but the first case from the working data file.
- FLIP transposes cases and variables, using the original variable names as values for a string variable called *case_lbl*.
- The macro then creates a logical variable, *varcheck*, that is set to 1 for any "case" in the transposed file that has a *case_lbl* value that matches the variable name specified in the macro call. Since string values are case sensitive, we convert the string values to all upper case so that case won't matter when we specify the variable name in the macro call.
- Sorting the data file in descending order by values of *varcheck* will put any "case" with a *case_lbl* value of the specified variable name at the top of the working data file.
- The outer DO IF structure limits the next commands to the first case.
- If the value of *varcheck* is 1, then the specified variable exists and the nested DO IF structure writes a comment to the command file *temp.sps* that indicates that no action is necessary.
- If the value of *varcheck* is 0 (or missing), then the specified variable doesn't exist, and a command to INCLUDE *var_not_exist.sps* is written to *temp.sps*.
- The EXECUTE command is then run in order to close the command file that was just written.

- Finally, the copy of the original data file (*tempdata.sav*) is loaded and the command file *temp.sps* is included, which will either in turn include the command file *var_not_exist.sps* or simply display a comment.

For a more general solution using macros, see "run syntax depending on variable type.sps" in "Other Macro Examples Included with SPSS" on p. 232 in Chapter 6.

Set Number of Macro Loops Based on Data

This examples sets the number of !DO loops in a macro to the sum of the values of *var1* for case that have an *id* value of 1.

```
*macro_loop_from_data.sps
*create some sample data.
DATA LIST LIST /id(F8) var1(F8).
BEGIN DATA.
1 1
1 3
1 2
2 20
2 25
3 15
3 25
END DATA.
SAVE OUTFILE='c:\temp\tempdata.sav'.
SET MPRINT=OFF.

***real job starts here***.
*use aggregate to find sum of var1 for id 1.
AGGREGATE
 /OUTFILE=*
 /BREAK=id
 /var1_1 = SUM(var1).

* Write a command file that defines a macro using the value of var1_1
as the end value for the !DO loop.
DO IF id=1.
WRITE OUTFILE 'c:\temp\temp.sps'
  /"DEFINE !LoopingMacro()"
 /  "!DO !cnt=1 !TO " var1_1
 /"COMPUTE !CONCAT(var,!cnt)=!cnt."
 /"!DOEND"
 /"!ENDDEFINE.".
END IF.
EXECUTE.

*open the original data file and run the include file that
 defines the macro.
GET FILE='c:\temp\tempdata.sav'.
```

```
INCLUDE 'c:\temp\temp.sps'.

SET MPRINT=ON.
* Invoke the macro then execute transformations.
!LoopingMacro.
EXECUTE.
```

- AGGREGATE is typically used to change the unit of analysis by combining cases and using various functions to define the variable values for the new aggregated cases. In this case, we simply want the value returned by one of those functions.
- Using *id* as the break variable and the function SUM(var1), the new working data file will contain one case for each value of *id*, and the variable *var1_1* will contain the sum of *var1* values for each *id* value.
- OUTFILE = * specifies that the aggregated data should become the working data file.

Figure 5-8
Original and aggregated data

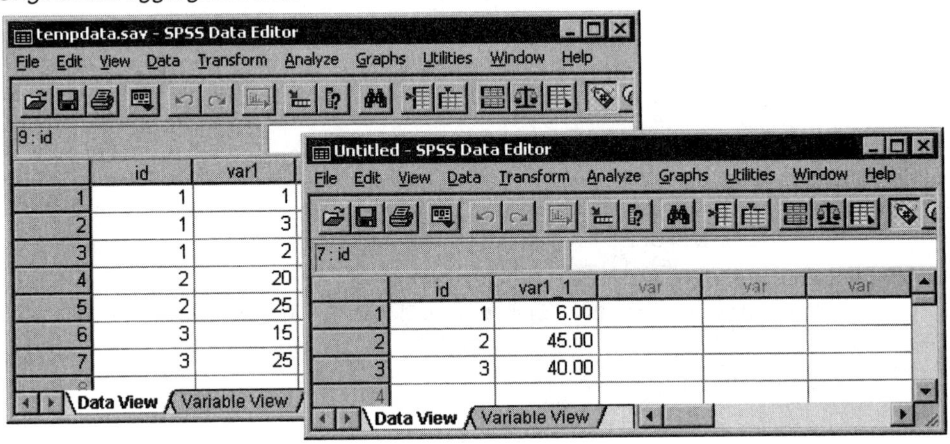

- For the aggregated case with an *id* value of 1, the DO IF structure writes out a text file that contains a macro definition.
- "!DO !cnt=1 !TO " var1_1 in the WRITE command writes a literal string followed by the value of *var1_1* for the aggregated case with an *id* value of 1—in this case, !DO !cnt=1 !TO 6.
- For each iteration of the macro !DO loop, a new variable will be created, with a name constructed from a concatenation of the literal string *var* and the current value of *!cnt*. The value of each variable will also be set to the current value of *!cnt*.

- Then we open the copy of the original data file and use INCLUDE to run the generated command file that contains the macro defintion.
- The "command" *!LoopingMacro* invokes the macro, generating the COMPUTE commands that create the new variables.
- SET MPRINT = ON displays the command generated by the macro in the Viewer log:

```
54 M>  COMPUTE var1 = 1.
55 M>
56 M>  COMPUTE var2 = 2.
57 M>
58 M>  COMPUTE var3 = 3.
59 M>
60 M>  COMPUTE var4 = 4.
61 M>
62 M>  COMPUTE var5 = 5.
63 M>
64 M>  COMPUTE var6 = 6.
```

Macro Exits Loop When There Is Convergence

Suppose that we have a macro with a !DO - !DOEND loop. The purpose of the loop is to repeat an iteration until the result converges within a predefined precision. Each iteration takes quite a long time, and we would like to stop the loop once the convergence criteria has been met.

To illustrate the a solution, we first use a macro that does *not* stop when convergence is reached. We will then modify it so that the macro exits the loop once convergence is reached. (Actually, the loop continues but without executing any commands.)

```
*no_exit_macro.sps.
*create some sample data.
DATA LIST FREE /a.
BEGIN DATA
1 2 3
END DATA.

SET SEED=12365985.
SET MPRINT=OFF.

***job starts here***.
DEFINE !loop1 (nb=!TOKENS(1))
!DO !cnt=1 !TO !nb
COMPUTE cnt=!cnt.
INCLUDE "c:\examples\commands\do_calc.sps".
!DOEND
!ENDDEFINE.
```

```
SET MPRINT=ON.
!loop1 nb=8. /* This macro continues to loop even when conver=1*/.
EXECUTE.
```

And here is the command syntax file called with the INCLUDE command in the macro, *do_calc.sps*:

```
DO IF $CASENUM=1.
COMPUTE conver=TRUNC(UNIFORM(10)).
ELSE.
COMPUTE conver=LAG(conver).
END IF.
EXECUTE.
```

- The command syntax file *do_calc.sps* is a just a proxy for the real calculation file that would be iterated. It simply generates a random integer value between 0 and 10, and we define "convergence" as the point at which the random value assigned to the variable *conver* is 1. In a real file, we would test the result at the end of the file and assign a value of 1 to the variable *conver* when we have attained the convergence.
- The *!loop1* macro simply calls the *do_calc.sps* file !nb times. Since no checks are performed on any values, the macro will always run *do_calc.sps* the number of times specified for !nb, even if the value of *conver* is 1 on an earlier iteration.

The following macro *!conver* is a modification of the *!loop1* macro so that the file *do_calc.sps* is no longer executed once convergence has been reached. The strategy is to:

- INCLUDE *do_calc.sps* and *check.sps* for the first iteration.
- Use *check.sps* to check to see if convergence has been reached.
- If convergence has not been reached, *check.sps* writes the file *do_calc2.sps*, which simply calls the file *do_calc.sps*, again using an INCLUDE command. It also writes a file, *check2.sps*, which calls the file *check.sps* using an INCLUDE command.
- If convergence is reached, *check.sps* writes different versions of the files *do_calc2.sps* and *check2.sps* containing nothing but comments.

So if convergence is reached, subsequent iterations of the *!conver* macro simply run two comment files.

```
*macro_convergence_exit.sps.

SET SEED=12365985.
SET MPRINT=OFF.
```

```
*get a data file (could be any data file).
GET FILE='c:\examples\data\employee data.sav'.

DEFINE !conv(maxIter=!TOKENS(1))
!DO !cnt=1  !TO !maxIter
COMPUTE cnt=!cnt.
!IF (!cnt = 1) !THEN
INCLUDE "c:\examples\commands\do_calc.sps".
INCLUDE "c:\examples\commands\check.sps".
!ELSE
INCLUDE "c:\temp\do_calc2.sps".
INCLUDE "c:\temp\check2.sps".
!IFEND
!DOEND
EXECUTE.
!ENDDEFINE.

!conv maxIter=10.
```

And here is the command file included by the macro that checks for convergence, *check.sps*:

```
*check.sps.
DO IF ($CASENUM=1 & conver=1).
- FORMATS conver (F2.0).
- PRINT RECORDS=5 //"Conver=1!!! ****"
 /"Conver=1!!! **** cnt=" cnt (F4) " conver="conver(F4)
 /"Conver=1!!! ****"/.
- WRITE OUTFILE='c:\temp\do_calc2.sps'
   /"*** Convergence achieved ***.".
- WRITE OUTFILE='c:\temp\check2.sps'
   /"*** No check needed ***.".
ELSE IF $CASENUM=1.
- WRITE OUTFILE='c:\temp\do_calc2.sps'
 /"INCLUDE 'c:\examples\commands\do_calc.sps'".
- WRITE OUTFILE='c:\temp\check2.sps'
 /"INCLUDE 'c:\examples\commands\check.sps'".
- PRINT RECORDS=5 //"Current values ****"
 /"Current values **** cnt=" cnt(F4) " conver="conver(F4)
 /"Current values ****"/ .
END IF.
EXECUTE.
```

- The macro *!conv* is simple: on the first iteration, it runs *do_calc.sps* and *check.sps*; on subsequent iterations, it runs *do_calc2.sps* and *check2.sps*. That's it.
- The included command file that checks for convergence, *check.sps*, consists of a single DO IF structure that only does something for the first case in the file.

- If the variable *conver* is not equal to 1, we have not yet achieved convergence, and we need to execute *check.sps* again. So we write the file *do_calc2.sps* and put a single command in that file: an INCLUDE command to run *do_calc.sps* again. When the macro *!conv* includes the file *do_calc2.sps* in its next iteration, it will run *do_calc.sps* again. This is what we need, since convergence has not been achieved.
- Now, the more interesting part is what *check.sps* does when there *is* convergence. In that case, it writes only a comment line in the file *do_calc2.sps*. Similarly, it also writes a comment line in *check2.sps*. So on subsequent iterations, the macro will not run *do_calc.sps* or *check.sps*. Once convergence is reached, only two comment syntax files are run for the remaining iterations of the macro.
- The PRINT commands provide a running log of what happens on each iteration of the macro until convergence is reached:

```
Current values ****
Current values **** cnt=    4 conver=    7
Current values ****
 ...
Current values ****
Current values **** cnt=    5 conver=    6
Current values ****
...
Conver=1!!! ****
Conver=1!!! **** cnt=    6 conver=    1
Conver=1!!! ****

6329   *** Convergence achieved ***.
6330
6332   * End of INCLUDE nesting level 01.
6334   *** No check needed ***.
6335
6337   * End of INCLUDE nesting level 01.
6340   *** Convergence achieved ***.
6341
6343   * End of INCLUDE nesting level 01.
6345   *** No check needed ***.
```

Executing Selective Portions of Command Syntax

One of the drawbacks of large, complicated command syntax projects is that they're...well, large and complicated. Sometimes you may want to run only a subset of reports in the project, or you may want to automatically exclude large sections of the project's command syntax under certain conditions.

Using a Master Command Syntax File with Modular Components

Suppose that you have a long command syntax file and want to exclude certain sections for a given run. A good solution is to break down the file into logical pieces and use a master command syntax file to run all of those pieces. For example:

```
* Master command syntax file.
INCLUDE 'c:\mydata\get data.sav'.
INCLUDE 'c:\mydata\standardize data.sps'.
INCLUDE 'c:\mydata\regional sales report.sps'.
INCLUDE 'c:\mydata\global sales report.sps'.
INCLUDE 'c:\mydata\expenses report.sps'.
INCLUDE 'c:\mydata\projections.sps'.
INCLUDE 'c:\mydata\quaterly reports.sps'.
```

Once the master file is set up, it is a simple matter to exclude some of these sections by putting asterisks in front of the INCLUDE commands for the command files you don't want to run. For more information on master command syntax files, see "Using INCLUDE with a Master Command Syntax File" on p. 26 in Chapter 2.

Selection Based On Macro Variables

Assume that we have a more complicated situation in which the master syntax file has 40–50 INCLUDE commands and many of these commands need to be executed only if some macro variables have predetermined values. More specifically, say we have a macro variable, *!qtity*, that indicates whether the variable *quantity* is in the data file or not. When the variable exists, and only when the variable exists, a specified command syntax file should be run.

```
* include_based_on_macro_var.sps.
SET MPRINT=OFF.

*create sample command syntax files.
DO IF $CASENUM=1.
- WRITE OUTFILE='c:\temp\temp1.sps'
   /"* This is the syntax if the variable exists.".
- WRITE OUTFILE='c:\temp\temp2.sps'
   /"* Command file not run because required variables not present.".
END IF.
EXECUTE.

***real job starts here***.
DEFINE !incl (testvar=!TOKENS(1) /sname=!CMDEND)
!IF (!testvar="YES") !THEN
INCLUDE !QUOTE(!CONCAT('c:\temp\',!sname)).
!ELSE
```

```
INCLUDE 'c:\temp\temp2.sps'.
!IFEND
!ENDDEFINE.

SET ERRORS=OFF.

DEFINE !qtity()YES!ENDDEFINE.
!incl testvar=!qtity sname=temp1.sps.

DEFINE !qtity()NO!ENDDEFINE.
!incl testvar=!qtity sname=temp1.sps.

SET ERRORS=ON.
```

- The DO IF structure simply creates two sample command syntax files.
- The *!incl* macro has two arguments, testvar and sname, which will be set to the values passed by the macro call. Based on the value of testvar passed to the macro, it will then either run the command syntax file passed by the sname argument or run *temp2.sps*.
- When the macro *!qtity* is defined to have the value YES, then testvar=!qtity on the subsequent *!incl* macro call evaluates *!qtity* as YES, and the *!incl* macro runs the command syntax file specified on the sname argument in the macro call.
- When the macro *!qtity* is defined to have the value NO, then testvar=!qtity on the subsequent *!incl* macro call evaluates *!qtity* as NO, and the command syntax file *temp2.sps* is run.
- The display of error and warning messages is turned off temporarily because defining the same macro more than once in the same session results in a warning message every time the macro definition is run.

Here are the results displayed in the Viewer log:

```
DEFINE !qtity()YES!ENDDEFINE.
!incl testvar=!qtity sname=temp1.sps.
7146  * This is the syntax if the variable exists.
7146
7148  * End of INCLUDE nesting level 01.

DEFINE !qtity()NO!ENDDEFINE.
!incl testvar=!qtity sname=temp1.sps.
7156  * Command file not run because required variables not present.
7156
7158  * End of INCLUDE nesting level 01.
```

Excluding Variables from Analysis

Let's say that you have a master command syntax file designed to work under various conditions, including:

- Some variables may not exist in all data files.
- Some variables are not relevant for a particular customer or report.
- Some variables contain confidential information that should be excluded from some reports.

Obvious, but inefficient, solutions are to modify the command syntax files each time to add/remove references to those variables or to maintain two different sets of command syntax files.

A better solution is to create a separate command syntax file that defines how to treat certain variables. You could then include this file as the first command file in the master file, and any changes you make in that definition file could automatically modify the behavior of all of the other command files in the project.

Example

This example uses a macro file to define how to treat the variable *salary*, using a macro variable in place of *salary* in subsequent command files. In this example, we have inserted the INCLUDE command for the macro definition file in the subsequent command file. In a more practical application, this INCLUDE would probably be one of the first commands in a master command syntax file.

```
*macro_include_var.sps.

*This macro definition needs to be all on one line.
DEFINE !v_salary()!IF(!EVAL(!salary)="YES")!THEN salary !IFEND!ENDDEFINE.
*This next macro should be changed from YES to NO when you want to
  exclude the variable.
DEFINE !salary() YES !ENDDEFINE.
```

And here's the command file that runs the macro definition via an INCLUDE command:

```
*use_macro_include_var.sps.

INCLUDE FILE = 'c:\examples\commands\macro_include_var.sps'.

GET FILE='c:\examples\data\employee data.sav'.

SUMMARIZE
  /TABLES=id !v_salary gender educ
  /FORMAT=LIST   LIMIT=6
  /TITLE='Salary Included'
  /CELLS=COUNT .

*Redefine !salary macro to exclude variable.
DEFINE !salary() NO !ENDDEFINE.

*Same as above but different results.
SUMMARIZE
  /TABLES=id !v_salary gender educ
  /FORMAT=LIST   LIMIT=6
  /TITLE='Salary Omitted'
  /CELLS=COUNT .
```

- The macro definition file contains two macros. The first one, *!v_salary,* inserts the variable name *salary* wherever the macro call appears in a command if the value of *!salary* is YES. Otherwise, it does nothing.
- The *!salary* macro is currently set to YES, indicating that the variable *salary* should be inserted wherever the macro call *!v_salary* appears. If *salary* should be excluded, you can change the value of *!salary* to NO.
- The INCLUDE command in the subsequent command file runs the two macro definitions.
- The two SUMMARIZE commands demonstrate what happens when *!salary* is set to YES and NO. (*Note*: You would normally change the definition of the *!salary* macro in the macro definition file.)

Figure 5-9

Variable included or excluded based on macro definition

Salary Included

	Case Number	Employee Code	Current Salary	Gender	Educational Level (years)
1	1	1	$57,000	Male	15
2	2	2	$40,200	Male	16
3	3	3	$21,450	Female	12
4	4	4	$21,900	Female	8
5	5	5	$45,000	Male	15
6	6	6	$32,100	Male	15
Total N		6	6	6	6

Salary Omitted

	Case Number	Employee Code	Gender	Educational Level (years)
1	1	1	Male	15
2	2	2	Male	16
3	3	3	Female	12
4	4	4	Female	8
5	5	5	Male	15
6	6	6	Male	15
Total N		6	6	6

There are two important limitations to this macro approach:

- The *!v_salary* macro definition must be specified entirely on a single line.
- A command line should not end with the macro call if the command is continued on additional lines. For example:

```
SUMMARIZE
  /TABLES=id gender educ !v_salary
  /FORMAT=LIST LIMIT=6.
```

will generate an error (unless the SUMMARIZE command is inside a macro). A simple workaround for this latter limitation is to change the variable order or, if the macro call is the only variable, move part or all of the next continuation line up to the same line as the line containing the macro call, as in:

```
SUMMARIZE
  /TABLES=!v_salary /FORMAT=LIST LIMIT=6.
```

In the above example, the macro either inserts the variable name or does nothing; and if the macro call is the only variable specified, an error will result if the macro does nothing.

Debugging Command Syntax

Beyond usually descriptive error messages, there aren't a lot of built-in tools to help you debug command syntax. There are, however, a number of common error conditions that you can easily avoid. (See "Customizing the Programming Environment" on p. 11 in Chapter 2 for additional tips and tools.)

Errors Caused by Different Syntax Rules for Different Operational Modes

Interactive and batch/include processing have slightly different syntax rules, leading to situations in which commands that run without any problems in one mode cause errors when the same commands are run in the other mode.

- In interactive mode, if a command does not end with a command terminator (a period), the first word on the next line is read as a continuation line even if it begins in the first column.
- In batch/include mode, any word that starts in the first column of a line is read as a command name regardless of the presence or absence of a command terminator on the previous line.

Example

```
*Interactive error because COMPUTE command doesn't
 have a command terminator.
COMPUTE newvar=1
VARIABLE LABEL
jobcat "A new label for this variable".

>Error # 4381 in column 1.  Text: VARIABLE
>The expression ends unexpectedly.
>This command not executed.

*Error in include file because a continuation line
 starts in first column.
INCLUDE 'c:\examples\commands\temp_include.sps'.
  78  COMPUTE newvar=1
  79  VARIABLE LABEL
  80  jobcat "A new label for this variable".

>Error # 1 on line 80.  Command name: jobcat
>The first word in the line is not recognized as an SPSS command.
>This command not executed.
```

To avoid these error conditions, always end commands with a command terminator and always indent continuation lines. Commands pasted from dialog boxes follow these guidelines and should work in both interactive and batch/include mode. For more information, see "Syntax Rules" on p. 7 in Chapter 1.

Calculations Affected by Low Default MXLOOPS Setting

A LOOP with an end point defined by a logical condition (for example, END LOOP IF varx > 100) will loop until the defined end condition is reached or until the number of loops specified on SET MXLOOPS is reached, whichever comes first. The default value of MXLOOPS is only 40, which may produce undesirable results or errors that can be hard to locate for looping structures that require a larger number of loops to function properly.

Example

This example generates a data file with 1,000 cases, where each case contains the number of random numbers—uniformly distributed between 0 and 1—that have to be drawn to obtain a number less than 0.001. Under normal circumstance, you would expect the mean value to be around 1,000 (randomly drawing numbers between 0 and 1 will result in a value of less than 0.001 roughly once every thousand numbers), but the low default value of MXLOOPS would give you misleading results.

```
* set_mxloops.sps.

SET MXLOOPS=40.     /* Default value. Change to 10000 and compare.
SET SEED=02051242.
INPUT PROGRAM.
LOOP cnt=1 TO 1000. /*indexing clause not affected by MXLOOPS.
+ COMPUTE n=0.
+ LOOP.
+   COMPUTE n=n+1.
+ END LOOP IF UNIFORM(1)<.001. /*Loops limited by MXLOOPS setting.
+ END CASE.
END LOOP.
END FILE.
END INPUT PROGRAM.

DESCRIPTIVES VARIABLES=n
  /STATISTICS=MEAN  MIN MAX.
```

- All of the commands are syntactically valid and produce no warnings or error messages.
- SET MXLOOPS=40 simply sets the maximum number of loops to the default value.

- The seed is set so that the same result occurs each time the commands are run.
- The outer LOOP generates 1,000 cases. Since it uses an indexing clause (cnt=1 TO 1000), it is unconstrained by the MXLOOPS setting.
- The nested LOOP is *supposed* to iterate until it produces a random value of less than 0.001.
- Each case includes the case number (*cnt*) and *n*, where *n* is the number of times we had to draw a random number before getting a number less than 0.001. There is 1 chance in 1,000 of getting such a number.
- The DESCRIPTIVES command shows that the mean value of *n* is only 39.2—far below the expected mean of close to 1,000. Looking at the maximum value gives you a hint as to why the mean is so low. The maximum is only 40, which is remarkably close to the mean of 39.2; and if you look at the values in the Data Editor, you can see that nearly all of the values of *n* are 40, because the MXLOOPS limit of 40 was almost always reached before a random uniform value of 0.001 was obtained.
- If you change the MXLOOPS setting to 10, 000 (SET MXLOOPS=10000), however, you get very different results. The mean is now 980.9, fairly close to the expected mean of 1,000.

Figure 5-10
Different results with different MXLOOPS settings

MXLOOPS = 40

	N	Minimum	Maximum	Mean
n	1000	1.00	40.00	39.2100
Valid N (listwise)	1000			

cnt	n
1.00	40.00
2.00	40.00
3.00	40.00
4.00	40.00
5.00	40.00
6.00	40.00
7.00	40.00
8.00	29.00
9.00	40.00
10.00	40.00

MXLOOPS = 10000

	N	Minimum	Maximum	Mean
n	1000	2.00	8223.00	980.9090
Valid N (listwise)	1000			

cnt	n
1.00	309.00
2.00	2261.00
3.00	800.00
4.00	2595.00
5.00	1850.00
6.00	281.00
7.00	244.00
8.00	1064.00
9.00	386.00
10.00	1718.00

Missing Values in DO IF - ELSE IF - END IF Structures

Missing values can affect the results from DO IF structures because if the expression evaluates to missing, then control passes immediately to the END IF command at that point. To avoid this type of problem, you should attempt to deal with missing values first in the DO IF structure before evaluating any other conditions.

```
* doif_elseif_missing.sps.

*create sample data with missing data.
DATA LIST FREE (",") /a.
BEGIN DATA
1, , 1 , ,
END DATA.

COMPUTE b=a.

* The following does NOT work since the second condition
  is never evaluated.
DO IF a=1.
 COMPUTE a1=1.
ELSE IF MISSING(a).
 COMPUTE a1=2.
END IF.

* On the other hand the following works.
DO IF MISSING(b).
 COMPUTE b1=2.
ELSE IF b=1.
 COMPUTE b1=1.
END IF.
EXECUTE.
```

- The first DO IF will never yield a value of 2 for *a1*, because if *a* is missing, then DO IF a=1 evaluates as missing, and control passes immediately to END IF. So *a1* will either be 1 or missing.
- In the second DO IF, however, we take care of the missing condition first; so if the value of *b* is missing, DO IF MISSING(b) evaluates as true and *b1* is set to 2; otherwise, *b1* is set to 1.

In this example, DO IF MISSING(b) will always evaluate as either true or false, never missing, thereby eliminating the situation in which the first condition might evaluate as missing and pass control to END IF without evaluating the other condition(s).

Figure 5-11
DO IF results with missing values displayed in Data Editor

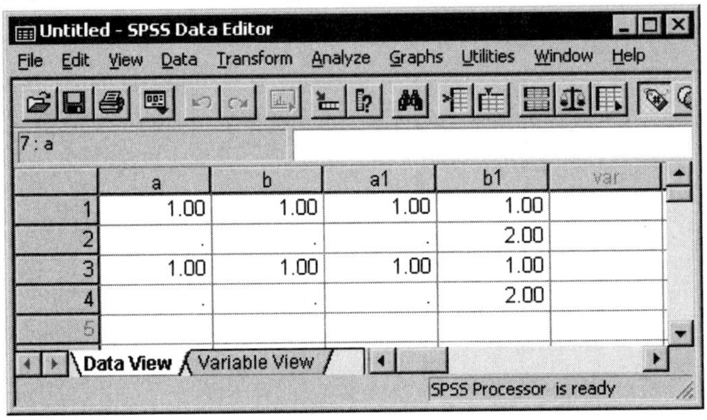

Disappearing Vectors

Vectors have a short lifespan; a vector lasts only until the next command that reads the data, such as a statistical procedure or the **EXECUTE** command. This can lead to problems under some circumstances, particularly when you are testing and debugging a command file. When you are creating and debugging long, complex command syntax jobs, it is often useful to insert **EXECUTE** commands at various stages to check intermediate results. Unfortunately, this kills any defined vectors that might be needed for subsequent commands, making it necessary to redefine the vector(s). However, redefining the vectors sometimes requires special consideration.

```
* vectors_lifespan.sps.

GET FILE='c:\examples\data\employee data.sav'.
VECTOR vec(5).
LOOP #cnt=1 TO 5.
+ COMPUTE vec(#cnt)=UNIFORM(1).
END LOOP.
EXECUTE.

*Vector vec no longer exists; so this will cause an error.
LOOP #cnt=1 TO 5.
+ COMPUTE vec(#cnt)=vec(#cnt)*10.
END LOOP.
```

```
*This also causes error because variables vec1 - vec5 now exist.
VECTOR vec(5).
LOOP #cnt=1 TO 5.
+ COMPUTE vec(#cnt)=vec(#cnt)*10.
END LOOP.

* This  redefines vector without error.
VECTOR vec=vec1 TO vec5.
LOOP #cnt=1 TO 5.
+ COMPUTE vec(#cnt)=vec(#cnt)*10.
END LOOP.
EXECUTE.
```

- The first VECTOR command uses the **short form** of the command to create five new variables as well as a vector named *vec* containing those five variable names: *vec1* to *vec5*.
- The LOOP assigns a random number to each variable of the vector.
- EXECUTE completes the process of assigning the random numbers to the new variables (transformation commands like COMPUTE aren't run until the next command that reads the data). Under normal circumstances, this may not be necessary at this point. However, you might do this when debugging a job to make sure that the correct values are assigned. At this point, the five variables defined by the VECTOR command exist in the working data file, but the vector that defined them is gone.
- Since the vector *vec* no longer exists, the attempt to use the vector in the subsequent LOOP will cause an error.
- Attempting to redefine the vector in the same way it was originally defined will also cause an error, since the short form will attempt to create new variables using the names of existing variables.
- VECTOR vec=vec1 to vec5 redefines the vector to contain the same series of variable names as before without generating any errors, because this form of the command defines a vector that consists of a range of contiguous variables that already exist in the working data file. See "VECTOR" on p. 140 for more information.

Locale-Sensitive Decimal Indicators

In many countries, a comma is used as a decimal indicator instead of a period. SPSS can read data that uses a comma as the decimal indicator (for example, using the DOT format) and will display results using a locale-sensitive decimal indicator (in Windows, this is specified in the Regional Options control panel). However, with the exception of commands that read data, command syntax recognizes only a period as the decimal indicator. For example:

```
COMPUTE NumVar=10,2.
```

will generate the following error message, regardless of the defined format of the variable or the regional/locale settings of your operating system.

```
>Error # 4026 in column 21.  Text: ,
>An expression contains a misplaced comma.
>Check the expression for omitted
>or extra operands, operators, and parentheses.
>Also check for a number specified with a comma as the
>decimal delimiter.  Commas cannot be used as
>decimal delimiters in transformations.
>This command not executed.
```

In the above example, the solution is simple and obvious: Replace the comma with a period. In other situations, however, the problem may require a more subtle solution.

Example

A very powerful technique illustrated in this book is the ability to use command syntax to write command files that are subsequently run via INCLUDE commands. Including the current value of a variable in a WRITE command, however, can cause errors if the defined format of the variable is DOT, which uses a comma as the decimal indicator, or if you use F format and the current Windows regional settings specify a comma as the decimal indicator.

```
*decimal_indicator.sps.

*create some dot format sample data.
DATA LIST FIXED /NumVar (DOT3.1).
BEGIN DATA
1,1
2,4
3,5
END DATA.
```

```
DO IF ($CASENUM = 1).
- WRITE OUTFILE='c:\temp\temp.sps'
     /"COMPUTE newVar=" NumVar ".".
END IF.
EXECUTE.

INCLUDE FILE='c:\temp\temp.sps'.

*override the default variable write format.
DO IF ($CASENUM=1).
- WRITE OUTFILE='c:\temp\temp.sps'
     /"COMPUTE newVar=" NumVar(COMMA18.16) ".".
END IF.
EXECUTE.

INCLUDE FILE='c:\temp\temp.sps'.
```

- The DOT format is used to read data where a comma is the decimal indicator.
- The WRITE command in the first DO IF structure will write a command syntax file that contains the literal string "COMPUTE newVar=" followed by the value of *NumVar* for the first case. However, in the absence of a different format specification, WRITE uses the defined format of the variable, which will result in:

  ```
  COMPUTE newVar=1,1.
  ```

  which will cause an error when the command file is invoked with an INCLUDE command, since a numeric value can't contain a comma in command syntax.
- The WRITE command in the second DO IF provides the solution to this problem: NumVar(COMMA18.16) specifies that the value of *NumVar* should be written in COMMA format, which always uses a period as the decimal indicator regardless of locale, which will result in:

  ```
  COMPUTE newVar=1.1000000000000000.
  ```

  which will correctly set the value of *newVar* to the first case value of *NumVar* without changing the defined format of the original variable.

Although you probably don't want all of those decimal places, we use a "tight" format specification to suppress any commas that COMMA format would insert as the grouping symbol if the defined width provided enough space for grouping symbols. A format of COMMA18.16 ensures that any extra space is allocated to additional decimal positions, and the grouping separator is never displayed. You could, of course, specify a shorter but equally "tight" format, such as COMMA5.3, but COMMA18.16 ensures maximum precision when you don't know how many significant digits the value may contain.

Chapter

6

Macros

Macros allow you to define a named piece of SPSS command syntax that you can then insert into an SPSS job by giving its name and optional arguments to be used in its expansion. The macro language includes conditional and looping statements and string manipulation functions so that a comparatively compact macro can expand into a substantial section of command syntax. Macros are usually part of the solution when you need to:

- Run the same analysis on many variables or data files.
- Run different analyses depending on certain parameters (for example, run an annual report versus quarterly reports).
- Do repetitive tasks, such as obtaining 1,000 random samples from a data file, calculating statistics for each sample, and summarizing the statistics obtained.

Macros are a significant productivity tool. Macros can:

- Speed up code development.
- Simplify code maintenance.
- Facilitate code recycling.

Documentation for the operations of macros keywords is contained in the *SPSS Command Syntax Reference* under the DEFINE - !ENDDEFINE command. Also, see the appendix "Using the Macro Facility" in that book for additional examples.

A Very Basic Macro

Let's start with an example of the simplest possible macro:

```
DEFINE !month() 5 !ENDDEFINE.
```

Once that line has run, any subsequent *!month* found in command syntax will be replaced by the number 5. For example:

```
SELECT IF MONTH = !month.
```

will become

```
SELECT IF MONTH = 5.
```

Using a simple macro allows you to set a value, such as month, at the start of a command file instead of searching through the commands for the place or places where you need to change the value.

Macro Arguments

Generally, you want to specify the values, variable names, or other information to be used in the macro execution at the time the macro is called. You define what these specifications (arguments) will be inside the parentheses that follow the macro name.

Example

This macro accepts a single argument: the sample size of a random sample.

```
DEFINE !getsamp (size=!TOKENS(1))
GET FILE="c:\Program Files\SPSS\Employee data.sav".
SAMPLE !size.
!ENDDEFINE.

SET MPRINT=ON.
* Call the macro with a value for the size argument.
!getsamp size=.1.
```

- The argument name in this macro is *size*, and the argument will be the one token that follows the argument name in the macro call. Note that when the name of the argument is used within the body of the macro, it is necessary to insert an exclamation mark (!) before the name.
- If you set MPRINT=ON (or YES), the log file will show the command that SPSS executes after the macro has been expanded.

Example

When you don't know the number of tokens that might be supplied for a macro argument, you can specify all tokens up to a particular character (!CHAREND), all tokens enclosed between two characters (!ENCLOSE), or all tokens up to the end of the command (!CMDEND), as in the following example. This macro gets samples of various sizes (for example, one sample of about 10% of the file, one of about 20%, and one of about 30%), and for each such sample, it runs the DESCRIPTIVES procedure on the variables named in the macro call.

```
SET PRINTBACK=ON MPRINT=ON.
DEFINE !stat3 (size=!CHAREND('/') /vnames=!CMDEND)
!DO !s !IN (!size)
GET FILE="c:\Program Files\SPSS\Employee data.sav".
SAMPLE !s.
DESCRIPTIVES
  VARIABLES=!vnames
  /STATISTICS=MEAN STDDEV MIN MAX .
!DOEND
!ENDDEFINE.

!stat3 size = .1 .2 .3 /vnames=jobcat salary.
```

Figure 6-1
Descriptive statistics produced by macro call

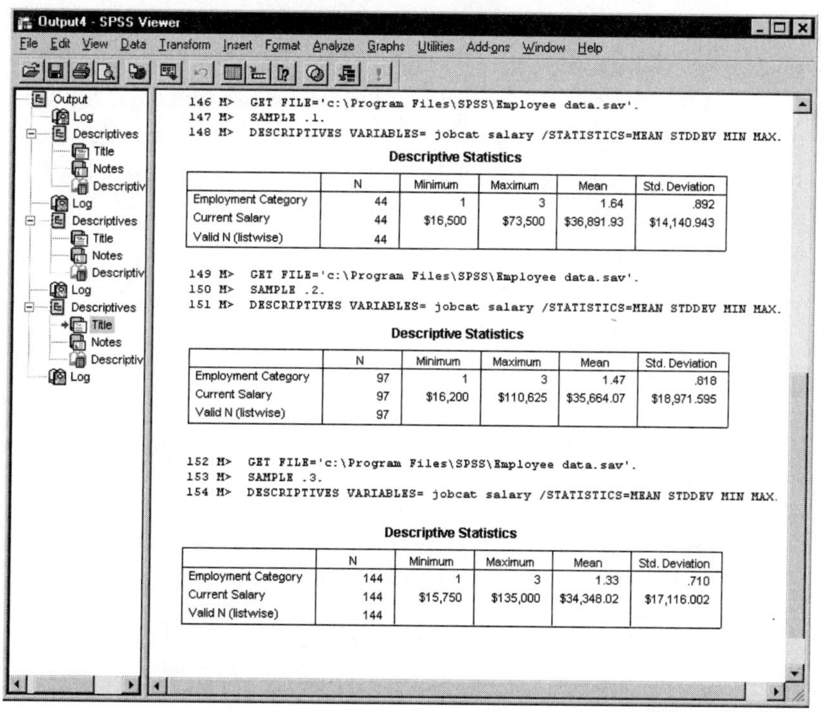

- The first argument (size) includes all tokens (in this case all numbers) up to the "/" character.
- The second argument includes all tokens (in this case all variable names) up to the command terminator.
- The !DO -!DOEND structure is executed three times (as many times as there are numbers in the size argument). The macro variable !s equals 0.1 the first time, 0.2 the second time, and 0.3 the last time.
- The DESCRIPTIVES command is executed using the variables contained in the macro argument *!vnames*.
- The log items display the results of the macro expansion.
- The Viewer window shows the three resulting tables. Note that the 20% sample does not have twice the number of cases as the 10% sample. This is because SAMPLE .2 does not take exactly 20% of the file; instead, each case in the file has a 20% probability of being retained.

Positional Arguments

Instead of using an argument name, you can use the keyword !POSITIONAL (which can be shortened to !POS) and then refer to the arguments as !1, !2... in the body of the macro. Named arguments have the following advantages over positional arguments:

- They can be specified in any order in the macro call (except if the argument is defined using !CMDEND).
- It is not necessary to specify all argument names in the macro call (it is possible to specify default values for named arguments that are not included in the macro call).

Tokens

Macro arguments contain one or more tokens. A token is a number, a contiguous set of characters other than delimiters, or a quoted string. Here are a few examples:

Original content	Resulting number of tokens
age group gender	3 (each word is a token)
1 2 8.1235 0.023	4 (each number is a token)
"age group" 18.256 'abc 12 ct2'	3 (items within single or double quotes are treated as a single token)
1,2	3 (the comma separating the two numbers is treated as a separate token)
C234	1
234C	2 (234 and C; to treat this as one token, enclose it in quotes)

You can use quotation marks and the !QUOTE and !UNQUOTE functions to control how tokens are handled. The macro parser interprets tokens according to the same rules as the command syntax parser:

- Anything inside of a set of quotation marks is a single token.
- Inside of single quotation marks, double quotation marks are treated as literal characters.
- Inside of single quotation marks, two consecutive single quotation marks are interpreted as one single quotation mark (or apostrophe).
- Inside of double quotation marks, single quotation marks are treated as literal characters.
- Inside of quotation marks, multiple spaces (blanks) are significant.
- Two quoted strings can be combined into a single quoted string by placing a plus sign between them. Thus, “a b” + “c d” is the single token “a b c d”. This is primarily useful for continuing long strings across multiple lines.
- A line that ends with an unclosed quoted string generates an error.
- The maximum length of a string (quoted or not) is 255 characters.

Outside of quotation marks, tokens are set off by delimiters.

- The blank is the most common delimiter. Multiple blanks are treated as a single blank.

- Special delimiters have various roles in command syntax. They are tokens in their own right, so that A+B is three tokens. The following are special delimiters:

  comma, parentheses, square brackets, braces, slash, equals sign (, ( ) [ ] { } / =)
  arithmetic operators (+ – * /)
  comparison operators (> < <= >= ~= <>)
  logical operators (~ & |)
  matrix arithmetic operators (&* &/).

  Blanks before and after special delimiters are not significant.
- Numbers are tokens and end when complete. Thus, 123, 12.33, and 1.5e12 are each one token, but 1.1.1 and 123C are each two tokens.
- Commas within numbers are delimiters. Thus, 1,234.00 is three tokens—two numbers and the comma. This is also true in locales where the comma is used as the decimal delimiter; within command syntax, decimals must be set off by periods, and commas are interpreted as delimiters.

Conditional Processing

It is often necessary to process certain sections of a macro only when certain conditions are met. The macro facility provides for conditional processing with the !IF...!THEN...!ELSE...!IFEND statements.

Example

The following macro converts a number such as 20031231 (form YMD) or 31122003 (form DMY) to a date variable. The macro extracts the year, month, and day from the number and then defines the date variable using the DATE.DMY function. Since the macro handles both the YMD and DMY format, that information is supplied in the macro call. The macro executes a different section of the code, depending on the value of the macro argument *form*. Purely for illustration, the macro uses numeric functions to separate the elements of YMD and string functions to separate the elements of DMY.

```
* macros_conditional_processing.sps.

NEW FILE.
DATA LIST LIST /num1 num2.
BEGIN DATA
20011231 31122001
20020503 8022002
END DATA.
```

```
DEFINE !datevar (form=!TOKENS(1).
  /num=!TOKENS(1) /newvar=!TOKENS(1))

!IF (!UPCASE(!form)=YMD) !THEN
COMPUTE #yr=TRUNC(!num/10000).
COMPUTE #mth=TRUNC(MOD(!num,10000)/100).
COMPUTE #day=MOD(!num,100).
PRINT /#yr #mth #day.
!ELSE !IF (!UPCASE(!form)=DMY) !THEN
STRING #datestr(A8).
COMPUTE #datestr=STRING(!num,F8).
COMPUTE #day=NUMBER(SUBSTR(#datestr,1,2),F4).
COMPUTE #mth=NUMBER(SUBSTR(#datestr,3,2),F4).
COMPUTE #yr=NUMBER(SUBSTR(#datestr,5),F4).
!IFEND
!IFEND

COMPUTE !newvar=DATE.DMY(#day,#mth,#yr).
FORMATS !newvar(DATE12).
VARIABLE WIDTH !newvar(11).
!ENDDEFINE.

!datevar form=ymd num=num1 newvar=date1.
!datevar form=DMY num=num2 newvar=date2.

EXECUTE.
```

Figure 6-2
Computed date-format variables displayed in Data Editor

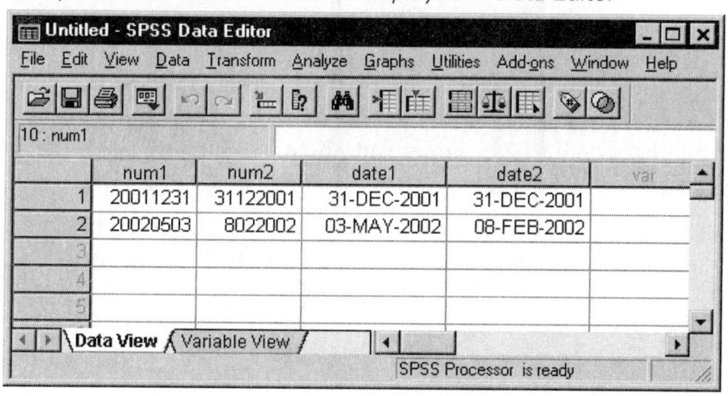

- DATA LIST reads two cases containing two numbers each. The first variable has the form YMD; the other has the form DMY. The macro will be called with the appropriate form.
- DEFINE has three argument names, each made up of a single token.

- !IF - !THEN checks whether !UPCASE(!form)=YMD. We could simply check whether !form=YMD, but using !UPCASE makes the macro more general; it can be called using !form=YMD, !form=ymd, or !form=Ymd and work in every case.
- The first macro call specifies !form=ymd; so the condition within the first !IF – !THEN is true, and the next three COMPUTE commands are expanded and become part of the command syntax that is executed.
- In the YMD format, COMPUTE #yr=TRUNC(!num/10000) extracts the year portion of the date, which is the truncated result of dividing the number by 10,000.
- COMPUTE #mth=TRUNC(MOD(!num,10000)/100) takes the remainder of dividing the number by 10,000, divides that value by 100, and truncates the result to yield the month.
- The day portion of the date in YMD format is simply the remainder after dividing the original number by 100: COMPUTE #day=MOD(!num,100).
- When !form=DMY, the !ELSE - !IF condition is true, and the STRING command and four COMPUTE commands are expanded by the macro.
- The STRING command defines the temporary string variable *#datestr*. Unlike numeric variables, strings must be defined before being used.
- The COMPUTE command is then used to convert the numeric variable into a string variable.
- In the DMY format, the day is the first two characters of the string. The SUBSTR function is used to extract a substring from the *#datestr* variable. The substring starts in position 1 and has a total of two characters. The NUMBER function converts the substring into a numeric variable using the format F4. We could have used any number equal to 2 or larger, instead of 4. Similarly, substring functions select the month and the year.
- Finally, the date variable with the name supplied to the NEWVAR argument is created with the DATE.DMY function and given a DATE12 format.

Looping Constructs

The macro facility provides two looping constructs: the index loop that iterates a fixed number of times and the list processing loop that iterates once for each item in a list. You can interrupt either of these loops with !BREAK in conjunction with conditional processing.

Example: Index Loop

This macro creates and saves a specified number of random samples of approximately 10%. It requires one argument, *nbsamp* (the number of random samples to create). The program uses a macro variable *!cnt*, which is initialized to 1 and incremented by 1 until it reaches the value *nbsamp*. The variable *!cnt* is concatenated to the end of samp to create the various filenames.

```
* macros_looping_construct_example01.sps

* Get n random samples and save them as separate files.

DEFINE !getrnd(nbsamp=!TOKENS(1))
!DO !cnt=1 !TO !nbsamp
GET FILE='c:\examples\data\Employee data.sav'.
SAMPLE .10.
SAVE OUTFILE=!QUOTE(!CONCAT('c:\temp\samp',!cnt,'.sav')).
!DOEND
!ENDDEFINE.

SET MPRINT=ON.
!getrnd nbsamp=4.
```

Figure 6-3
Macro expansion displayed in log

```
 44 M>  GET FILE='c:\examples\data\Employee data.sav'.
 45 M>  SAMPLE .10.
 46 M>  SAVE OUTFILE= 'c:\temp\samp1.sav'.
 47 M>
 48 M>  GET FILE='c:\examples\data\Employee data.sav'.
 49 M>  SAMPLE .10.
 50 M>  SAVE OUTFILE= 'c:\temp\samp2.sav'.
 51 M>
 52 M>  GET FILE='c:\examples\data\Employee data.sav'.
 53 M>  SAMPLE .10.
 54 M>  SAVE OUTFILE= 'c:\temp\samp3.sav'.
 55 M>
 56 M>  GET FILE='c:\examples\data\Employee data.sav'.
 57 M>  SAMPLE .10.
 58 M>  SAVE OUTFILE= 'c:\temp\samp4.sav'.
```

Since the macro is called using nbsamp=4, the !DO -!DOEND loop is executed four times.

Example: List Processing Loop

This macro is the same as the previous example, except that the argument is a list of filenames and it creates as many random samples as there are filenames.

```
* macros_looping_construct_example02.sps.
* create files whose names are given in the macro call.

DEFINE !getrnd2(filenam=!CMDEND)
!DO !name !IN (!filenam)
GET FILE='c:\examples\data\Employee data.sav'.
SAMPLE .10.
SAVE OUTFILE=!QUOTE(!CONCAT('c:\temp\',!name,'.sav')).
!DOEND
!ENDDEFINE.

SET MPRINT=ON.
!getrnd2 filenam=samp1 file5 data8.
```

Figure 6-4
Macro expansion displayed in log

```
216 M>  GET FILE='c:\examples\data\Employee data.sav'.
217 M>  SAMPLE .10.
218 M>  SAVE OUTFILE= 'c:\temp\samp1.sav'.
219 M>  GET FILE='c:\examples\data\Employee data.sav'.
220 M>  SAMPLE .10.
221 M>  SAVE OUTFILE= 'c:\temp\samp2.sav'.
222 M>  GET FILE='c:\examples\data\Employee data.sav'.
223 M>  SAMPLE .10.
224 M>  SAVE OUTFILE= 'c:\temp\samp3.sav'.
225 M>  GET FILE='c:\examples\data\Employee data.sav'.
226 M>  SAMPLE .10.
227 M>  SAVE OUTFILE= 'c:\temp\samp4.sav'.
```

- The macro variable *!name* successively assumes each of the filenames assigned to the argument *filenam* in the macro call.
- The SAVE command concatenates the path, the filename, and the extension to create the complete filename.
- The !QUOTE function encloses the complete file specification in quotes. As a general rule, file specifications should always be enclosed in single or double quotes.

Example: List Processing Loop with Different Handling of First Item

This example generates a CTABLES command (available with the Tables option) with stacked variables. It illustrates the use of the !HEAD and !TAIL functions to treat the first token in a list differently from the remaining ones—specifically, to place a plus sign (+) before each variable after the first.

```
*macros_varying_number_variables_in_table.sps.

GET FILE='c:\examples\data\employee data.sav'.

DEFINE !tab (title=!TOKENS(1) /vnames=!CMDEND)

!LET !h=!HEAD(!vnames)
!LET !t=!TAIL(!vnames)

CTABLES
  /VLABELS VARIABLES=!vnames DISPLAY=DEFAULT
  /TABLE !h [COUNT F40.0]
  !DO !var !IN (!t)!CONCAT(" + ",!var," [COUNT F40.0]") !DOEND
  /CATEGORIES VARIABLES=!vnames ORDER=A KEY=VALUE
   EMPTY=INCLUDE MISSING=EXCLUDE
  /TITLES TITLE=!title.

!ENDDEFINE.

PRESERVE.
SET MPRINT=ON PRINTBACK=ON.
* Call using 3 variables.
!tab title="Table with 3 variables" vnames=minority jobcat educ.
RESTORE.
```

The CTABLES command syntax generated by the macro call is:

```
CTABLES /VLABELS VARIABLES= minority jobcat educ DISPLAY=DEFAULT
  /TABLE minority [COUNT F40.0] + jobcat [COUNT F40.0] +
   educ [COUNT F40.0]
  /CATEGORIES VARIABLES= minority jobcat educ ORDER=A KEY=VALUE
   EMPTY=INCLUDE MISSING=EXCLUDE
  /TITLES TITLE="Table with 3 variables".
```

- The macro has two arguments: *title* (which should be enclosed in quotes) and *vnames*.
- The !HEAD function extracts the first token from the macro variable *!vnames* and assigns it to *!h*. Thus, *!h* equals *minority*.
- The function !TAIL assigns the remaining tokens to variable *!t*.

- Since we want to display the labels of all variables, we simply use *!vnames* in the VLABELS subcommand of the CTABLES command.
- In the TABLE subcommand, we first list the name of the first variable along with the corresponding required statistics and format. The !DO loop adds a plus sign (+), the variable name, statistics, and format for each of the remaining variables.
- The argument *!title* is used in the TITLES subcommand so that it gets printed at the top of the table.
- The PRESERVE command is used because we will change two SET parameters in the next line, and we do not want these changes to be permanent.
- SET ensures that the macro expansion is displayed in the log along with the other commands.
- The macro is called with the two required arguments.

Macro Expansion

By default, macro expansion is on during normal processing of SPSS command syntax. As the command stream is read, the macro parser considers whether a token could be a defined macro. If it is, the parser then examines tokens following the macro call to satisfy any arguments to the macro. Macro expansion continues during the collecting of arguments, so any other macros that occur during that stage are expanded, and their expansion is read as part of the arguments. The process is recursive until the arguments to all macros are satisfied (or an error occurs). When all of the arguments are satisfied, the body of the macro (the part between the argument definition header in parentheses and !ENDDEFINE) operates. Once the body has operated, the resulting command syntax is pushed back into the command stream ahead of any tokens not used to satisfy the arguments.

Macros that are included in the body of the macro may or may not be expanded. The arguments to macro functions are not scanned for possible macro calls. Thus, assuming that *!mac* is a defined macro, !LENGTH(!mac) is 4, regardless of the definition of *!mac*. Otherwise, macros within the body are expanded. If you have a reason not to expand a macro immediately within another macro, you can use the !NOEXPAND function; !NOEXPAND(!mac) is passed as !mac to the next level of processing. On the other hand, if you want to expand a macro that is an argument to a function, you can use the !EVAL function, as in the following example:

Example

```
DEFINE !year()2003!ENDDEFINE.

DEFINE !test()
STRING a(A8).
COMPUTE num=!year.
COMPUTE a=!QUOTE(!year).
COMPUTE a=!QUOTE(!EVAL(!year)).
!ENDDEFINE.

SET MPRINT=ON PRINTBACK ON.
!test.
EXECUTE.
```

Figure 6-5
Extract from Log

```
 483 M>  STRING a(A8).
 484 M>  COMPUTE num=2003.
 486 M>  COMPUTE a= '!year'.
 487 M>  COMPUTE a= '2003'
```

- In the first COMPUTE, *!year* is not used within a macro expression and is expanded.
- In the second COMPUTE, *!year* is used within a macro expression and the macro is not expanded, so the value of the string variable *a* is set to '!year'.
- In the third COMPUTE, the !EVAL function forces the macro parser to check whether *!year* is a macro. Since this is the case, !EVAL expands *!year* to 2003.

Doing Arithmetic with Macro Variables

The macro facility is a string processor designed to produce SPSS command syntax; it has no ability to do arithmetic using macro variables. For example, !LET !cnt=!cnt+1 is not a legal macro command. On infrequent occasions where arithmetic or other calculations are needed within the macro, you can employ one of two strategies. You can use the !BLANK(n) function to create strings the length of the numeric values of interest, concatenate the strings, and use the !LENGTH function to obtain the sum, as in this simple example:

```
* macros_doing_arithmetic.sps.

SET MPRINT=ON.
DATA LIST LIST /a.
BEGIN DATA
1
END DATA.
```

```
* A macro to add 2 positive numbers.
DEFINE !add(!POS=!TOKENS(1) /!POS=!TOKENS(1))
COMPUTE total=!LENGTH(!CONCAT(!BLANK(!1),!BLANK(!2))).
!ENDDEFINE.

* call the macro.
!add 5 7.
```

The macro call expands to COMPUTE total=12.

As a variation on that strategy, you can use the !SUBSTR function to subtract numbers. Examples can be found in the file *macros_doing_arithmetic.sps* on the CD that comes with this book.

As an alternative strategy, you can use the SPSS transformation language, most likely COMPUTE, to perform more complicated operations, write the resulting variable to a file (limiting WRITE to just one case), and INCLUDE the file back into the macro syntax. For an example, see *macros_beyond_arithmetic.sps* on the accompanying CD.

Macro Examples

Importing from MS Access

When variables from a database have hundreds of value labels, it is very convenient to have command syntax available to retrieve the labels and assign them automatically to the relevant SPSS variables.

Example

This example assumes that value labels are stored in separate tables in MS Access. The macro retrieves the values and value labels and writes a command syntax file to apply the labels to the values of the SPSS variables.

This macro works only for numeric variables (see the explanation for ADD VARIABLE LABELS below). Revising it for string variables is straightforward, but making it general would require an argument for the variable type, since the macro facility has no direct information about variable types.

Figure 6-6
Relationship between three Access tables

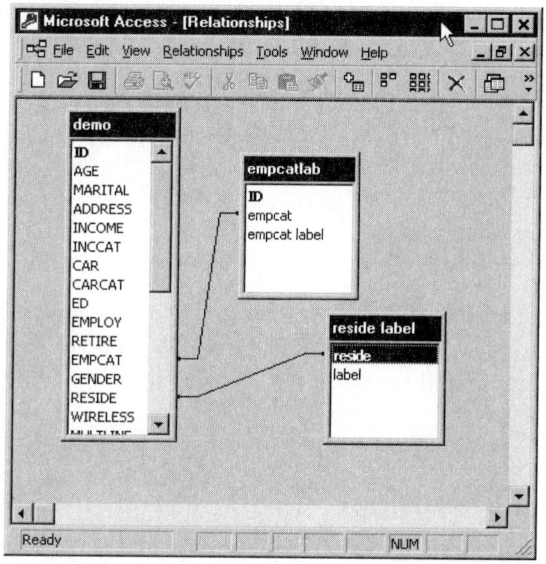

```
* macros_import_value_labels_from_access.sps.

GET DATA
  /TYPE=ODBC
  /CONNECT=  'DSN=MS Access Database;'
      'DBQ=C:\examples\data\demo.mdb;'
  /SQL =   'SELECT * FROM demo;'.
SAVE OUTFILE='c:\temp\data from access.sav'.

DEFINE !getlab (table=!TOKENS(1) /vname=!TOKENS(1)
  /vlabel=!TOKENS(1))

  /* table = name of MS Access table containing values
   and value labels  */
  /* vname = name of SPSS variable whose value labels
   will be defined    */
  /* vlabel= the access table Field Name containing
   the labels of !vname  */

GET DATA
  /TYPE=ODBC
  /CONNECT=  'DSN=MS Access Database;'
      'DBQ=C:\examples\data\demo.mdb;'
  /SQL =   'SELECT * '
      !QUOTE(!CONCAT("FROM [",!UNQUOTE(!table),"];")).
```

```
WRITE OUTFILE=!QUOTE(!CONCAT('c:\temp\define ',!vname,'.sps'))
  /"ADD VALUE LABELS " !QUOTE(!vname) " " !vname " '" !vlabel"'.".
EXECUTE.
!ENDDEFINE.

SET MPRINT=ON.
* Call macro: once for empcat and once for reside.
!getlab table =empcatlab  vname=empcat vlabel=empcatlabel.
!getlab table ='reside label' vname=reside vlabel=label.
SET MPRINT=no.

GET FILE='c:\temp\data from access.sav'.
INCLUDE 'c:\temp\define empcat.sps'.
INCLUDE 'c:\temp\define reside.sps'.
```

- The GET DATA command reads the Access database. If you are unsure of how to specify the CONNECT string, you can use the Database Wizard (File menu, Open Database) and paste the command syntax at the last step to obtain a valid CONNECT string.
- The SQL statement imports all fields from the *demo* table of the *demo.mdb* file.
- The data are then saved in SPSS format in *c:\temp\data from access.sav*.
- We then start to define the macro *!getlab*. The three arguments required by the macro are described in comment lines after the DEFINE line.
- GET DATA imports all fields from the table containing the values and value labels.
- WRITE creates a command syntax file containing an ADD VALUE LABELS command for each case in the data file. We could have used a single ADD VALUE LABELS command with many values but used separate commands for each label for simplicity.
- When we call the macro with the argument vname=empcat, the name of the command syntax file is *define empcat.sps*.
- The construction of ADD VALUE LABELS places quotes around the name of the variable and the value label but not the value itself. Thus, it works only for numeric variables.
- The macro is called twice, once per variable for which we need to retrieve the value labels.
- We then load the SPSS-format version of the data file and use an INCLUDE command to run the two command syntax files created by the macro.

Defining a List of Variables between Two Variables

Sometimes we cannot use references such as var1 TO xyz5; we have to actually list all of the variables of interest. One example is when a macro argument containing variable names is used in a !DO !var !IN (!!list) construct. Giving the explicit list of variables can be tedious when we are dealing with a large number of variables.

Example

The following macro creates a new macro, *!list1*, which contains the names of all variables between any two given variable names. The following general approach is used: all variables outside of the range of interest are deleted. The file is then flipped, which gives us the list of all variables. We then write a syntax file in which we define a macro containing the list of all of the variables. We can then use the macro *!list* whenever we need an explicit list of variables between any two variables.

```
* macros_examples_define_list_of_variables.

SET MPRINT=no.
DEFINE !DefList (var1=!TOKENS(1)
     /var2=!TOKENS(1)
     /fname=!CMDEND)

GET FILE=!fname.
N OF CASES 1.
* Keep only the variables we need.
ADD FILES FILE=* /KEEP=!var1 TO !var2.
FLIP.

COMPUTE nobreak=1.
* Flag the first and last case.
MATCH FILES FILE=* /BY nobreak /FIRST=first /LAST=last.

* Write a macro which contains the variable names.
DO IF first.
- WRITE OUTFILE='c:\temp\list1.sps' / 'DEFINE !list1()' .
END IF.
WRITE OUTFILE='c:\temp\list1.sps' / " "case_lbl.
DO IF last.
- WRITE OUTFILE='c:\temp\list1.sps' /' !ENDDEFINE.'.
END IF.
EXECUTE.

GET FILE=!fname.
* Define the macro.
INCLUDE 'c:\temp\list1.sps'.
!ENDDEFINE.
```

```
* Only 6 variables are used to illustrate the procedure.
DATA LIST LIST /id g x345 v3 k b.
BEGIN DATA.
1 1.21 . 3.01 5.51 41.98
2 2.33 5.67 . 4.22 6.02
END DATA.

SAVE OUTFILE='c:\temp\mydata.sav'.
EXECUTE.
SET MPRINT=ON.

* Call the macro..
!DefList var1=g var2=k fname="c:\temp\mydata.sav".
SET MPRINT=no.
```

The generated command syntax file, *list1*, contains the macro definition for the variable list:

```
DEFINE !list1()
 g
 x345
 v3
 k
 !ENDDEFINE.
```

- The macro *!DefList* needs three arguments: the first and last variables and the complete path of the data file.
- GET FILE reads the data file.
- N OF CASES retains the first case and discards all of the rest, since at this point we need only the variable names, not the data values. Note that for large files, N OF CASES 1 is more efficient than SELECT IF $CASENUM=1 because N OF CASES takes effect immediately (it does not need to go through the entire file).
- ADD FILES is used to delete all variables other than those between *!var1* and *!var2*.
- FLIP transposes the file. Variable names are stored in the variable *case_lbl*.
- COMPUTE defines the variable *nobreak* and sets it to 1. (Any other constant would also work.) This number is used as the BY variable in the next command.
- MATCH FILES creates two new variables: *first* equals 1 for the first case in the data file (0 for all other cases), and *last* equals 1 for the last case in the file (0 for all other cases).
- We then start to write the command syntax file, where we define a macro containing the names of all variables between *var1* and *var2*.

- First we write 'DEFINE !list()', using DO IF to do this only for the first case. Note that 'DO IF first' has the same effect as 'DO IF first=1'.
- Then we write each of the variable names, which are the values of the variable *case_lbl*.
- Then, for the last case, we write '!ENDDEFINE.'.
- EXECUTE creates the file.
- We then load the data file and run the *!list* macro using the INCLUDE command.

It would be easy to modify the macro to pass as an argument the name of the macro to be created.

Changing Variable Formats

We frequently have to change formats of variables—for example, numeric values might be imported as strings, or string variables might have 255 characters when we need only the first 8. The first example here changes string to numeric and numeric to string, while the second changes the format of long string variables to accommodate the longest string actually in the data.

Example

This macro applies the same format modification to any number of variables while retaining the original variable names and labels. Since it is not possible to directly change the format of a variable from string to numeric (or vice versa), the following approach is used:

- A new variable having the desired format is created.
- The information from the original variable is converted to the desired format and transferred to the new variable.
- The variable label from the original variable is copied to the new variable.
- The original variable is deleted.
- The new variable is renamed to the name of the original variable.

Creating a new string variable requires specification of the format for the new string. This macro uses the ability to set a default for a macro argument to differentiate between string-to-numeric conversions and numeric-to-string conversions.

```
* macros_exchange_variable_formats.sps.
SET MPRINT OFF.
DEFINE !convert (variables=!CHAREND("/")
  /format=!TOKENS(1)
  /stringformat= !DEFAULT('NONE') !TOKENS(1) )
*  variables = the names of the numeric or string
   variables to convert;
   format = the numeric format to read the string as a number
   or the format in which to represent the numeric variable
   in a string;
   stringformat = the format for the new string (required when
   converting numeric to string).
!DO !vname !IN (!variables)
!IF (!stringformat='NONE') !THEN
NUMERIC temp1234(!format).
COMPUTE temp1234=NUMBER(!vname,!format).
!ELSE
STRING temp1234(!stringformat).
COMPUTE temp1234=LTRIM(STRING(!vname,!format)).
!IFEND
APPLY DICTIONARY FROM=*
  /SOURCE VARIABLES=!vname /TARGET VARIABLES=temp1234.
MATCH FILES FILE=* /DROP=!vname.
RENAME VARIABLE (temp1234=!vname).
!DOEND
!ENDDEFINE.

* Test the macro.
DATA LIST LIST /var1(A12) var2(A12) customer_ID(F8).
BEGIN DATA
'1,235.23' '762.00' 181254
'5,3261.32' '1,265.85' 011618
END DATA.
VARIABLE LABEL var1 'Account value'
  /var2 'Recent purchase'
  / customer_ID 'Customer ID #'.
SUMMARIZE /TABLES=var1 var2 customer_ID
  /FORMAT=LIST /CELLS=NONE.
SET MPRINT=ON PRINTBACK=ON.
!convert variables= var1 var2 / format=DOLLAR10.2.
!convert variables=customer_ID
  /format=F8 stringformat=A8.
SET MPRINT=OFF.
SUMMARIZE /TABLES=var1 var2 customer_ID
  /FORMAT=LIST /CELLS=NONE.
```

Figure 6-7
Summarize results before and after running macro

Before Running Macro

	Case Number	Account value	Recent purchase	Customer ID #
1	1	1,235.23	762.00	181254
2	2	5,3261.32	1,265.85	11618

After Running Macro

	Case Number	Account value	Recent purchase	Customer ID #
1	1	$1,235.23	$762.00	181254
2	2	$53,261.32	$1,265.85	11618

- Although this macro handles both string-to-numeric conversions and numeric-to-string conversions, each call of the macro can handle only one; and it assumes that the formats of the converted variables will be the same for all variables being converted in one call. It requires two arguments when converting strings to numeric variables and a third argument when converting numeric to string variables. The presence or absence of that third argument determines what kind of conversion it attempts.
- The !DO - !DOEND structure loops as many times as there are variable names in *!variables*.
- The default for !stringformat (the format for a resulting string) is 'NONE'. Thus, if !stringformat is not specified in the macro call, the macro executes the NUMERIC and COMPUTE commands to create a new numeric variable, *temp1234*, reading the string variable with the format specified in !format and applying that format to the new variable.
- If !stringformat has been specified, then the macro proceeds to commands following !ELSE and executes the STRING and COMPUTE commands to create a new string variable with the width specified in !stringformat, representing the numeric variable in the format specified in !format.
- APPLY DICTIONARY copies the variable label from the original variable to the new variable. A warning message for each converted variable tells us that other dictionary information cannot be copied because the formats of the variables are different.
- MATCH FILES deletes the original variable, and the new variable is then renamed to the original variable.

- Two macro calls are used to demonstrate the two different conversions. The tables from SUMMARIZE show that the values of *var1* and *var2* have been converted to numeric and are shown in DOLLAR format, while the values of *customer_ID* have been converted to strings.

Note that the order of variables is changed by the macro. If we want the order of the variables to remain unchanged, we could define the macro *!list1* using the macro *!DefList*, described in the previous section, and use ADD FILES FILE=* /KEEP=!list1 after having called the macro *!convert*.

Reducing a String to Minimum Length

For various reasons, we often find ourselves with strings of greater length than necessary. The following macro contains the commands needed to reduce the defined length of a string to the length needed to represent its meaningful contents.

Example

This example finds the maximum number of characters (excluding trailing spaces) contained in a given string variable, creates a new string variable with the correct format, drops the original variable, and renames the new string to the original name.

```
*macros_reduce_string_length.sps.

DEFINE !ReformatString (variables=!CMDEND)
!DO !var !IN (!variables)
COMPUTE strlength=LENGTH(RTRIM(!var)).
SORT CASES BY strlength (D).
DO IF ($casenum = 1).
WRITE OUTFILE = 'c:\temp\temp.sps'
  /"STRING temp1234  (A"strlength(N3)")."
END IF.
EXECUTE.
INCLUDE FILE = 'c:\temp\temp.sps'.
COMPUTE temp1234 = !var.
APPLY DICTIONARY FROM=*
  /SOURCE VARIABLES=!var  /TARGET VARIABLES=temp1234.
MATCH FILES FILE=* /DROP !var strlength.
RENAME VARIABLE (temp1234=!var).
EXECUTE.
!DOEND
!ENDDEFINE.

DATA LIST FREE /string1 (A10) string2 (A10) string3(A10).
BEGIN DATA
a ab abc
a abcde ab
abcdef abcdefgh abcdefghi
END DATA.

!ReformatString variables=string1 string2 string3.
```

- This macro loops through a list of variables; all commands are applied to each variable at a time.
- Strlength is the length of *!var* when all trailing blanks are removed.
- Sorting by strlength places the longest trimmed string value of *!var* as the first case. The WRITE command writes a temporary file containing the STRING command specifying the width equal to strlength for the first case. The N3 format guarantees that strlength will be expressed with leading zeros to ensure that the format specification will not contain blanks.
- EXECUTE is required, since WRITE is a transformation and we need to execute it before we read another file.
- We then include the file with the necessary string format, apply the dictionary format from the original variable to the temporary variable, drop the original variable and strlength from the file, and rename the temporary variable to the original variable's name.

Including a Procedure in a Loop

Because LOOP - END LOOP and DO REPEAT - END REPEAT are transformation commands, it is not possible to have procedures inside such constructs. Macros are an elegant solution in those cases.

Example: Listing in a Loop

Say our variables of interest go from *v191* to *v247* and variables *v191*, *v192*, and *v193* form a group, variables *v194*, *v195*, and *v196* form a group, and so on. For each group, we want to list those cases where the first variable of the group equals 1 and the second variable equals 0.

The example uses INPUT PROGRAM to create a data file for illustration purposes. The data file of 20 cases is generated so that the first and second variables of each group have an equal probability of being either 0 or 1.

The macro itself is made up of a !DO - !DOEND loop, which loops once per group. !CONCAT statements are used to obtain the name of the applicable variables, and a flag is set to 1 when the first variable is 1 and the second is 0. A filter is applied using the flag, and resulting applicable cases are listed.

```
* macros_examples_listing_in_a_loop.sps.
SET MPRINT ON PRINTBACK ON.
* Create a dummy file for illustration purposes.
NEW FILE.
INPUT PROGRAM.
SET SEED=11171942.
NUMERIC v191 TO v247.
VECTOR v=v191 TO v247.
* create 20 cases.
LOOP v1=1 TO 20   /* v1 is the case id */.
- LOOP #cnt=1 TO 57.
-   DO IF MOD(#cnt,3)=0.
-    COMPUTE v(#cnt)=UNIFORM(1).
-   ELSE.
-    COMPUTE v(#cnt)=UNIFORM(1)>.5.
-   END IF.
- END LOOP.
- END CASE.
END LOOP.
END FILE.
END INPUT PROGRAM.
EXECUTE.

* define a macro to do the job.

DEFINE !listvar()

!DO !cnt=191 !TO 247 !BY 3
- FILTER OFF.
- COMPUTE flag=0.
  !LET !a1=!CONCAT('v',!cnt)
  !LET !a2=!CONCAT('v',!LENGTH(!CONCAT(!BLANKS(!cnt)," ")))
  !LET !a3=!CONCAT('v',!LENGTH(!CONCAT(!BLANKS(!cnt),"  ")))
- IF ( !a1=1 & !a2=0 ) flag=1.
- FILTER BY flag.
- LIST v1 !a1 !a2 !a3.
!DOEND

!ENDDEFINE.

*Call macro.
!listvar.
```

- NEW FILE clears any existing data file.
- Since SET SEED is used, the syntax generates the same results each time it is executed.
- Variables *v191* to *v247* are defined and then assigned to the vector *v*. Thus, element *v(1)* of the vector refers to variable *v191*.
- The first LOOP is executed 20 times; the END CASE immediately before the corresponding END LOOP creates one case for each execution of the loop.

- The second LOOP is executed 57 times in order to assign a value to each of the variables from *v191* to *v247*.
- MOD(#cnt,3) equals 0 only when #cnt equals a multiple of 3—in other words, only for the third variable of each group of three variables. For those cases, the variable is set to a pseudo-random number uniformly distributed between 0 and 1.
- The ELSE portion of the DO IF sets the first two variables of each group to the result of UNIFORM(1) > .5. The result of this comparison is either true (1) or false (0). Thus, the first two variables are equal to either 0 or 1.
- The macro *!listvar* does not require any arguments.
- The !DO loop is executed once for each group of variables. Note the use of the !BY keyword, which increments the variable *!cnt* by 3 after each iteration.
- FILTER OFF is used to ensure that the next commands are applied to all cases.
- COMPUTE sets the flag to 0. This variable will flag which cases need to be listed.
- During the first loop, the first !LET produces *!a1=v191*.
- Note how the macro variable *!a2* is defined. For example, when !cnt=191, we create a string having 191 blanks, concatenate it with an additional blank (space), calculate the length of the resulting string (which is, of course, 192), and concatenate that number to the letter *v* to form the name of the variable *v192*.
- IF sets the flag to 1 when the condition is satisfied—that is, when the first variable equals 1 and the second equals 0.
- FILTER BY flag "hides" cases where flag=0.
- LIST lists the ID and the three variables of the group for all cases where the condition is satisfied.

Figure 6-8
Portion of output from listing in a loop

```
68 M>   - FILTER OFF.
69 M>   COMPUTE flag=0.
70 M>   - IF ( v200 =1 & v201 =0 ) flag=1.
71 M>   FILTER BY flag.
72 M>   LIST v1 v200 v201 v202.

      v1       v200       v201       v202

    3.00       1.00        .00        .44
    4.00       1.00        .00        .45
    5.00       1.00        .00        .86
    6.00       1.00        .00        .33
   18.00       1.00        .00        .76
```

```
Number of cases read:  5    Number of cases listed:  5

  73 M>  - FILTER OFF.
  74 M>  COMPUTE flag=0.
  75 M>  - IF ( v203 =1 & v204 =0 ) flag=1.
  76 M>  FILTER BY flag.
  77 M>  LIST v1 v203 v204 v205.

      v1     v203     v204     v205

    1.00     1.00      .00      .03
    3.00     1.00      .00      .36
    4.00     1.00      .00      .78
   10.00     1.00      .00      .50
   15.00     1.00      .00      .88
   16.00     1.00      .00      .14

Number of cases read:  6    Number of cases listed:  6
```

Counting Distinct Values across Variables

Example

This macro counts the number of distinct values across a set of consecutive variables.

```
* macros_count_distinct_values_across_variables.SPS.
SET MPRINT ON PRINTBACK ON.
DATA LIST LIST (",") /var1 var2 var3 varn.
BEGIN DATA
1, 2, 3, 4
1, 1, 1, 1
1.37, 1.37, 2, 4
2, 3, 2, 2
, 1,, 1
END DATA.

DEFINE !nb(nbvars=!TOKENS(1) /v1=!TOKENS(1) /v2=!TOKENS(1))

VECTOR v=!v1 TO !v2 /#val(!nbvars).
LOOP #cnt=1 TO !nbvars.
- COMPUTE #val(#cnt)=v(#cnt).
END LOOP.

LOOP #cnt1 = 1 TO !nbvars - 1.
- DO IF ~MISSING(#val(#cnt1)).
-   LOOP #cnt2 = #cnt1 + 1 TO !nbvars.
-     IF #val(#cnt2)=v(#cnt1) #val(#cnt2)=$SYSMIS.
-   END LOOP.
- END IF.
END LOOP.
```

```
COMPUTE distinct=!nbvars - NMISS(#val1 TO !CONCAT('#val',!nbvars)).
FORMATS distinct (F5).
!ENDDEFINE.

* Call macro.
!nb nbvars=4 v1=var1 v2=varn.
EXECUTE.
```

Figure 6-9
Results in Data Editor

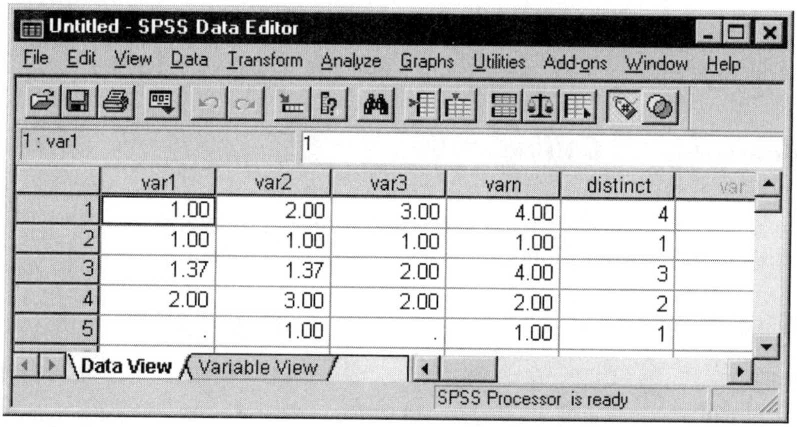

- The macro has three arguments: the number of variables, the name of the first variable, and the name of the last variable. It would be easy to have the macro count the number of variables, but for simplicity, the number is supplied as an argument.
- VECTOR sets vector *v* to comprise all variables of interest. A scratch vector *#val* of the same length is also defined.
- The first LOOP - END LOOP copies all values from vector *v* to vector *#val.*
- The *#cnt1* parameter of the second LOOP - END LOOP goes from 1 to !nbvars-1. We will follow what happens when #cnt1=1 and we are on the third case.
- The condition of the DO IF is true, since *var1* contains the number 1.37 and hence *#val(#cnt1)* is not missing.
- The LOOP - END LOOP inside the DO IF is executed, and the LOOP tests whether any variable after the current variable is equal to 1.37. When that is true, the variable is set to $SYSMIS. Thus, the LOOP sets *#val(2)* to $SYSMIS. Since the other variables do not equal 1.37, they are left unchanged.
- The parameter *#cnt1* is then incremented to 2. This time, the condition of the DO IF is false (*#val(2)* is missing). So the parameter *#cnt1* is incremented to 3.

- Since the value of *#val(3)* is 2, the condition of the DO IF is satisfied and the inner LOOP checks whether the last variable equals 2. This is not the case, so the value of the last variable is left unchanged.
- The result of the above LOOP - END LOOP is that the vector *#val* includes only one occurrence of every distinct value per case.
- COMPUTE calculates the number of distinct values as the number of variables (*!nbvars*) minus the number of missing values across all cases.
- !ENDDEFINE signals the end of the macro definition.
- The macro is called with required parameters.

Recursive Macro (Macro Calling Itself)

Recursive functions are often used in programming languages. They usually result in shorter code. This technique can be used with SPSS macros.

Example: Flagging Ties

The macro *!flgties* flags cases where any of the given variables have the same value.

```
* macros_examples_recursive_macro.gif.
SET MPRINT OFF.
DATA LIST LIST (",") /var1 var2 var3 var4.
BEGIN DATA
1, 2, 3, 3
1, 2, 3, 4
1, 1, 2, 2
1, 1, 1, 1
3, 3, 2, 2
 ,  ,  ,
4, 1.7, 2, 1.7
END DATA.

* Flag ties (cases where some of the variables have the same value).

DEFINE !flgties(listvar=!CMDEND)

!IF (!listvar !NE !NULL) !THEN
 !LET !testval=!HEAD(!listvar)
 !LET !other=!TAIL(!listvar)
 !DO !var !IN (!other)
-  COMPUTE flag=SUM(!var = !testval, flag).
 !DOEND
!flgties listvar=!other.
!IFEND

!ENDDEFINE.
```

```
COMPUTE flag=0.
SET MPRINT ON PRINTBACK ON.
!flgties listvar=var1 var2 var3 var4.
COMPUTE flag2=MIN(flag,1).
EXECUTE.

* Flag = the number of ties.
* Flag2 = 1 when any of the variables var1 to var4 have the same
value.
```

Figure 6-10

Portion of Log showing the macro expansion

```
332 M>  - COMPUTE flag=SUM( var2 = var1 , flag).
333 M>  - COMPUTE flag=SUM( var3 = var1 , flag).
334 M>  - COMPUTE flag=SUM( var4 = var1 , flag).
337 M>  - COMPUTE flag=SUM( var3 = var2 , flag).
338 M>  - COMPUTE flag=SUM( var4 = var2 , flag).
341 M>  - COMPUTE flag=SUM( var4 = var3 , flag).
```

Figure 6-11

Data Editor after running !flgties

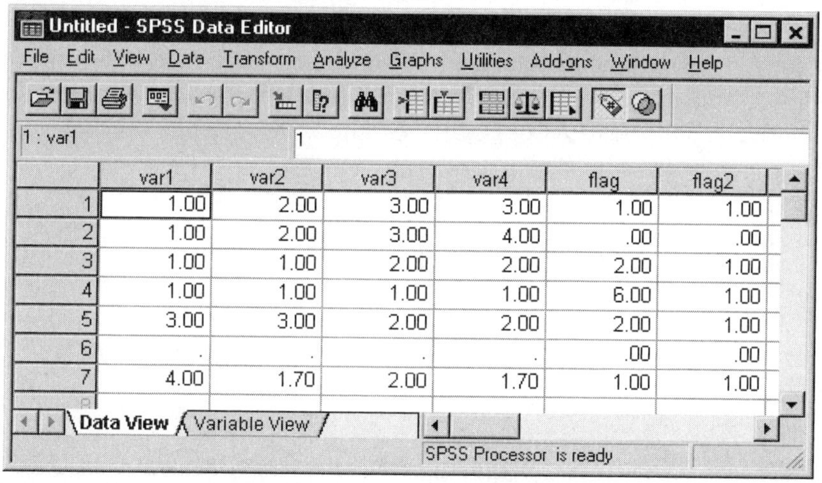

- If the list of variables is empty, the macro exits. Otherwise, the first variable is assigned to the macro variable *!testval* and the remaining variables are assigned to *!other*.
- The value of *!testval* is compared to the value of each of the *!other* variables. Each time the value matches, the result of the comparison is 1, and the function SUM adds 1 to the variable *flag*.
- The macro then calls itself using *!other* as the argument.

By default, the maximum number of nesting levels is 50. If more than 50 are required (for example, if we have 90 variables), we could increase the maximum allowed using SET MNEST=100 before calling the macro. Alternatively, we could add the following code at the beginning of the macro:

```
!LET !mnest=50
!IF (!BLANKS(!nbvars) !GT !BLANKS(50)) !THEN !LET !mnest=!nbvars
!IFEND
SET MNEST=!mnest.
```

Random Samples and Selections

In this section, we look at various ways of taking random samples from a given population.

Example: Random Sorts

The first example shows how to obtain a large number of random sorts of a list for an assessment field test. The macro requires one argument: the number of random sorts required. A loop is executed the required number of times. Each time, the variable *draw* is assigned a random number. The list is sorted by values of *draw*, and the file is printed. Note that because a SUMMARIZE procedure is used, the macro could not be replaced by a DO REPEAT or LOOP structure.

```
* macros_print_thousands_of_random_sorts.sps*.
SET MPRINT=OFF.
*Create and print thousands of random sorts of a
  list for an assessment field test.

DEFINE !random(nb=!TOKENS(1))

!DO !cnt=1 !TO !nb
COMPUTE draw=UNIFORM(1).
SORT CASES BY draw.
SUMMARIZE
  /TABLES=ALL
  /FORMAT=VALIDLIST NOCASENUM  NOTOTAL LIMIT=10
  /TITLE='First Ten Cases'
  /CELLS=COUNT .
!DOEND

!ENDDEFINE.

GET FILE='c:\examples\data\employee data.sav'.
SET MPRINT=ON PRINTBACK ON.
!random nb=3.
```

The macro is very simple. Since it is called with the argument nb=3, the code inside the !DO loop is executed three times.

Randomly Selecting Cases Based on Given Criteria

Example

Two groups of cases must be randomly selected from a data file. Macro arguments give the number of cases in each group and the criteria used to determine whether a given case is included in the population to be sampled for each group.

```
* macros_random_samples_based_on_criteria.SPS.
* Create indicator variables of cases randomly selected based
  on given criteria.
SET MPRINT=OFF.

DEFINE !select (
    nb1=!TOKENS(1)    /crit1=!ENCLOSE('(',')')
   /nb2=!TOKENS(1)    /crit2=!ENCLOSE('(',')')
   /FPath=!TOKENS(1) /RPath=!TOKENS(1))
GET FILE=!FPath.
COMPUTE casenum=$CASENUM.
SAVE OUTFILE='c:\temp\temp.sav'.
SHOW SEED.
!DO !cnt=1 !TO 2
- SELECT IF !IF (!cnt=1) !THEN !crit1 !ELSE !crit2 !IFEND.
- COMPUTE draw=UNIFORM(1).
- SORT CASES BY draw.
- N OF CASES !IF (!cnt=1) !THEN !nb1 !ELSE !nb2 !IFEND.
- SORT CASES BY casenum.
- SAVE OUTFILE=!QUOTE(!CONCAT('c:\temp\group',!cnt,'.sav.')).
- GET FILE='c:\temp\temp.sav'.
!DOEND
MATCH FILES FILE=*
   /FILE='c:\temp\group1.sav'
   /IN=ingrp1
   /FILE='c:\temp\group2.sav'
   /IN=ingrp2
   /BY=casenum
  /DROP=draw.
SAVE OUTFILE=!RPath.
!ENDDEFINE.

SET MPRINT=ON.
!select nb1=5  crit1=(gender='m' AND jobcat=1 AND educ<16)
        nb2=7  crit2=(gender='f' AND jobcat=1 AND educ>11)
        FPath= 'c:\examples\data\employee data.sav'
        RPath= 'c:\temp\results.sav'.

* List cases selected by criteria 1.
DO IF ingrp1=1.
+ PRINT /id ingrp1 gender jobcat educ.
END IF.
EXECUTE.
```

- The macro has six arguments: the number of required cases for group 1 and the criteria to determine if a case is eligible to participate in group 1; similar information for group 2; the name and path of the initial data file and the result file.
- The arguments *crit1* and *crit2* are contained within parentheses.
- The macro loads the original data file, creates the variable *casenum,* which is used as the ID variable, and saves the file.
- The !DO loop is executed twice, once for each group.
- When *!cnt* equals 1, the first line of the loop becomes
  SELECT IF !crit1.
  and only cases meeting those criteria are retained in the working data file.
- A random number is drawn for each case; then the file is sorted in increasing order of that random variable. The effect is to sort the file of eligible cases into a random order.
- When *!cnt* equals 1, the next line becomes
  N OF CASES !nb1.
  and only the first *!nb1* cases are kept. We thus have the required number of cases for group 1 (unless there are fewer than *!nb1* cases that satisfy the criteria assigned to *!crit1*).
- Cases are then sorted by *casenum*, because we will later MATCH the file with the original data file and use *casenum* as the BY variable.
- The file is saved with the name *group1.sav*.
- The above steps are repeated for *!cnt* equals 2 to create the file *group2.sav*.
- MATCH FILES merges the two files with the initial data file, using *casenum* as the BY variable. The variable *ingrp1* is 1 for cases that are present in file group1 (0 for other cases). Similarly, the variable *ingrp2* indicates the cases that are in group 2.
- !ENDDEFINE signals the end of the macro definition.
- The macro is called with the six arguments.
  In group1, we want five cases satisfying the criteria assigned to *crit1*.
  In group2, we want seven cases satisfying the criteria assigned to *crit2*.
  The name and path of both data files are given.

Random Assignment of Control Subjects with Given Characteristics

Example

Say the file *population.sav* contains the variables *id*, *age* at a given date, *sex, fup* (period of follow-up, in years), *event* (1 when event occurred; 0, otherwise), and for cases where the event occurred, the *evtday, evtmonth*, and *evtyear.*

For each case where the event occurred, the objective is to randomly select *n* control cases where the event did not occur. The selected controls must have the same sex and age (or be within *x* years of that age), and their period of follow-up must be at least equal to that of the case for which the event occurred. A given control subject cannot be assigned to more than one case. Control cases must then be given the same *evtday*, *evtmonth*, and *evtyear* as their corresponding case. The ID of the case to which they relate must also be shown.

The strategy used is to create the macro *!do_one*, which, for a given case where the event occurred, gets the list of possible control subjects, randomly selects *n* control subjects, removes those subjects from the list of possible control subjects, and adds the controls to the *.sav* file of controls found up to now.

Once the macro is created, *population.sav* is loaded into memory. Cases with event=1 are selected, and a syntax file is created using a WRITE command. Each line of the syntax file is a call to the macro *!do_one*, and each line contains the arguments required to randomly select control cases for the given ID.

The syntax file is then executed using an INCLUDE command:

```
* macros_match_cases_with_controls.sps.

DEFINE !pathd()'c:\temp\'!ENDDEFINE.

* Generate sample data for illustration purposes.
SET SEED=01251701.
NEW FILE.
INPUT PROGRAM.
LOOP id=1 TO 300./* generate 300 cases*/
+ COMPUTE sex=1 + (UNIFORM(1)>.5).
+ COMPUTE age=TRUNC(50+UNIFORM(20)).
+ COMPUTE event=UNIFORM(1)>.96./* 1=case, 0=potential control */
+ COMPUTE fup  =UNIFORM(10).
+ DO IF event=1.
+   COMPUTE evtday  =RND(UNIFORM(28)).
+   COMPUTE evtmonth=RND(.5 + UNIFORM(12)).
+   COMPUTE evtyear =RND(1993 + UNIFORM(10)).
+   COMPUTE fup=(CTIME.DAYS(DATE.DMY(evtday,evtmonth,evtyear) -
  DATE.DMY(1,1,1993)))/365.25.
+ END IF.
+ END CASE.
```

```
END LOOP.
END FILE.
FORMATS id TO event evtday TO evtyear (F5) fup(F4.2).
END INPUT PROGRAM.
FREQ VAR=event.
SAVE OUTFILE=!pathd + "population.sav".

* Define macro which finds control subjects for a given id.
DEFINE !do_one (id=!TOKENS(1) /age=!TOKENS(1) /delta=!TOKENS(1)
  /fup=!TOKENS(1)  /sex=!TOKENS(1)  /first=!TOKENS(1))
GET FILE=!pathd + "remaining pop.sav".
SELECT IF (event=0) AND
  RANGE(age,!age - !delta, !age + !delta) AND
  (fup>!fup) AND
  (sex=!sex).
COMPUTE draw=UNIFORM(1).
SORT CASES BY draw.
/* keep only 3 controls (Change number as required) */
N OF CASES 3.
COMPUTE matchid=!id.
ADD FILES FILE=* /DROP=evtmonth evtyear evtday.
SORT CASES BY id.
SAVE OUTFILE=!pathd + "control.sav" /DROP=draw.
* Add controls to list of those found.
!IF (!first !NE 1) !THEN
ADD FILES FILE=*
  /FILE=!pathd + "all control.sav".
!IFEND
SAVE OUTFILE=!pathd + "all control.sav".
* Remove those control from main file.
MATCH FILES FILE=!pathd + "control.sav"
  /IN=control
  /FILE=!pathd + "remaining pop.sav"
  /BY=id.
SELECT IF control=0.
SAVE OUTFILE=!pathd + "remaining pop.sav" /DROP=control.
!ENDDEFINE.

*Change next number or comment the line to obtain different results.
SET SEED=987654321 PRINTBACK=ON.
GET FILE=!pathd + "population.sav".
SORT CASES BY id.
SAVE OUTFILE=!pathd + "remaining pop.sav".
SHOW SEED.

* Write syntax to call macro for each case where event=1.
SELECT IF event=1.
COMPUTE first=($CASENUM=1).
COMPUTE delta=1 /* Change value of delta as required */.
TEMPORARY.
FORMATS first(F1) delta(F3) fup(COMMA8.3).
WRITE OUTFILE=!pathd + "call macro.sps"
  /"!do_one id="id" age="age" delta="delta" fup="fup
  " sex="sex" first="first".".
EXECUTE.
```

```
SET MPRINT=ON.
* Call macro for each case where event=1.
INCLUDE !pathd + "call macro.sps".
* We need matchid to be able to match cases and control.
GET FILE=!pathd + "remaining pop.sav".
COMPUTE matchid=id.
SAVE OUTFILE=!pathd + "remaining pop.sav".
* Add evtday evtmonth and evtyear to control subjects.
GET FILE=!pathd + "all control.sav" /DROP=draw.
SORT CASES BY matchid.
FORMATS matchid(F5).
MATCH FILES FILE=*
  /TABLE=!pathd + "remaining pop.sav"
  /BY=matchid.
* Add control cases to remaining population.
ADD FILES FILE=*
  /FILE=!pathd + "remaining pop.sav".
SORT CASES BY matchid(A) event(D) id(A).
* Show # of control subjects found per id.
TEMPORARY.
SELECT IF NOT MISSING(evtyear).
SUMMARIZE
  /TABLES=fup  BY matchid
  /FORMAT=NOLIST TOTAL
  /TITLE='matchid with N=1 have no control subjects'
  /MISSING=VARIABLE
  /CELLS=COUNT MIN.
```

Figure 6-12

Portion of data file with matched controls

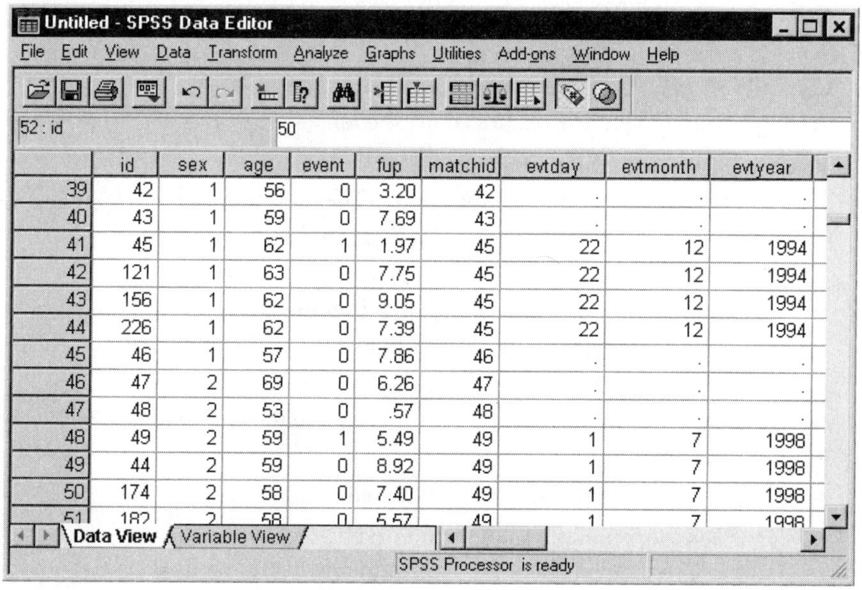

	id	sex	age	event	fup	matchid	evtday	evtmonth	evtyear
39	42	1	56	0	3.20	42	.	.	.
40	43	1	59	0	7.69	43	.	.	.
41	45	1	62	1	1.97	45	22	12	1994
42	121	1	63	0	7.75	45	22	12	1994
43	156	1	62	0	9.05	45	22	12	1994
44	226	1	62	0	7.39	45	22	12	1994
45	46	1	57	0	7.86	46	.	.	.
46	47	2	69	0	6.26	47	.	.	.
47	48	2	53	0	.57	48	.	.	.
48	49	2	59	1	5.49	49	1	7	1998
49	44	2	59	0	8.92	49	1	7	1998
50	174	2	58	0	7.40	49	1	7	1998
51	182	2	58	0	5.57	49	1	7	1998

Figure 6-13
Number of control subjects found per ID

matchid with N=1 have no control subjects

fup

matchid	N	Minimum
45	4	1.97
49	4	5.49
68	4	7.58
126	4	5.70
169	1	10.13
177	1	10.00
202	4	4.46
231	4	2.82
283	4	3.68
Total	30	1.97

Comments on the INPUT PROGRAM

- Since the *ID* parameter of the LOOP goes from 1 to 300, and since the END CASE command is immediately before the END LOOP command, this creates a file with 300 cases.
- We assume that *sex* should be 1 for males and 2 for females. To generate a file with the same expected number of each gender, we compare a UNIFORM(1) and 0.5; a uniformly distributed random number between 0 and 1 is 50% likely to exceed 0.5. When the comparison is false (0), *sex* equals 1; when it is true (1), *sex* equals 2.
- The variable *age* is uniformly distributed between 50 and 70. We then truncate the value to the lower integer.
- The event of interest occurs (that is, event=1) in about 4% of cases.
- The period for which the case was followed up is a number between 0 and 10.
- DO IF calculates other variables when event=1. In that case, we need a day, month, and year of the event. The variable *fup* is recalculated to be consistent with the date just created.
- To calculate *fup* in years, we assume that the study started on 1/1/1993, so the duration in years from the start of the study to the date of the event is the distance in days divided by 365.25.
- END FILE closes the file. Variables are formatted, and END INPUT PROGRAM completes the structure.
- The frequencies of event are calculated.
- The file is saved in the folder specified by the *!pathd* macro, which is defined at the beginning of the syntax. This technique is useful if the working folder changes from time to time.

Comments on the Macro !do_one

- The purpose of this macro is to randomly select the required number of control subjects that fit the characteristics of a given case.
- The macro requires six arguments: *id, age, sex*, and *fup* of the case as well as *delta* (ages in the range from *age – delta* to *age + delta* are acceptable control subjects; *delta* could be 0) and *first,* which indicates whether this is the first call of *!do_one* or not.
- The macro gets the file *remaining pop.sav*. At any given time, this file includes the cases of the original *population.sav other than* those that have already been selected to be control subjects.
- The SELECT IF command retains only potential control subjects (where event=0) having an *age* in the acceptable range, a *fup* that exceeds that given in the macro call, and the same *sex* as given in the macro call.
- COMPUTE assigns a random number draw. The file is then sorted by draw. Hence, the file is now in a random order.
- N OF CASES keeps the first three cases. (We would change that number if you needed to assign a different number of control subjects to each case where event=1.)
- We have now found three or fewer control subjects. These cases are saved in *control.sav*. Note that it may happen that none of the cases in *remaining pop.sav* satisfies all of the requirements.
- !IF - !IFEND tests whether this is the first time the macro is called. If it is the first time, it is not necessary to add the control subjects we just selected to the list of those already selected. We therefore skip the ADD FILES command. If is not the first time, the newly assigned control subjects are added to the list of cases assigned by previous macro calls.
- The combined file of all control subjects is then saved to *all control.sav*.
- We now need to remove the newly assigned control subjects from the file *remaining pop.sav* (since we do not want to assign them to another case).
- The two files are matched by ID. The MATCH FILES command creates the variable *control,* which equals 1 when a case is in *control.sav* and 0, otherwise.
- SELECT IF keeps only cases of *remaining pop.sav* that are not in *control.sav*. We then save *remaining pop.sav* but without the *control* variable.
- !ENDDEFINE signals the end of the macro definition.

Comments on Remaining Section of Syntax

- The original data file is loaded, sorted, and saved under the another name.
- The next paragraph of the syntax writes a syntax file containing a macro call for each case where event=1.
- SELECT IF keeps only cases for which we need to create a macro call. The variable *first* equals 1 for the first case and 0 for all others.
- We assume that a delta age of 1 is acceptable (for example, a case with age 56 requires control subjects aged 55, 56, or 57). We would change the value of delta as required.
- TEMPORARY is used because we do not want to permanently modify the format of existing variables. We need the modifications made in the next command only for the next WRITE command.
- We format the variables *first* and *delta*. In the case of *delta*, this format is purely cosmetic, whereas it is required for the variable *first*. Since we define first to have no decimals, the WRITE command will write either 0 or 1 for *first*. When the macro tests the condition !IF (!first=1), the result will be *true*. If the format of *first* were F8.2 (the default format), then the macro would test whether 1.00=1, and the result would be *false*. The macro is a string parser; it would compare the string 1 and the string 1.00, which are not the same.
- The change of format is critical for variables with decimals, such as *fup* in this example. Since syntax requires a period as decimal delimiter, for this syntax to work in locales where comma is the decimal delimiter, we need to change the format to one that forces a period. COMMA format uses a period as the decimal delimiter; to avoid any commas appearing in the number, you can specify a number of decimal places two or three less than the width, such as COMMA(12.9).
- WRITE writes one line of syntax for each variable where event=1. The line is a macro call with all required arguments.
- EXECUTE forces the creation of the syntax file.
- SET MPRINT=ON is used to see the result of macro expansions in the log of the output window.
- INCLUDE loads the syntax *call macro.sps*.
- The variable *matchid* is added to *remaining pop.sav*. This is done because this file includes the cases with event=1. Matching this file and *all control.sav* on the basis of *matchid* allows us to add the *evtday*, *evtmonth*, and *eventyear* of the case to the assigned control subjects.

- ADD FILES adds the control subjects to *remaining pop.sav*.
- We then sort the cases in order to have subjects follow their related case. Figure 6-12 shows a portion of a data file with matched controls displayed in the Data Editor. Note that ID 45 has event=1 and that three control subjects were found that have the same sex as ID 45, their ages are within 1 year from age 62, and their *fup* exceeds 1.97. Content of variables *evtday*, *evtmonth*, and *evtyear* were copied from the case to the control subjects.
- SUMMARIZE lists the *matchid* of cases where event=1 and displays the total number of cases with the same *matchid*. A value of 1 means that no control subjects were found for that case. A value of *n* means that *n*–1 controls were found. We see that no control cases were found for IDs 169 and 177. The *fup* value for these two cases is high, making it impossible to find control subjects.

Generating Simulated Data

It is often necessary (or convenient) to generate data files in order to test the variability of results, bootstrap statistics, or work on code development before the actual data file is available. For an example, see "Random Assignment of Control Subjects with Given Characteristics" on p. 207. While a macro is not required in order to generate data, using a macro makes it easy to create repeated and varying data files.

Example

This example generates simulated data for assessment given by each member of a work group to each other member of the group. This INPUT PROGRAM requires three nested loops. The outer loop covers the number of groups, the middle loop covers the raters, and the inner loop covers the ratees. An END CASE is executed only when the rater is not the ratee.

```
* macros_generate_data01.sps.
SET MPRINT OFF.
* simulate ratings assigned by each member of workgroup
  to other members of the group.

DEFINE !simul (nbgrps=!TOKENS(1)
              /nbpers=!TOKENS(1)
              /mxscore=!TOKENS(1))
INPUT PROGRAM.
LOOP group=1 TO !nbgrps.
+LOOP rater=1 TO !nbpers.
+ LOOP ratee=1 TO !nbpers.
+ LEAVE group rater ratee.
* Change next command to fit requirements.
```

```
+ COMPUTE score1=RND(UNIFORM(!mxscore)+.5).
+ DO IF rater<>ratee /* exclude self rating */.
+  END CASE.
+ END IF.
+ END LOOP.
+END LOOP.
END LOOP.
END FILE.
END INPUT PROGRAM.
FORMATS ALL(F4).
!ENDDEFINE.

SET MPRINT=ON PRINTBACK ON.
* Simulate 10 groups of 6 persons where scores are
   between 1 and 7.
!simul nbgrps=10 nbpers=6 mxscore=7.
FREQ VAR=score1.
```

Figure 6-14
Simulated data from the !simul macro

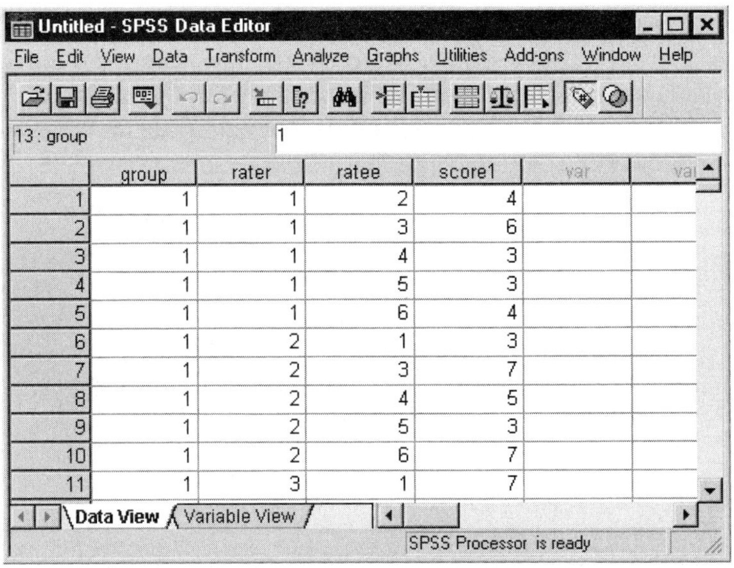

	group	rater	ratee	score1	var	var
1	1	1	2	4		
2	1	1	3	6		
3	1	1	4	3		
4	1	1	5	3		
5	1	1	6	4		
6	1	2	1	3		
7	1	2	3	7		
8	1	2	4	5		
9	1	2	5	3		
10	1	2	6	7		
11	1	3	1	7		

- The macro has three arguments: the number of groups, the number of persons in each group, and the maximum score that may be assigned.
- Three nested loops are required to generate the *group* number, *rater*, and *ratee*.
- LEAVE is used to retain the value of *group* and *rater* when we change *ratee*.

- COMPUTE generates a score for every combination of *rater* and *ratee*. This includes cases for self-rating. The formula generates integers between 1 and *!mxscore*, and each integer has an equal probability of being generated.Of course, any appropriate distribution formula could be used instead of the uniform distribution.
- In an INPUT PROGRAM, a case is created when the END CASE command is encountered. Here, END CASE is executed only when the rater is different from the ratee. When rater and ratee are the same person, the loop continues, no case is written, and the results are replaced by those of the next pair of rater-ratee.
- FORMATS ALL (F4) formats all variables to no decimal.
- The macro is called using the three required arguments.
- We can see that the data does not include cases for self assessments.

Working with Many Files

The examples in this section show how to apply the same macro (or syntax file) to:

- many *.sav* files with consecutive names (for example, *file1*, *file2*, ... *file10*).
- all data files whose names are in *.sav* files.
- all data files in a given folder.

Applying a Macro to Many Known SPSS Data Files

Example

This example shows how to apply a given macro or a given syntax file to many consecutively named data files.

```
* macros_many_files_apply01.sps.
SET MPRINT OFF.
* Apply the same macro (or syntax) to several data files.

DEFINE !runall (fpath=!TOKENS(1) /fname=!TOKENS(1)
  /nb1=!TOKENS(1) /nb2=!TOKENS(1))
!DO !var=!nb1 !TO !nb2.
GET FILE=!QUOTE(!CONCAT(!UNQUOTE(!fpath),"\",!fname,!var,".sav")).

* Call macro to do analysis.
!dowork.
```

```
* Run the master syntax on the file.
INCLUDE "c:\temp\master syntax.sps".

!DOEND.
!ENDDEFINE.

* This macro does the analysis of each file.
DEFINE !dowork()
/* replace next command by whatever is required */
LIST.
!ENDDEFINE.

*Next line starts the process.
SET MPRINT=ON.
!runall fpath="c:\temp" fname=file nb1=1 nb2=10.
```

- The macro requires four arguments: the path for the files, the fixed portion of the filenames, and the first and last numeric portions.
- The macro *!runall* has a loop that is executed 10 times, since the *nb1* and *nb2* arguments are 1 and 10, respectively.
- On the first iteration, the result of the !CONCAT function is *c:\temp\file1.sav*. The !QUOTE function adds quotes on each side of the complete path and filename.
- The macro *!dowork* is then called. Thus, the macro *!runall* calls another macro. We say that *!dowork* is nested inside *!runall.*
- The effect of the INCLUDE is similar to actually pasting the content of the file *master syntax.sps* into the macro. We say *similar* because a file executed using INCLUDE must comply with special syntax rules. If we were pasting the syntax inside the macro, the syntax would not have to comply with those rules. See the section "Running Commands" in "Universals" in the *SPSS Command Syntax Reference* for a description of these syntax rules. Another difference is that a file executed using INCLUDE stops on the first error encountered.
- Note that since *file1.sav* to *file10.sav* are not supplied on the data disk, the above syntax will generate errors, although you can run it to see how the macro expands into syntax.

Combining Many Files with the Same Variables

Example

We have many SPSS data files containing the same variables, and we need to combine them in a single file. The following example assumes that the files have consecutive names.

```
* macros_many_files_combine01.SPS.
SET MPRINT OFF.
* Create some files for illustration purposes.
DATA LIST FREE /var1 var2.
BEGIN DATA
1 2 1 4 5 1 2 4 5 2 2 5 4 1 5 4
END DATA.

DEFINE !save (!POS=!TOKENS(1) /!POS=!TOKENS(1))
!DO !cnt=!1 !TO !2
COMPUTE yr=!cnt.
SAVE OUTFILE=!QUOTE(!CONCAT('c:\temp\file',!cnt,'.sav.')).
!DOEND
!ENDDEFINE.

SET MPRINT ON.
!save 1995 2002.

DEFINE !merge (fname=!TOKENS(1) /nb1=!TOKENS(1) /nb2=!TOKENS(1))

/* fname the constant portion of the file names (file)*/
/* nb1 the first file number (1995)                   */
/* nb2 the last file number (2002)                    */

!DO !var=!nb1 !TO !nb2.
!IF (!var = !nb1) !THEN
GET FILE=!QUOTE(!CONCAT("c:\temp\file",!var,".sav")).
COMPUTE !CONCAT(!fname,!var)=1.
!ELSE
ADD FILES /FILE=*
 /FILE=!QUOTE(!CONCAT("c:\temp\file",!var,".sav"))
 /IN=!CONCAT(!fname,!var).
!IFEND
!DOEND
FORMATS ALL(F8).
RECODE !CONCAT(!fname,!nb1) TO !CONCAT(!fname,!nb2) (SYSMIS=0).
EXECUTE.

!ENDDEFINE.

*call macro.
!merge fname=file nb1=1995 nb2=2002.
```

Figure 6-15
Data Editor displaying portion of final file

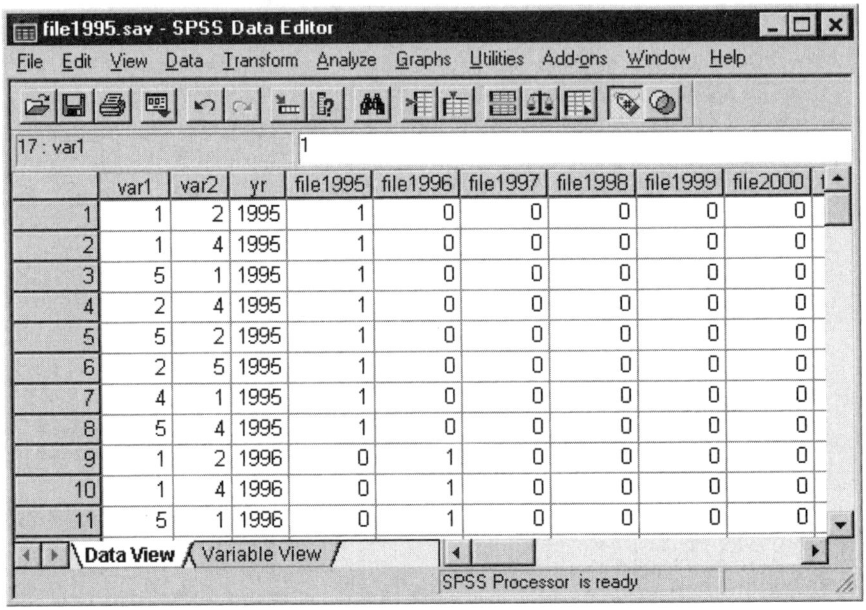

- DATA LIST reads a small data file. For illustration purposes, it is sufficient to save that data in files named *file1995* to *file2002*.
- The macro *!save* is called with the arguments *1995* and *2002*. The macro variable *!cnt* takes each value from 1995 to 2002. For each such value, the variable *yr* is set to *!cnt*. A file is created with the name *file1995* when !cnt=1995, *file1996* when !cnt=1996, and so on.
- The macro *!merge* combines all of the SPSS data files that we have just created.
- The !DO loop combines all of the files. The macro variable *!var* goes from 1995 to 2002. When *!var=!nb1* (for the first file), it executes a GET command and computes an indicator variable named by concatenating *!fname* and *!var*. For each subsequent value of *!var*, it adds the corresponding file to the current file. An indicator variable is created each time a new file is added.
- When all files have been added, all variables are given the format F8.0, and the indicator variables are recoded so that the system-missing values become 0.

Saving Multiple Files Based on a Split Variable.

Example

This example shows how to split an SPSS data file into distinct SPSS data files on the basis of the values of a given categorical variable (called *filevar* in this example). The program:

- Defines a macro that saves cases where *filevar* equals a given value.
- Finds the distinct values.
- Writes a syntax file that calls the macro for each of the distinct values.
- Gets the original data file and uses an INCLUDE command to run the syntax written by the program.

```
* macros_split_file_by_cat_var_numeric.SPS.
SET MPRINT OFF.
* Initial file has category variable cat1 which has
  n different values.
* Objective is to create n different files.
* The syntax works for any different values of cat1.

* This creates a data file for illustration purposes.
* The categorical variable cat1 has up to 10 different values.
NEW FILE.
INPUT PROGRAM.
LOOP id=1 TO 500.
- COMPUTE cat1=TRUNC(UNIFORM(10)).
- END CASE.
END LOOP.
END FILE.
END INPUT PROGRAM.
SAVE OUTFILE='c:\temp\mydata.sav'.

* Start the job.

DEFINE !split (filevar=!TOKENS(1) /value=!TOKENS(1))
TEMPORARY.
SELECT IF (!filevar=!value).
SAVE OUTFILE=!QUOTE(!CONCAT('c:\temp\temp',!value,'.sav.')).
!ENDDEFINE.

*Find all different values of cat1 which exist.
SORT CASES BY cat1.
AGGREGATE OUTFILE=*
 /PRESORTED
 /BREAK=cat1
 /notused = N.
FORMAT cat1(F8.0).
```

```
* Write a syntax file which will call the above macro.
WRITE OUTFILE='c:\temp\call macro.sps'
  /'!split filevar=cat1 value=' cat1 '.'.
EXECUTE.

* Get the original data file and do the macro calls.
GET FILE='c:\temp\mydata.sav'.
SET MPRINT=ON.
INCLUDE 'C:\temp\call macro.sps'.
```

Figure 6-16

Content of call macro.sps:

```
!split filevar=cat1 value=       0.
!split filevar=cat1 value=       1.
!split filevar=cat1 value=       2.
!split filevar=cat1 value=       3.
!split filevar=cat1 value=       4.
!split filevar=cat1 value=       5.
!split filevar=cat1 value=       6.
!split filevar=cat1 value=       7.
!split filevar=cat1 value=       8.
!split filevar=cat1 value=       9.
```

- A file is created to illustrate the solution.
- NEW FILE is always recommended when working with INPUT PROGRAM because it clears any pending operations and/or errors.
- The LOOP structure generates 500 cases consisting of random integers between 0 and 9. There is only one variable.
- The macro has two arguments: *filevar* and *value*. We want to call this macro once for each distinct value of *filevar*. We do not need to know what those values are; we will get them from the data when we generate the macro calls.
- TEMPORARY is used because we do not want the SELECT IF to be permanent.
- SELECT IF then keeps only cases whose value of *cat1* equals the value given in the macro call.
- SAVE OUTFILE saves these cases with the name *temp0.sav* when *value* equals 0, *temp1.sav* when *value* equals 1, and so on.
- AGGREGATE finds the distinct values of *filevar*. Since AGGREGATE expects the definition of a new variable, we define the variable *notused* and set it to the function *N*, the number of cases in each file.
- FORMATS declares *cat1* as having no decimals. This is done because the values of *cat1* will become part of the filename, and removing decimals makes for better filenames.

- For each case in the data file—that is, for each distinct value of *cat1*—WRITE writes a line in a syntax file. The line is a call to the macro *!split*, and it contains the two arguments required by that macro.
- EXECUTE is required to close the syntax file.
- We then get the original data file and include the syntax file, which calls the macro *!split*. The content of that file is shown.

This job assumes a numeric categorical variable for the split. For a string variable, it is necessary to use a combination of !QUOTE and !UNQUOTE functions because string values are expressed in command syntax as quoted strings. For an example, see *macros_split_file_by_cat_var_string.sps* on the accompanying CD.

Finding All Combinations of Three Letters Out of N

Example

This example finds all combinations of three characters out of *n* in which each character can appear only once. The macro call includes the list of all letters or characters to be used. The macro counts the number of characters (there are 12 in the example) and assigns each one to a different variable (variables *v1* to *v12* are used).

Three nested loops are needed to obtain all combinations of characters. The outer loop counter *#cnt1* goes from variable 1 to 10. (It cannot go beyond 10 because, at that point, we need the 11th and 12th characters to complete the trio.) The middle loop counter *#cnt2* goes from #cnt1+1 to #cnt1+11. The inner loop counter *#cnt3* goes from #cnt2+1 to #cnt2+12. The characters corresponding to the three loop counters are concatenated to form the combination.

```
* macros_combinations_three_letters_out_of_N.SPS.

* Get all combinations of 3 letters out of N where N > 3.

SET MPRINT=OFF.
DATA LIST FREE /nbers.
BEGIN DATA
1
END DATA.

DEFINE !Comb3L (!POS=!CMDEND)
!LET !x=!NULL
STRING ans1 TO ans3 answer (A8).
!DO !var !IN (!1)
   !LET !x=!CONCAT(!x,!BLANKS(1))
+  STRING !CONCAT('V',!LENGTH(!x)) (A8).
```

```
+  COMPUTE !CONCAT('V',!LENGTH(!x))=!QUOTE(!var).
!DOEND
!LET !lastv1=!LENGTH(!SUBSTR(!x,3))
!LET !lastv2=!LENGTH(!SUBSTR(!x,2))
!LET !lastv3=!LENGTH(!SUBSTR(!x,1))
VECTOR vec=v1 TO !CONCAT('V',!LENGTH(!x)).
LOOP #cnt1=1 TO !lastv1.
+ COMPUTE ans1=vec(#cnt1).
+ LOOP #cnt2=#cnt1+1 TO !lastv2.
+   COMPUTE ans2=vec(#cnt2).
+   LOOP #cnt3=#cnt2+1 TO !lastv3.
+     COMPUTE ans3=vec(#cnt3).
+     COMPUTE answer=CONCAT(RTRIM(ans1),RTRIM(ans2),RTRIM(ans3)).
+     XSAVE OUTFILE='c:\temp\temp.sav' /KEEP=answer.
+   END LOOP.
+ END LOOP.
END LOOP.
EXECUTE.
GET FILE='c:\temp\temp.sav'.
!ENDDEFINE.

SET MPRINT ON.
!Comb3L A B C D E F U V W X Y Z.
```

Figure 6-17
Portion of syntax generated by macro expansion

```
 877 M>  + STRING V10 (A8).
 878 M>  COMPUTE V10 = 'X'.
 879 M>  + STRING V11 (A8).
 880 M>  COMPUTE V11 = 'Y'.
 881 M>  + STRING V12 (A8).
 882 M>  COMPUTE V12 = 'Z'.
 883 M>  VECTOR vec=v1 TO V12.
 884 M>  LOOP #cnt1=1 TO 10.
 885 M>  COMPUTE ans1=vec(#cnt1).
 886 M>  LOOP #cnt2=#cnt1+1 TO 11.
 887 M>  COMPUTE ans2=vec(#cnt2).
 888 M>  LOOP #cnt3=#cnt2+1 TO 12.
 889 M>  COMPUTE ans3=vec(#cnt3).
 890 M>  COMPUTE
answer=CONCAT(RTRIM(ans1),RTRIM(ans2),RTRIM(ans3)).
 891 M>  XSAVE OUTFILE='c:\temp\temp.sav' /KEEP=answer.
 892 M>  END LOOP.
 893 M>  END LOOP.
 894 M>  END LOOP.
 895 M>  EXECUTE.
 896 M>  GET FILE='c:\temp\temp.sav'
```

Figure 6-18
Combinations of three letters Out of N

- The macro *!Comb3L* requires one argument, which contains an unknown number of letters or characters.
- The macro variable *!x* is used to count the number of characters assigned to the positional argument. It starts as an empty string, and then in the !DO loop, a blank space is added to the string for each character in the positional argument.
- In the !DO loop, we also define a string variable for each character. Variables are named *v1*, *v2*, ... *v12*, since we have 12 characters in the example. The index numeric portion of the variable name is obtained by measuring the length of the macro variable *!x*.
- We want the outer loop to go to the last character minus 2 and the middle loop to go to the last character minus 1. To simplify the coding of the loops, we calculate the values for the end of each loop first. For the outer loop, *!lastv1* is the substring of *!x* starting with the third character, and so on, for *!lastv2* and *!lastv3*.

- COMPUTE then assigns the current character to the corresponding variable. The vector *vec* corresponds to variables *v1* to *v12*.
- The three LOOP commands find all possible combinations. The index for the middle loop starts with the current value of the index for the outer loop plus 1, and the index for the inner loop starts with the current value of the index for the middle loop plus 1. The extract of the log produced by the macro shows clearly what is going on.
- The Data Editor shows a portion of the resulting data file.

Creating Variables Containing Bounds of the CI for the Mean

It is often useful to create statistics across all cases in a file (or for each group within a file) and save those statistics back as variables so that individual cases can be compared to the statistic for the group. This is frequently done using AGGREGATE to write an SPSS data file containing the desired statistic and MATCH FILES with a table lookup to add the calculated values back into the original file. For statistics not available in AGGREGATE, other strategies are available. The following two examples both create two new variables containing the lower and upper bounds of the 95% (or other percentage) confidence interval for the mean of a given variable. The first uses the COMPUTE function to calculate the statistics. The second uses the EXAMINE command and the new (as of SPSS 12.0) Output Management System (OMS) to write an output file that can be matched back into the original data.

Example: Calculate Statistics with AGGREGATE and Computation Language

The strategy in this example is to use AGGREGATE to create for all cases in the file the values needed to compute the confidence intervals. Then compute the CI limits and save the one-case file. Finally, match that new file back into the original data.

```
*macros_new_variables_containing_bounds_of_CI_for_mean.sps.

DEFINE !AddCInt (vname=!TOKENS(1)
                /conf=!TOKENS(1)
                /fname=!TOKENS(1))
GET FILE=!fname.
SELECT IF NOT MISSING(!vname).
/* next command is only for checking purposes */
```

```
EXAMINE
  VARIABLES=!vname
  /COMPARE GROUP /PLOT=NONE
  /STATISTICS DESCRIPTIVES
  /CINTERVAL !conf
  /MISSING LISTWISE
  /NOTOTAL.
COMPUTE nobreak=1.
AGGREGATE OUTFILE=*
  /BREAK=nobreak
  /N=n /sd_var=SD(!vname) /mean_var=MEAN(!vname).
COMPUTE se_mean=sd_var/SQRT(n).
/* Compute lower and upper CI limit. */
COMPUTE lowCI=mean_var - se_mean * IDF.T(1-(100-!conf)/200,n-1).
COMPUTE upCI=mean_var + se_mean * IDF.T(1-(100-!conf)/200,n-1).
VARIABLE LABELS
  lowCI !QUOTE(!CONCAT("Lower ",!conf,"% CI for mean ",!vname)).
VARIABLE LABELS
  upCI !QUOTE(!CONCAT("Upper ",!conf,"% CI for mean ",!vname)).
SAVE OUTFILE='c:\temp\temp.sav' /KEEP=nobreak lowCI upCI.
GET FILE=!fname.
COMPUTE nobreak=1.
MATCH FILES FILE=*
  /TABLE='c:\temp\temp.sav'
  /BY=nobreak
  /DROP=nobreak.
EXECUTE.
!ENDDEFINE.

** Example (95% CI for a large sample).
!addCInt vname=salary conf=95
  fname='c:\examples\data\Employee data.sav'.

** Example (90% CI for a small sample).
GET FILE='c:\examples\data\Employee data.sav'.
N OF CASES 15.
SAVE OUTFILE='c:\temp\eee data.sav'.
!addCInt vname=salbegin conf=90
  fname='c:\temp\eee data.sav'.
```

- The macro requires three arguments: the name of the variable for which the CI must be calculated, the desired confidence level, and the full path and name of the data file.
- We load the data file and keep only cases with non-missing values. The number of valid cases (n) will serve to derive the number of degrees of freedom of the *t* distribution.
- EXAMINE serves only to compute the bounds of the confidence interval to check the result obtained by the macro.

- To calculate the mean, we have to aggregate all cases into a single case. For this, we need a constant as the break variable, and we use *nobreak* for that purpose.
- AGGREGATE replaces the working data file with a single case with three variables.
- We compute the standard error of the mean and then the lower and upper bound of the confidence interval. When conf=95, we need the inverse distribution function of *t* at 0.975. There are n–1 degrees of freedom.
- In saving the file, we obviously keep the two variables containing the upper and lower bounds, but we also need *nobreak* in order to match the file with the original data file.
- We then load the original file and compute a *nobreak* variable.
- MATCH adds the upper and lower bound variable; we drop *nobreak* since it is no longer useful.
- The first macro call generates a 95% confidence interval for the variable *salary*.
- The second macro call generates a 90% confidence interval of *salbegin* based on the first 15 cases of the *Employee data.sav* file.

Example: Retrieve Statistics Using OMS

The strategy in this example is to use OMS to direct the desired statistics created by the EXAMINE procedure to a temporary file and match that file back into the original file, much as in the previous example.

```
*macros_new_variables_containing_bounds_oms.sps.

DEFINE !AddCInt (vname=!TOKENS(1) /conf=!TOKENS(1)
/fname=!TOKENS(1))
GET FILE=!fname.
OMS SELECT TABLES
  /IF SUBTYPES=['Descriptives']
  /DESTINATION FORMAT=SAV OUTFILE='c:\temp\temp.sav'
  /COLUMNS SEQUENCE=[r2].
EXAMINE
  VARIABLES=!vname
  /COMPARE GROUP /PLOT=NONE
  /STATISTICS DESCRIPTIVES
  /CINTERVAL !conf
  /MISSING LISTWISE
  /NOTOTAL.
OMSEND.
STRING Var2 (a10).
COMPUTE Var2="Statistic".
```

```
MATCH FILES FILE=*
  /TABLE='c:\temp\temp.sav'
  /BY Var2
  /DROP Command_ to Mean, @5TrimmedMean to Kurtosis.
EXECUTE.
DELETE VARIABLES Var2.
!ENDDEFINE.

** Example (95% CI for a large sample).
!addCInt   vname=salary conf=95
    fname='c:\examples\data\Employee data.sav'.

** Example (90% CI for a small sample).
GET FILE='c:\examples\data\Employee data.sav'.
N OF CASES 15.
SAVE OUTFILE='c:\temp\eee data.sav'.
!addCInt  vname=salbegin  conf=90
    fname='c:\temp\eee data.sav'.
```

Figure 6-19

Descriptives table from EXAMINE

Descriptives

			Statistic	Std. Error
Current Salary	Mean		$34,419.57	$784.311
	95% Confidence Interval for Mean	Lower Bound	$32,878.40	
		Upper Bound	$35,960.73	
	5% Trimmed Mean		$32,455.19	
	Median		$28,875.00	
	Variance		291578214.45	
	Std. Deviation		$17,075.661	
	Minimum		$15,750	
	Maximum		$135,000	
	Range		$119,250	
	Interquartile Range		$13,163	
	Skewness		2.125	.112
	Kurtosis		5.378	.224

- The arguments for this example are identical to those for the previous example, identifying the file and variable and the confidence level desired.
- The OMS command selects a table identified as "Descriptives," which is the name of the table from EXAMINE containing the statistics of interest. It specifies that the output should go to an SPSS data file. The COLUMNS specification instructs OMS to create variables from the rows identified in the second column of the table. Compare the output from EXAMINE to the OMS command to see how the specifications are derived.

- The OMSEND command cancels the OMS specifications so that subsequent Descriptives tables will be handled normally.
- The generated data file will have a variable with the generic name *Var2* that contains the original row element label (*Statistic*), so we can use that to match cases by creating the same variable with the same value in the active file.
- All that remains is to drop the variables containing the statistics that we do not need. The names of these variables are the same as appear in the rows of the table.
- In creating the data file, OMS automatically created variable labels for *LowerBound* and *UpperBound*. For the upper bound, the variable label is *95% Confidence Interval for Mean Upper Bound*.

Debugging Macros

Errors in macros are most often errors in the syntax resulting from unexpected expansion of the macro specifications. Finding the cause may require some detective work.

Printback of the Expanded Syntax

The most important tool for debugging a macro is to print the expanded command syntax. To display expanded macros in the log, you need to specify that commands and expanded macros should be displayed in the log:

```
SET PRINTBACK=ON MPRINT=ON.
```

- PRINTBACK=ON displays commands in the log.
- MPRINT=ON includes expanded macros in the commands displayed in the log.

Print Arguments

One of the first things to do when a macro does not behave as expected is to add lines to the macro to verify the content of the arguments. In the following example, the COMPUTE command contains all of the arguments in the printback.

Example

```
DEFINE !macro (arga=!TOKENS(1) /argb=!TOKENS(1) /argz=!TOKENS(1))
COMPUTE test=ANY("Any string",!arga,!argb,!argz).
!ENDDEFINE.
!macro arga=jobcat argb=125 argz=educ.
```

Figure 6-20
Error message

```
 208  0 M>  COMPUTE TEST=ANY('Any string', jobcat , 125 , educ )

>Error # 4325 in column 52.  Text: )
>The arguments to the ANY and RANGE functions must be either all
strings (or
>string expressions) or all numeric variables (or numeric
expressions).
>This command not executed.
```

- Often, an error is caused by spelling mistakes in the arguments to the macro call. To ensure that mistakes are caught, when you write the (temporary) command to see the content of the arguments, copy the argument names from the beginning of the macro (that is, from the DEFINE line) and paste them into the COMPUTE test line.
- The log confirms that the arguments have been correctly read by the parser and that the argument names are correctly spelled.
- The error message is caused by the fact that 125 is not a string. We simply ignore this error message since it is caused by our COMPUTE test command, which we delete in the final version of the macro.

Examples of Error Messages

The macros used in the following examples do not do anything useful; their purpose is simply to illustrate some error messages and explain the solutions.

Example

```
DEFINE !save (!POS=!TOKENS(1) !POS=!TOKENS(1))
!DO !cnt=!1 !TO !2
SAVE OUTFILE=!QUOTE(!CONCAT('c:\temp\file',!cnt,'.sav.')).
!DOEND
!ENDDEFINE.
```

Figure 6-21
Error message

```
>Error # 6819 in column 26.  Text: !POS
>The DEFINE command includes an invalid keyword specification.  The
>recognized specifications are !DEFAULT, !NOEXPAND, !TOKENS, !CMDEND,
>!CHAREND, and !ENCLOSE.
>This command not executed.
```

The forward slash (/) is missing before the second !POS in the DEFINE line.

Example

```
DEFINE !merge (fname=!TOKENS(1))
GET FILE=!QUOTE(!CONCAT('C:\temp\'!fname'.sav')).
COMPUTE !fname=1.
!ENDDEFINE.
```

Figure 6-22
Error message

```
>Error # 6834 in column 35.  Text: !FNAME
>In a macro expression, an operand was not preceded by an operator.
>This command not executed.
```

A comma is missing on both sides of *!fname*.

Example

```
DEFINE !test(vara=!TOKENS(1) /varb=!TOKENS(1))
STRING a(A8).
COMPUTE a=!QUOTE(!vara).
COMPUTE z1=1.
COMPUTE b=!varb.
COMPUTE z2=1.
!ENDDEFINE.
!test vara=12345X varb=56.
```

Figure 6-23
Error message

```
 152   0 M>   STRING VARA(A8).
 153   0 M>   COMPUTE A= '12345'.
 154   0 M>   COMPUTE Z1=1.
 155   0 M>   COMPUTE B=.

>Error # 4007 in column 256.  Text: (End of Command)
>The expression is incomplete.  Check for missing operands, invalid
>operators, unmatched parentheses or excessive string length.
>This command not executed.
```

```
 156   0 M>   COMPUTE Z2=1
 157   0 M>     X varb=56.

>Error # 4381 in column 2.  Text: X
>The expression ends unexpectedly.
>This command not executed.
```

- When the macro parser expands a macro call, it first reads all of the arguments supplied to the macro. In this case, there are potentially two arguments. The parser finds 'vara' but when reading the value '12345X', it splits that value into two tokens. This is easy to see, since the log contains the line COMPUTE A='12345'. See "Tokens" on p. 179.
- The macro parser assigns '12345' to !vara and continues its search for 'varb' but finds 'X'. The parser concludes that 'varb' has not been supplied, and it assigns a null string to !varb. This is confirmed by the line COMPUTE B=.
- Remember that the macro facility replaces the macro call with text. In this case, the macro call is only the section !test vara=12345; the remaining portion of the line X varb=56 is not part of the macro call. Thus, when the macro has finished replacing !test vara=12345 with the macro expansion, the second expression X varb=56 still exists and remains as is. This explains why we find it at the end of the macro.
- Note that the above macro works as expected when the argument *vara* is enclosed in single quotes in the macro call !test vara='12345X' varb=56.

Example

```
DEFINE !rwo (nstudy=!TOKENS(1) /vname=!TOKENS(1))
!DO !study= 1 !TO !nstudy
GET FILE='c:\temp\data.sav'.
SELECT IF i<>!study.
AGGREGATE OUTFILE=!QUOTE(!CONCAT('c:\temp\i',!study,'.sav')
  /PRESORTED
  /BREAK=nobreak
  /vbar=MEAN(!vname).
EXECUTE.
!DOEND
!ENDDEFINE.
```

Figure 6-24
Error message

```
>Error # 6838 in column 3.  Text: /
>A macro expression includes an operator which is syntactically correct but
>which has not yet been implemented in the macro language.  This is probably
>an instance of an attempt to use an arithmetic operator such as addition or
>subtraction.
>This command not executed.
```

A closing parenthesis is missing at the end of the first line of the AGGREGATE command.

Other Macro Examples Included with SPSS

run syntax depending on variable type.sps. This example allows you to run different command syntax depending on whether a given variable is numeric, string, or not defined in the active data file.

run syntax only when there are cases.sps. This macro allows you to run a given syntax file only when there is at least one case that meets given criteria. This is useful to avoid runtime errors.

make variable names on the fly.sps. This is useful when the length of vectors is not constant from one run to the next. For example, the number of repeated measures or months may vary from one job to the next. The result of !makevar a 7 is *a7*. The result of !makevar var 25 is *var25*.

macros_example_reorder_vector_names.sps. Suppose that you have variables *a1* to *a50*, *b1* to *b50* and you need to reorder the variables as follows *a1 b1 a2 b2 ... a50 b50*. This macro illustrates how it can be done.

macros_examples_define_various_lists_of_variables.sps. This macro is very general and allows you to obtain a list of all variables, all string variables, or all numeric variables. In each case, you can obtain a list of only those variables between two given variables; and in each case, it is possible to exclude a list of variables.

macros_many_files_combine04.sps. SPSS commands for merging data files, such as MATCH FILES and ADD FILES, are limited to a maximum of 50 files specified on a single command. This macro combines any number of consecutively named SPSS data files (*.sav* files), 50 at a time.

macros_print_histo_or_bar_depending_on_data.sps. If you have numeric variables with just a few different values (say, fewer than 10) and other variables with many different values, it makes sense to generate histograms for the first group and a histogram for the second group. This macro accepts variable names and a breakpoint (10 in this case) and then produces histograms or bar charts, depending on the actual number of distinct values in each variable.

rename_var_of_fileA_to_those_of_fileX.sps. Suppose that you have two data files with the same variables in the same order, but variable names are different. This macro renames variables in *fileA* to the corresponding names in *fileX*.

Chapter

7

Scripting

Introduction

The SPSS scripting facility provides a language similar to Microsoft VBA (Visual Basic for Applications) for programming tasks that cannot readily be done with SPSS command syntax, including macros. It is primarily useful for manipulating output that appears in the Viewer. For example, you can use scripts to apply special data-dependent formatting to a pivot table or to implement a search function in the Viewer. However, scripts can also access the SPSS data dictionary and run SPSS command syntax; so, they can be used to generate command syntax dynamically in cases where the particular variables in a data set are not known in advance.

Scripts can generate actions based on results appearing in the Viewer. They can also be used to control other applications being used with SPSS, and they can manipulate files and directories. For example, you can write a script to create a Microsoft PowerPoint presentation from objects in the SPSS Viewer by using both SPSS and PowerPoint automation methods. Command syntax can invoke a script and pass parameters to it via the SCRIPT command. Autoscripting allows scripts to be invoked automatically when particular kinds of objects are created in the Viewer.

Scripting can create custom dialog boxes in order to interact with the user, and it can open particular SPSS dialog boxes and run the resulting commands when the user clicks OK. This capability can be used to direct a user through a prespecified set of tasks or to build a custom application on top of SPSS.

Unlike SPSS command syntax, which is executed by the SPSS Processor, scripts are executed in the context of the SPSS front end. This means that in distributed mode, scripts see only the client-side file system, whereas command syntax sees the server-side file system, and an SPSSB job cannot execute a script. (The SCRIPT command is ignored in that context.) However, production mode jobs do support scripting, whether in distributed or local mode.

Scripts operate asynchronously from command syntax. Scripts are not available in SPSS for Macintosh.

Scripting uses Microsoft Windows OLE automation and VBA commands, and SPSS includes a VBA IDE. This chapter presumes familiarity with these technologies. See the *SPSS Base User's Guide* or the SPSS scripting and automation Help topics for more information.

You can find useful scripts and tips online at the SPSS Script Exchange (*http://www.spss.com/tech/scptxchg*), and you can make contributions to the exchange as well.

Scripting or OMS?

The SPSS Output Management System (OMS), which was introduced in SPSS 12.0, provides alternative, syntax-driven ways of controlling SPSS output. To determine whether the scripting or the OMS approach is more appropriate for a task, consider the following differences:

- When in distributed mode, OMS runs in the server context and therefore does not require a client; it is always synchronized with the command syntax, whereas scripts run in the client context and run asynchronously.
- OMS commands follow the rules for SPSS syntax, whereas scripts use VBA syntax.
- OMS has no control over the presentation of output (except that it can suppress it), whereas scripts have full control.
- OMS can produce output as XML and SPSS *.sav* files, among other formats, whereas scripts can use the export methods available in the Viewer to produce output in HTML, text, Word, Excel, and various chart formats. The HTML produced by OMS is free of style information, whereas the HTML produced by script exports uses the styles applied in the Viewer. OMS XML can be processed with XSLT to produce the desired presentation. HTML for presentation can be created from OMS HTML with CSS.
- OMS cannot be applied to output created by the IGRAPH or MAPS commands.
- Scripts can interact with the user via dialog boxes and alerts.
- OMS has no access to OLE automation methods for SPSS or other applications.
- SPSS OLE automation methods can also be used by external applications written in languages that support OLE, such as Microsoft Visual Basic and C++.

Tasks for Scripting

The following are examples of tasks that can be automated using scripts:

- Save or close the output documents (other than at the end of a job).
- Open new output documents.
- Switch between the Draft Viewer and regular Viewer windows.
- Modify pivot tables (change column or row labels, make totals bold, add footnotes, change fonts or colors) beyond the formatting available in the general TableLook facility.
- Use a Windows dialog box to get input from the user and run user-selected tasks on a selected data file.
- Export selected objects from the Viewer to other applications, preserving the formatting applied in the Viewer.
- Modify interactive charts (created by the IGRAPH command).
- Automatically run a script or command syntax file every time SPSS starts.
- Locate error messages in the logs of the Viewer window.

Automation Objects

SPSS scripts are written in Sax ActiveX Basic Engine (Sax Basic). Sax Basic works with **objects**. The following are examples of SPSS objects:

- The SPSS application itself
- The data document (contents of the Data Editor window)
- The syntax windows
- The output documents (contents of the Viewer windows)

Objects can contain other objects—for example, an output document might contain objects, such as pivot tables, interactive charts, and text objects, and most of these objects can contain other objects—for example, pivot tables can contain titles, labels, and data cell objects.

To see the tree of objects, open a new script window. From the menus, choose:

File
  New
    Script

Then, close the Use Starter Script dialog box and select Objects from the Help menu in the script window.

Figure 7-1
Tree of automation objects

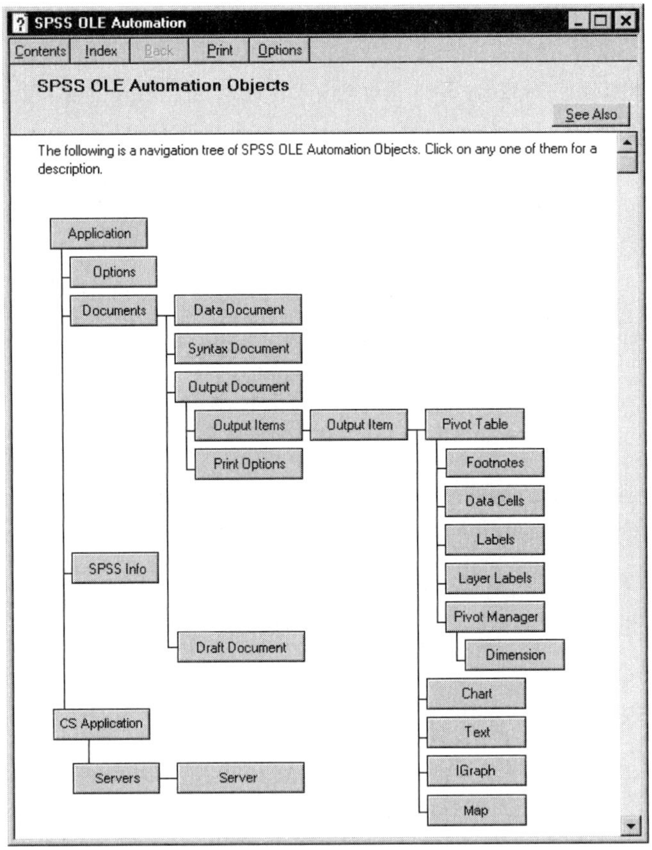

Clicking on any of these objects gives you access to a definition of the object, examples of code using the object, and information about the object's properties and methods.

Generally, properties describe a characteristic, whereas methods perform an action. In practice, this distinction is sometimes difficult to see, but it does not generally cause a problem because both are referred to in the same way.

Properties can be used on either side of an equals sign. For example:

```
objPivotTable.TextColor = vbBlue
```

sets the color to blue.

And:

```
lngColor = objPivotTable.TextColor
```

assigns the color to the variable *lngColor.*

Some properties, however, can only be read.

This chapter is concerned with using the Sax Basic scripting language, but the automation interfaces can be accessed with any language that supports automation; you can control SPSS from another application in the same way that you can use SPSS scripting to control other applications.

Script Window

Scripts are created, edited, and debugged in the script window, which also provides access to the Help topics for the scripting language and the object model. Scripts can be run from the script window or directly from the Utilities menu. See the chapter "SPSS Scripting Facility" in the *SPSS Base User's Guide* for more information.

Tip: When writing or modifying scripts, make the status bar at the bottom of the script window visible in order to see error messages. To do this, select Status Bar from the View menu.

Figure 7-2
Error message displayed in the status bar

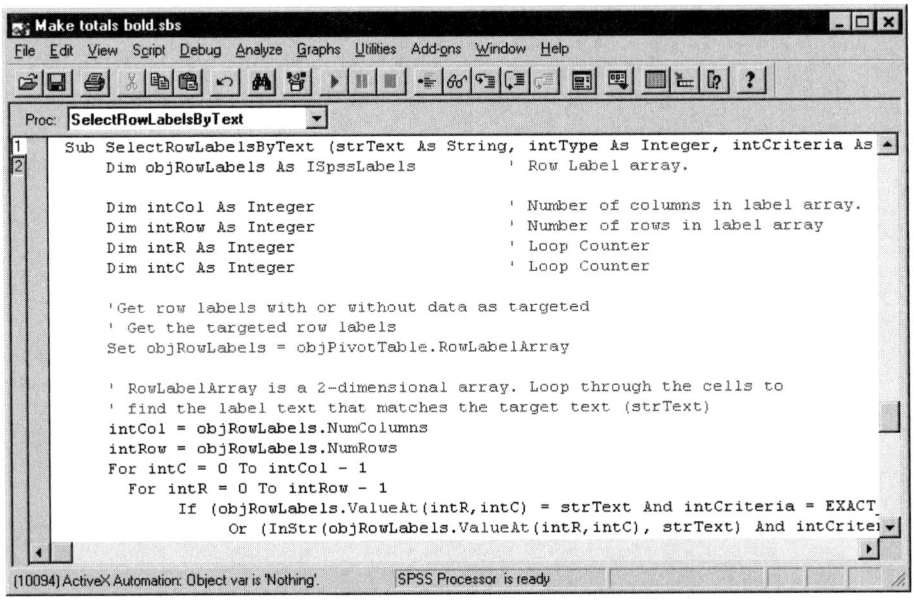

In the script above, the reference to a pivot table object (objPivotTable) causes an error because the script assumes that a pivot table object is already selected in the Viewer window and fails if no pivot table is selected. The line turns red when you run the script, and the error message is shown in the status bar. The message indicates that the object variable (objPivotTable) has the value *nothing*.

Tip: Use Option Explicit in your scripts in order to catch spelling errors in variable names.

Global Scripts

When you open a script, you actually open both that script and the global script file, *global.sbs* by default, in an associated window. The numbers on the left side of the script window show which window is current. The contents of the global script file are in scope for all scripts. You can add code to it that you need to call from more than one script. Besides functions and subroutines, global constants and variables can be added. Variables in the global file, however, do not retain their values after a script terminates.

The name and location of the global file is controlled by the Scripts tab in the Options dialog box (Edit menu, Options).

Installing a new version of SPSS overwrites *global.sps* in the standard location. Save a copy before installing SPSS in the same location, or change the filename.

You can also call a script that is stored in a different file from the one that is currently executing with the Sax Basic MacroRun command. MacroRun does not pass arguments like an ordinary subroutine, but you can pass a command line that the invoked code can access with the command function.

Invoking a Script

Scripts can be invoked in four ways:

- Interactively from the Utilities menu or from a custom toolbar button
- From command syntax using the SCRIPT command
- Implicitly by using autoscripting
- Using MacroRun

You should consider how the script will typically be invoked and what context it requires when designing it.

- You probably do *not* want to include a dialog box in a script that will be run from command syntax, since it may need to complete without user interaction.
- The SCRIPT command can pass parameters to a script, whereas menu invocation cannot.
- A script invoked by SCRIPT runs asynchronously from the subsequent command syntax stream, so its context may be unpredictable; subsequent command syntax should not assume that the script has finished.
- Autoscripts execute automatically when their associated events occur. An event is usually the creation of a particular kind of object in the Viewer, such as using the FREQUENCIES command to obtain a Statistics table. There is also an event associated with starting SPSS. The event provides the context. Reformatting a particular table type beyond what you can do by applying a TableLook is best done with an autoscript.

Control over whether or not an autoscript is executed when its event occurs is handled in the SPSS user interface on the Scripts tab (Edit menu, Options), so users can easily enable or disable the script.

Autoscripts cannot be passed parameters (except for the standard autoscript parameters that indicate its context); however, they can be given information indirectly through SPSS command syntax. See "An Autoscript That Accepts a Parameter from Syntax" on p. 247 for more information.

Debugging a Script

The SPSS script window provides tools for debugging that are very similar to those provided with Microsoft Visual Basic or VBA. The *SPSS Base User's Guide* and the online Help explain how to use these tools. With these tools, you can:

- Set breakpoints.
- Step through code line by line.
- Inspect variable values in an immediate window or by using a watch.
- Use the `debug.print` method to display script output in the immediate window.
- Set the next line to be executed.
- Hover over a variable when a script is paused to show the value as a ToolTip.

You cannot debug an autoscript. An autoscript is always run from the saved autoscript file, which cannot contain breakpoints, and the debugging windows do not display while it is executing. Remember to save your changes before attempting to test an autoscript. You can use a `MsgBox` to display useful information about the script state. You can also create a small autoscript shell that calls a regular script, which can be debugged in the usual way. See the *AutoExperiment.sbs* script on the accompanying CD for an example. It works on the first pivot table in a selection and generates the arguments that an autoscript would get.

Scripts Included with SPSS

When you install SPSS, some scripts are installed in the *Scripts* folder. To see the available scripts, select Run Script from the Utilities menu.

Figure 7-3
Scripts contained in the Scripts folder

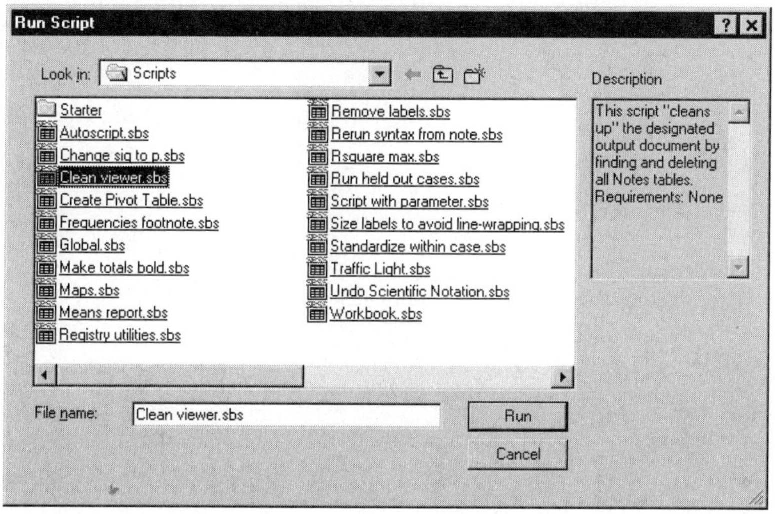

A short description of the currently selected script is displayed in the Description window. You can see that the script *Clean viewer.sbs* finds and deletes all Notes tables from the current designated output window. Clicking the Run button will execute the script.

Some of the scripts expect that an item in the output window has been selected (such as a pivot table or an interactive graph). For example, the script *Make totals bold.sbs* requires that a pivot table be selected in the output window before running the script.

The *Starter* folder contains well-documented scripts that can be modified by a user with no prior experience in SPSS scripting.

Sample Scripts

Add File Date to Filename

Example

This example illustrates the most basic scripting features. It adds the modification date to the filename of all output files in a specified directory. For example, a file named *test.spo* that was last modified on May 12, 2003, at 8:54 would be renamed *test 12-05-2003 8:54.spo*. If the modification date is already in the filename, it is not renamed.

```
'addDateToFileName.SBS

'BEGIN DESCRIPTION
'Add modification date to the names of all spo files in
'a particular directory
'END DESCRIPTION


Sub Main

Dim Path As String, T As String, F As String
Dim first As Boolean

 On Error GoTo date_error

 first = True

 While (Dir(Path, vbDirectory) = "")
  Path = InputBox(IIf(first,"Specify the directory to process", _
        "Specified directory does not exist.  Please respecify"), _
     "Add Modification Date to spo Files", Path)
  If (Path = "") Then
   Exit Sub
  End If
  first = False
 Wend
 F = Dir(Path & "*.spo")
```

```
  While F <> ""
   T=CStr(FileDateTime(Path & F))
   T=Replace (T,"/","-")
   T=Replace(T, ":", ";")
   If (InStr(F, T) = 0) Then  'if date is not already present in name
    Name Path & F As _
     Path & Left(F, Len(F)-4) & " "  & T & ".spo"
   End If
   F = Dir()
  Wend
  Exit Sub
date_error:
  MsgBox Err.Number & ":" & Err.Description & vbCrLf & F
  Resume Next
End Sub
```

- The script starts with structured description comments between BEGIN DESCRIPTION and END DESCRIPTION. These will appear in the Run Script dialog box (Utilities menu, Run Script). They must appear first in the file.
- This example uses a simple input box to get the directory to process and loops until the directory choice is valid or the user cancels the dialog box.
- FileDateTime is a function that returns a date variable containing the date and time of the most recent file modification—for example, 12/05/2003 8:10:12 AM. However, the format may depend on your Windows locale settings. Its formatting behavior is not identical to the Microsoft VBA function of the same name.
- Invalid characters in filenames are replaced.
- The statement Name oldname As newname is used to rename the file unless the modification date is already part of the name.
- The rename operation could fail because, for example, the new name is too long or there is already a file with that name in the directory. The error handler displays the error and then continues with the next file.

Run Simple Statistics on All Variables

This script illustrates dynamically generating and executing command syntax. It examines the list of variables in the active data file and generates either frequency tables or simple descriptive statistics for each one based on the declared measurement level of the variable.

```
'RunSimpleStats.sbs
'BEGIN DESCRIPTION
'Run FREQUENCIES on all categorical variables and DESCRIPTIVES on all scale variables.
'END DESCRIPTION

Option Explicit

Sub Main

Const TITLE="Run Simple Statistics on All Variables"
' get variables
 Dim objDataDoc As ISpssDataDoc
 Dim objDocuments As ISpssDocuments
 Set objDocuments = objSpssApp.Documents

 ' Declare variables to receive the variable information.
 Dim numVars As Long
 Dim vrtVarNames As Variant
 Dim vrtVarLabels As Variant
 Dim vrtVarTypes As Variant
 Dim vrtVarMsmtLevels As Variant
 Dim vrtLabelCounts As Variant
 Dim CatVarlist As String, ScaleVarlist As String

 ' Get the SPSS data file.
 Set objDataDoc = objDocuments.GetDataDoc(0)

 ' Get the number of variables and the variable information.
 numVars = objDataDoc.GetVariableInfo(vrtVarNames, vrtVarLabels, _
      vrtVarTypes, vrtVarMsmtLevels, vrtLabelCounts)
 If (numVars = 0) Then
   MsgBox "A data file must be opened before this script is run", _
         vbOkOnly, TITLE
   Exit Sub
 End If
```

```
' Find all nonscale variables
Dim i As Integer
For i = 0 To numVars-1
  If (vrtVarMsmtLevels(i) <> SpssMsmtLevelScale) Then
    CatVarlist = CatVarlist & " " & vrtVarNames(i)
  Else
    ScaleVarlist = ScaleVarlist & " " & vrtVarNames(i)
  End If
Next
If (Len(CatVarlist) > 0) Then
  objSpssApp.ExecuteCommands "FREQUENCIES " & CatVarlist & ".", _
          False  'run cmd asynchronously
End If
If (Len(ScaleVarlist) > 0) Then
  objSpssApp.ExecuteCommands "DESCRIPTIVES " & ScaleVarlist & ".", _
          False
End If

End Sub
```

- objSPSSApp is automatically provided as the SPSS application.
- The ISPSSDataDoc object is used to get the variable dictionary.
- If there are no variables, the user is alerted and the script stops; otherwise, it iterates through the zero-based arrays returned by the GetVariableInfo method and builds variable lists of categorical and scale variables.
- The ExecuteCommands method of the SPSS application object is used to run the generated syntax commands. Note that each command must end with a period.

This example interfaces with the SPSS Processor through command syntax. It is also possible for a script or another application to open an SPSS dialog box and either run or retrieve the command syntax generated by that dialog box.

The InvokeDialogAndExecuteSyntax and InvokeDialogAndReturnSyntax methods can be used with the Data Editor, syntax, and Viewer objects. The dialog box to execute is specified using its menu path (omitting the keyboard mnemonic indicator, &) separating the menu levels with >. This path is specific to the user interface language of the product, and while syntax is kept compatible in newer versions of SPSS, the user interface structure is not guaranteed to remain compatible across SPSS versions. Changes that would affect these methods include moving a dialog box to a different menu item or even eliminating it altogether. However, such changes are infrequent.

Using a Parameter in the Script Command

This example illustrates how to pass a parameter to a script invoked with the SCRIPT command. It also illustrates using methods of the syntax window object to execute a file containing syntax formatted for a batch INCLUDE using interactive rules. Command syntax in an INCLUDE file has certain formatting restrictions that do not apply interactively, and such command syntax stops at the first error. This script executes an INCLUDE file interactively.

Following is the original command syntax. It runs two command syntax files. If there are any errors, syntax processing stops at that point in the INCLUDE file and resumes with the next INCLUDE.

```
INCLUDE 'c:\temp\file1.sps'.
INCLUDE 'c:\temp\file2.sps'.
```

To make the included files continue after the point of an error, they are run by this SCRIPT command instead. Note that the parameters must be enclosed in parentheses.

```
SCRIPT 'c:\examples\scripts\RunImmediateMode.SBS' ('c:\temp\file1.sps').
SCRIPT 'c:\examples\scripts\RunImmediateMode.SBS' ('c:\temp\file2.sps').
```

```
' RunImmediateMode.sbs
Option Explicit

Sub Main
' Interactively run the syntax file passed as the script parameter.
On Error GoTo exit_sub
Dim objSyntaxDoc As ISpssSyntaxDoc
Set objSyntaxDoc = _
  objSpssApp.OpenSyntaxDoc(objSpssApp.ScriptParameter(0))
objSyntaxDoc.Run
objSyntaxDoc.Close

exit_sub:
Set objSyntaxDoc = Nothing
Exit Sub
End Sub
```

- The script gets the parameter from syntax using the ScriptParameter method and opens the named file in a syntax window. The SCRIPT command allows only a single parameter, which must be quoted. The script could, however, interpret the single string as a list and split it up to get more than one parameter.

- Then the script runs the contents and closes the window. Because it is run from a syntax window, interactive syntax rules apply.
- As a side effect, this script may change the designated syntax window. You can prevent this by first getting the designated window with:
  objSPSSApp.GetDesignatedSyntaxDoc
  and setting the Designated property of that window to True after the Close. If there is an error in the script because no parameter was given or the named file does not exist, an alert is raised by the OpenSyntaxDoc method, and the script then terminates.
- This script is not designed to work synchronously with syntax. If that is needed, see "Synchronizing Scripts and Syntax" on p. 281.

If you need this functionality frequently, you could wrap it in a macro and invoke it as follows:

```
* Define a macro for convenience to run syntax in immediate mode.
DEFINE !INCLUDE (!POS=!TOKENS(1))
SCRIPT 'C:\temp\RunImmediateMode.SBS' (!1).
!ENDDEFINE.


!INCLUDE 'c:\temp\file1.SPS'.
```

An Autoscript That Accepts a Parameter from Syntax

This script illustrates how an autoscript works and how to pass a parameter using procedure syntax, since the parameter passing mechanism of the SCRIPT command is unavailable in this context.

Autoscripts are invoked implicitly by a creation event for a particular object type. They reside in the autoscript file (*autoscript.sbs* by default) and are created by right-clicking on an example of the associated object in the Viewer. They are enabled or disabled on the Scripts tab (Edit menu, Options). The list of autoscripts that appears on the Scripts tab is maintained automatically by SPSS for Windows.

Autoscripts have three standard parameters: the activated object itself, the Viewer document, and the index of the object. While there is no way to change this parameter list, procedure syntax can sometimes be used to the same effect. This script uses the TITLE subcommand of the SUMMARIZE command for this.

```
SUMMARIZE
  /TABLES=educ  BY jobcat
  /FORMAT TOTAL
  /TITLE='/bold/Case Summaries'
  /MISSING=VARIABLE  /CELLS=COUNT .
```

```
'Summarize_Table_Report_Create.sbs
Sub Summarize_Table_Report_Create(objTable As Object, _
    objOutputDoc As Object, _
    lngIndex As Long)

' Autoscript
' Trigger Event: Report Table Creation after running Summarize procedure.
' Effects: Goes through the Row Labels and finds "Total" rows and turns
' "Total" and associated data cells bold
' if the title begins with "/bold/"

 Dim bolSelection As Boolean
 Dim i As Integer
 Dim objitem As ISpssItem

 Set objitem = objOutputDoc.Items.GetItem(lngIndex)

 With objitem
 If (Left(.Label,1) = "/") Then
  i = InStr(2, .Label, "/")
  If (i > 0) Then
   If (Mid(.Label,2, i-2) = "bold") Then
    Call SelectRowLabelsAndData(objTable, cTOTAL, _
            bolSelection)
    If bolSelection = True Then
     objTable.TextStyle = 2 'make text bold
    End If
   End If
   .Label = Mid(.Label, i+1)
   objTable.TitleText = Mid(objTable.TitleText, i+1)
  End If
 End If
 End With
End Sub
```

- The lngIndex parameter is used to get a reference to the Case Summaries table in order to access the associated outline label.
- The label is inspected for initial text enclosed in "/". If found, the body of the script makes the font bold for totals. Otherwise, the text is not made bold.
- The parameter is removed from the label. Since the title text also appears within the pivot table, the pivot table object TitleText property is accessed to remove the parameter from there as well.
- The text "Total" is represented by the constant cTOTAL defined at the top of the autoscript file in order to facilitate translation. The subroutine:
  SelectRowLabelsAndData
  is defined elsewhere in the standard autoscript file.
- When SPSS for Windows is installed, a standard autoscript file is copied into the installation *Scripts* folder. If you have written autoscripts that you want to preserve, save a copy of your old autoscript file before installing a new version of SPSS.
- Another way to pass a parameter is to use a dictionary property, such as a variable label, for a predetermined extra variable: set the label in syntax and retrieve it using the data document object.

Set Data Editor Column Width to Match Data

Example

This script illustrates accessing the data dictionary and manipulating the Data Editor window. Often, when data are imported from other applications, long string variables result. To facilitate browsing the imported data, it is convenient to reduce the Data Editor column width. This can be done with the VARIABLE WIDTH command. This has no effect on the data. This script allows the user to set minimum and maximum values for the width.

```
'SetDataEditorColumnWidthToMatchVariableLength.SBS
'Begin Description
'This script changes the column width of the data editor to match the
'number of bytes in each variable.
'End Description

' Define min and max column width
Const IntMinLength As Integer = 7
Const IntMaxLength As Integer = 15
```

```
Option Explicit

Sub Main()

 Dim objDocuments As ISpssDocuments
 Dim objDataDoc As ISpssDataDoc
 Dim objSpssInfo As ISpssInfo
 Dim varName As String
 Dim varList As String
 Dim intLength As Integer
 Dim varCount As Integer
 Dim i As Integer

 Set objDocuments = objSpssApp.Documents

 'Get the data document
 Set objDataDoc = objDocuments.GetDataDoc(0)
 Set objSpssInfo = objSpssApp.SpssInfo

 'Get the number of variables
 varCount = objSpssInfo.NumVariables

 With objSpssInfo
 For i = 0 To varCount - 1
   varName = .VariableAt(i)
   'Uncomment next line if you only want to change column width of strings
   'If .VarType(i) = SpssDataString Then

   ' Comment next line if you only want to change column width of strings
   If 1 Then
    'Make column width equal to length of this string variable
    '(subject to the min and max specified above)
    intLength = .VarLength(i)
    If IntMaxLength < .VarLength(i) Then intLength = IntMaxLength
    If IntMinLength > .VarLength(i) Then intLength = IntMinLength
    objSpssApp.ExecuteCommands ("VARIABLE WIDTH " & varName & _
      " (" & intLength & ").",True)
   End If
  Next i
 End With

 Set objDataDoc = Nothing
 Set objDocuments = Nothing
End Sub
```

- The column width of each variable will be set to the declared width of the variable (subject to a minimum of 7 characters and a maximum of 15 characters).
- Since Option Explicit is specified, all variables and objects must be defined before being used.
- A With–End With structure is used to reference elements of the SPSSInfo object. This shortens the commands, since you can then write VariableAt(i) instead of having to write objSpssInfo.VariableAt(i); the initial period stands in for the object mentioned in the With line. This form of reference is also more efficient.
- The loop counter, *I*, goes from 0 to the number of variables minus 1, so all variables are being checked. If there are no variables (there is no open data file), the loop will never be executed.
- intLength equals the length of the variable. It is modified, as required in order to be between the minimum and maximum widths specified at the beginning of the script.
- objSpssApp.ExecuteCommands executes the syntax command that sets the column width to the desired number of characters.
- objDataDoc and objDocuments are set to Nothing before exiting the script. This ensures that the memory held by these objects is released.

Set the Length of All String Variables to the Maximum Length of the Data

Example

This script illustrates working with the case data, which is usually a job for syntax. Often, when data are imported from other applications, long string variables result. The script redefines string variables to have a length matching the maximum length found in the data. It illustrates using the actual data in a script and writing a file of syntax that is then executed. Note that this script makes a data pass for each string variable in the file, and it holds the values for a single variable in memory, so it is not intended for large data sets.

The macro *!conver*, described in Chapter 6, is used to actually make the change.

```
' SetDimOfStringVarToMaxDataValue.SBS
'BEGIN DESCRIPTION
' This script changes all string variables to have the minimum width
' required to hold the data.  Trailing blanks are not counted, but leading
' blanks are preserved.
```

```
' Requirements:
' Data must be present in the data editor and
' the macro !conver must have been defined (run) before running this script.
'END DESCRIPTION
Option Explicit

Sub Main
 Dim objDocuments As ISpssDocuments
 Dim objDataDoc As ISpssDataDoc
 Dim objSpssInfo As ISpssInfo
 Dim varName As String
 Dim varList As String
 Dim intLength As Integer, intMaxLen As Integer
 Dim i As Integer
 Dim SPSSTextData As Variant
 Dim varCount As Integer
 Dim lngNbCases As Long  'number of cases
 Dim tempDir As String
 Dim changeKt As Long

 Set objDocuments = objSpssApp.Documents

 Set objDataDoc = objDocuments.GetDataDoc(0)
 Set objSpssInfo = objSpssApp.SpssInfo

 varCount = objSpssInfo.NumVariables
 Debug.Print "varCount =" & varCount
 lngNbCases = objDataDoc.GetNumberOfCases
 If (varCount = 0 Or lngNbCases = 0) Then
  MsgBox "There are no variables in data file or there are no cases!"
   Exit Sub
 End If
 tempDir = getTempDir()
 If (tempDir = "") Then
  MsgBox "No valid temporary directory was found."
  Exit Sub
 End If

  Open tempDir & "\ SetDimOfStringVar.sps" For Output As #1
  Print #1, "* Generated by SetDimOfstringVarToMaxDataValue.SBS on " & Now() & "."

  With objSpssInfo
  For i = 0 To varCount - 1
```

```
    If .VarType(i) = SpssDataString Then
     varName = .VariableAt(i)
     intLength = .VarLength(i)
     SPSSTextData = objDataDoc.GetTextData (varName, varName, _
                  1, lngNbCases )
     'MaxLength() is a function which is defined after this Sub
     intMaxLen = MaxLength(SPSSTextData, lngNbCases, intLength)

     If intLength <>intMaxLen Then
      Debug.Print ("Dim of " & varName & _
       " will be changed from "  & intLength  & " to " & intMaxLen)
       Print #1,"!conver type=ss _
             nformat=A" & intMaxLen & _
              " vnames=" & varName & "."
       changeKt = changeKt + 1
     End If
    End If
   Next i
   End With

  Print #1, "EXECUTE."
  Close #1

  Set objDataDoc = Nothing
  Set objDocuments = Nothing
  If (changeKt > 0) Then
   objSpssApp.ExecuteCommands ("INCLUDE '" & tempDir & "\ SetDimOfStringVar.sps'",False)
  Else
   MsgBox "All string variables already have their minimum widths"
  End If
End Sub

Function MaxLength(SPSSTextData As Variant,_
     lngNbCases As Long, _
     intLength As Integer) As Integer

' SPSSTextData contains the value of the variable of interest for every case in the file
' lngNbCases contains the number of cases in the active data file
' intLength is the currently defined length of the variable

Dim casenb As Integer
Dim intCurrentMax As Integer
 intCurrentMax = 1
```

```
 For casenb=0 To lngNbCases -1
  If (Len(SPSSTextData(0,casenb))> intCurrentMax) Then
        intCurrentMax=Len(SPSSTextData(0,casenb))
  'Debug.Print casenb & " " & intCurrentMax
  If intCurrentMax=intLength Then Exit For
 Next casenb
 MaxLength=intCurrentMax
End Function

Function getTempDir As String
Rem returns temporary directory or an empty string
 getTempDir = Environ("temp")
 If (Dir(getTempDir, vbDirectory) = "") Then
  getTempDir = objSpssApp.CurrentDirectory
  If (Dir(getTempDir, vbReadOnly) <> "") Then  ' make sure writeable
    getTempDir= ""
  End If
 End If
End Function
```

- The script goes over each variable one by one. If it is a string variable, it gets the variable name and its declared length. The list of values is then retrieved and assigned to the variant variable SPSSTextData.
- In the function MaxLength, intCurrentMax is initialized to 1, which is the minimum legal width.
- If the maximum found equals the currently defined dimension of the variable, the data scan stops. Trailing blanks are not counted.
- Back to the main subroutine, if the number returned by the MaxLength function differs from the current dimension of the variable, a line of syntax is written to the file #1.
- Once all variables have been processed, an EXECUTE statement is added to the file and it is closed.
- The syntax is then executed. The command syntax file is not deleted because the script runs asynchronously from the syntax.
- Here, the script creates a command syntax file that is then run using an INCLUDE command. The accompanying CD includes a modified version of the file that executes the code on the fly without creating an intermediate command syntax file.

Modify Page Title in Left Pane of Output Window

Example

This script illustrates working with objects in the Viewer. It is useful for finding items in the left pane of a long output window. The script finds every occurrence of SPSSPageTitle objects contained in the Viewer. For each such object, it reads the content of the corresponding object in the right pane and replaces the label Page Title with the content of the right pane. To make the outline titles more prominent, start the title text with a special string, such as ***, or modify the script to do that automatically.

```
'ReplaceLeftPanePageTitle.SBS
'BEGIN DESCRIPTION
'Replace "Page Title" in the Output left pane by a portion of the content of the title.
' This is useful to place quick references in the left pane to locate given areas
' of the output.  It has no effect if no page titles have been created or if there is
' not a designated regular Viewer window.
' Page titles are different from the object titles that also appear in the outline.
' They are created by the TITLE command or, in the Viewer, by Insert/Page Title
' Requirement: the Output Document must be open.
' It is convenient to call this script from syntax using the command
'   SCRIPT "\path\script name.SBS"
'END DESCRIPTION

Option Explicit

Sub Main()
'Each PageTitle in the left pane is replaced by the content of right pane
' Acts on currently designated output window
Const MAXLEN=30    ' truncation point for text
 Dim objOutputDoc As ISpssOutputDoc
 Dim objOutputItems As ISpssItems  'the collection of items
 Dim objOutputItem As ISpssItem    'a specific item
 Dim cnt As Integer         'loop counter

 On Error Resume Next

 'Get designated output document and items collection
 Set objOutputDoc = objSpssApp.GetDesignatedOutputDoc
 Set objOutputItems = objOutputDoc.Items
 If (Err.Number <> 0) Then  'no output doc or draft
  Exit Sub
 End If
```

```
For cnt = 0 To objOutputItems.Count - 1
  Set objOutputItem = objOutputItems.GetItem(cnt)
  With objOutputItem
    If (.SPSSType = SPSSPageTitle) Then
'Get right pane content and set outline text
      .Label = Left(.ActivateText.Text,MAXLEN)
      If (Len(.Label) = MAXLEN) Then
       .Label = .Label & "..."
      End If
      .Deactivate
    End If
  End With
 Next cnt

 Set objOutputDoc = Nothing
 Set objOutputItems = Nothing
 Set objOutputItem = Nothing

End Sub
```

Figure 7-4
Output before and after running script

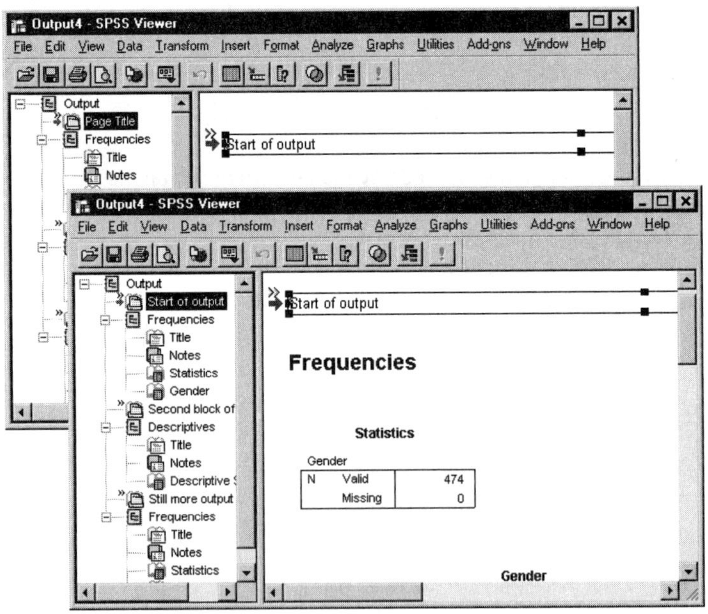

- The first three Dim statements are required each time you need to work with output items.
- On Error Resume Next is used to allow explicit error handling in the code. If there is no designated output window or if it is the Draft Viewer rather than the regular Viewer, accessing its items will fail and the script will silently stop.
- The line starting with Set objOutputDoc assigns the currently designated output window to the variable *objOutputDoc*.
- The next line assigns all items in *objOutputDoc* to the variable *objOutputItems*.
- The For–Next loop checks every item of *objOutputItems* to see whether it is of the type SPSSPageTitle. The counter *cnt* starts at 0 and ends at the number of items minus 1.
- If the SPSSType of an item is SPSSPageTitle, the content of its right pane window is assigned to the Label property. To get the item's text, it must first be activated (this is equivalent to double-clicking on the object to bring it into edit mode). The text is truncated at 30 bytes (declared in a constant). If it is used with an output language in which characters can be more than one byte, such as Japanese, there is a risk that the truncation will leave a partial character at the end. For such situations, it is best to eliminate the truncation feature or to rewrite it to handle character boundaries correctly.

Print Syntax with Path, Date, and Page Numbers

This script illustrates working with Viewer objects and a cooperating application. Using the Print menu or the Print button in the syntax window toolbar prints the currently designated syntax window without any file path, date stamp, or page numbers. *PrintSyntaxFile.sbs* uses Microsoft Word automation methods to read the command syntax file and print it with the these attributes. You can replace the standard Print button or add a new button attached to this script using the Customize dialog box (View menu, Toolbars).

The script includes some code that was initially generated by the Word macro recorder. Some of these commands include Word VBA constants, such as wdFieldDate and wdfieldPage. When the code is subsequently pasted into an SPSS script, these constants need to be defined and set equal to the value they have in Word.

```
' PrintSyntaxFile.sbs
'BEGIN DESCRIPTION
' Save, then print the currently designated Syntax window.
' The file name, path ,date, timestamp and page numbers are printed
' If the file has never been saved, the user is prompted for the file name and path
' It has been tested with Word 2000 (English version)
'END DESCRIPTION

Sub Main
' This saves then prints the currently Designated Syntax file along
' with the file name, path ,date, time and page numbers.

' Assign this script to a custom button in your Syntax window toolbar

 Dim objSyntaxDoc As ISpssSyntaxDoc
 Dim strDocPath As String

 On Error Resume Next
 Set objSyntaxDoc = objSpssApp.GetDesignatedSyntaxDoc
 If Err Then 'There is no opened syntax file
  strDocPath = GetFilePath (,"sps",,"Select the syntax file to be printed", 0)
  If strDocPath = "" Then
   Exit Sub  'User cancelled Dialog box
  End If
  Err.Clear
  Call PrintSyntax(strDocPath)
  Exit Sub
 End If

 On Error GoTo Error_PrintSyntaxDoc

 strDocPath = objSyntaxDoc.GetDocumentPath

 Dim GotOK As Boolean
 If (strDocPath = "") Then   'Syntax has never been saved, ask for path
  strDocPath = GetFilePath (,"sps",,"Select folder and enter name for the syntax file", 3)
  If (strDocPath = "") Then
   Exit Sub  'User Cancelled the dialog box
  End If
  GotOK = True
 Else
  GotOK = MsgBox ("Save designated syntax to " & strDocPath & vbCr _
        & "and print it?",vbYesNo) = vbYes
```

```
 End If
  ' Save the current version of the syntax file
 If (GotOK) Then
  objSyntaxDoc.SaveAs (strDocPath)
  Call PrintSyntax(strDocPath)
 End If
 Exit Sub

Error_PrintSyntaxDoc:
 MsgBox Err & ": " & Err.Description      'Alert user
 Exit Sub
End Sub


' Define some word constants
Const wdAlignPageNumberRight = 0
Const wdOpenFormatAuto = 0
Const wdSeekMainDocument = 0
Const wdSeekCurrentPageHeader = 9
Const wdSeekCurrentPageFooter = 10
Const wdFieldDate = 31
Const wdfieldPage = 33
Const wdFieldTime = 32
Const wdPrintView = 3
Const wdFieldNumPages = 26
Const wdAlignParagraphCenter  = 1
Const vbTab =Chr(9)
Const wdDoNotSaveChanges =0

Sub PrintSyntax(strDocPath As String)
Dim WordApp As Object
On Error GoTo Error_PrintSyntax

  'launch Microsoft Word
  Set WordApp=CreateObject("Word.Application")
  With WordApp
   ' Load syntax file in word
  .Documents.Open FileName:=strDocPath, _
     ConfirmConversions:=False, ReadOnly:=False, AddToRecentFiles:=False, _
     PasswordDocument:="", PasswordTemplate:="", Revert:=False, _
     WritePasswordDocument:="", WritePasswordTemplate:="", Format:= wdOpenFormatAuto
```

```
  .ActiveWindow.View.Type = wdPrintView
   .ActiveWindow.ActivePane.View.SeekView = wdSeekCurrentPageHeader
  ' Add path and file name to header
  With .selection
    .TypeText Text:= vbTab & strDocPath
  End With
   .ActiveWindow.ActivePane.View.SeekView = wdSeekCurrentPageFooter

  ' Add date, time and page number to footer
  With .selection
    .Fields.Add Range:=.Range, Type:=wdFieldDate
    .TypeText Text:=" "
    .Fields.Add Range:=.Range, Type:=wdFieldTime
    .TypeText Text:=" " & vbTab
    .Fields.Add Range:=.Range, Type:=wdfieldPage
    .TypeText Text:=" of "
    .Fields.Add Range:=.Range, Type:=wdFieldNumPages
  End With

   .ActiveWindow.ActivePane.View.SeekView = wdSeekMainDocument
   .ActiveDocument.PrintOut Background:= False
  ' Close document without saving changes
  .ActiveDocument.Close SaveChanges:=False
 End With

  WordApp.Quit SaveChanges:=wdDoNotSaveChanges

  Set WordApp = Nothing
  Exit Sub

Error_PrintSyntax:
 MsgBox Err.Number & ": " & Err.Description
 Exit Sub
End Sub
```

Comments on Sub Main

- If an error occurs, control simply continues with the next line.
- The GetDesignatedSyntaxDoc method of the objSpssApp object is used to retrieve the designated syntax.

- When there is no open command syntax file, an error occurs and the next If–End If block is executed. A dialog box gives the user an opportunity to browse to and select the required command syntax file. An empty path means that the user canceled the dialog box, in which case the script terminates. Otherwise, the error flag is cleared and the PrintSyntax subroutine is called.
- Otherwise, it uses the GetDocumentPath method to obtain the path of the designated syntax file.
- That method returns an empty string if the file has never been saved. In that case, the user is asked to select a folder and enter the name to be used to save the currently designated syntax file. If that variable is empty, it means that the user canceled the dialog box and the script terminates.
- The script displays the full path and filename of the designated syntax window and asks for confirmation that this is the file that is to be printed if the user has not already been asked.
- The file is then saved. However, if an error occurs, the script terminates after informing the user.

Comments on Sub PrintSyntax

- The subroutine requires a string argument containing the full path and name of the command syntax file.
- If an error occurs, the subroutine terminates after alerting the user. A general error handler is used here because there could be unanticipated problems when controlling another application.
- The Word script was initially recorded using the Word macro recorder and then pasted into the Sax Basic script window. Constants such as wdFieldDate are used by Word. These constants are predefined in Word but do not exist in the Sax Basic environment. It is therefore necessary to define these constants (as done above) immediately before the Sub PrintSyntax. Alternatively, object library references can be added to the Sax Basic standard list, although they do not display in the user interface. See the topic "Reference" in the scripting language Help for instructions on how to do this.
- The main modification that is required to run native Word code inside Sax Basic is that every Word command must be prefaced by the name of the Word object (WordApp in our example). The easiest way to do this is to enclose the whole word syntax within a With–End With structure and to add a period (.) at the beginning of the Word commands.

See your Word documentation for explanations of the Word commands.

Create PowerPoint Presentation

This script illustrates working with chart and table objects in the Viewer and interacting with another application. It also illustrates how to write a script in a style that allows for easy translation of its user interface into other languages.

```
' CreatePowerPointPresentation.sbs
'BEGIN DESCRIPTION
'Create a PowerPoint presentation from the tables, charts, interactive graphs,
'and maps visible in the designated Viewer window.  The script requires that
'PowerPoint is installed.  It does not work with the Draft Viewer.
'END DESCRIPTION

Rem Create PowerPoint slides from Designated Output Window
Rem Copyright (c) SPSS Inc., 2003.  All rights reserved.

Rem Translatable strings
Const CREATEPP = "Create PowerPoint Presentation"
Const DLGINST = "Select the Viewer object types to copy to a new PowerPoint Presentation." _
& "  All visible objects of those types will be included."
Const DLGTBL ="&Pivot Tables"
Const DLGCHT = "&Charts"
Const DLGIG = "&Interactive Graphs"
Const DLGMAP = "&Maps"
Const DLGINCLUDETITLES = "I&nclude title on slide"
Const MSGWKDIR = "Working directory is read only.  Charts will not be exported"
Const MSGRESULT = "Number of slides created: "
Const MSGNOPPT = "Cannot start PowerPoint.  No slides will be created."
Const MSGNOVIEWER = "There is no designated Viewer window, or there are no objects." _
& "  No slides will be created."

Dim objOutput As ISpssOutputDoc
Dim tempDir As String
Dim tables As Boolean, charts As Boolean, igraphs As Boolean, maps As Boolean
Dim titles As Boolean
Dim continue As Boolean

Sub Main
  On Error Resume Next

  If (Not getTempDir) Then  ' find a place for temp files
    Exit Sub
```

```
  End If

  If (Not setAgenda) Then    ' get user requests
   Exit Sub
  End If

  CreatePptSlides     ' make the presentation

End Sub

Function setAgenda As Boolean
Rem Determine what object types to export to PowerPoint

  Begin Dialog UserDialog 330,224,CREATEPP,.dlgControls ' %GRID:10,7,1,1
   GroupBox 10,56,310,105,"Contents",.GroupBox1
   Text 20,7,290,49,DLGINST,.Text1
   OKButton 70,196,80,21
   CancelButton 180,196,80,21
   CheckBox 20,77,290,14,DLGTBL,.Tables
   CheckBox 20,98,290,14,DLGCHT,.Charts
   CheckBox 20,119,290,14,DLGIG,.Igraphs
   CheckBox 20,140,290,14,DLGMAP,.Maps
   CheckBox 20,168,290,14,DLGINCLUDETITLES,.Titles
  End Dialog

  Dim Dlg As UserDialog
  Dialog Dlg
  setAgenda = continue
End Function

Private Function dlgControls(DlgItem$, Action%, SuppValue&) As Boolean
 Select Case Action%
 Case 1 ' Dialog box initialization
  DlgValue "Tables", True
  DlgValue "Charts", True
  DlgValue "IGraphs", True
  DlgValue "Maps", True
  DlgValue "Titles", True
 Case 2 ' Value changing or button pressed
  Select Case DlgItem
   Case "OK"
    continue = True
    tables = DlgValue("Tables")
```

```
      charts = DlgValue("Charts")
      igraphs = DlgValue("IGraphs")
      maps = DlgValue("Maps")
      titles = DlgValue("Titles")
     Case "Cancel"
      continue = False
     Case Else
      DlgEnable "OK", DlgValue("Tables") Or DlgValue("Charts") _
        Or DlgValue("igraphs") Or DlgValue("maps")
    End Select
  End Select
End Function

Function getTempDir As Boolean
Rem returns true if successful
  getTempDir = True
  tempDir = Environ("temp")
  If (Dir(tempDir, vbDirectory) = "") Then
   tempDir = objSpssApp.CurrentDirectory
   If (Dir(tempDir, vbReadOnly) <> "") Then  ' make sure writeable
    If (MsgBox(MSGWKDIR, vbOkCancel,CREATEPP) + vbCancel) Then
     getTempDir= False
    End If
   End If
  End If
End Function

Sub CreatePptSlides
Rem make Ppt slides containing all visible objects of the selected types

Dim objPpt As Object
Dim objPresent As Object
Dim objItems As ISpssItems
Dim objItem As ISpssItem
Dim objSPSSChart As ISpssChart
Dim objSPSSIGraph As ISpssIGraph
Dim objMap As Object
Dim item, slide, vertOffset, dataAreaVert, horizOffset, dataAreaHoriz As Long
Dim scaleFactorV As Double, scaleFactorH As Double, scaleFactor As Double
Dim lastShape As Integer, toplabel As String

Rem names for temp graphics files
```

```
Const CHARTFILE = "\g_name~~.bmp"
Const IGFILE = "\ig_name~~.bmp"

 On Error Resume Next

 Set objPpt = CreateObject("Powerpoint.Application")
 If (objPpt Is Nothing) Then
  MsgBox MSGNOPPT, vbOK, CREATEPP
  GoTo Exit_createppt
 End If
 objPpt.Visible = True    ' otherwise Paste does not work
  Set objPresent = objPpt.Presentations.Add

 slide = 0

  Set objOutput = objSpssApp.GetDesignatedOutputDoc
  If (objOutput Is Nothing) Then
   MsgBox MSGNOVIEWER, vbOkOnly, CREATEPP
  GoTo Exit_createppt
 End If

  Set objItems = objOutput.Items
  objOutput.ClearSelection  ' tables and maps use clipboard, so must clear selection.

  For item = 0 To objItems.Count - 1
   Set objItem = objItems.GetItem(item)
   If (objItem Is Nothing) Then
   MsgBox MSGNOVIEWER, vbOkOnly, CREATEPP
  GoTo Exit_createppt
 End If

  If (objItem.Level = 1) Then
   toplabel = objItem.Label
  End If
  If ((objItem.SPSSType = SPSSPivot And tables) _
     Or (objItem.SPSSType = SPSSChart And charts) _
     Or (objItem.SPSSType = SPSSIGraph And igraphs) _
     Or (objItem.SPSSType = SPSSIMap And maps)) And objItem.Visible Then
   slide = slide + 1
    objPresent.Slides.Add slide,12   ' new slide
    objPpt.ActiveWindow.View.GotoSlide slide
```

```
    With objPresent.slides(slide)
     objPresent.slides(slide).layout = 11 'ppLayouttitleonly
      If Not .shapes.HasTitle Then
         .shapes.AddTitle.TextFrame.TextRange _
         .shapes.Text = IIf(titles, toplabel & ": " & objItem.Label, "")
      Else
         .Shapes.Title.TextFrame.TextRange.Text = _
               IIf(titles,toplabel & ": " & objItem.Label, "")
      End If
     vertOffset = .shapes.Title.Top+.shapes.Title.Height + 6
     dataAreaVert = .shapes.application.Height - vertOffset
     dataAreaHoriz =  .shapes.application.Width
    End With
    objItem.Deactivate
    objItem.Selected = True

Rem make object fit vertically and horizontally in data area - do not enlarge

   scaleFactorV = dataAreaVert/objItem.Height
   scaleFactorH = dataAreaHoriz/objItem.Width
   scaleFactor = IIf(scaleFactorV > scaleFactorH, scaleFactorH, scaleFactorV)
   If (scaleFactor > 1) Then
     scaleFactor = 1
   End If
   horizOffset = (dataAreaHoriz - objItem.Width*scaleFactor)/2  ' center horizontally
   If (horizOffset <0) Then horizOffset = 0

Rem copy current item to Ppt slide

   If ((objItem.SPSSType = SPSSChart And charts) _
     Or (objItem.SPSSType = SPSSIGraph And igraphs)) Then
     If (objItem.SPSSType = SPSSChart) Then    ' VE Chart
      Set objSPSSChart = objItem.ActivateChart
      objSPSSChart.ExportChart (tempDir & CHARTFILE, "Windows Bitmap")
      objPresent.slides(slide).shapes.addpicture _
      tempDir & CHARTFILE, False, True, horizOffset,vertOffset, _
                    objItem.Width*scaleFactor, objItem.Height*scaleFactor
      objItem.Deactivate
     Else
      Set objSPSSIGraph = objItem.GetIGraphOleObject  'IGraph
      objSPSSIGraph.ExportChartPercent tempDir & IGFILE, "Windows Bitmap", _
      scaleFactor*100, 0, 1
      objPresent.slides(slide).shapes.addpicture _
```

```
      tempDir & IGFILE, False, True, horizOffset,vertOffset, _
      objItem.Width*scaleFactor, objItem.Height*scaleFactor
     End If
    ElseIf (objItem.SPSSType = SPSSPivot And tables) Then
      Clipboard ""       ' table
       objOutput.Copy
       objPpt.ActiveWindow.View.Paste
       lastShape = objPresent.slides(slide).shapes.Count
' 'adjust below title
     objPresent.slides(slide).shapes(lastShape).Top = vertOffset
      ElseIf (objItem.SPSSType = SPSSIMap And maps) Then
       Clipboard ""
       Set objMap = objItem.Activate
       'miPaperUnitConstants: miPaperUnitPoint=11
     objMap.paperunit = 11
       objMap.exportmap "CLIPBOARD", 1    , _
        CDbl(objItem.Width*scaleFactor), CDbl(objItem.Height*scaleFactor)  'miFormatBMP
     objItem.Deactivate
     Set objMap = Nothing
     objPpt.activewindow.view.Paste
     lastShape = objPresent.slides(slide).shapes.Count
     objPresent.slides(slide).shapes(lastShape).Top = vertOffset
      End If
      objItem.Selected = False
     End If
    Next item

objPpt.ActiveWindow.View.GotoSlide 1

Kill tempDir & CHARTFILE  ' clean up
Kill tempDir & IGFILE

MsgBox MSGRESULT & slide, vbOK ,CREATEPP

exit_createppt:
Set objPresent = Nothing
Set objPpt = Nothing

End Sub
```

- The script first elicits from the user the types of objects that should be exported to the Microsoft PowerPoint presentation; then it creates one slide for each appropriate object, optionally including the title from the Viewer on the slide. Charts are resized by the script to fit the slide.
- All of the text for the user interface is extracted from the body of the code and placed at the top in Consts. If the script user interface needs to be translated into another language, this makes it easier. The dialog box control fields are generously oversized for English, but since text generally expands significantly in translation, the dialog box layout may still need to be adjusted. Similarly, for a script intended to work with different SPSS output languages, you may want to extract text referring to the output or SPSS user interface.
- Automatic error notifications are suppressed in this script, but certain critical error checks are made explicitly in the code.
- The function dlgControls handles the dialog box operation. First, it initializes the dialog box; then, it handles events that occur; and, finally, it records whether to proceed or not. On each action event in the dialog box, the handler resets the enabled status of the OK button appropriately.
- The script needs to write temporary files. The function getTempDir locates a temporary directory based on a Windows environment variable or falls back to the current directory, which must then be writeable.
- The subroutine CreatePptSlides does most of the work. First, it launches a new PowerPoint session; then, it iterates through the objects in the Viewer and creates a slide for each appropriate one. Then it resizes the object if necessary and either copies it to PowerPoint using the clipboard or, for graphics, exports the object in the best format for display in PowerPoint. This step cannot use the clipboard because Copy places several graphical object formats on the clipboard and PowerPoint does not have a Paste Special automation method to select the format needed. The PowerPoint Paste method happens *not* to select the best format for SPSS charts.
- Finally, the script reports the result to the user and cleans up temporary files and object variables.

Utilities

This section presents scripts that are useful when developing code or running SPSS command syntax.

Empty Designated Output Window

This script empties the designated output window and then executes a SHOW MXERRS command. It is convenient to attach this script to a button on the toolbar and (when writing or debugging syntax) click on it before running command syntax.

The command SHOW MXERRS produces output of the form:

```
MXERRS = 100  (42 encountered so far)
```

where the number within the parentheses indicates the total number of errors that occurred since the beginning of the session; that is, since SPSS was loaded in memory. When you ensure that the first and last command executed in the Viewer is SHOW MXERRS, you can quickly determine if there have been errors in the run by simply comparing the two values in parentheses. Note that although the command is called MXERRS (for maximum errors), the first number shown in the output (100 in this case) has no effect. The processor does not stop after 100 errors, and the function continues to count errors even after that number of errors has occurred.

```
' EmptyDesignatedOutputWindow.sbs
'BEGIN DESCRIPTION
'This script empties the designated regular output document
'and displays the number of errors so far.
'END DESCRIPTION

Option Explicit

Sub Main()
'Empty the Designated Output Window

 Dim objOutputDoc As ISpssOutputDoc
 On Error Resume Next


 Set objOutputDoc = objSpssApp.GetDesignatedOutputDoc
 objOutputDoc.Items.GetItem(0).Selected = True
 objOutputDoc.Remove

 objSpssApp.ExecuteCommands "SHOW MXERRS." & vbCr,False
 set objOutputDoc = Nothing
End Sub
```

- Item 0 is the root of the Viewer, so selecting it selects the entire Viewer contents.
- The Remove method deletes the selected items, so it empties the Viewer window.
- The ExecuteCommands method is then used to run the SHOW MXERRS command.

Extension

This short script runs a SHOW MXERRS command and then selects the result in the Viewer window. Thus, you do not have to navigate to the end of the Viewer window to see the total number of errors in the session.

```
' ShowMXERRS.SBS
Option Explicit

Sub main
 Call ShowMXERRS()
End Sub

Sub ShowMXERRS()
' Acts on designated output window
 Dim objOutputDoc As ISpssOutputDoc
 Dim objOutputItems As ISpssItems
 Dim objOutputItem As ISpssItem

 objSpssApp.ExecuteCommands ("SHOW MXERRS." & vbCrLf.",True)

 'Get designated output document and items collection
 Set objOutputDoc = objSpssApp.GetDesignatedOutputDoc
 objOutputDoc.WindowState=SpssNormal
 objOutputDoc.Visible =True
 Set objOutputItems = objOutputDoc.Items

 objOutputDoc.ClearSelection
 ' Go to the last MXERRS item
 Set objOutputItem = objOutputItems.GetItem(objOutputItems.Count - 2)
 objOutputItem.Selected = True
End Sub
```

- The SHOW MXERRS command is executed.
- You make sure the that Viewer window is not minimized and then make it visible.
- Since you know that the result is at the end of the window, simply select that item.

An extended version of this script, *ShowMXERRS_2.sbs*, which also searches for warnings and offers to go to the first error message or warning, is included on the accompanying CD.

Count Number of Errors

This script counts the number of errors that occurred between the first and the last SHOW MXERRS commands that were executed in the designated Viewer. This script is useful either to verify that no errors occurred or, when errors occurred, to locate where in the code they occurred.

Note that if you needed only to compare the first and last SHOW MXERRS results, you would not really need a script to do it. The script comes in handy when there are errors in the run and you need to locate them. A good strategy is to insert SHOW MXERRS at various places within the command stream. The difficulty of locating an error then becomes much easier.

```
' CountNumberOfErrors.SBS
'Begin Description
'This assumes that syntax file(s) were ran and the SHOW MXERRS command was
' used at least at the beginning and end of the syntax file
' This script compares the number of errors reported in the first and last MXERRS output
' and displays the information in the last MXERRS object label (in the left pane).
' The script then modifies the MXERRS output so that upon subsequent run, the comparison
' is done using the last MXERRS in the current Output
'Requirement: the Output Document must be open.
'Restriction: Before running this, you must have run a syntax file with a SHOW MXERRS
'End Description

Option Explicit

Sub main()
 Call CountErrors
End Sub

Sub CountErrors()

 Dim objOutputDoc As ISpssOutputDoc
 Dim objOutputItems As ISpssItems
 Dim objOutputItem As ISpssItem
 Dim strTitle As String
```

```
Dim cnt As Integer
Dim lngNbErrBegin As Long  '# of errors reported in first (unprocessed) MXERRS
Dim lngNbErrEnd As Long   '# of errors reported in last MXERRS
Dim lngNbErr As Long   'Number of errors since this script was last run
Dim lngTemp As Long
Dim lngFirstItemNumber As Long 'Item number containing first unprocessed MXERRS
Dim bolTest As Boolean   'Test level 2 SPSSText items only when bolTest is True
On Error GoTo Oopps

'Get designated output document and items collection
Set objOutputDoc = objSpssApp.GetDesignatedOutputDoc
Set objOutputItems = objOutputDoc.Items

' Find # errors in first MXERRS
For cnt = 0 To objOutputItems.Count - 1
 Set objOutputItem = objOutputItems.GetItem(cnt)

  If objOutputItem.Level=1 Then bolTest=objOutputItem.Label="Show"

  'If Text Output is under a Show Header, test for MXERRS
  If objOutputItem.SPSSType = SPSSText And bolTest Then
  strTitle = objOutputItem.ActivateText.Text
  lngTemp=InStr(strTitle,"(") + 1
   If Left(strTitle,6) = "MXERRS" And lngTemp > 1 _
     Then 'this MXERRS has not yet been processed
    lngFirstItemNumber = cnt
    lngNbErrBegin = CLng(Mid$(strTitle,lngTemp, _
     InStr(lngTemp,strTitle,"encountered")-lngTemp-1))
     lngNbErrBegin & " errors"     Debug.Print cnt & " " & "First MXERRS has " & _
    objOutputItem.Deactivate
    objOutputItem.Label = lngNbErrBegin & " Errors in session"
    Exit For
   End If
  objOutputItem.Deactivate
  objOutputItem.Selected=False
  End If
 Next

' Find # errors in last MXERRS
lngNbErrEnd = -1  ' -1 means have not found the last MXERRS yet
For cnt = objOutputItems.Count - 1 To lngFirstItemNumber Step -1
 Set objOutputItem = objOutputItems.GetItem(cnt)
 Debug.Print cnt & " " & objOutputItem.SPSSType & " " & objOutputItem.Label _
```

```
  & " " & objOutputItem.Height
 If objOutputItem.SPSSType = SPSSText And objOutputItem.Height < 35 And _
  (cnt=lngFirstItemNumber Or objOutputItem.Label="Text Output") Then
  strTitle = objOutputItem.ActivateText.Text
  If Left(strTitle,6) = "MXERRS" Then
   If lngNbErrEnd = -1 Then  'we have found last MXERRS
    lngTemp=InStr(strTitle,"(") + 1
    lngNbErrEnd = CLng(Mid$(strTitle,lngTemp, _
     InStr(lngTemp,strTitle,"encountered")-lngTemp-1))
    Debug.Print "Last MXERRS shows " & lngNbErrBegin & " errors"
    objOutputItem.Deactivate

    If lngNbErrEnd - lngNbErrBegin > 0 Then
     objOutputItem.Label = ">>> # of Errors to explain: " & _
      CStr(lngNbErrEnd - lngNbErrBegin)
     Else
     objOutputItem.Label = ">>> NO ERRORS!"
    End If
   Else
    lngTemp=InStr(strTitle,"(") + 1
    If lngTemp  > 1 Then
     lngNbErr = CLng(Mid$(strTitle,lngTemp, _
      InStr(lngTemp,strTitle,"encountered")-lngTemp-1))
     Debug.Print "MXERRS has " & lngNbErr & " errors"
     ' Replace "(" by "[" in the MXERRS message
     Mid(strTitle,lngTemp - 1 ,1 ) = "["
     objOutputItem.ActivateText.Text = strTitle
     Debug.Print strTitle
     objOutputItem.Deactivate
     objOutputItem.Label = lngNbErr & " Errors in session"
    End If
   End If
 End If
 objOutputItem.Deactivate
 objOutputItem.Selected=False
 End If
Next
If lngNbErrEnd - lngNbErrBegin = 0 Then
 MsgBox "There were NO ERRORS!"
Else
 MsgBox CStr(lngNbErrEnd - lngNbErrBegin) & _
  " ERRORS since this script was last run"
End If
```

```
Exit Sub

Oopps:
 MsgBox Err.Number & " " & Err.Description    'inform user
 Debug.Print Err.Number & " " & Err.Description 'for future reference
 'Resume Next 'Comment this line when not debugging this script
 Exit Sub
End Sub
```

Figure 7-5
Running count of errors displayed in outline pane

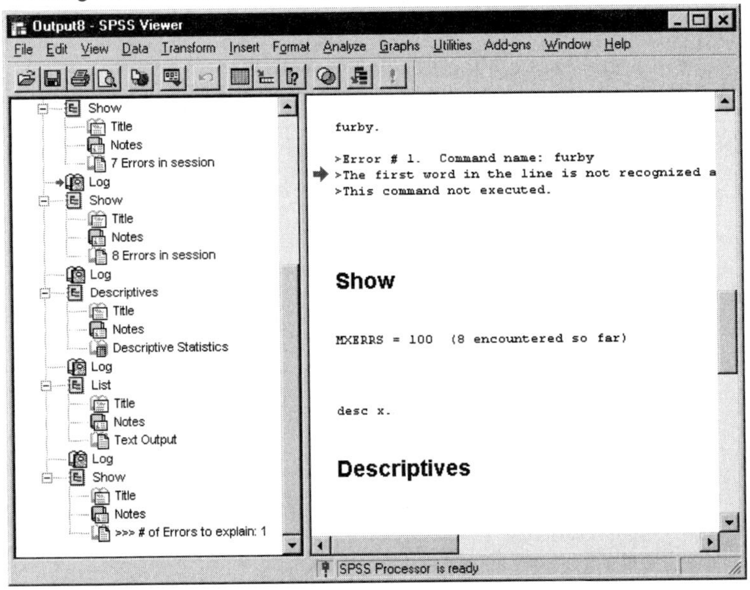

- SHOW MXERRS reports the number of errors that occurred during the current session; that is, since the last time SPSS has been started. The message has the format:

  `MXERRS = n    (n encountered so far)`

  where the values of n are integers. The first number is not relevant here (and this setting is honored only by SPSSB, available with the server version of SPSS). The second number is used by the script.

- The script finds the first MXERRS message in the output that it has not previously processed. When the script processes a MXERRS, it replaces the left parenthesis in the error message with a left square bracket ([).

- It then starts at the end of the output and looks for the last MXERRS message. The difference is the number of errors that occurred in this output since the script was last run. This information is printed in the outline label of the last MXERRS message.
- The outline label of the last SHOW MXERRS message is replaced with
  ">>> # Errors to explain: n"
  The outline labels of the other SHOW MXERRS messages are replaced with
  "n Errors in session"
  where n is the corresponding number of errors encountered so far (as found in the right pane of that object).
- When the length of the outline pane contents is only two or three screens, it is easy to see the area where the number of errors increases and to subsequently find the code that produced the errors.
- When the length of the left pane of the window is many screens, it is easier to use the script described in the next section to search for the errors. With that script, it takes a few seconds to locate the errors in a very long output document.
- If OMS is being used to suppress the appearance of some items in the Viewer, this script will not, of course, find associated errors. It can see only objects that actually appear in the Viewer, although they do not have to be visible.

Find String in the Viewer Outline

This script searches for user-specified text in the labels in the outline panel of the Viewer starting with the current item. Each time it finds a match, it selects the item and makes it current. The user can stop the search or continue to find other occurrences. The search does not wrap to the start of the Window.

The script uses an Input box to obtain the string from the user. If the user closes the window or returns an empty string, the script exits. When a non-empty string is supplied, the script loops through every item in the left pane of the window; for each such item, the function InStr is used to find the position of the strTitle inside the label of the item. Comparison strings are converted to upper case in order to make the search case insensitive.

When InStr returns 0, the search string is not present in the label, and the loop continues with the next object. When InStr returns a positive integer, the search string is present in the label.

```
' FindOutlineText.sbs
'BEGIN DESCRIPTION
'Search the outline of the Designated Output window for specified text
'starting with the current item.
'The search is not case sensitive.
'For convenience attach this script to a toolbar button
'END DESCRIPTION

Option Explicit

Sub Main()
' PageTitle in left pane is replaced by content of right pane
' Acts on designated output window

  Dim objOutputDoc As ISpssOutputDoc
  Dim objOutputItems As ISpssItems
  Dim objOutputItem As ISpssItem
  Dim bolFound As Boolean
  Dim strTitle As String
  Dim cnt As Long, start As Long

  Const TITLE="Find Outline Text"

  On Error GoTo Error_SearchOutline
  bolFound = False

  ' Request search string
  strTitle=UCase(InputBox("Enter text to find",TITLE))
  If Len(strTitle)=0 Then  Exit Sub

  'Get designated output document and items collection
  Set objOutputDoc = objSpssApp.GetDesignatedOutputDoc
  Set objOutputItems = objOutputDoc.Items
  'objOutputDoc.WindowState =SpssMaximized
  objOutputDoc.ClearSelection
```

```
'Find current item and start search there
For start = 0 To objOutputItems.Count-1
 If (objOutputItems.GetItem(start).Current) Then
  Exit For
 End If
Next start

' Check every item
For cnt = start To objOutputItems.Count - 1
 Set objOutputItem = objOutputItems.GetItem(cnt)
 If InStr(UCase(objOutputItem.Label),strTitle) > 0 Then
  bolFound = True
  objOutputItem.Selected = True
  objOutputItem.Current = True
  If (MsgBox("Find Next?", vbYesNo, TITLE)  =vbNo) Then
   Exit Sub
  End If
  objOutputItem.Selected = False
  bolFound = False
 End If
Next
If bolFound =False Then
 MsgBox("Text not found.",vbOkOnly,TITLE)
End If
Exit Sub

Error_SearchOutline:
 MsgBox Err.Number & " " & Err.Description, vbOkOnly, TITLE    'inform user
 Debug.Print Err.Number & " " & Err.Description 'for future reference
 'Resume Next 'use Resume Next when debugging script
End Sub
```

Figure 7-6
Finding outline text in the Viewer

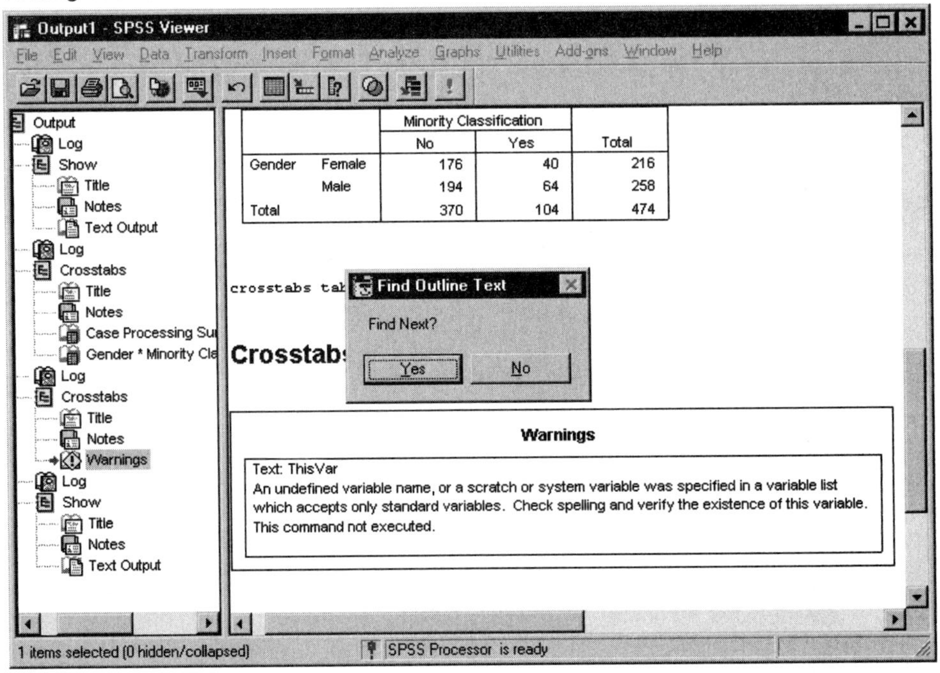

The script can search for any label in the outline pane. For illustration purposes, we entered “warnings” as the search word. The script found and selected the first instance of “Warnings” in the outline pane. Selecting the item in the outline also selects the Warnings object in the content pane. (Note that the search is not case sensitive.)

Check Viewer for Errors

This script scans all visible log objects and text output objects in the designated Viewer window and either stops with the text ">Error #" highlighted or displays a message that no errors were found. As it scans the log objects, it makes them invisible when there are no errors.

```
' findErrorMessage.sbs
'BEGIN DESCRIPTION
'Find error messages in logs and text blocks.
'Warnings objects and items that are not visible are not included.
'Requirement: the Output Document must be open.
'END DESCRIPTION
Option Explicit

Sub Main()
' Find error messages in visible LOG or Text Output
 Dim objOutputDoc As ISpssOutputDoc  'The Output Viewer
 Dim objOutputItems As ISpssItems  'The collection of all Output items
 Dim objOutputItem As ISpssItem    'A particular Output Items
 Dim cnt As Integer          'A loop counter
 Dim strLOG As String        'Will hold the content of the Log
 On Error GoTo error_FindErrorMsg

 'Get designated output document and items collection
 Set objOutputDoc = objSpssApp.GetDesignatedOutputDoc
 Set objOutputItems = objOutputDoc.Items
 objOutputDoc.Visible =True
 If objOutputDoc.WindowState=SpssMinimized Then _
   objOutputDoc.WindowState=SpssNormal
 For cnt = 0 To objOutputItems.Count - 1
   Set objOutputItem = objOutputItems.GetItem(cnt)
   With objOutputItem
    If (.SPSSType=SPSSLog Or .SPSSType = SPSSText) And .Visible Then
    strLOG=.ActivateText.Text
    If (InStr(strLOG,">Error #") >0) Then
     SendKeys ("^F>Error #~{Tab}{Tab}{Tab}{Tab}~")
     Wait 1
     Exit Sub
    ElseIf (InStr(strLOG,">Note # 213") >0) Then
     SendKeys ("^F>Note # 213~{Tab}{Tab}{Tab}{Tab}~")
     Wait 1
     Exit Sub
    End If
    .Deactivate
    If .SPSSType=SPSSLog Then .Visible=False
    End If
  End With
```

```
 Next cnt
 MsgBox "There were no error messages in the visible Log and Text Output!", vbOkOnly, "Find
Errors"
Exit Sub

Error_FindErrorMsg:
 MsgBox Err.Number & ": " & Err.Description    'inform user
 Exit Sub
End Sub
```

- If the WindowState property of the output document is set to SpssMinimized, it is set to SpssNormal. SpssMinimized and SpssNormal are predefined constants. To see the list of all constants available, place the cursor on the property (in this case, on the word WindowState) and press F1.
- The Visible property of the objOutputDoc is set to True. The visible property determines whether the window is hidden or not.
- The For–Next loop checks every item in the Viewer window. If the type of the object is Log or Text Output and the object is visible, then the script searches the item for the string ">Error #". If the script used the Label text in this check instead, it would be sensitive to the output language setting.
- If InStr finds an error, you know that there is an error in the current log.
- Manually, you can press Ctrl-F (or use the Edit menu, Find) to open the Find dialog box. You would then type ">Error #" in the Find What text box and press Enter. After finding the error, you would then click Cancel to close the dialog box. Note that the Cancel button does not have a shortcut key. One way to enable the Cancel button without using the mouse is to press the Tab key four times. Try it. Another way is to close the dialog box by pressing the Escape key (Esc) once.
- The Sax Basic function SendKeys is used to perform the same action as described in the above bullet. SendKeys sends keys to the processor exactly as if you were pressing the keys yourself.
- To get a description of the codes used by SendKeys, place the cursor on the word SendKeys and press F1.
- The script waits one second and then terminates. Once you have noted or corrected that error, you can modify the ">Error #" expression so that the script will not recognize it, then exit the edit mode, and restart the script.
- Note that error messages are not always displayed in the log. Sometimes they appear in text output. The script is designed to find errors in both log and text output objects.

A modified version of this script, *findErrorMessage_2.sbs*, which also searches for Warnings objects (that may contain error messages) and text and log objects that contain the text string ">Note # 213", is included on the accompanying CD.

A Challenge: Missing Labels

Suppose that you have a large data file with thousands of numeric variables, and there are many categorical variables with defined value labels, as well as scale variables for which fewer than three value labels are defined. You need to find all variables for which the data contain values without value labels.

Hints:

- Use a script to write a text file containing variable names and values with value labels. (However, exclude from the list any variable having fewer than three value labels).
- Using command syntax, read the text file and write a command syntax file that, for each variable, will set to SYSMIS all values having value labels. Reread the text file and write command syntax that will drop any variable not listed in the text file (this will drop variables with three or fewer value labels). Load the original data file and INCLUDE the two command syntax files. Use CTABLES (requires the Tables option) to list variables and values in the data (exclude missing categories).
- For a complete solution, see:
  – *Challenge_Find_Variables_With_Missing_Labels.SPS*
  and
  – *Challenge_Find_Variables_With_Missing_Labels.SBS*
  on the accompanying CD.

Synchronizing Scripts and Syntax

Illustration of the Problem

As previously explained, it is possible to run command syntax from a script and, conversely, it is possible to run scripts from a command syntax file. When command syntax runs a script by using the SCRIPT command or a script runs syntax using ExecuteCommands or a similar method, you sometimes would like this process to be synchronous; that is, you would like the SPSS Processor or script to pause until the invoked operation has completed. This would be necessary if the result is needed by the invoking code for further processing or because there is a dependency on a volatile context. For example, a script that was intended to work with the most recently created pivot table might fail because syntax generated another table before the script got to the point of working with the table. In many cases, autoscripting can solve this problem, but for some problems, this is not sufficient.

As the online Help for the script ExecuteCommands method of the objSpssApp explains, if you invoke syntax synchronously in your script, it regains control only when that syntax completes, whereas if you invoke it asynchronously, the script regains control immediately. With SPSS, making asynchronous calls and using the IsBusy method to query the status of the process results in significant performance gains.

The following script executes a syntax command and waits until the Processor has completed the task. In this example, in fact, the script does not really depend on the Processor having completed the task, but it could have further parts that use the results of the executed syntax.

```
' asynchro_example1.SBS
'This script works only when run in 'immediate' mode (that is when script
'is not directly or indirectly called from a syntax file)

Sub Main
 Dim strCmd As String, strVar1 As String
 strVar1 = InputBox$("Enter value of var1:")
 strCmd = "COMPUTE var1=" & strVar1 & "." & vbCrLf & "EXECUTE." & vbCrLf
 objSpssApp.ExecuteCommands ( strCmd, False)
 While objSpssApp.IsBusy
  Wait .1
 Wend
 MsgBox ("The SPSS Processor is no longer busy")
End Sub
```

- The ExecuteCommands method requires two parameters: a string containing the syntax to be executed, and an indication of whether the syntax is to be run synchronously or not.
- The syntax is run asynchronously and the script loops until the Processor's IsBusy method returns False (which means the SPSS Processor is free).

If the script is invoked from command syntax, however, there is the possibility of deadlock, where the command syntax is waiting for the script to complete and the script is waiting for the command syntax to complete, so neither one ever does.

Suppose this script is invoked as follows:

```
* asynchro_example1.SPS.
* Call a script that checks whether the SPSS processor is busy.

GET FILE='c:\examples\data\employee data.sav'.
SCRIPT 'C:\examples\scripts\asynchro_example1.SBS'.
COMPUTE var2=1.
EXECUTE.
```

- The command syntax opens a data file and then calls the script of the preceding example.
- The command syntax then immediately creates *var2*; it does *not* wait for the script to be completed. In fact *var2*, created by the command *following* the SCRIPT command, may be created *before var1*, created by the script.
- The Processor then has nothing else to do, but since the SCRIPT command has not yet completed, it waits.
- During that time, the script has indeed completed its main task but the condition objSpssApp.IsBusy is always True, since the Processor has not received a completion indication from the script. SPSS must be terminated (Ctrl-Alt-Delete) in order to break out of this loop.
- In this example, the commands that follow the SCRIPT call do not depend on the result of the script, so you could solve the problem by simply removing the Processor-busy text from the script. In some cases, however, the command stream needs the result of the script before it can continue. For example, there are problems if the following occur:
  - *var2* is a function of *var1*.
  - There is an INCLUDE command that needs to read a file created by the script.
  - The script is supposed to modify or act upon a specific pivot table, interactive graph, or other object just created by the command syntax. If the command syntax continues to generate output without waiting until the script has completed its tasks, the script might end up modifying the wrong object.

Conclusion: Never invoke a script with the SCRIPT command if it relies on IsBusy.

Synchronizing without the IsBusy Method

The solution to the deadlock problem depends on whether the script needs to wait for the syntax or the syntax needs to wait for the script. It involves inspecting a dictionary property that is modified in syntax and waiting for it to have a value set in the script. There is a third kind of synchronization that is not addressed here: If the problem involves synchronizing a script with the creation of a pivot table in the Viewer, consider using the following instead:

- An autoscript
- OMS
- A Wait loop in the script based on the appearance of a particular object in the Viewer

First, consider the case where the script needs to wait for the syntax it submits to complete. It would seem at first that just running it synchronously would work. However, this causes a deadlock when the script is run by SCRIPT. Instead, the following approach can be used:

```
*asynchro_example1a.sps.
GET FILE='c:\program files\spss\employee data.sav'.
NUMERIC flag.
VARIABLE LABELS flag 'working'.
SCRIPT 'C:\examples\scripts\asynchro_example1a.SBS'.
```

```
' asynchro_example1a.SBS
' This script synchronizes using a variable named "flag"
' which is assumed to already exist and initally
' to have a label different from "completed".

Sub Main
 Dim strCmd As String, strVar1 As String

 strVar1 = InputBox$("Enter value of var1:")
 strCmd = "COMPUTE var1=" & strVar1 & "." & vbCrLf
 objSpssApp.ExecuteCommands ( strCmd, False)  ' async
 Call WaitOnFlag
 MsgBox ("The SPSS Processor is no longer busy")
End Sub
Sub WaitOnFlag
Dim objSpssInfo As ISpssInfo
```

```
Set objSpssInfo = objSpssApp.SpssInfo

objSpssApp.ExecuteCommands "EXECUTE." & vbCrLf & "variable label flag 'completed'." &
vbCrLf, False
Dim I As Integer, found As Boolean

For I = 0 To objSpssInfo.NumVariables-1
 If (objSpssInfo.VariableAt(I) = "flag") Then
  found = True
  Exit For
 End If
Next
If (Not found) Then
 MsgBox "ERROR: The synchronization variable, 'flag' does not exist'
 Exit Sub
End If
While objSpssInfo.VariableLabelAt(I) <> "completed"
 Wait 1
Wend
End Sub
```

- The command syntax creates a variable named *flag* whose label will be used for synchronization. The NUMERIC command should not be repeated in the job, since it cannot be applied to an existing variable. However, it does not require a data pass. You could put the label resetting and script invocation commands into a macro for regular use.
- The variable label is set to *working*. This command should be repeated every time a synchronized script is invoked.
- WaitOnFlag runs command syntax to change the variable label and waits until this has occurred. The command syntax it runs begins with an EXECUTE command in order to ensure that all the values of the new variable have been realized before the syntax is deemed completed. If you do not need the values for subsequent use in the script, this part of the ExecuteCommands code could be removed. Add the WaitOnFlag subroutine to your copy of *global.sbs* if you need to use it with different scripts. The script is the same as before except that it calls the subroutine WaitOnFlag for synchronization.
- The synchronization process in this example does not guarantee that the Viewer has finished constructing and displaying the pivot table. To do this, determine the number of the last preceding object in the Viewer and loop, checking newer objects for an appropriate property, such as a label. You can retrieve the last object in the Viewer with code such as the following:

```
Set item = _
objSpssApp.GetDesignatedOutputDoc.Items.GetItem(objSpssApp.GetDesignatedOutput-
Doc.Items.Count-1)
```

Next, consider the case where the command syntax needs to wait for the script to complete. This requires additional measures, since the SPSS Processor will go on to the command following SCRIPT as soon as it has invoked the script. To prevent this, end the command syntax file with the SCRIPT command requiring synchronization, and put the remaining command syntax in another file. Then pass the name of that file to the script as a parameter on the SCRIPT command. After the script has done its other work, including any necessary waiting for completion, pass the second portion of the syntax to the SPSS Processor by using the ExecuteInclude method of the SPSS application object.

Other Scripts Included on the CD

define_variables.sbs. This script takes a *.sav* file and writes command syntax that could be used to define the following properties of every variable in the file:

- Variable label
- Value labels
- Variable level
- Missing value definitions

In other words, it creates the syntax equivalent of the major properties of the dictionary.

ExportViewerToSingleExcelSheet.sbs. This script exports visible pivot tables, charts, and interactive graphs to a single Microsoft Excel sheet. Each item is "grouped" by the script so that it can be collapsed to a single line by clicking on the – symbol, which is on the left side of the Excel sheet.

Export_SPSSdataToAccess.SBS. This script exports data from SPSS to a Microsoft Access file. A separate table of value labels is created in Access for each variable with value labels in SPSS. By linking these tables with the master data file, labels can be displayed in Access output.

ConvertSyntaxToScript.sbs. This script converts the syntax of the designated syntax window into a script format. The new code is inserted at the end of the designated syntax window. It can then be copied and pasted into a subroutine.

Write reverse autorecode syntax.SBS. This script requires two arguments: the names of the variables that must be "reversed autorecode," and the name of the new variable created by the script. For example, when the file *Employee data.sav* is in the Data Editor and the script is called using the following:

```
Call ReverseAutorecode("gender","gender2")
```

the following code is generated and pasted into a new syntax window:

```
STRING gender2(A6).
RECODE gender
 ("f"="Female")
 ("m"="Male") (ELSE=COPY) INTO gender2.
```

The code is also executed by the script, so the variable *gender2* exists when the script has finished.

Chapter

8

Exporting Data and Results

You can export and save both data and results in a variety of formats for use by other applications, including:

- Save data in SAS, Excel, and text format.
- Write data to a database.
- Export results in HMTL, Word, Excel, and text format.
- Save results in XML and SPSS data file (*.sav*) format.

Output Management System

The Output Management System (introduced in SPSS 12.0) provides the ability to automatically write selected categories of output to different output files in different formats. Formats include:

SPSS data file format (SAV). Output that would be displayed in pivot tables in the Viewer can be written out in the form of an SPSS data file, making it possible to use output as input for subsequent commands.

XML. Tables, text output, and even many charts can be written out in XML format.

HTML. Tables and text output can be written out in HTML format.

Text. Tables and text output can be written out as tab-delimited or space-separated text.

The examples provided here are also described in the SPSS Help system, and they barely scratch the surface of what is possible with the OMS command. For a detailed description of the OMS command and related commands (OMSEND, OMSINFO, and OMSLOG), see the *SPSS Command Syntax Reference*.

Using Output Results as Input Data

Using the OMS command, you can save pivot table output to SPSS-format data files, and then use that output as input in subsequent commands or sessions. This can be useful for many purposes. This section provides examples of two possible ways to use output as input:

- Generate a table of group summary statistics (percentiles) not available with the AGGREGATE command and then merge those values into the original data file.
- Draw repeated random samples with replacement from a data file, calculate regression coefficients for each sample, save the coefficient values in a data file, and then calculate confidence intervals for the coefficients (bootstrapping).

Adding Group Percentile Values to a Data File

Using the AGGREGATE and MATCH FILES commands, you can compute various group summary statistics and then merge those summary values into the original data file. For example, you could compute mean, minimum, and maximum income by job category and then include those values in the original data file. (For more information, see "Aggregating Data" on p. 96 in Chapter 4.) Some summary statistics, however, are not available with the AGGREGATE command. This example uses OMS to write a table of group percentiles to a data file and then merges the data in that file with the original data file.

The command syntax used in this example is *oms_percentiles.sps*, located in the *tutorial\sample_files* folder of the SPSS installation folder.

```
***oms_percentiles.sps***.

GET
  FILE='c:\Program Files\spss\Employee data.sav'.
PRESERVE.
SET TVARS=NAMES TNUMBERS=VALUES.
***split file by job category to get group percentiles.
SORT CASES BY jobcat.
SPLIT FILE LAYERED BY jobcat.
OMS
  /SELECT TABLES
  /IF COMMANDS=['Frequencies'] SUBTYPES=['Statistics']
  /DESTINATION FORMAT=SAV
   OUTFILE='c:\temp\temp.sav'
  /COLUMNS SEQUENCE=[L1 R2].
FREQUENCIES
  VARIABLES=salary
  /FORMAT=NOTABLE
  /PERCENTILES= 25 50 75.
OMSEND.
***restore previous  SET settings.
RESTORE.
MATCH FILES FILE=*
  /TABLE='c:\temp\temp.sav'
  /rename (Var1=jobcat)
  /BY jobcat
 /DROP command_ TO salary_Missing.
EXECUTE.
```

- The PRESERVE command saves your current SET command specifications.
- SET TVARS=NAMES TNUMBERS=VALUES specifies that variable names and data values, not variable or value labels, should be displayed in tables. Using variable names instead of labels is not technically necessary in this example, but it makes the new variable names constructed from column labels somewhat easier to work with. Using data values instead of value labels, however, is required to make this example work properly because we will use the job category values in the two files to merge them together.
- SORT CASES and SPLIT FILE are used to divide the data into groups by job category (*jobcat*). The LAYERED keyword specifies that results for each split-file group should be displayed in the same table rather than in separate tables.
- The OMS command will select all statistics tables from subsequent FREQUENCIES commands and write the tables to an SPSS-format data file.

- The COLUMNS subcommand will put the first layer dimension element and the second row dimension element in the columns.
- The FREQUENCIES command produces a statistics table that contains the 25th, 50th, and 75th percentile values for salary. Since split-file processing is on, the table will contain separate percentile values for each job category.

Figure 8-1
Default and pivoted statistics table

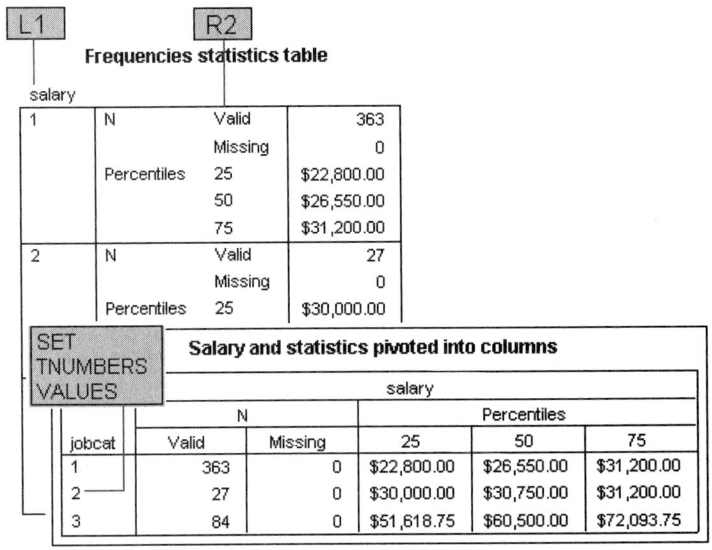

Frequencies statistics table

salary

1	N	Valid	363
		Missing	0
	Percentiles	25	$22,800.00
		50	$26,550.00
		75	$31,200.00
2	N	Valid	27
		Missing	0
	Percentiles	25	$30,000.00

Salary and statistics pivoted into columns

	salary				
	N		Percentiles		
jobcat	Valid	Missing	25	50	75
1	363	0	$22,800.00	$26,550.00	$31,200.00
2	27	0	$30,000.00	$30,750.00	$31,200.00
3	84	0	$51,618.75	$60,500.00	$72,093.75

- In the statistics table, the variable *salary* is the only layer dimension element; so the L1 specification in the OMS COLUMNS subcommand will put *salary* in the column dimension.
- The table statistics are the second (inner) row dimension element in the table; the R2 specification in the OMS COLUMNS subcommand will put the statistics in the column dimension, nested under the variable *salary.*
- The data values 1, 2, and 3 are used for the categories of the variable *jobcat* instead of the descriptive text value labels because of the previous SET command specifications.
- OMSEND ends all active OMS commands. Without this, we could not access the data file *temp.sav* in the subsequent MATCH FILES command, because the file is not written until the OMS command is ended either by an OMSEND command or the end of the session.

Figure 8-2
Data file created from pivoted table

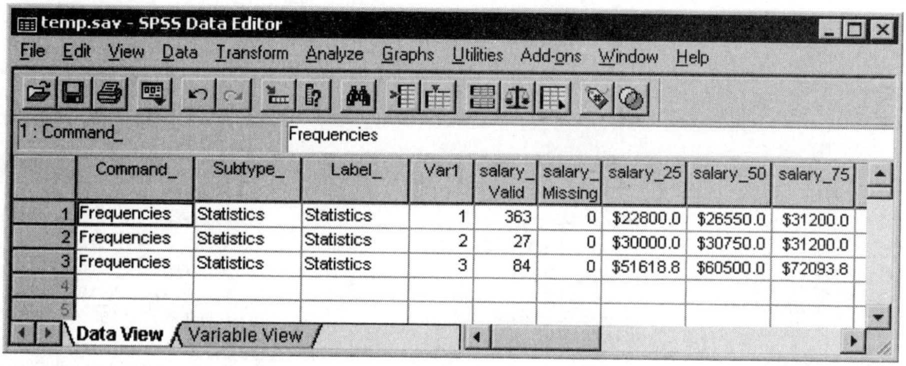

- The MATCH FILES command merges the contents of the data file created from the statistics table with the original data file. New variables from the data file created by OMS will be added to the original data file.
- FILE=* specifies the current working data file, which is still the original data file.
- TABLE='c:\temp\temp.sav' identifies the data file created by OMS as a table lookup file. A table lookup file is a file in which data for each "case" can be applied to multiple cases in the other data file(s). In this example, the table lookup file contains only three cases: one for each job category.
- In the data file created by OMS, the variable that contains the job category values is named *Var1*, but in the original data file the variable is named *jobcat*. RENAME (Var1=jobcat) compensates for this discrepancy in the variable names.
- BY jobcat merges the two files together by values of the variable *jobcat*. The three cases in the table lookup table will be merged with every case in the original data file with the same value for *jobcat* (*Var1* in the table lookup file).
- Since we do not need the three table identifier variables automatically included in every data file created by OMS or the two variables that contain the information on valid and missing cases, we use the DROP subcommand to omit these from the merged data file.

The end result is three new variables containing the 25th, 50th, and 75th percentile salary values for each job category.

Figure 8-3
Percentiles added to original data file

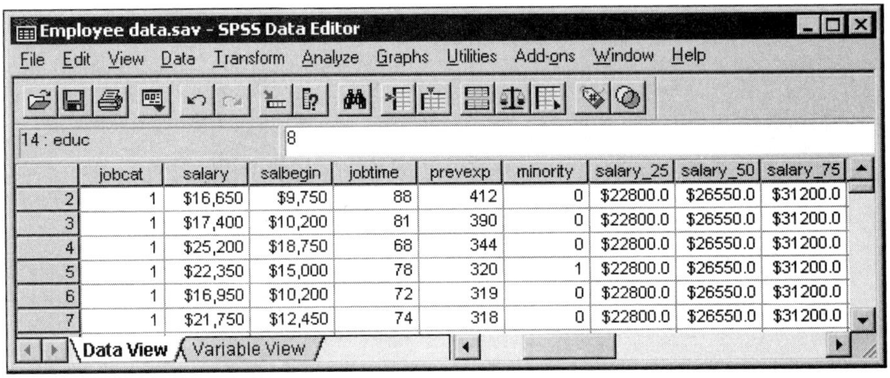

	jobcat	salary	salbegin	jobtime	prevexp	minority	salary_25	salary_50	salary_75
2	1	$16,650	$9,750	88	412	0	$22800.0	$26550.0	$31200.0
3	1	$17,400	$10,200	81	390	0	$22800.0	$26550.0	$31200.0
4	1	$25,200	$18,750	68	344	0	$22800.0	$26550.0	$31200.0
5	1	$22,350	$15,000	78	320	1	$22800.0	$26550.0	$31200.0
6	1	$16,950	$10,200	72	319	0	$22800.0	$26550.0	$31200.0
7	1	$21,750	$12,450	74	318	0	$22800.0	$26550.0	$31200.0

Bootstrapping with OMS

Bootstrapping is a method for estimating population parameters by repeatedly "resampling" the same sample, computing some test statistic on each sample, and then looking at the distribution of the test statistic over all the samples. Cases are selected randomly, with replacement, from the original sample to create each new sample. Typically, each new sample has the same number of cases as the original sample—but some cases may be randomly selected multiple times and others not at all.

In this example, we:

- Use a macro to draw repeated random samples with replacement.
- Run the REGRESSION command on each sample.
- Use the OMS command to save the regression coefficients tables to a data file.
- Produce histograms of the coefficient distributions and a table of confidence intervals, using the data file created from the coefficient tables.

The command syntax file used in this example is *oms_bootstrapping.sps*, located in the *tutorial\sample_files* folder of the SPSS installation folder.

OMS Commands to Create a Data File of Coefficients

Although the command syntax file may seem long and/or complicated, the OMS commands that create the data file of sample regression coefficients are short and simple:

```
PRESERVE.
SET TVARS NAMES.
OMS /DESTINATION VIEWER=NO /TAG='suppressall'.
OMS
  /SELECT TABLES
  /IF COMMANDS=['Regression'] SUBTYPES=['Coefficients']
  /DESTINATION FORMAT=SAV OUTFILE='c:\temp\temp.sav'
  /COLUMNS DIMNAMES=['Variables'  'Statistics']
  /TAG='reg_coeff'.
```

- The PRESERVE command saves your current SET command specifications, and SET TVARS NAMES specifies that variable names, not labels, should be displayed in tables. Since variable names in data files created by OMS are based on table column labels, using variable names instead of labels in tables tends to result in shorter, less cumbersome variable names.
- The first OMS command prevents subsequent output from being displayed in the Viewer, until an OMSEND is encountered. This is not technically necessary, but if you are drawing hundreds or thousands of samples, you probably do not want to see the output of the corresponding hundreds or thousands of REGRESSION commands.
- The second OMS command will select Coefficients tables from subsequent REGRESSION commands.
- The COMMANDS keyword in the IF subcommand restricts the selection to the specified command(s). The keyword COMMANDS must be followed by an equals sign (=) and a list of quoted command identifiers enclosed in square brackets. Command identifiers are usually—but not always—the same as the actual command name, as in this example. You can use the OMS Identifiers dialog box (Utilities menu) to copy and paste command identifiers.
- The SUBTYPES keyword restricts the selection to the specified table types. The keyword SUBTYPES must be followed by an equals sign (=) and a list of quoted subtype identifiers enclosed in square brackets. You can use the OMS Identifiers dialog box (Utilities menu) to copy and paste subtype identifiers.
- All the selected tables will be saved in a single SPSS-format data file: *temp.sav*.

- The COLUMNS subcommand specifies that both the Variables and Statistics dimension elements of each table should appear in the columns. Since a regression coefficients table is a simple two-dimensional table with variables in the rows and statistics in the columns, if both dimensions appear in the columns, then there will be only one row (case) in the generated data file for each table. This is equivalent to pivoting the table in the Viewer so that both variables and statistics are displayed in the column dimension.

Figure 8-4
Variables dimension element pivoted into column dimension

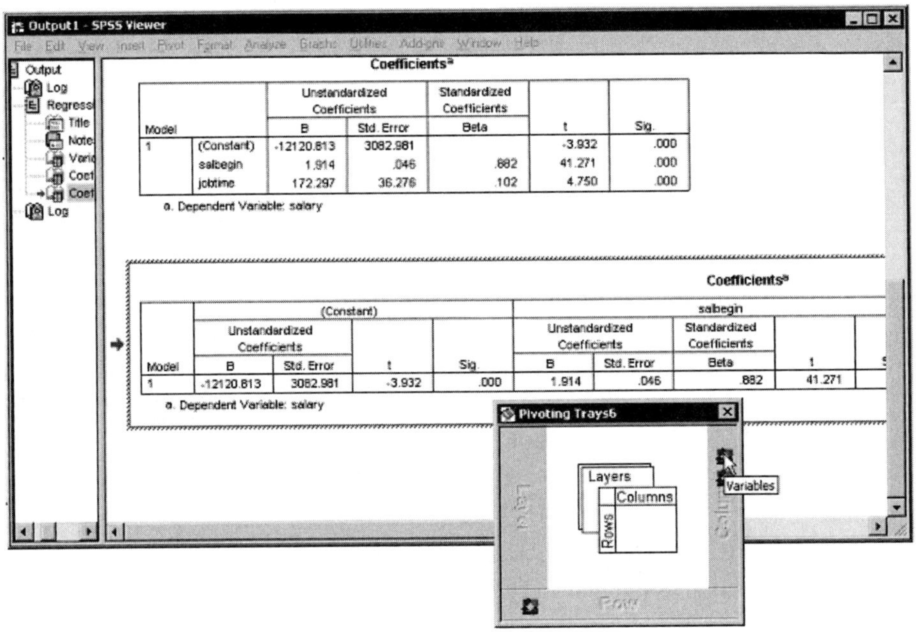

Sampling with Replacement and Regression Macro

The most complicated part of the OMS bootstrapping example has nothing to do with the OMS command. A macro routine is used to generate the samples and run the REGRESSION commands. Only the basic functionality of the macro is discussed here. For detailed information on macros, see Chapter 6.

```
DEFINE regression_bootstrap (samples=!TOKENS(1)
                             /depvar=!TOKENS(1)
                             /indvars=!CMDEND)

COMPUTE dummyvar=1.
AGGREGATE
  /OUTFILE='c:\temp\aggrtemp.sav'
  /BREAK=dummyvar
  /filesize=N.
MATCH FILES FILE=* /TABLE='c:\temp\aggrtemp.sav'
  /BY dummyvar.
!DO !other=1 !TO !samples
SET SEED RANDOM.
WEIGHT OFF.
FILTER OFF.
DO IF $casenum=1.
- COMPUTE #samplesize=filesize.
- COMPUTE #filesize=filesize.
END IF.
DO IF (#samplesize>0 and #filesize>0).
- COMPUTE sampleWeight=rv.binom(#samplesize, 1/#filesize).
- COMPUTE #samplesize=#samplesize-sampleWeight.
- COMPUTE #filesize=#filesize-1.
ELSE.
- COMPUTE sampleWeight=0.
END IF.
WEIGHT BY sampleWeight.
FILTER BY sampleWeight.
REGRESSION
  /STATISTICS COEFF
  /DEPENDENT !depvar
  /METHOD=ENTER !indvars.
!DOEND
!ENDDEFINE.

GET FILE='c:\Program Files\SPSS\Employee data.sav'.

regression_bootstrap
   samples=100
   depvar=salary
   indvars=salbegin jobtime.
```

- A macro named *regression_bootstrap* is defined. It is designed to work with arguments similar to SPSS subcommands and keywords.
- Based on user-specified number of samples, dependent variable, and independent variable, the macro will draw repeated random samples with replacement and run the REGRESSION command on each sample.
- The samples are generated by randomly selecting cases with replacement and assigning weight values based on how many times each case is selected. If a case has a value of 1 for *sampleWeight*, it will be treated like one case. If it has a value of 2, it will be treated like two cases, and so on. If a case has a value of 0 for *sampleWeight*, it will not be included in the analysis.
- The REGRESSION command is then run on each weighted sample.
- The macro is invoked by using the macro name like a command. In this example, we generate 100 samples from the *employee data.sav* file. You can substitute any file, number of samples, and/or analysis variables.

Ending the OMS Requests

Before you can open the generated data file in SPSS and analyze it, you need to end the OMS request that created it, because the file is not written until you end the OMS request. At that point, the basic job of creating the file of sample coefficients is complete, but we've added some histograms and a table that displays the 2.5th and 97.5th percentile values of the bootstrapped coefficient values, which indicate the 95 percent confidence intervals of the coefficients.

```
OMSEND.
GET FILE 'c:\temp\temp.sav'.
FREQUENCIES
  VARIABLES=salbegin_B salbegin_Beta jobtime_B jobtime_Beta
  /FORMAT NOTABLE
  /PERCENTILES= 2.5 97.5
  /HISTOGRAM  NORMAL.
RESTORE.
```

- OMSEND without any additional specifications ends all active OMS requests. In this example, there were two: one to suppress all Viewer output and one to save regression coefficients in a data file. If you do not end both OMS requests, you either will not be able to open the data file or will not see any results of your subsequent analysis.
- The job ends with a RESTORE command that restores your previous SET specifications.

Figure 8-5
95% confidence interval (2.5th and 97.5th percentiles) and coefficient histograms

Statistics

		salbegin_B	salbegin_Beta	jobtime_B	jobtime_Beta
N	Valid	100	100	100	100
	Missing	0	0	0	0
Percentiles	2.5	1.71305	.83828	87.69077	.05271
	97.5	2.10343	.90552	254.97741	.14664

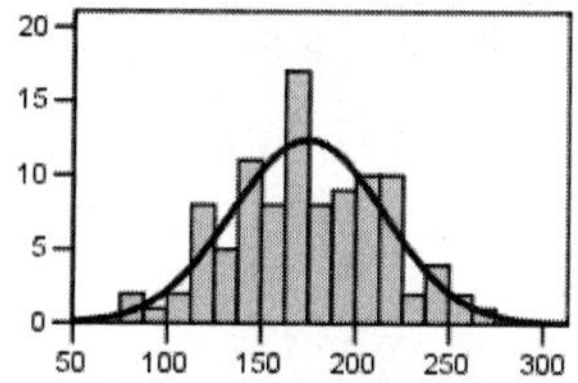

jobtime Unstandardized Coefficients B

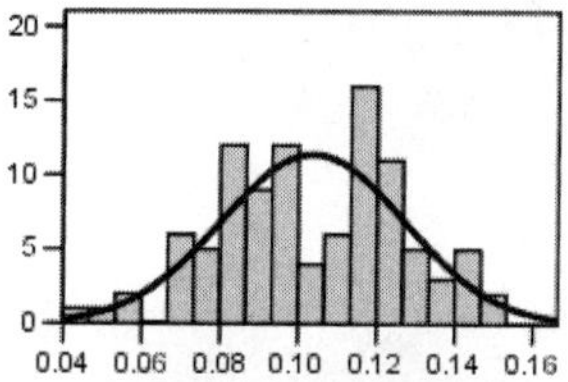

jobtime Standardized Coefficients Beta

Transforming OXML with XSLT

Using the OMS command, you can route output to OXML, which is XML that conforms to the SPSS Output XML schema. This section provides a few basic examples of using XSLT to transform OXML.

- These examples assume some basic understanding of XML and XSLT. If you have not used XML or XSLT before, this is not the place to start. There are numerous books and Internet resources that can help you get started.
- All the XSLT style sheets presented here are installed in the *tutorial\sample_files* folder of the SPSS installation folder.
- The SPSS Output XML schema is documented in *SPSSOutputXML_schema.htm*, located in the *help\main* folder of the SPSS installation folder.

OMS Namespace

Output XML produced by OMS contains a namespace declaration:

```
xmlns="http://xml.spss.com/spss/oms"
```

In order for XSLT style sheets to work properly with OXML, the XSLT style sheets must contain a similar namespace declaration that also defines a prefix that is used to identify that namespace in the style sheet. For example:

```
<xsl:stylesheet xmlns:xsl="http://www.w3.org/1999/XSL/Transform"
  version="1.0" xmlns:oms="http://xml.spss.com/spss/oms">
```

This defines oms as the prefix that identifies the namespace; therefore, all the XPath expressions that refer to OXML elements by name must use oms: as a prefix to the element name references. All the examples presented here use the oms: prefix, but you could define and use a different prefix.

"Pushing" Content from an XML File

In the "push" approach, the structure and order of elements in the transformed results are usually defined by the source XML file. In the case of OXML, the structure of the XML mimics the nested tree structure of the Viewer outline, and we can construct a simple XSLT transformation to reproduce the outline structure.

This example generates the outline in HTML, but it could just as easily generate a simple text file. The XSLT style sheet is *oms_simple_outline_example.xsl*, located in the *tutorial\sample_files* folder of the SPSS installation folder.

Figure 8-6
Viewer outline pane

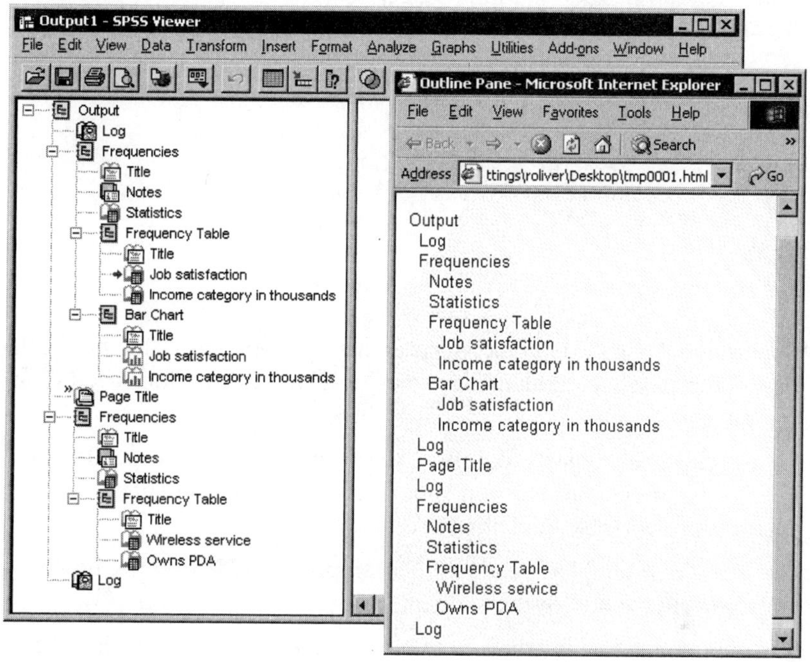

Figure 8-7
oms_simple_outline_example.xsl

```
<?xml version="1.0" encoding="UTF-8"?>
<xsl:stylesheet xmlns:xsl="http://www.w3.org/1999/XSL/Transform"
 version="1.0" xmlns:oms="http://xml.spss.com/spss/oms">
<xsl:template match="/">
 <HTML>
  <HEAD>
   <TITLE>Outline Pane</TITLE>
  </HEAD>
  <BODY>
  <br/>Output
   <xsl:apply-templates/>
  </BODY>
 </HTML>
</xsl:template>
<xsl:template match="oms:command|oms:heading">
 <xsl:call-template name="displayoutline"/>
  <xsl:apply-templates/>
</xsl:template>
<xsl:template
match="oms:textBlock|oms:pageTitle|oms:pivotTable|oms:chartTitle">
 <xsl:call-template name="displayoutline"/>
```

```
</xsl:template>
<!--indent based on number of ancestors:
two spaces for each ancestor-->
<xsl:template name="displayoutline">
 <br/>
 <xsl:for-each select="ancestor::*">
  <xsl:text>  </xsl:text>
 </xsl:for-each>
 <xsl:value-of select="@text"/>
 <xsl:if test="not(@text)">
  <!--no text attribute, must be page title-->
  <xsl:text>Page Title</xsl:text>
 </xsl:if>
</xsl:template>
</xsl:stylesheet>
```

- xmlns:oms="http://xml.spss.com/spss/oms" defines oms as the prefix that identifies the namespace; so all element names in XPath expressions need to include the prefix oms:.
- The style sheet consists mainly of two <template match> specifications that cover each type of element that can appear in the outline: command, heading, textBlock, pageTitle, pivotTable, and chartTitle.
- Both of those templates call another template that determines how far to indent the text attribute value for the element.
- The command and heading elements can have other outline items nested under them, so the template for those two elements also includes <xsl:apply-templates/> to apply the template for the other outline items.
- The template that determines the outline indentation simply counts the number of "ancestors" the element has, which indicates its nesting level, and then inserts two spaces (is a "non-breaking" space in HTML) before the value of the text attribute value.
- <xsl:if test="not(@text)"> selects <pageTitle> elements, because this is the only specified element that does not have a text attribute. This occurs wherever there is a TITLE command in the SPSS command file. In the Viewer, it inserts a page break for printed output and then inserts the specified page title on each subsequent printed page. In OXML, the <pageTitle> element has no attributes; we use <xsl:text> to insert the text "Page Title" as it appears in the Viewer outline.

Viewer Outline "Titles"

You may notice that there are a number of "Title" entries in the Viewer outline that do not appear in the generated HTML. These should not be confused with page titles. There is no corresponding element in OXML because the actual "title" of each output block (the text object selected in the Viewer if you the click the "Title" entry in the Viewer outline) is exactly the same as the text of the entry directly above the "Title" in the outline, which is contained in the text attribute of the corresponding command or heading element in OXML.

"Pulling" Content from an XML File

In the "pull" approach, the structure and order of elements in the source XML file may not be relevant for the transformed results. Instead, the source XML is treated like a data repository from which selected pieces of information are extracted, and the structure of the transformed results is defined by the XSLT style sheet.

The "pull" approach typically uses <xsl:for-each> to select and extract information from the XML.

Simple <xsl:for-each> "Pull" Example

This example uses <xsl:for-each> to "pull" selected information out of OXML output and create customized HTML tables.

Although you can easily generate HTML output using DESTINATION FORMAT=HTML on the OMS command, you have very little control over the HTML generated beyond the specific object types included in the HTML file. Using OXML, however, you can create customized tables. This example:

- Selects only frequency tables in the OXML file.
- Displays only valid (non-missing) values.
- Displays only the *Frequency* and *Valid Percent* columns.
- Replaces the default column labels with *Count* and *Percent*.
- The XSLT style sheet used in this example is *oms_simple_frequency_tables.xsl*, located in the *tutorial\sample_files* folder of the SPSS installation folder.

Figure 8-8
Frequencies pivot table in Viewer

Variable One

		Frequency	Percent	Valid Percent	Cumulative Percent
Valid	One	19	18.1	26.0	26.0
	Two	28	26.7	38.4	64.4
	3.00	26	24.8	35.6	100.0
	Total	73	69.5	100.0	
Missing	99.00	17	16.2		
	System	15	14.3		
	Total	32	30.5		
Total		105	100.0		

var2

		Frequency	Percent	Valid Percent	Cumulative Percent
Valid	Female	63	60.0	60.0	60.0
	Male	42	40.0	40.0	100.0
	Total	105	100.0	100.0	

Figure 8-9
Customized HTML frequency tables

Variable One

Category	Count	Percent
One	19	26.0
Two	28	38.4
3.00	26	35.6
Total	73	100.0

var2

Category	Count	Percent
Female	63	60.0
Male	42	40.0
Total	105	100.0

Figure 8-10
XSLT style sheet: oms_simple_frequency_tables.xsl

```
<?xml version="1.0" encoding="UTF-8"?>

<xsl:stylesheet xmlns:xsl="http://www.w3.org/1999/XSL/Transform"
  version="1.0" xmlns:oms="http://xml.spss.com/spss/oms">
<!--enclose everything in a template, starting at the root node-->
<xsl:template match="/">
<HTML>
<HEAD>
<TITLE>Modified Frequency Tables</TITLE>
</HEAD>
<BODY>
<!--Find all Frequency Tables-->
<xsl:for-each select="//oms:pivotTable[@subType='Frequencies']">
<xsl:for-each select="oms:dimension[@axis='row']">
 <h3>
  <xsl:value-of select="@text"/>
 </h3>
</xsl:for-each>
<!--create the HTML table-->
<table border="1">
 <tbody align="char" char="." charoff="1">
 <tr>
  <!--
  table header row; you could extract headings from
  the XML but in this example we're using different header text
  -->
  <th>Category</th><th>Count</th><th>Percent</th>
 </tr>
 <!--find the columns of the pivot table-->
 <xsl:for-each select="descendant::oms:dimension[@axis='column']">
   <!--select only valid, skip missing-->
    <xsl:if test="ancestor::oms:group[@text='Valid']">
     <tr>
     <td>
       <xsl:choose>
        <xsl:when test="not((parent::*)[@text='Total'])">
         <xsl:value-of select="parent::*/@text"/>
        </xsl:when>
        <xsl:when test="((parent::*)[@text='Total'])">
         <b><xsl:value-of select="parent::*/@text"/></b>
        </xsl:when>
       </xsl:choose>
     </td>
     <td>
      <xsl:value-of select=
       "oms:category[@text='Frequency']/oms:cell/@text"/>
     </td>
     <td>
      <xsl:value-of select=
       "oms:category[@text='Valid Percent']/oms:cell/@text"/>
```

```
      </td>
     </tr>
   </xsl:if>
   </xsl:for-each>
  </tbody>
 </table>
<!--Don't forget possible footnotes for split files-->
<xsl:if test="descendant::*/oms:note">
<p><xsl:value-of select="descendant::*/oms:note/@text"/></p>
</xsl:if>
</xsl:for-each>
</BODY>
</HTML>
</xsl:template>
</xsl:stylesheet>
```

- xmlns:oms="http://xml.spss.com/spss/oms" defines oms as the prefix that identifies the namespace; all element names in XPath expressions need to include the prefix oms:.
- The XSLT primarily consists of a series of nested <xsl:for-each> statements, each drilling down to a different element and attribute of the table.
- <xsl:for-each select="//oms:pivotTable[@subType='Frequencies']"> selects all tables of the subtype 'Frequencies'.
- <xsl:for-each select="oms:dimension[@axis='row']"> selects the row dimension of each table.
- <xsl:for-each select="descendant::oms:dimension[@axis='column']"> selects the column elements from each row. OXML represents tables row by row, so column elements are nested within row elements.
- <xsl:if test="ancestor::oms:group[@text='Valid']"> selects only the section of the table that contains valid, non-missing values. If there are no missing values reported in the table, then this will include the entire table. This is the first of several XSLT specifications in this example that rely on attribute values that differ for different output languages. If you do not need solutions that work for multiple output languages, this is often the simplest, most direct way to select certain elements. Many times, however, there are alternatives that do not rely on localized text strings.
- <xsl:when test="not((parent::*)[@text='Total'])"> selects column elements that are not in the *Total* row. Once again, this selection relies on localized text, and the only reason we make the distinction between total and non-total rows in this example is to make the row label *Total* bold.

- <xsl:value-of select="oms:category[@text='Frequency']/oms:cell/@text"/> gets the content of the cell in the *Frequency* column of each row.
- <xsl:value-of select="oms:category[@text='Valid Percent']/oms:cell/@text"/> gets the content of the cell in the *Valid Percent* column of each row. Both this and the previous code for obtaining the value from the *Frequency* column rely on localized text.

Figure 8-11
XPath expressions for selected frequency table elements

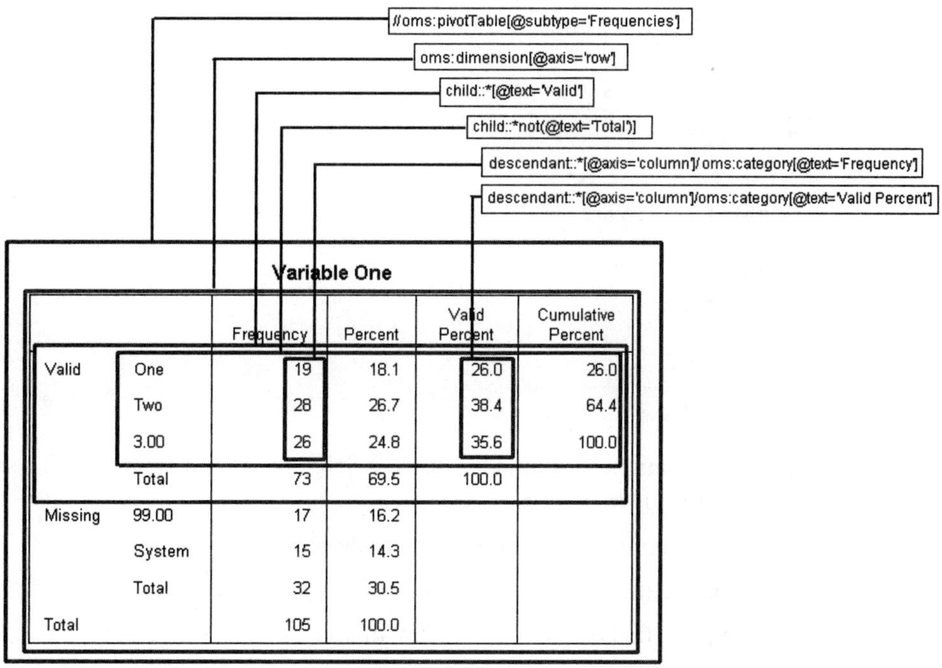

Advanced xsl:for-each "Pull" Example

This example builds on the basics described in the previous example. In addition to selecting and displaying only selected parts of each frequency table in HTML format, this example:

- Does not rely on any localized text.
- Always shows both variable names and labels.
- Always shows both values and value labels.
- Rounds decimal values to integers.

The XSLT style sheet used in this example is *customized_frequency_tables.xsl*, located in the *tutorial\sample_files* folder of the SPSS installation folder.

Figure 8-12
Customized HTML with values rounded to integers

Variable Name: var1

Variable Label: Variable One

Category	Count	Percent
1: One	19	26
2: Two	28	38
3	26	36
Total	73	100

Variable Name: var2

Category	Count	Percent
f: Female	63	60
m: Male	42	40
Total	105	100

The simple example contained a single XSLT <template> element. This style sheet contains multiple templates:

- A "main" template that selects the table elements from the OXML
- A template that defines the display of variable names and labels
- A template that defines the display of values and value labels
- A template that defines the display of cell values as rounded integers

Main template. Since this XSLT style sheet produces tables with essentially the same structure as the simple <xsl:for-each> example, the main template is similar to the one used in the simple example.

```
<?xml version="1.0" encoding="UTF-8"?>
<xsl:stylesheet xmlns:xsl="http://www.w3.org/1999/XSL/Transform"
  version="1.0" xmlns:oms="http://xml.spss.com/spss/oms">
```

```
<!--enclose everything in a template, starting at the root node-->
<xsl:template match="/">
<HTML>
<HEAD>
<TITLE>Modified Frequency Tables</TITLE>
</HEAD>
<BODY>
<xsl:for-each select="//oms:pivotTable[@subType='Frequencies']">
<xsl:for-each select="oms:dimension[@axis='row']">
 <h3>
  <xsl:call-template name="showVarInfo"/>
 </h3>
</xsl:for-each>
<!--create the HTML table-->
<table border="1">
 <tbody align="char" char="." charoff="1">
 <tr>  <th>Category</th><th>Count</th><th>Percent</th>
 </tr>
 <xsl:for-each select="descendant::oms:dimension[@axis='column']">
   <xsl:if test="oms:category[3]">
    <tr>
     <td>
       <xsl:choose>
        <xsl:when test="parent::*/@varName">
         <xsl:call-template name="showValueInfo"/>
        </xsl:when>
        <xsl:when test="not(parent::*/@varName)">
          <b><xsl:value-of select="parent::*/@text"/></b>
        </xsl:when>
       </xsl:choose>
     </td>
     <td>
      <xsl:apply-templates select=
       "oms:category[1]/oms:cell/@number"/>
     </td>
     <td>
      <xsl:apply-templates select=
       "oms:category[3]/oms:cell/@number"/>
     </td>
    </tr>
  </xsl:if>
  </xsl:for-each>
 </tbody>
</table>
<xsl:if test="descendant::*/oms:note">
<p><xsl:value-of select="descendant::*/oms:note/@text"/></p>
</xsl:if>
</xsl:for-each>
</BODY>
</HTML>
</xsl:template>
```

This template is similar to the one for the simple example. The main differences are:

- <xsl:call-template name="showVarInfo"/> calls another template to determine what to show for the table title instead of simply using the text attribute of the row dimension (oms:dimension[@axis='row']).
- <xsl:if test="oms:category[3]"> selects only the data in the *Valid* section of the table, instead of <xsl:if test="ancestor::oms:group[@text='Valid']">. The positional argument used in this example does not rely on localized text. It also relies on the fact that the basic structure of a frequency table is always the same—and the fact that OXML does not include elements for empty cells. Since the *Missing* section of a frequency table contains only values in the first two columns, there are no oms:category[3] column elements in the *Missing* section; so the test condition is not met for the *Missing* rows.
- <xsl:when test="parent::*/@varName"> selects the nontotal rows instead of <xsl:when test="not((parent::*)[@text='Total'])">. Column elements in the nontotal rows in a frequency table contain a *varName* attribute that identifies the variable, whereas column elements in total rows do not. So, this selects nontotal rows without relying on localized text.
- <xsl:call-template name="showValueInfo"/> calls another template to determine what to show for the row labels instead of <xsl:value-of select="parent::*/@text"/>.
- <xsl:apply-templates select="oms:category[1]/oms:cell/@number"/> selects the value in the *Frequency* column instead of
<xsl:value-of select="oms:category[@text='Frequency']/oms:cell/@text"/>.
A positional argument is used instead of localized text (the *Frequency* column is always the first column in a frequency table), and a template is applied to determine how to display the value in the cell. Percent values are handled the same way, using oms:category[3] to select the values from the *Valid Percent* column.

Controlling variable and value label display. The display of variable names and/or labels and values and/or value labels in pivot tables is determined by the current settings for SET TVARS and SET TNUMBERS; the corresponding text attributes in the OXML also reflect those settings. The system default is to display labels when they exist and names/values when they do not. The settings can be changed to always show names/values and never show labels or always show both.

The XSLT templates *showVarInfo* and *showValueInfo* are designed to ignore those settings and always show both names/values and labels (if present).

```
<!--display both variable names and labels-->
<xsl:template name="showVarInfo">
 <p>
 <xsl:text>Variable Name: </xsl:text>
 <xsl:value-of select="@varName"/>
 </p>
 <xsl:if test="@label">
  <p>
   <xsl:text>Variable Label: </xsl:text>
   <xsl:value-of select="@label"/>
  </p>
 </xsl:if>
</xsl:template>

<!--display both values and value labels-->
<xsl:template name="showValueInfo">
 <xsl:choose>
 <!--Numeric vars have a number attribute,
  string vars have a string attribute -->
  <xsl:when test="parent::*/@number">
   <xsl:value-of select="parent::*/@number"/>
  </xsl:when>
  <xsl:when test="parent::*/@string">
   <xsl:value-of select="parent::*/@string"/>
  </xsl:when>
 </xsl:choose>
 <xsl:if test="parent::*/@label">
   <xsl:text>: </xsl:text>
   <xsl:value-of select="parent::*/@label"/>
 </xsl:if>
</xsl:template>
```

- <xsl:text>Variable Name: </xsl:text> and <xsl:value-of select="@varName"/> display the text "Variable Name:" followed by the variable name.
- <xsl:if test="@label"> checks to see if the variable has a defined label.
- If the variable has a defined label, <xsl:text>Variable Label: </xsl:text> and <xsl:value-of select="@label"/> display the text "Variable Label:" followed by the defined variable label.
- Values and value labels are handled in a similar fashion, except instead of a *varName* attribute, values will have either a number attribute or a string attribute.

Controlling decimal display. The text attribute of a <cell> element in OXML displays numeric values with the default number of decimal positions for the particular type of cell value. For most table types, there is little or no control over the default number of decimals displayed in cell values in pivot tables, but OXML can provide some flexibility not available in default pivot table display.

In this example, the cell values are rounded to integers, but we could just as easily display five or six or more decimal positions because the number attribute may contain up to 15 significant digits.

```
<!--round decimal cell values to integers-->
<xsl:template match="@number">
 <xsl:value-of select="format-number(.,'#')"/>
</xsl:template>
```

- This template is invoked whenever <apply-templates select="..."/> contains a reference to a number attribute.
- <xsl:value-of select="format-number(.,'#')"/> specifies that the selected values should be rounded to integers with no decimal positions.

Positional Arguments versus Localized Text Attributes

Whenever possible, it is always best to avoid XPath expressions that rely on localized text (text that differs for different output languages) or positional arguments. You will probably find, however, that this is not always possible.

Localized Text Attributes

Most table elements contain a text attribute that contains the information as it would appear in a pivot table in the current output language. For example, the column in a frequency table that contains counts is labeled *Frequency* in English but *Frecuencia* in Spanish. If you do not need XSLT that will work in multiple languages, XPath expressions that select elements based on text attributes (for example, @text='Frequency') will often provide a simple, reliable solution.

Positional Arguments

Instead of localized text attributes, for many table types you can use positional arguments that are not affected by output language. For example, in a frequency table the column that contains counts is always the first column, so a positional argument of category[1] at the appropriate level of the tree structure should always select information in the column that contains counts.

In some table types, however, the elements in the table and order of elements in the table can vary. For example, the order of statistics in the columns or rows of table subtype 'Report' generated by the MEANS command is determined by the specified order of the statistics on the CELLS subcommand. In fact, two tables of this type may not even display the same statistics at all. So in one table, category[1] might select the category that contains mean values, but median values in another table, and nothing at all in another table.

Layered Split-File Processing

Layered split-file processing can alter the basic structure of tables that you might otherwise assume have a fixed default structure. For example, a standard frequency table has only one row dimension (dimension axis="row"), but a frequency table of the same variable when layered split-file processing is in effect will have multiple row dimensions, and the total number of dimensions—and row label columns in the table—depends on the number of split-file variables and unique split-file values.

Figure 8-13
Standard and layered frequency tables

Standard Frequency Table

		Frequency	Percent	Valid Percent	Cumulative Percent
Valid	One	19	18.1	26.0	26.0
	Two	28	26.7	38.4	64.4
	3.00	26	24.8	35.6	100.0
	Total	73	69.5	100.0	
Missing	99.00	17	16.2		
	System	15	14.3		
	Total	32	30.5		
Total		105	100.0		

Frequency Table with Layered Split-File Processing

var2			Frequency	Percent	Valid Percent	Cumulative Percent
Female	Valid	One	14	22.2	29.2	29.2
		Two	20	31.7	41.7	70.8
		3.00	14	22.2	29.2	100.0
		Total	48	76.2	100.0	
	Missing	System	15	23.8		
	Total		63	100.0		
Male	Valid	One	5	11.9	20.0	20.0
		Two	8	19.0	32.0	52.0
		3.00	12	28.6	48.0	100.0
		Total	25	59.5	100.0	
	Missing	99.00	17	40.5		
	Total		42	100.0		

Exporting Data to Other Applications and Formats

You can save the contents of the working data file in variety of formats, including SAS and Excel. You can also write data to a database.

Saving Data in SAS Format

With the SAVE TRANSLATE command, you can save data as SAS v6, SAS v7, and SAS transport files. A SAS transport file is a sequential file written in SAS transport format and can be read by SAS with the XPORT engine and PROC COPY or the DATA step.

- Certain characters that are allowed in SPSS variable names are not valid in SAS, such as @, #, and $. These illegal characters are replaced with an underscore when the data are exported.
- SPSS variable labels containing more than 40 characters are truncated when exported to a SAS v6 file.
- Where they exist, SPSS variable labels are mapped to the SAS variable labels. If no variable label exists in the SPSS data, the variable name is mapped to the SAS variable label.
- SAS allows only one value for missing, whereas SPSS allows the definition of numerous missing values. As a result, all missing values in SPSS are mapped to a single missing value in the SAS file.

Example

```
*save_as_SAS.sps.
GET FILE='c:\examples\data\employee data.sav'.
SAVE TRANSLATE OUTFILE='c:\examples\data\sas7datafile.sas7bdat'
  /TYPE=SAS  /VERSION=7  /PLATFORM=WINDOWS
  /VALFILE='c:\examples\data\sas7datafile_labels.sas' .
```

- The active data file will be saved as a SAS v7 data file.
- PLATFORM=WINDOWS creates a data file that can be read by SAS running on Windows operating systems. For UNIX operating systems, use PLATFORM=UNIX. For platform independent data files, use VERSION=X to create a SAS transport file.

- The VALFILE subcommand saves defined value labels in a SAS formats file. Unlike SPSS, SAS variable and value labels are not saved with the data; they are stored in separate file.

For more information, see the SAVE TRANSLATE command in the *SPSS Command Syntax Reference*.

Saving Data in Excel Format

To save data in Excel format, use the SAVE TRANSLATE command with /TYPE=XLS.

Example

```
*save_as_excel.sps.
GET FILE='c:\examples\data\employee data.sav'.
SAVE TRANSLATE OUTFILE='c:\examples\data\exceldata.xls'
  /TYPE=XLS /VERSION=8
  /FIELDNAMES
  /CELLS=VALUES.
```

- VERSION=8 saves the data file in Excel 97–2000 format.
- FIELDNAMES includes the variable names as the first row of the Excel file.
- CELLS=VALUES saves the actual data values. If you want to save descriptive value labels instead, use CELLS=LABELS.

Writing Data Back to a Database

SAVE TRANSLATE can also write data back to an existing database. You can create new database tables or replace or modify existing ones. As with reading database tables, writing back to a database uses ODBC, so you need to have the necessary ODBC database drivers installed.

The command syntax for writing back to a database is fairly simple—but, just like reading data from a database, you need the somewhat cryptic CONNECT string. The easiest way to get the CONNECT string is to use the Database Wizard to read data from the database, and paste the generated command syntax at the last step of the wizard.

For more information on ODBC drivers and CONNECT strings, see Chapter 3.

Example

This example reads a table from an Access database, creates a subset of cases and variables, and then writes a new table to the database containing that subset of data.

```
*write_to_access.sps.
GET DATA /TYPE=ODBC /CONNECT=
 'DSN=MS Access Database;DBQ=C:\examples\data\dm_demo.mdb;'+
 'DriverId=25;FIL=MS Access;MaxBufferSize=2048;PageTimeout=5;'
 /SQL = 'SELECT * FROM CombinedTable'.
EXECUTE.
DELETE VARIABLES Income TO Response.
N OF CASES 50.
SAVE TRANSLATE
  /TYPE=ODBC /CONNECT=
   'DSN=MS Access Database;DBQ=C:\examples\data\dm_demo.mdb;'+
   'DriverId=25;FIL=MS Access;MaxBufferSize=2048;PageTimeout=5;'
  /TABLE='CombinedSubset'
  /REPLACE
  /UNSELECTED=RETAIN
  /MAP.
```

- The CONNECT string in the SAVE TRANSLATE command is exactly the same as the one used in the GET DATA command, and that CONNECT string was obtained by pasting command syntax from the Database Wizard. TYPE=ODBC indicates that the data will be saved in a database. The database must already exist; you cannot use SAVE TRANSLATE to create a database.
- The TABLE subcommand specifies the name of the database table. If the table does not already exist in the database, it will be added to the database.
- If a table with the name specified on the TABLE subcommand already exists, the REPLACE subcommand specifies that this table should be overwritten.
- You can use APPEND instead of REPLACE to append data to an existing table, but there must be an exact match between variable and field names and corresponding data types. The table can contain more fields than variables being written to the table, but every variable must have a matching field in the database table.
- UNSELECTED=RETAIN specifies that any filtered, but not deleted, cases should be included in the table. This is the default. To exclude filtered cases, use UNSELECTED=DELETE.
- The MAP subcommand provides a summary of the data written to the database. In this example, we deleted all but the first three variables and first 50 cases before writing back to the database, and the output displayed by the MAP subcommand indicates that three variables and 50 cases were written to the database.

Figure 8-14
MAP subcommand summary displayed in Viewer

```
Data written to CombinedSubset.
3 variables and 50 cases written.
Variable: ID                  Type: Number   Width: 11   Dec: 0
Variable: AGE                 Type: Number   Width:  8   Dec: 2
Variable: MARITALSTATUS       Type: Number   Width:  8   Dec: 2
```

Saving Data in Text Format

You use the SAVE TRANSLATE command to save data as tab-delimited text or the WRITE command to save data as fixed-width text. See the *SPSS Command Syntax Reference* for more information.

Exporting Results to Other Applications and Formats

The OMS command (discussed earlier in this chapter) is the method of choice for exporting results in XML or text format. For HTML format, OMS is currently limited by the fact that all charts are excluded, and OMS is not appropriate if you want to export results to Microsoft Word or Excel.

To export results to Word or Excel or to include charts in HTML, you need to use the Export facility in the Viewer. There is no command syntax alternative, although it is possible to write scripts to accomplish this in an automated fashion. For more information on scripting, see Chapter 7.

To export results in HTML, Word, or Excel format, from the menus in the Viewer window, choose:

File
  Export

For detailed examples, see the tutorials installed with SPSS. From the menus, choose:

Help
  Tutorial

In the Tutorial table of contents, choose:

Working with Output
  Using the Viewer
    Using Results in Other Applications

A sample script for exporting results to Excel—*Scripts_ExportViewerToSingleExcelSheet.sbs*—is included in the *examples\scripts* folder.

Customizing HTML

In addition to including charts with HTML, the Export facility also provides another feature not currently available with OMS:—the ability to automatically customized exported HTML results.

To customize HTML documents, you need to modify the text file *htmlfram.txt*, located in the SPSS installation folder. Replace the comments in the "fields" on the lines between the double open brackets (<<) with the text or HTML code that you want to insert in your exported HTML documents, and then save the text file.

Chapter

9

SPSS for SAS Programmers

This chapter shows the SPSS code and SAS equivalents for a number of basic data management tasks. This is not a comprehensive comparison of the two applications. The purpose of this chapter is to provide a point of reference for users familiar with SAS who are making the transition to SPSS; it is not intended to demonstrate how one application is better or worse than the other.

Reading Data

Both SPSS and SAS can read data stored in a wide variety of formats, including numerous database formats, Excel spreadsheets, and text files. All of the SPSS examples presented in this section are discussed in greater detail in Chapter 3.

Reading Database Tables

Both SAS and SPSS rely on Open Database Connectivity (ODBC) to read data from relational databases. Both applications read data from databases by reading database tables. You can read information from a single table or merge data from multiple tables in the same database.

Reading a Single Database Table

The structure of a database table is very similar to the structure of an SPSS data file or SAS data set: records (rows) are cases, and fields (columns) are variables.

Figure 9-1
SPSS code to read a single database table

```
*access1.sps.
GET DATA /TYPE=ODBC /CONNECT=
 'DSN=MS Access Database;DBQ=C:\examples\data\dm_demo.mdb;'+
 'DriverId=25;FIL=MS Access;MaxBufferSize=2048;PageTimeout=5;'
 /SQL = 'SELECT * FROM CombinedTable'.
EXECUTE.
```

Figure 9-2
SAS code to read a single database table

```
proc sql;
connect to odbc(dsn=dm_demo uid=admin pwd=admin);
create table sasdata1 as
  select *
  from connection to odbc(
  select *
  from CombinedTable
  );
quit;
```

- The SPSS code allows you to input the parameters for the name of the database and the path directly into the code. SAS assumes that you have used the Windows Administrative Tools to set up the ODBC path. For this example, SAS assumes that the ODBC DSN for the database *c:\examples\data\dm_demo.mdb* is defined as *dm_demo*.
- Another difference that you will notice is that SPSS does not use a data set name. This is because once the data is read, it is immediately the active data set in SPSS. For this example, the SAS data set is given the name *sasdata1*.
- In SPSS, the CONNECT string and all SQL statements must be enclosed in quotes.
- SAS converts the spaces in field names to underscores in variable names, while SPSS removes the spaces without substituting any character. Where SAS uses all of the original variable names as labels, SPSS provides labels for only the variables not conforming to SPSS standards. So, in this example the variable *ID* will be named *ID* in SPSS with no label and will be named *ID* in SAS with a label of *ID*. The variable *Marital Status* will be named *Marital_Status* in SAS and *MaritalStatus* in SPSS, with a label of *Marital Status* in both SPSS and SAS.

Reading Multiple Tables

Both SPSS and SAS support reading and merging multiple database tables, and the code in both languages is very similar.

Figure 9-3
SPSS code for reading multiple database tables

```
*access_multtables1.sps.
GET DATA /TYPE=ODBC /CONNECT=
 'DSN=MS Access Database;DBQ=C:\examples\data\dm_demo.mdb;'+
  'DriverId=25;FIL=MS Access;MaxBufferSize=2048;PageTimeout=5;'
 /SQL =
 'SELECT  * FROM DemographicInformation, SurveyResponses'
 ' WHERE DemographicInformation.ID=SurveyResponses.ID'.
EXECUTE.
```

Figure 9-4
SAS code for reading multiple database tables

```
proc sql;
connect to odbc(dsn=dm_demo uid=admin pwd=admin);
create table sasdata2 as
  select *
  from connection to odbc(
  select *
  from DemographicInformation, SurveyResponses
  where DemographicInformation.ID=SurveyResponses.ID
  );
quit;
```

Outer Joins

Both languages also support both left and right outer joins, and one-to-many record matching between database tables.

Figure 9-5
SPSS code for one-to-many left outer join

```
*sqlserver_outer_join.sps.
GET DATA /TYPE=ODBC
 /CONNECT= 'DSN=SQLServer;UID=;APP=SPSS For Windows;'
  'WSID=ROLIVERLAP;Network=DBMSSOCN;Trusted_Connection=Yes'
 /SQL =
  'SELECT  SurveyResponses.ID,  SurveyResponses.Internet,'
  ' [Value Labels].[Internet Label]'
  ' FROM SurveyResponses LEFT OUTER JOIN [Value Labels]'
  ' ON SurveyResponses.Internet'
  ' = [Value Labels].[Internet Value]'.
```

Figure 9-6
SAS code for one-to-many left outer join

```
proc sql;
connect to odbc(dsn=sql_survey uid=admin pwd=admin);
create table sasdata3 as
  select *
  from connection to odbc(
  select SurveyResponses.ID,
     SurveyResponses.Internet,
     "Value Labels"."Internet Label"
  from SurveyReponses left join "Value Labels"
     on SurveyReponses.Internet =
     "Value Labels"."Internet Value"
     );
quit;
```

The left outer join works similarly for both languages.

- The resulting data set will contain all the records from the *SurveyResponses* table, even if there is not a matching record in the *Value Labels* table.
- SPSS requires the syntax LEFT OUTER JOIN, and SAS requires the syntax left join to perform the join.
- Both languages support the use of either quotes or square brackets to delimit table and/or variable names that contain spaces. Since SPSS requires that each line of SQL be quoted, square brackets are used here for clarity.

Reading Excel Files

SPSS and SAS can read individual Excel worksheets and multiple worksheets in the same Excel workbook.

Reading a Single Worksheet

As with reading a single database table, the basic mechanics of reading a single worksheet are fairly simple: rows are read as cases and columns are read as variables.

Figure 9-7
SPSS code for reading an Excel worksheet

```
*readexcel.sps.
GET DATA
   /TYPE=XLS
   /FILE='c:\examples\data\sales.xls'
   /SHEET=NAME 'Gross Revenue'
   /CELLRANGE=RANGE 'A2:I15'
   /READNAMES=on .
```

Figure 9-8
SAS code for reading an Excel worksheet

```
proc import datafile='c:\examples\data\sales.xls'
  dbms=excel2000 replace out=SASdata4;
   sheet="Gross Revenue";
   range="A2:I15";
   getnames=yes;
   run;
```

- Both languages require the name of the Excel file, worksheet name, and range of cells.
- Both provide the choice of reading the top row of the range as variable names. SPSS accomplishes this with the READNAMES subcommand, and SAS accomplishes this with the GETNAMES option.
- SAS requires an output data set name. The data set name *SASdata4* has been used in this example. SPSS has no corresponding requirement.
- Both languages convert spaces in variable names to underscores. SAS uses all of the original variable names as labels, and SPSS provides labels for the variable names not conforming to SPSS variable naming rules. In this example, both languages convert *Store Number* to *Store_Number* with a label of *Store Number*.

- The two languages use different rules for assigning the variable type (for example, numeric, string, date). SPSS searches the entire column to determine each variable type. SAS searches to the first non-missing value of each variable to determine the type. In this example, the *Toys* variable contains dollar-formatted data with the exception of one record containing a value of "NA." SPSS assigns this variable the string data type preserving the "NA" in record five, whereas SAS assigns it a numeric dollar format and sets the value for *Toys* in record five to missing.

Reading Multiple Worksheets

Both SPSS and SAS rely on ODBC to read multiple worksheets from a workbook.

Figure 9-9
SPSS code for reading multiple worksheets

```
*readexcel2.sps.
GET DATA
  /TYPE=ODBC
  /CONNECT=
    'DSN=Excel Files;DBQ=c:\examples\data\sales.xls;' +
    'DriverId=790;MaxBufferSize=2048;PageTimeout=5;'
    /SQL =
    'SELECT  Location$.[Store Number], State, Region, City,'
    ' Power, Hand, Accessories,'
    ' Tires, Batteries, Gizmos, Dohickeys'
    ' FROM [Location$], [Tools$], [Auto$]'
    ' WHERE [Tools$].[Store Number]=[Location$].[Store Number]'
    ' AND [Auto$].[Store Number]=[Location$].[Store Number]'.
```

Figure 9-10
SAS code for reading multiple worksheets

```
proc sql;
connect to odbc(dsn=salesxls uid=admin pwd=admin);
create table sasdata5 as
  select *
  from connection to odbc(
  select Location$."Store Number", State, Region, City,
    Power, Hand, Accessories, Tires, Batteries, Gizmos,
    Dohickeys
  from "Location$", "Tools$", "Auto$"
  where "Tools$"."Store Number"="Location$"."Store Number"
  and "Auto$"."Store Number"="Location$"."Store Number"
  );
quit;;
```

- For this example, both SPSS and SAS treat the worksheet names as table names in the From statement.

- Both require the inclusion of a "$" after the worksheet name.
- As in the previous ODBC examples, quotes could be substituted for the square brackets in the SPSS code and vice-versa for the SAS code.

Reading Text Data

Both SPSS and SAS can read a wide variety of text format data files. This example shows how the two applications read comma separated values (CSV) files. A CSV file uses commas to separate data values, and encloses values that include commas in quotation marks. Many applications export text data in this format.

Figure 9-11
CSV text data file

```
ID,Name,Gender,Date Hired,Department
1,"Foster, Chantal",f,10/29/1998,1
2,"Healy, Jonathan",m,3/1/1992,3
3,"Walter, Wendy",f,1/23/1995,2
```

Figure 9-12
SPSS code for reading CSV text data

```
*delimited_csv.sps.
GET DATA  /TYPE = TXT
  /FILE = 'C:\examples\data\CSV_file.csv'
  /DELIMITERS = ","
  /QUALIFIER = '"'
  /ARRANGEMENT = DELIMITED
  /FIRSTCASE = 2
  /VARIABLES = ID F3 Name A15 Gender A1
   Date_Hired ADATE10 Department F1.
```

Figure 9-13
SAS code for reading CSV text data

```
data csvnew;
  infile "c:\examples\data\csv_file.csv" DLM=',' Firstobs=2 DSD;
  informat name $char15. gender $1. date_hired mmddyy10.;
  input id name gender date_hired department;
  run;
```

- The SPSS DELIMITERS and SAS DLM values identify the comma as the delimiter.
- SAS uses the DSD option on the infile statement to handle the commas within quoted values, and SPSS uses the QUALIFIER subcommand.

- SPSS uses the format ADATE10, and SAS uses the format mmyydd10 to properly read the date variable.
- The SPSS FIRSTCASE subcommand is equivalent to the SAS Firstobs specification, indicating that the data to be read start on the second line/record.

Merging Data Files

Both SPSS and SAS can merge two or more data sets together. All of the SPSS examples presented in this section are discussed in greater detail in "Merging Data Files" on p. 87 in Chapter 4.

Merging Files with the Same Cases but Different Variables

One of the types of merges supported by both applications is a **match merge**: two or more data sets that contain the same cases but different variables are merged together. Records from each data set are matched based on the values of one or more key variables. For example, demographic data for survey respondents might be contained in one data set, and survey responses for surveys taken at different times might be contained in multiple additional data sets. The cases are the same (respondents), but the variables are different (demographic information and survey responses).

Figure 9-14
SPSS code for match merge

```
*match_files2.sps.
GET FILE='C:\examples\data\match_response1.sav'.
SORT CASES BY id.
SAVE OUTFILE='C:\examples\data\match_response1.sav'.
GET FILE='C:\examples\data\match_response2.sav'.
SORT CASES BY id.
SAVE OUTFILE='C:\examples\data\match_response2.sav'.
GET FILE='C:\examples\data\match_demographics.sav'.
SORT CASES BY id.
MATCH FILES /FILE=*
  /FILE='C:\examples\data\match_response1.sav'
  /FILE='C:\examples\data\match_response2.sav'
  /RENAME  opinion1=opinion1_2 opinion2=opinion2_2
   opinion3=opinion3_2 opinion4=opinion4_2
  /BY id.
EXECUTE.
```

Figure 9-15
SAS code for match merge

```
libname in "c:\examples\data";
proc sort data=in.match_response1;
  by id;
  run;
proc sort data=in.match_response2;
  by id;
  run;
proc sort data=in.match_demographics;
  by id;
  run;
data match_new;
  merge match_demographics
        match_response1
        match_response2 (rename=(opinion1=opinion1_2
          opinion2=opinion2_2 opinion3=opinion3_2
          opinion4=opinion4_2));
  by id;
  run;
```

- SPSS uses the GET FILE command to open each data file prior to sorting. SAS uses libname to assign a working directory for each data set that needs sorting.
- Both require that each data set be sorted by values of the BY variable used to match cases.
- In SPSS, the last data file opened with the GET FILE command is the active data file. So in the MATCH FILES command, FILE=* refers to the data file *match_demographics.sav*, and the merged working data file retains that filename (but if you do not explicitly save the file with the same filename, the original file is not overwritten). SAS requires a data set name for the DATA step. In this example, the merged data set is given the name *match_new*.
- Both SPSS and SAS allow you to rename variables when merging. This is necessary because *match_response1* and *match_response2* contain variables with the same names. If the variables were not renamed for the second data set, then the variables merged from the first data set would be overwritten.

Merging Files with the Same Variables but Different Cases

You can also merge two or more data sets that contain the same variables but different cases, appending cases from each data set. For example, regional revenue for two different company divisions might be stored in two separate data sets. Both files have the same variables (region indicator and revenue) but different cases (each region for each division is a case).

Figure 9-16
SPSS code for appending cases/records

```
*add_files1.sps.
ADD FILES
  /FILE = 'c:\examples\data\catalog.sav'
  /FILE =' c:\examples\data\retail.sav'
    /IN = Division.
EXECUTE.
VALUE LABELS Division 0 'Catalog' 1 'Retail Store'.
```

Figure 9-17
SAS code for appending cases/records

```
libname in "c:\examples\data";
proc format;
  value divfmt
        0='Catalog'
        1='Retail Store' ;
  run;
data append_new;
  set in.catalog (in=a) in.retail (in=b);
  format division divfmt.;
  if a then division=0;
     else if b then division=1;
  run;
```

- In the SPSS code, the IN subcommand after the second FILE subcommand creates a new variable *Division* with a value of 1 for cases from *retail.sav* and a value of 0 for cases from *catalog.sav*. To achieve this same result in SAS requires the Format procedure to create a user-defined format where 0 represents the catalog file and 1 represents the retail file.
- In SAS, the SET statement is required to append the files so that the system variable *IN* can be used in the data step to assist with identifying which data set contains each observation.
- The SPSS VALUE LABELS command assigns descriptive labels to the values 0 and 1 for the variable *Division*, making it easier to interpret the values of the variable that identifies the source file for each case. In SAS, this would require a separate formats file.

Aggregating Data

SPSS and SAS can both aggregate groups of cases, creating a new data set in which the groups are the cases. In this example, information was collected for every person living in a selected sample of households. In addition to information for each individual, each case contains a variable that identifies the household. You can change the unit of analysis from individuals to households by aggregating the data based on the value of the household ID variable.

Figure 9-18
SPSS code for aggregating and merging

```
*aggregate2.sps.
DATA LIST FREE (" ")
  /ID_household (F3) ID_person (F2) Income (F8).
BEGIN DATA
101 1 12345 101 2 47321 101 3 500 101 4 0
102 1 77233 102 2 0
103 1 19010 103 2 98277 103 3 0
104 1 101244
END DATA.
SORT CASES BY ID_household.
SAVE OUTFILE = 'c:\temp\tempdata.sav'.
AGGREGATE
  /OUTFILE = *
  /BREAK = ID_household
  /per_capita_Income = MEAN(Income)
  /Household_Size = N.
***merge the two files together***.
MATCH FILES
  /FILE = 'c:\temp\tempdata.sav'
  /TABLE = *
  /BY ID_Household.
EXECUTE.
```

Figure 9-19
SAS code for aggregating and merging

```
data tempdata;
  informat id_household 3. id_person 2. income 8.;
  input ID_household ID_person Income @@;
cards;
101 1 12345 101 2 47321 101 3 500 101 4 0
102 1 77233 102 2 0
103 1 19010 103 2 98277 103 3 0
104 1 101244
;
run;
proc sort data=tempdata;
  by ID_household;
  run;
proc summary data=tempdata;
  var Income;
  by ID_household;
  output out=aggdata
    mean=per_capita_Income
    n=Household_Size;
  run;
data new;
  merge tempdata aggdata (drop=_type_ _freq_);
  by ID_Household;
  run;
```

- SAS uses the Summary procedure for aggregating, whereas SPSS has a specific command for aggregating data: AGGREGATE.
- The SPSS BREAK subcommand is equivalent to the SAS By Variable command.
- In SPSS, you specify the aggregate summary function and the variable to aggregate in a single step, as in: per_capita_Income=MEAN(Income). In SAS, this requires two separate statements: var Income and mean=per_capita_Income.
- Both SPSS and SAS allow you to drop unnecessary variables when merging the data sets. In this example, that is not necessary for SPSS, since the aggregated data file contains only the specific variables requested on the AGGREGATE command. The SAS aggregated data set, however, contains two automatically generated variables that you probably do not want in the merged result.

Assigning Variable Properties

In addition to basic data type (numeric, string, date, etc.) you can assign other properties that describe the variables and their associated values. In a sense, these properties can be considered **metadata**: data that describe the data. All of the SPSS examples provided here are discussed in greater detail in "Variable Properties" on p. 71 in Chapter 4.

Variable Labels

Both SPSS and SAS provide the ability to assign descriptive variable labels that have less restrictive rules than variable naming rules. For example, variable labels can contain spaces and special characters not allowed in variable names.

Figure 9-20
SPSS code for assigning variable labels

```
VARIABLE LABELS
  Interview_date "Interview date"
  Income_category "Income category"
  opinion1 "Would buy this product"
  opinion2 "Would recommend this product to others"
  opinion3 "Price is reasonable"
  opinion4 "Better than a poke in the eye with a sharp stick".
```

Figure 9-21
SAS code for assigning variable labels

```
label Interview_date = "Interview date";
label Income_category = "Income category";
label opinion1="Would buy this product";
label opinion2="Would recommend this product to others";
label opinion3="Price is reasonable";
label opinion4="Better than a poke in the eye with a sharp stick";
```

- In SPSS, all the variable labels can be defined in a single VARIABLE LABELS command. In SAS, a separate label statement is required for each variable.
- In SPSS, VARIABLE LABELS commands can appear anywhere in the command stream, and the labels are attached to the variables at that point in the command processing; so you can assign labels to newly created variables and/or change labels for existing variables at any time. In SAS, the label statements must be contained in the data step.

Value Labels

You can also assign descriptive labels for each value of a variable. This is particularly useful if your data file uses numeric codes to represent non-numeric categories. For example, *income_category* uses the codes 1 through 4 to represent different income ranges, and the four opinion variables use the codes 1 through 5 to represent level of agreement/disagreement.

Figure 9-22
SPSS code for assigning value labels

```
VALUE LABELS
  Gender "m" "Male" "f" "Female"
  /Income_category 1 "Under 25K" 2 "25K to 49K"
   3 "50K to 74K" 4 "75K+" 7 "Refused to answer"
   8 "Don't know" 9 "No answer"
  /Religion 1 "Catholic" 2 "Protestant" 3 "Jewish"
   4 "Other" 9 "No answer"
  /opinion1 TO opinion4 1 "Strongly Disagree" 2 "Disagree"
   3 "Ambivalent" 4 "Agree" 5 "Strongly Agree" 9 "No answer".
```

Figure 9-23
SAS code for assigning value labels

```
proc format;
  value $genfmt
    'm'='Male'
          'f'='Female'
          ;
  value incfmt
    1='Under 25K'
    2='25K to 49K'
    4='75K+'    3='50K to 74K'
    7='Refused to answer'
    8='Don''t know'
    9='No answer'
    ;
  value relfmt
    1='Catholic'
    2='Protestant'
    3='Jewish'
    4='Other'
    9='No answer'
    ;
```

```
  value opnfmt
    1='Strongly Disagree'
    2='Disagree'
    3='Ambivalent'
    4='Agree'
    5='Strongly Agree'
    9='No answer'
    ;
  run;
data new;
  format Gender $genfmt.
    Income_category incfmt.
    Religion relftm.
    opinion1 opinion2 opinion3 opinion4 opnfmt.;
  input Gender $ Income_category Religion opinion1-opinion4;
cards;
m 3 4 5 1 3 1
f 3 0 2 3 4 3
;
run;
```

- In SPSS, assigning value labels is relatively straightforward. You can insert VALUE LABELS commands (and ADD VALUE LABELS commands to append additional value labels) at any point in the command stream; those value labels, like variable labels, become metadata that is part of the data file, saved with the data file.
- In SAS, you need to define a format and then apply the format to specified variables within the data step.

Cleaning and Validating Data

Real data frequently contain real errors—and SPSS and SAS both have features that can help identify invalid or suspicious values. All of the SPSS examples provided in this section are discussed in detail.

Finding and Displaying Invalid Values

All the variables in a file may have values that appear to be valid when examined individually, but certain combinations of values for different variables may indicate at least one of the variables has either an invalid value or at least one that is suspect. For example, a pregnant male clearly indicates an error in one of the values, whereas a pregnant female older than 55 may not be invalid but should probably be double-checked.

Figure 9-24
SPSS code for finding and displaying invalid values

```
*invalid_data3.sps.
DATA LIST FREE /age gender pregnant.
BEGIN DATA
25 0 0
12 1 0
80 1 1
47 0 0
34 0 1
9 1 1
19 0 0
27 0 1
END DATA.
VALUE LABELS gender 0 'Male' 1 'Female'
  /pregnant 0 'No' 1 'Yes'.
COMPUTE valueCheck = 0.
DO IF pregnant = 1.
- DO IF gender = 0.
-   COMPUTE valueCheck = 1.
- ELSE IF gender = 1.
-   DO IF age > 55.
-      COMPUTE valueCheck = 2.
-   ELSE IF age < 12.
-      COMPUTE valueCheck = 3.
-   END IF.
- END IF.
END IF.
VALUE LABELS valueCheck
  0 'No problems detected'
  1 'Male and pregnant'
  2 'Age > 55 and pregnant'
  3 'Age < 12 and pregnant'.
FREQUENCIES VARIABLES = valueCheck.
```

Figure 9-25
SAS code for finding and displaying invalid values

```
proc format;
  value genfmt
    0='Male'
    1='Female'
    ;
  value pregfmt
    0='No'
    1='Yes'
    ;
  value vchkfmt
    0='No problems detected'
    1='Male and pregnant'
    2='Age > 55 and pregnant'
    3='Age < 12 and pregnant'
    ;
  run;
data new;
  format gender genfmt.
    pregnant pregfmt.
    valueCheck vchkfmt.
    ;
  input age gender pregnant;
  valueCheck=0;
  if pregnant then do;
     if gender=0 then valueCheck=1;
     else if gender then do;
       if age > 55 then valueCheck=2;
       else if age < 12 then valueCheck=3;
     end;
  end;
cards;
25 0 0
12 1 0
80 1 1
47 0 0
34 0 1
9 1 1
19 0 0
27 0 1
;
run;
proc freq data=new;
  tables valueCheck;
  run;
```

- DO IF pregnant = 1 in SPSS is equivalent to if pregnant then do in SAS. As in the SAS example, you could simplify the SPSS code to DO IF pregnant, since this resolves to Boolean "true" if the value of *pregnant* is 1.

- END IF in SPSS is equivalent to end in SAS in this example.
- To display a frequency table of *valueCheck*, SPSS uses a simple FREQUENCIES command, whereas in SAS you need to call a procedure separate from the data processing step.

Finding and Filtering Duplicates

In this example, each case is identified by two ID variables: *ID_house*, which identifies each household, and *ID_person*, which identifies each person within the household. If multiple cases have the same value for both variables, then they represent the same case. In this example, that is not necessarily a coding error, since the same person may have been interviewed on more than one occasion. The interview date is recorded in the variable *int_date*, and for cases that match on both ID variables, we want to ignore all but the most recent interview.

The SPSS code used in this example was generated by pasting and editing command syntax generated by the Identify Duplicate Cases dialog box (Data menu, Identify Duplicate Cases).

Figure 9-26
SPSS code for finding and filtering duplicates

```
* duplicates_filter.sps.
GET FILE='c:\examples\data\duplicates.sav'.
SORT CASES BY ID_house(A) ID_person(A) int_date(A) .
MATCH FILES  /FILE = *
  /BY ID_house ID_person /LAST = MostRecent .
FILTER BY MostRecent .
EXECUTE.
```

Figure 9-27
SAS code for finding and filtering duplicates

```
libname in "c:\examples\data";
proc sort data=in.duplicates;
  by ID_house ID_person int_date;
  run;
data new;
  set in.duplicates;
  by ID_house ID_person;
  if last.ID_person;
  run;
```

- Like SAS, SPSS is able to identify the last record within each sorted group. In this example, both assign a value of 1 to the last record in each group and a value of 0 to all other records.
- SAS uses the temporary variable *last.* to identify the last record in each group. This variable is available for each variable in the by statement following the set statement within the data step, but it is not saved to the data set.
- SPSS uses a MATCH FILES command with a LAST subcommand to create a new variable, *MostRecent*, that identifies the last case in each group. This is not a temporary variable, so it is available for future processing.
- Where SAS uses an if statement to select the last case in each group, SPSS uses a FILTER command to filter out all but but the last case in each group. The new SAS data step does not contain the duplicate records. SPSS retains the duplicates but does not include them in reports or analyses unless you turn off filtering (but you could use SELECT IF to delete instead of filter unselected cases). SPSS displays these records in the Data Editor with a slash through the row number.

Transforming Data Values

In both SPSS and SAS you can perform data transformations ranging from simple tasks, such as collapsing categories for reports, to more advanced tasks, such as creating new variables based on complex equations and conditional statements. All of the SPSS examples presented in this section are discussed in greater detail in "Transforming Data Values" on p. 112 in Chapter 4.

Recoding Data

There are many reasons why you might need or want to recode data. For example, questionnaires often use a combination of high-low and low-high rankings. For reporting and analysis purposes, however, you probably want these all coded in a consistent manner.

Figure 9-28
SPSS code for recoding data values

```
*recode.sps.
DATA LIST FREE /opinion1 opinion2.
BEGIN DATA
1 5
2 4
3 3
4 2
5 1
END DATA.
RECODE opinion2
 (1 = 5) (2 = 4) (4 = 2) (5 = 1)
 (ELSE = COPY)
 INTO opinion2_new.
EXECUTE.
VALUE LABELS opinion1 opinion2_new
  1 'Really bad' 2 'Bad' 3 'Blah'
  4 'Good' 5 'Terrific!'.
```

Figure 9-29
SAS code for recoding data values

```
proc format;
  value opfmt
        1='Really bad'
        2='Bad'
        3='Blah'
        4='Good'
        5='Terrific!'
        ;
  run;
data recode;
  format opinion1 opinion2_new opfmt.;
  input opinion1 opinion2;
  if opinion2=1 then opinion2_new=5;
  else if opinion2=2 then opinion2_new=4;
  else if opinion2=4 then opinion2_new=2;
  else if opinion2=5 then opinion2_new=1;
  else opinion2_new=opinion2;
cards;
1 5
2 4
3 3
4 2
5 1
;
run;
```

- SPSS uses a single RECODE command to create a new variable *opinion2_new* with the recoded values of the original variable *opinion_2*.
- SAS uses a series of if/else if/else statements to assign the recoded values, which requires a separate conditional statement for each value.
- ELSE=COPY in the SPSS RECODE command covers any values not explicitly specified and copies the original values to the new variable. This is equivalent to the last else statement in the SAS code.

Banding Data

Creating a small number of discrete categories from a continuous scale variable is sometimes referred to as **banding**. For example, you can band salary data into a few salary range categories.

Although it is not difficult to write code in SPSS or SAS to band a scale variable into range categories, in SPSS we recommend you try the Visual Bander, available on the Transform menu, because it can help you make the best recoding choices by showing the actual distribution of values and where your selected category boundaries occur in the distribution. It also provides a number of different banding methods and can automatically generate descriptive labels for the banded categories. The SPSS command syntax in this example was generated by the Visual Bander.

Figure 9-30
SPSS code for banding scale values into discrete categories

```
*visual_bander.sps.
GET FILE = 'c:\examples\data\employee data.sav'.
***commands generated by Visual Bander***.
RECODE salary
   ( MISSING = COPY ) ( LO THRU 25000 =1 ) ( LO THRU 50000 =2 )
   ( LO THRU 75000 =3 ) ( LO THRU HI = 4 )
   INTO salary_category.
VARIABLE LABELS salary_category 'Current Salary (Banded)'.
FORMAT salary_category (F5.0).
VALUE LABELS salary_category
   1  '<= $25,000'
   2  '$25,001 - $50,000'
   3  '$50,001 - $75,000'
   4  '$75,001+'
   0   'missing'.
MISSING VALUES salary_category ( 0 ).
VARIABLE LEVEL salary_category ( ORDINAL ).
EXECUTE.
```

Figure 9-31
SAS code for banding scale values into discrete categories

```
libname in "c:\examples\data";
proc format;
  value salfmt
        1='<= $25,000'
        2='$25,001 - $50,000'
        3='$50,001 - $75,000'
        4='$75,001+'
        0='missing'
        ;
  run;
data recode;
  set in.employee_data;
  format salary_category salfmt.;
  label salary_category = "Current Salary (Banded)";
  if 0<salary and salary<=25000 then salary_category=1;
  else if 25000<salary and salary<=50000 then salary_category=2;
  else if 50000<salary and salary<=75000 then salary_category=3;
  else if 75000<salary then salary_category=4;
  else salary_category=salary;
run;
```

- The SPSS Visual Bander generates RECODE command syntax similar to the code in the previous recoding example. It can also automatically generate appropriate descriptive value labels (as in this example) for each banded category.
- As in the recoding example, SAS uses a series of if/else if/else statements to accomplish the same thing.
- The SPSS RECODE command supports the keywords LO and HI to ensure that no values are left out of the banding scheme. In SAS, you can obtain similar functionality with the standard <, <=, >, and >= operators.

Numeric Functions

In addition to simple arithmetic operators (for example, +, -, /, *), you can transform data values in both SPSS and SAS with a wide variety of functions, including arithmetic and statistical functions.

Figure 9-32
SPSS code with arithmetic and statistical functions

```
*numeric_functions.sps.
DATA LIST LIST (",") /var1 var2 var3 var4.
BEGIN DATA
1, , 3, 4
5, 6, 7, 8
9, , , 12
END DATA.
COMPUTE Square_Root = SQRT(var4).
COMPUTE Remainder = MOD(var4, 3).
COMPUTE Average = MEAN.3(var1, var2, var3, var4).
COMPUTE Valid_Values = NVALID(var1 TO var4).
COMPUTE Trunc_Mean = TRUNC(MEAN(var1 TO var4)).
EXECUTE.
```

Figure 9-33
SAS code with arithmetic and statistical functions

```
data new;
  input var1 var2 var3 var4;
  Square_Root=sqrt(var4);
  Remainder=mod(var4,3);
  x=nmiss(var1,var2,var3,var4);
  if x<=1 then Average=mean(var1,var2,var3,var4);
  Valid_Values=4-x;
  Trunc_Mean=int(mean(var1,var2,var3,var4));
cards;
1 . 3 4
5 6 7 8
9 . . 12
;
run;
```

- SPSS and SAS use the same function names for the square root (SQRT) and remainder (MOD) functions.
- SPSS allows you to specify the minimum number of non-missing values required to calculate any numeric function. For example, MEAN.3 specifies that at least three of the variables (or other function arguments) must contain non-missing values.
- In SAS, if you want to specify the minimum number of non-missing arguments for a function calculation, you need to calculate the number of non-missing values using the function nmiss, and then use this information in an if statement prior to calculating the function.
- The SPSS NVALID function returns the number of non-missing values in an argument list. To achieve comparable functionality with SAS, you need to use the

NMISS function to calculate the number of missing values and then subtract that value from the total number of arguments.

- The SAS INT function is equivalent to the SPSS TRUNC function.

Random Number Functions

Random value and distribution functions generate random values based on various distributions.

Figure 9-34
SPSS code for random number functions

```
*random_functons.sps.
NEW FILE.
SET SEED 987987987.
*create 1,000 cases with random values.
INPUT PROGRAM.
- LOOP #I=1 TO 1000.
-   COMPUTE Uniform_Distribution = UNIFORM(100).
-   COMPUTE Normal_Distribution = RV.NORMAL(50,25).
-   COMPUTE Poisson_Distribution = RV.POISSON(50).
-   END CASE.
- END LOOP.
- END FILE.
END INPUT PROGRAM.
EXECUTE.
```

Figure 9-35
SAS code for random number functions

```
data new;
  seed=987987987;
  do i=1 to 1000;
     Uniform_Distribution=100*ranuni(seed);
     Normal_Distribution=50+25*rannor(seed);
     Poisson_Distribution=ranpoi(seed,50);
     output;
     end;
  run;
```

- Both SAS and SPSS allow you to set the seed to start the random number generation process.
- Both languages allow you to generate random numbers using a wide variety of statistical distributions. This example generates 1,000 observations using the uniform distribution with a mean of 100, the normal distribution with a mean of 50 and standard deviation of 25, and the poisson distribution with a mean of 50.

- SPSS allows you to provide parameters for the distribution functions, such as the mean and standard deviation for the RV.NORMAL function.
- SAS functions are generic and require that you use equations to modify the distributions.
- SPSS does not require the seed as a parameter in the random number functions as does SAS.

String Concatenation

You can combine multiple string and/or numeric values to create new string values. For example, you could combine three numeric variables for area code, exchange, and number into one string variable for telephone number with dashes between the values.

Figure 9-36
SPSS code for concatenating string values

```
*concat_string.sps.
DATA LIST FREE /tel1 tel2 tel3 (3F4).
BEGIN DATA
111 222 3333
222 333 4444
333 444 5555
END DATA.
STRING telephone (A12).
COMPUTE telephone =
  CONCAT((STRING(tel1, N3)), "-",
         (STRING(tel2, N3)), "-",
         (STRING(tel3, N4))).
EXECUTE.
```

Figure 9-37
SAS code for concatenating string values

```
data new;
   input tel1 4. tel2 4. tel3 4.;
   telephone=
     (translate(right(put(tel1,$3.)),'0',' '))||"-"||
     (translate(right(put(tel2,$3.)),'0',' '))||"-"||
     (translate(right(put(tel3,$4.)),'0',' '))
  ;
cards;
111 222 3333
222 333 4444
333 444 5555
;
run;
```

- SPSS uses the CONCAT function to concatenate strings together, and SAS uses "||" for concatenation.
- The SPSS STRING function converts a numeric value to a character value, like the SAS put function.
- The SPSS N format converts spaces to zeroes, like the SAS translate function.

String Parsing

In addition to being able to combine strings, you can also take them apart. For example, you could take apart a 12-character telephone number, recorded as a string (because of the embedded dashes), and create three new numeric variables for area code, exchange, and number.

Figure 9-38
SPSS code for parsing a string value

```
*substr_index.sps.
DATA LIST FREE (",") /telephone (A16).
BEGIN DATA
111-222-3333
222 - 333 - 4444
 333-444-5555
444 - 555-6666
555-666-0707
END DATA.
COMPUTE tel1 =
  NUMBER(SUBSTR(telephone, 1, INDEX(telephone, "-")-1), F5).
COMPUTE tel2 =
  NUMBER(SUBSTR(telephone, INDEX(telephone, "-")+1,
  RINDEX(telephone, "-")-(INDEX(telephone, "-")+1)), F5).
COMPUTE tel3 =
  NUMBER(SUBSTR(telephone, RINDEX(telephone, "-")+1), F5).
EXECUTE.
FORMATS tel1 tel2 (N3) tel3 (N4).
```

Figure 9-39
SAS code for parsing a string value

```
data new;
   input telephone $16.;
   format tel1 tel2 3. tel3 z4.;
   tel1=substr(compress(telephone,'- '),1,3);
   tel2=substr(compress(telephone,'- '),4,3);
   tel3=substr(compress(telephone,'- '),7,4);
cards;
111-222-3333
222 - 333 - 4444
333-444-5555
444 - 555-6666
555-666-0707
;
run;
```

- SPSS uses substring (SUBSTR) and index (INDEX, RINDEX) functions to search the string for specified characters and to extract the appropriate values.
- SAS allows you to name the characters to exclude from a variable using the compress function and then take a substring (substr) of the resulting value.
- The SPSS N format is comparable to the SAS z format. Both formats write leading zeros.

Working with Dates and Times

Dates and times come in a wide variety of formats, ranging from different display formats (for example, 10/28/1986 vs. 28-OCT-1986) to separate entries for each component of a date or time (for example, a day variable, a month variable, and a year variable). Both SPSS and SAS can handle date and times in a variety of formats, and both applications provide features for performing date/time calculations.

Calculating and Converting Date and Time Intervals

A common date calculation is the elapsed time between two dates and/or times. Assuming you have assigned the appropriate date, time, or date/time format to the variables, SPSS and SAS can both perform this type of calculation.

Figure 9-40
SPSS code for calculating date/time intervals

```
*date_functions.sps.
DATA LIST FREE (",")
  /StartDate (ADATE12) EndDate (ADATE12)
  StartDateTime(DATETIME20) EndDateTime(DATETIME20)
  StartTime (TIME10) EndTime (TIME10).
BEGIN DATA
3/01/2003, 4/10/2003
01-MAR-2003 12:00, 02-MAR-2003 12:00
09:30, 10:15
END DATA.
COMPUTE days = CTIME.DAYS(EndDate-StartDate).
COMPUTE hours = CTIME.HOURS(EndDateTime-StartDateTime).
COMPUTE minutes = CTIME.MINUTES(EndTime-StartTime).
EXECUTE.
```

Figure 9-41
SAS code for calculating date/time intervals

```
data new;
   infile cards dlm=',' n=3;
   input StartDate : MMDDYY10. EndDate : MMDDYY10.
     #2 StartDateTime : DATETIME17. EndDateTime : DATETIME17.
     #3 StartTime : TIME5. EndTime : TIME5.
     ;
     days=EndDate-StartDate;
     hours=(EndDateTime-StartDateTime)/60/60;
     minutes=(EndTime-StartTime)/60;
cards;
3/01/2003, 4/10/2003
01-MAR-2003 12:00, 02-MAR-2003 12:00
09:30, 10:15
;
run;
```

- SPSS stores all date and time values as a number of seconds, and subtracting one date or time value returns the difference in seconds. You can use CTIME functions to return the difference as number of days, hours, or minutes.
- In SAS, simple dates are stored as a number of days, but times and dates with a time component are stored as a number of seconds. Subtracting one simple date from another will return the difference as a number of days. Subtracting one date/time from another, however, will return the difference as a number of seconds, and if you want the difference in some other time measurement unit, you must provide the necessary calculations.

Adding to or Subtracting from One Date to Find Another Date

Another common date/time calculation is adding or subtracting days (or hours, minutes, etc.) from one date to obtain another date. For example, let's say prospective customers can use your product on a trial basis for 30 days, and you need to know when the trial period ends—and, just to make it interesting—if the trial period ends on a Saturday or Sunday, you want to extend it to the following Monday.

Figure 9-42
SPSS code for adding to/subtracting from a date value

```
*date_functions2.sps.
DATA LIST FREE (" ") /StartDate (ADATE10).
BEGIN DATA
10/29/2003 10/30/2003
10/31/2003 11/1/2003
11/2/2003 11/4/2003
11/5/2003 11/6/2003
END DATA.
COMPUTE expdate = StartDate + TIME.DAYS(30).
execute.
FORMATS expdate (ADATE10).
***if expdate is Saturday or Sunday, make it Monday***.
DO IF (XDATE.WKDAY(expdate) = 1).
+  COMPUTE expdate = expdate + TIME.DAYS(1).
ELSE IF (XDATE.WKDAY(expdate) = 7).
+  COMPUTE expdate = expdate + TIME.DAYS(2).
END IF.
EXECUTE.
```

Figure 9-43
SAS code for adding to/subtracting from a date value

```
data new;
  format expdate date10.;
     input StartDate : MMDDYY10. @@ ;
     expdate=StartDate+30;;
  if weekday(expdate)=1 then expdate+1;
  else if weekday(expdate)=7 then expdate+2;
cards;
10/29/2003 10/30/2003
10/31/2003 11/1/2003
11/2/2003 11/4/2003
11/5/2003 11/6/2003
;
run;
```

- Since all SPSS date values are stored as a number of seconds, you need to use the TIME.DAYS function to add or subtract days from a date value. In SAS, simple dates are stored as a number of days, so you do not need a special function to add or subtract days.
- The SPSS XDATE.WKDAY function is equivalent to the SAS weekday function, and both return a value of 1 for Sunday and 7 for Saturday.

Extracting Date and Time Information

A great deal of information can be extracted from date and time variables. For example, in addition to the day, month, and year, a date is associated with a specific day of the week, week of the year, and quarter.

Figure 9-44
SPSS code for extracting information from a date value

```
*date_functions3.sps.
DATA LIST FREE (",")
  /StartDateTime (datetime25).
BEGIN DATA
29-OCT-2003 11:23:02
1 January 1998 1:45:01
21/6/2000 2:55:13
END DATA.
COMPUTE dateonly=XDATE.DATE(StartDateTime).
FORMATS dateonly(ADATE10).
COMPUTE hour=XDATE.HOUR(StartDateTime).
COMPUTE DayofWeek=XDATE.WKDAY(StartDateTime).
COMPUTE WeekofYear=XDATE.WEEK(StartDateTime).
COMPUTE quarter=XDATE.QUARTER(StartDateTime).
EXECUTE.
```

Figure 9-45
SPSS code for extracting information from a date value

```
data new;
  format dateonly mmddyyy10.;
     input StartDateTime & : DATETIME25. ;
     dateonly=datepart(StartDateTime);
     hour=hour(StartDateTime);
     DayofWeek=weekday(dateonly);
     quarter=qtr(dateonly);
cards;
29-OCT-2003 11:23:02
;
run;
```

- SPSS uses one main function, XDATE, to extract the date, hour, weekday, week, and quarter from a datetime value.
- SAS uses separate functions to extract the date, hour, weekday, and quarter from a datetime value.
- The SPSS XDATE.DATE function is equivalent to the SAS datepart function. The SPSS XDATE.HOUR function is equivalent to the SAS hour function.
- SAS requires a simple date value (with no time component) to obtain weekday and quarter information, requiring an extra calculation, whereas SPSS can extract weekday and quarter directly from a datetime value.

Index

ADD FILES (command), 90
ADD VALUE LABELS (command), 76
AGGREGATE (command), 96
aggregating data, 96
APPLY DICTIONARY (command), 78
arguments
  macros, 176
  positional, 178
automation objects, 235
autoscripts, 239
average
  mean, 117

banding scale variables, 113
Basic, 233
bootstrapping
  OMS command, 294

case
  changing case of string values, 120
case number
  system variable $casenum, 22
$casenum
  with SELECT IF command, 22
cases
  case number, 22
  finding first or last case in a group, 150
  weighting cases to replicate crosstabulation, 99
CASESTOVARS (command), 106
categorical variables, 77
cleaning data, 78
combining
  strings, 151
combining data files, 87
command syntax
  auto-adjusting command syntax, 152
  batch rules, 166
  creating command syntax files, 19
  debugging, 166
  interactive rules, 166
  invoking command file with INCLUDE command, 26
  master command file with modular components, 161
  rules for different modes, 166
  syntax rules for INCLUDE files, 26
  using command syntax to write command syntax, 150
commands
  displaying in the log, 11
COMMENT (command), 24
  macro names, 24
comments, 24
COMPUTE (command), 116
CONCAT (function), 121, 151
concatenating string values, 120, 151
conditional loops, 146
conditional processing, 152
  based on presence/absence of a variable, 161
  in macros, 180
  including/excluding variables based on macro parameters, 163
  number of macro loops based on data values, 155
confidence intervals
  macro to create confidence interval variables, 224
connect string
  reading databases, 33
CSV data, 48
CTIME.DAYS (function), 131
CTIME.HOURS (function), 131

CTIME.MINUTES (function), 131
customizing
  toolbars, 13

data
  generating simulated data with macros, 213
data files
  aggregating, 96
  making cases from variables, 108
  making variables from cases, 106
  merging, 87, 90
  read-only, 16
  transposing, 102
  updating, 94
DATA LIST (command)
  delimited data, 45
  fixed-width data, 49
  freefield data, 45
databases
  connect string, 33
  Database Wizard, 32
  GET DATA (command), 33
  installing drivers, 31
  outer joins, 36
  reading data, 31
  reading multiple tables, 35
  selecting tables, 33
  SQL statements, 33
  writing data to a database, 315
DATE.MDY (function), 130
DATE.MOYR (function), 130
dates, 126
  combining multiple date components, 130
  computing intervals, 131
  converting numbers to dates, 180
  extracting date components, 133
  functions, 130
  input and display formats, 127
days
  calculating number of days, 132
debugging command syntax, 166
debugging macros, 228
debugging scripts, 240
decimal indicator
  errors caused by localized decimal indicators, 172
  reading data with comma as decimal indicator, 173
DEFINE (command), 175
  !CHAREND, 177
  !CMDEND, 177
  !DO-!DOEND, 182
  !ENCLOSE, 177
  !EVAL, 186
  !IF-!ELSE-!IFEND, 180
  !TOKENS, 179
  arguments, 176
  positional arguments, 178
  tokens, 179
DO IF (command)
  conditions that evaluate to missing, 169
DO REPEAT (command), 136
DOT format
  reading data with comma as decimal indicator, 173
duplicate cases
  filtering, 82
  finding, 82

Errors, 166
errors
  script for counting errors, 271
  script for finding command syntax errors, 278
Excel
  reading Excel files, 38
  saving data in Excel format, 315
EXECUTE (command), 20
exporting
  data and results, 289
  data in Excel format, 315
  data in SAS format, 314
  data to a database, 315
  HTML, 289
  output as *.sav* files, 290
  Output Management System, 289
  text, 289
  XML, 289, 299

FILE HANDLE (command)
  defining wide records with LRCL, 53
FILTER (command), 84
filtering duplicates, 82
FIRST (subcommand)
  MATCH FILES command, 150
FLIP (command), 102
FORMATS (command), 128
functions
  arithmetic, 117
  date and time, 130
  random distribution, 118
  statistical, 117

GET DATA (command)
  TYPE=ODBC subcommand, 33
  TYPE=TXT subcommand, 48
  TYPE=XLS subcommand, 38
global scripts, 238
global.sbs, 238
grouped text data, 57

hierarchical text data, 60
HTML
  creating custom HTML output with OMS and XSLT, 303
  exporting output in HTML format, 317

importing data, 31
  Excel, 38
  SAS format, 67
  text, 43
INCLUDE (command), 26
INCLUDE files
  command syntax rules, 26
  conditional processing, 152
  error handling, 27
INDEX (function), 123

invalid values
  excluding, 81
  finding, 78

labels
  value, 75
  variables, 75
LAG (function), 21
LAST (subcommand)
  MATCH FILES command, 83
leading zeros
  preserving with N format, 121
LENGTH (function), 125
level of measurement, 77
log
  displaying commands, 11
long records
  defining with FILE HANDLE command, 53
lookup file, 90
loops
  conditional, 146
  default maximum number of loops, 167
  in macros, 182
  including a procedure in a loop, 197
  indexing clause, 143
  LOOP (command), 142
  nested, 143
  using XSAVE to build a data file, 148
LOWER (function), 120

macros, 175
  arguments, 176
  arithmetic, 187
  calculate all three-letter combinations, 221
  change variable format, 193
  conditional processing, 180
  converting numbers to dates, 180
  count distinct values across variables, 200
  create variables containing confidence intervals, 224
  creating a variable list, 191
  debugging, 228

define string variable width, 196
displaying expanded macros in log, 228
expansion, 186
generate simulated data, 213
include a procedure in a loop, 197
looping constructs, 182
macro names in comments, 24
positional arguments, 178
random samples, 204
recursive, 202
save *n* random samples, 183
setting number of loops based on data value, 155
tokens, 179
value labels from variable values, 188

MATCH FILES (command), 87
finding first or last case in each group, 150
LAST subcommand, 83

MEAN (function), 117

measurement level, 77

merging data files, 87
same cases, different variables, 87
same variables, different cases, 90
table lookup file, 90

missing values
in DO IF structures, 169
user-missing, 76

MISSING VALUES (command), 23, 76

mixed format text data, 56

MOD (function), 117

modulus, 117

N format, 121

namespace
OMS, 300

nested loops, 143

nested text data, 60

nominal variables, 77

normal distribution, 119

NUMBER (function), 122, 129

NVALID (function), 117

objects
automation objects, 235

ODBC, 31
installing drivers, 31

OMS
vs. scripting, 234

OMS (command)
bootstrapping, 294
controlling row and column display, 296
ending, 298
exporting output from selected commands, 295
exporting pivot tables to *.sav* files, 290
exporting results, 289
exporting selected table types, 295
suppressing selected output types, 295

OMS namespace, 300

OMSEND (command), 292, 298

ordinal variables, 77

outer joins
reading databases, 36

output
suppressing selected types with OMS, 295

parsing string values, 121

PERMISSIONS (subcommand)
SAVE command, 16

pivot tables
exporting selected table types, 295
saving as data files, 290

Poisson distribution, 119

positional arguments
in macros, 178

PowerPoint
script for creating a PowerPoint presentation, 262

protecting data, 16

random distribution functions, 118

random samples
macros, 204
reproducing with SET SEED, 25

reading data, 31
  database tables, 31
  Excel, 38
  SAS format, 67
  text, 43
RECODE (command), 113
  INTO keyword, 113
recoding
  categorical variables, 113
  scale variables, 113
records
  defining wide records with FILE HANDLE, 53
  system variable $casenum, 22
recursive macros, 202
remainder, 117
repeating text data, 66
results
  suppressing selected types with OMS, 295
RINDEX (function), 123
RTRIM (function), 125
RV.NORMAL (function), 119
RV.POISSON (function), 119

sampling
  with replacement (macro), 297
SAS
  reading SAS format data, 67
  saving data in SAS format, 314
SAS vs. SPSS
  aggregating data, 329
  arithmetic functions, 340
  banding scale data, 339
  calculating date/time differences, 345
  cleaning and validating data, 333
  dates and times, 345
  extracting date/time parts, 348
  finding duplicate records, 336
  finding invalid values, 334
  merging data files, 326
  random number functions, 342
  reading database tables, 319
  reading Excel files, 323
  reading text data files, 325
  recoding categorical data, 337
  statistical functions, 340
  string concatenation, 343
  string parsing, 344
  value labels, 332
  variable labels, 331
SAVE (command)
  PERMISSIONS subcommand, 16
SAVE TRANSLATE (command), 314
saving
  data in SAS format, 314
  output as data, 290
Sax Basic, 233
scale variables, 77
  recoding (banding), 113
scratch variables, 18
SCRIPT (command), 239
script window, 237
scripting, 233
  asynchronous problem with command syntax, 281
  autoscripts, 239
  counting command syntax errors, 271
  creating a PowerPoint presentation, 262
  debugging scripts, 240
  finding command syntax errors, 278
  global, 238
  invoking scripts from command syntax, 239
  running command syntax from scripts, 245
  synchronization, 281
  vs. OMS, 234
SELECT IF (command)
  with $casenum, 22
SET (command)
  MPRINT subcommand, 228
  PRINTBACK subcommand, 228
  SEED subcommand, 25
SQL
  reading databases, 33
SQRT (function), 117
square root, 117
STRING (command)
  declaring new string variables, 151

string values
- changing case, 120
- changing defined width, 125
- combining, 120
- concatenating, 120, 151
- converting numeric strings to numbers, 122
- converting string dates to date-format numeric values, 129
- declaring new string variables, 151
- LTRIM function, 151
- macro for defining string width, 196
- parsing, 121
- removing trailing blanks, 125
- substrings, 121

SUBSTR (function), 122, 147

substrings, 121

syntax
- creating command syntax files, 19

table lookup file, 90

TEMPORARY (command), 17

temporary transformations, 17

temporary variables, 18

text data
- comma-separated values, 48
- complex text data files, 56
- CSV format, 48
- delimited, 43
- fixed width, 44, 49
- GET DATA vs. DATA LIST, 44
- grouped, 57
- hierarchical, 60
- mixed format, 56
- nested, 60
- reading text data files, 43
- repeating, 66
- wide records, 53

TIME.DAYS (function), 132

TIME.HMS (function), 130

times, 126
- computing intervals, 131
- functions, 130
- input and display formats, 127

tokens
- in macros, 179

toolbars
- customizing, 13

transaction files, 94

transformations
- date and time, 126
- numeric, 116
- statistical functions, 117
- string, 119

transposing cases and variables, 102

TRUNC (function), 117

truncating values, 117

UNIFORM (function), 119

uniform distribution, 119

UPCASE (function), 120

UPDATE (command), 94

updating data files, 94

user-missing values, 76

using case weights to replicate crosstabulations, 101

valid cases
- NVALID function, 117

validating data, 78

value labels, 75
- adding, 76
- creating from variable values, 188

VALUE LABELS (command), 75

variable labels, 75

VARIABLE LABELS (command), 75

VARIABLE LEVEL (command), 77

variables
- conditional inclusion based on macro parameters, 163
- conditional processing based on presence/absence of a variable, 161
- creating with VECTOR command, 142
- declaring new string variables, 151
- macro for changing format, 193

macro for defining a variable list, 191
macro for defining string width, 196
making variables from cases, 106
measurement level, 77
VARSTOCASES (command), 108
VBA, 233
VECTOR (command), 140
creating variables, 142
short form, 171
vectors, 140
errors caused by disappearing vectors, 170
Viewer
suppressing selected output types, 295
visual bander, 113

WEIGHT (command), 99
weighting data, 99, 101
wide records
defining with FILE HANDLE command, 53
WRITE (command), 24, 151

XDATE.DATE (function), 134
XML
exporting results as XML, 299
XSAVE (command), 24
building a data file with LOOP and XSAVE, 148
XSLT
positional arguments vs. localized text attributes, 312
pulling content, 303
pushing content, 300

years
calculating number of years between dates, 131

zeros
preserving leading zeros, 121